PHIL'S PHOTO

HOMAGE to the ALPHABET

SECOND EDITION

Copyright © 1980, 1985 Phil's Photo, Inc.
2380 Champlain Street NW
Washington, DC 20009
Telephones: 202-293-2214,
1-800-424-2977

First published in the United States by
Rockport Publishers, Inc.
P.O. Box 396
5 Smith Street
Rockport, Massachusetts 01966
Telephone: 508-546-9590
Telex: 5106019284
Fax: 508-546-7141

Distributed by
North Light Books
1507 Dana Avenue
Cincinnati, Ohio 45207
Telephone: 1-800-289-0963

Library of Congress Catalog No. 85-60114

International Standard Book No. 0-935603-47-6

Printed in the United States

CONTENTS

SECTION 1

Spacing and Effects Guides

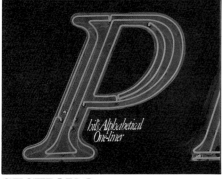

SECTION 2

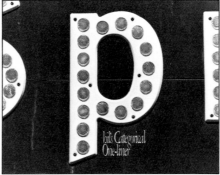

SECTION 3

*One-line index classified
by characteristics*

SECTION 4

SECTION 5

The Supplements.
Originally three additional books containing
newer releases, the supplements have been
bound in. Their indexes have been
integrated in sections

SECTION 6

*Alphabetical index
of typeface names*

ACKNOWLEDGMENTS

Designer: James Hellmuth.

Production manager and chief
type philosopher: Bob Bair.

Production staff: Lynn Bernardi, Margery
Berringer, Michael Bourgois, Virginia Daley,
Pamela R. Johnson, Earle Miller, Lee Norwood,
Bill Santry.

Typographers: Diana Boger, Mark Colliton,
Welton Doby, John Eckert, Paul Grant,
Pamela R. Johnson, Peggy Kelly, Sue Langholz,
Mike Martin, Lee Norwood, Ralph Smith,
Gene Vernon, Harold Baldus, Phil Baldus.

Photo credits: Most of the letters were shot by
John Burwell, with the following exceptions:
D, H, T are by Andrew Bartlett: G, K, N are by
James Hellmuth; Y, Steve Smith.

Written by James Hellmuth, Phil Baldus,
Paul Grant.

There should be a special award for people like
Bob Bair who are driven to the brink putting
type books together. Imagine the thrill of hang-
ing those dinky 6 point Futura "2"s under a
couple of thousand alternate characters (twice,
actually, since we didn't like the first go 'round);
or discovering that all the allotted space for ITC
Bookman Bold is used up and you're sitting
there staring at the "XYZ" in your hand; or
distributing 1488 one-liners many times over
many categories (Bob also named the categories
and decided which faces went in which). Imagine doing nothing else for a year and a half.

Besides being a nut for technical accuracy, his
knowledge and feel for typefaces and typography eclipses that of anyone we know, probably
the result of working in his parents' typehouse
in Philadelphia since the age of fourteen.

In addition to his usual superlative design work
evident throughout, James Hellmuth lent much
conceptual advice and lots of moral support. It
was *he* who convinced *us* that we would actually
finish this book someday.

Against his better instincts, between "serious"
assignments, John Burwell undertook to photo-
graph "interesting environmental letters in a
horizontal format." Only about 20% of his efforts
are shown here and we hope some day we can
find an excuse to publish the rest.

Sincerely, Phil & Harold Baldus

where all the letters came from

three index books

P   Webster's Deluxe Unabridged Dictionary
P   Peoples Drug Store, D.C.
P   Sign on U.S. 495
I   International Harvester truck

divider pages

A   Silver Spring Motel, Md.
B   Baltimore & Ohio freight car
C   Old Yellow Cab sign, Md.
D   Madison Square Garden, coming events sign
E   E.E. Ruebush, veterinarian
F   '66 Ford pickup
G   Grandmas, Wildwood, N.J. (now deceased)
H   Co-op overlooking Central Park, N.Y.
I   Ice Machine, Elde's Beer & Wine
J   Johnny B. Quick, plumbers
K   K Mart, El Centro, Ca.
L   Lions Club, every city in the U.S.A.
M   McDonald's, Route 7, Va.
N   Pinball parlor, Wildwood, N.J.
O   Back lot,, Silver Spring Plymouth
P   Metro construction, Bethesda, Md.
Q   27th & Q, N.W., D.C.
R   Little Tavern employee parking, Md.
S   Mrs. Smith's Pies, Pottstown, Pa.
T   The Big Kitchen, World Trade Center, N.Y.
U   Luau Hut, Silver Spring
V   '64 Valiant
W   Western Termite Control, D.C.
Z   Hollywood Sign, Hollywood, Ca.
Z   Zebra Room, D.C.

Ordering and Shipping

We take orders by phone and fax, and have a pick-up and delivery serice for larger orders (included in our price, for most of the D.C. metro area). Our service is overnight, with a two-hour and four-hour rush service available locally. (See price list.) Out of town orders will be shipped the same day via Federal Express (overnight or two-day service) at discounted rates. First Class Mail or UPS will be shipped next business day.

Ordering

Since jobs are finished faster and more efficiently if they are clearly spec'd, you might find the following guidelines helpful when ordering.

Typeface

Everything shown in this book is available for immediate use, and 3000 more faces have been added since the book's publication. Fonts can also be special ordered. Be certain to specify the complete name and weight, (and the designation ITC or WTC where applicable, since those faces frequently resemble older faces in name and appearance). Alphabets are shown in their entirety. If alternates, numbers and/or punctuation do not appear, they do not occur.

Irregularities

Faces with variations in the weight of their letters are labeled (WV), as are faces that are soft (S), rough (R), have an irregular baseline (IB), or cost more money (CMM). These qualifying notations are at the end of the alphabets, which are shown in their entirety.

Size

You can have any size up to our maximum paper size of 20x24, bearing in mind that we charge more for settings above 1⅛" cap height. Type can be ordered using any unit of measure, such as picas, agates, millimeters, fractions of inches, or points. (When using points, be sure to specify whether the measure is on the actual cap height or on the overall point size of the face.) We set to height or length, but can modify type to fit both dimensions at an extra charge.

Capitalization

Standard typographic shorthand is used: 'Caps' for all caps, 'C/lc' for caps and lower case, and 'C/sc' for caps and small caps. When ordering caps and lower case, please underscore with 3 lines the letters that are to be capitalized. Caps and small caps can be proportioned as you like—we find a ratio of 5:4 to be appealing.

Letterspacing

We will space it any way you want, but for the sake of clarity, refer to the spacing guide on pages SG-1 thru SG-4. These 28 representatives will give you our standards, though of course we accommodate the particular typeface, size and application. Feel free to provide us with a layout for most accurate reproduction of your ideas. If you do not specify, we will set for most even color according to our judgment.

Assembly

All type is provided galley. Positioning is done *only* upon request, for an additional charge. If no line breaks are indicated in the copy, we will break them where it is convenient.

Modifications and Special Effects

Modifications may be applied to any typeface or line image. Because no lenses are used in the process, quality and flexibility are considerable. These include condensing, extending, italicizing, backslanting, circles, curves, wavy lines and perspectives.

Special effects include outline, inline, shadow and airbrush. Existing faces are good points of reference when trying to determine suitable thickness or shadow angle and depth. If you are uncertain, we can provide a 2nd choice at about half the original cost when ordered at the same time. For more information about mods and effects, ask for our "Tricks" book.

Camera Services

Our copy camera is for enlargement or reduction of type, the making of film negatives and positives, and reverse prints. We keep your original type on file for 3 months should you need additional prints or resizing later.

Billing

All initial orders are C.O.D. or credit card. Credit applications are processed as quickly as possible. An itemized invoice accompanies each job, and is duplicated for our monthly statement. Terms are net 30 days.

Miscellaneous

Well, you can't think of everything at once. We charge by the word, irrespective of the number of characters, with a total of five loose characters counted as a word. Foreign languages cost more because they have to be proofread by character.

We are always happy to see our customers, whether for discussion of work or just to chat. Drop by and say hi.

2380 Champlain Street NW, Washington, DC 20009
202-293-2214/1-800-424-2977

INTRODUCTION

assive amounts of it pass before our eyes every day, and we don't see it.

Even the Big Eye doesn't infiltrate so many aspects of our lives.

But while we babble on about television and quarks and prime lending rates, nobody, outside of a small group of fanatics, even thinks about type.

We think it's time for typography to have a wider audience. People should use their eyes and appreciate what's under their noses.

Compare the round thin ones with the straight fat ones and the curved slanted ones. Why there are so many kinds we haven't the foggiest, but we find it an exceedingly rich field for study. It's almost as if humankind has embarked on a vast experiment to find out how many variations on 26 simple forms the mind can recognize. At what point does an I cease to be an I and become something else? Check out Lys Calligraph and Discus. The crossover point is very subtle.

Or try looking at type as a sort of heiroglyphic history of the last 300 years. See how it moves gradually away from handwritten forms as the machine age advances. Notice how the growing faith in technology as the great healer of all ills is accompanied by the almost complete elimination of the human hand in the sans serifs and notice how the hand is creeping back in now that we're not so sure.

Or why not have some of the pleasure of comparing the little idiosyncrasies of type faces in the ampersands and various dingbats? Often type designers really enjoy themselves down at the end of the font where nobody's looking too hard.

We could go on, but you get the idea. Anyhow, one of the fun things about type is finding your own games to play with it.

Philosophizing aside, *Homage to the Alphabet* masquerades by day as a working tool. To begin the agony and the ecstasy—the type selection process—we like to flip through the alphabetical showing until something pops out. Here, too, unexpected juxtapositions sometimes ring a bell. Then the categorical book can be used to compare others of similar characteristics.

Leafing through the main book, though time-consuming, can also be rewarding. We find that the clumped style of setting reveals hidden character by allowing each letter to socialize with its compatriots.

That's the most help we can give. Of course we hope we can also help when you get down to setting the type. Our business is to serve fellow lovers of letters in the most efficient and sympathetic way possible.

Phil's
PHOTO INC

2380 Champlain Street NW, Washington, DC 20009
202-293-2214/1-800-424-2977

Phil's
spacing &
effects guides

*Then, choose
a kerning
philosophy.*

1 Spend more on headlines
2 Spend more on headlines
3 Spend more on headlines
4 Spend more on headlines
5 Spend more on headlines
6 Spend more on headline
7 Spend more on headlin
8 S p e n d   m o r e   o n   h

(A)

Overlap for
even color.
Typesetter's
judgment

(B)

Minimum
of overlap.
Close big
holes only.

1 Spend more on headline

2 Spend more on headlin

3 Spend more on headlir

4 Spend more on headli

5 Spend more on headli

6 Spend more on head

7 Spend more on head

8 Spend more on h

No overlaps.
No touches
whatsoever.

*Or, you can
leave the whole
thing up to us.*

Capital letters spacing guide

1 SPEND MORE ON HEADL

2 SPEND MORE ON HEAD

3 SPEND MORE ON HEAD

4 SPEND MORE ON HEAI

5 SPEND MORE ON HEA

6 SPEND MORE ON HEA

7 SPEND MORE ON HE

8 S P E N D   M O R E   (

Modifications

Condense (−) Expand (+)

−34%	Spend more (
−26%	Spend more (
−19%	Spend more (
−12%	Spend more (
−8%	Spend more (
Normal	Spend more (
+8%	Spend more (
+15%	Spend more (
+25%	Spend more (
+35%	Spend more (

1 SPEND MORE ON HEAD

2 SPEND MORE ON HEA

3 SPEND MORE ON HEA

4 SPEND MORE ON HE

5 SPEND MORE ON HE

6 SPEND MORE ON HE

7 SPEND MORE ON H

8 SPEND MORE ON

Italicize/Backslant

24° *Spend more o*

20° *Spend more o*

16° *Spend more o*

12° *Spend more o*

8° *Spend more o*

Normal Spend more o

8° Spend more o

12° Spend more o

16° Spend more o

24° Spend more o

These are some of the tricks the mod' maker has up its sleeve. There are more. Whatever shape your inspiration comes in, we'll be glad to make it for you.

Original

Outlines

inlines

Both examples came from the same typeface. Some faces look better outlined, some inlined. If you have doubts, we can help.

Contour lines

Any thickness.
Any number.

Shadows

Shadows can be any length and any angle. The shadowed faces shown in the book cost less to set than the ones we custom make.

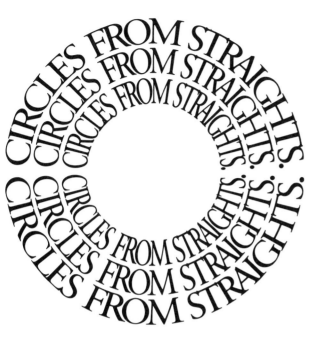

CIRCLES FROM STRAIGHTS.

Curves and waves

Curves and waves can be made in a number of standard shapes. Please look at our selection before designing.

Or all of the above

_hil's Alphabetical
One-liner_

1 Aachen AACHEN MED.	8 American AMER GOTHIC MED.	15 Anzeigen ANZEIGEN GROTESK BOLD
1 Aachen AACHEN BOLD	8 American AMER GOTHIC BOLD	15 Apollo APOLLO
1 Aachen AACHEN BOLD OUT.	8 American TYPEWR TYPE-WRITER LT. (ITC)	15 Aquarius2 AQUARIUS
2 Abbott ABBOTT O.S.	9 American TYPEW TYPE-WRITER MED. (ITC)	16 Aquarius4 AQUARIUS
2 Adagio ADAGIO	9 American TYPE TYPE-WRITER BOLD (ITC)	16 Aquarius 5 AQUARIUS
2 Advertisers ADVERTISE GOTHIC LT.	9 American TYPE TYPE-WRITER OUT. (ITC)	16 Aquarius 6 AQUARIUS
3 Advertisers ADVER GOTHIC	10 American TYPEWRITE TYPE-WRITER LT. COND. (ITC)	17 Aquarius7 AQUARIUS
3 Advertisers Gothic ADVERTIS GOTHIC COND.	10 American TYPEWRITE TYPE-WRITER MED. COND. (ITC)	17 Aquarius 8 AQUARIUS
3 Affiche Moderne AFF	10 American TYPEWRI TYPE-WRITER BOLD COND. (ITC)	17 Aquarius AQUARIUS OUT.
4 AKI LINES AKI LINES (ITC)	11 American TYPEWRITE TYPE-WRITER SHAD. (ITC)	18 Archie ARCHIE
4 Albertus ALBERTUS LT.	11 Americana AMER	18 Argent ARGENT
4 Albertus ALBERTUS	11 Americana AMERI ITAL.	18 Argent Open ARGENT OPEN
5 Albertus ALBERTUS BOLD	12 Americana AMER BOLD	19 Argentica ARGENTICA BOOK
5 Albertus ALBERTUS OUT.	12 Americana AMEI X-BOLD	19 Argentica ARGENTICA MED.
5 Alfereta ALFERETA	12 Americana AMEI BLK.	19 Argentica ARGENTICA DEMI
5 ALGERIAN ALGERI	13 Americana AME OUT.	20 Argentica ARGENTICA BOLD
6 Allegro ALLEGRO	13 Andrich Minerva ANI	20 Arpad ARPAD MED.
6 ALPHA MIDNIGI MIDNIGHT	13 Annlie ANNLIE X-BOLD	20 Arrow ARROW
7 Alternate Gothic ALTERNATE G NO. 3	14 ANTIETAM	21 Art Gothic ART GOTHIC
7 Amelia AMELIA	14 Antique No. 14 AN	21 Artcraft ARTCRAFT
7 American AMERIC GOTHIC LT.	14 Antique ANTIQUE ROMAN	21 Artcraft ARTCRAFT BOLD

22 Aster ASTER	29 **Avon AVON** BLK	37 **Baskerville BASKE** BOLD NO 312
22 **Aster ASTER** BOLD	31 BABY FAT BLACK	38 Bauer Bodoni BAUER BOI
22 **Aster ASTER** X BOLD	31 BABY TEETH	38 *Bauer Bodoni BAUER BC* ITAL
23 **Aster ASTER** BLK	31 Baker Danmark1 BAKE	38 **Bauer Bodoni BAUEI** X-BOLD
23 Aster ASTER OUT	32 Baker Danmark2 BAF	39 ***Bauer Bodoni BAUI*** X-BOLD ITAL
23 ASTRA ASTRA ASTRA	32 Baker Danmark3 BA	39 Bauer Classic BAUER ROMAN
24 Athenaeum ATHENAEU	32 Baker Danmark4 B	39 BAUER TEXT INITIALS
24 AUGUSTEA INLINE INLINE	33 **Baker Danmark5 B**	40 Bauer Text BAUER TEX
24 Aurora AURORA AURORA COND.	33 **Baker Danmark6 F** 6	40 **Bauer Text BAUER TEXT** BOLD
25 **Aurora AURORA** GROTESK IX	33 Baker Danmark BAI OUT	40 Bauhaus BAUHAUS LT. (ITC)
25 Avant Garde AVANT GARD GOTHIC X-LT. (ITC)	34 Baker Danmark BAI SHAD	41 Bauhaus BAUHAUS MED. (ITC)
25 Avant Garde AVANT GARL GOTHIC BOOK (ITC)	34 Baker Signet BAKER SIGN	41 **Bauhaus BAUHAUS** DEMI (ITC)
26 Avant Garde AVANT GARL GOTHIC MED. (ITC)	34 **Baker Signet BAKI** BLK	41 **Bauhaus BAUHAUS** BOLD (ITC)
26 Avant Garde AVANT GAR GOTHIC DEMI (ITC)	35 *BALLOON*	42 **Bauhaus BAUHAUS** HVY. (ITC)
26 **Avant Garde AVANT G** GOTHIC BOLD (ITC)	35 ***BALLOON*** BOLD	42 Bauhaus BAUHAUS HVY. OUT. (ITC)
27 Avant Garde AVANT GARDE GOTHIC BOOK COND. (ITC)	35 BANDANERO	42 **Bazaar BAZAAR**
27 Avant Garde AVANT GARDE GOTHIC MED. COND. (ITC)	36 *BANK NOTE* ITAL	43 *Belvedere BELVEDERE* SCRIPT
27 **Avant Garde AVANT GARDE** GOTHIC DEMI COND. (ITC)	36 Banque Job BANQUE JOB BANQUE JOB	43 Belwe BELWE LT.
28 **Avant Garde AVANT GARDE** GOTHIC BOLD COND. (ITC)	36 Basilea BASILEA	43 **Belwe BELWE** MED.
28 Avon AVON REG	37 Baskerville BASKERVIL	44 **Belwe BELWE** BOLD
28 **Avon AVON** BOLD	37 **Baskerville BASKERV** BOLD	44 Belwe BELWE BOLD SHAD

44 Bembo BEMBO
45 *Bembo BEMBO* ITAL.
45 **Bembo BEMBO** BOLD
45 **Bembo BEMBO** BLK.
46 Benguiat BENGUIAT BOOK (ITC)
46 Benguiat BENGUIAT MED. (ITC)
46 **Benguiat BENGU** BOLD (ITC)
47 *Benguiat BENGUIAT* BOOK ITAL. (ITC)
47 *Benguiat BENGUIAT* MED. ITAL. (ITC)
47 ***Benguiat BENGU*** BOLD ITAL. (ITC)
48 Benguiat BENGUIAT BOOK COND. (ITC)
48 Benguiat BENGUIAT MED. COND. (ITC)
48 **Benguiat BENGUIAT** BOLD COND. (ITC)
49 *Benguiat BENGUIAT* BOOK COND. ITAL. (ITC)
49 *Benguiat BENGUIAT* MED. COND. ITAL. (ITC)
49 ***Benguiat BENGUIAT*** BOLD COND. ITAL. (ITC)
50 Benton BENTON
50 Berling BERLING ANTIQUA
50 **Bernase BERNASE** ROMAN (ITC)
50 Bernhard BEERNNHAF FASHION
51 **Bernhard BERNH** FAT

51 Bernhard BERNHARD GOTHIC LT.
52 Bernhard BERNHARD GOTHIC MED.
52 **Bernhard BERNHAR** GOTHIC X-HVY.
52 Bernhard BERNHARD MODERN ROMAN
53 **Bernhard BERNHARD** BOLD COND.
53 Bernhard BERNHARD TANGO
53 **Beton BETON** X-BOLD
54 Beton BETON MED. COND.
54 **Beton BETON** BOLD COND.
54 **Binner BINNER**
55 Blippo BLIPPO BOLD
55 **Blippo BLIPPO** BLK.
55 Blippo BLIPPO BLK. OUT.
56 **Block Engraving BLOCK**
56 *Blue Skies BLUE*
56 Bocklin BOCKLIN
57 Bodoni BODONI
57 **Bodoni BODONI** BOLD
57 **Bodoni BODONI** ULTRA
58 *Bodoni BODONI* ITAL.
58 *Bodoni BODONI* BOLD ITAL.

58 **Bodoni BODONI** ULTRA X-COND.
59 Bodoni BODONI OPEN
59 BOLD EDGE
59 **Bolt BOLT** BOLD (ITC)
60 Book LSC BOOK REG. (ITC)
60 **Book LSC BOOK** BOLD (ITC)
60 **Book LSC BOOK** X-BOLD (ITC)
61 ***Book LSC BOOK*** X-BOLD ITAL. (ITC)
61 *Book Jacket BOOK JACKET* ITAL.
62 Bookman BOOKMA LT. (ITC)
62 Bookman BOOKM MED. (ITC)
63 **Bookman BOOKM** DEMI (ITC)
63 **Bookman BOOK** BOLD (ITC)
64 *Bookman BOOKM* LT. ITAL. (ITC)
64 *Bookman BOOKM* MED. ITAL. (ITC)
65 *Bookman BOOK* DEMI ITAL. (ITC)
65 ***Bookman BOOK*** BOLD ITAL. (ITC)
66 Bookman BOOKM BOLD OUT. (ITC)
66 **Bookman BOOKM** BOLD CONT. (ITC)
67 **Bookman BOOKMAN** BOLD SHAD. (ITC)
67 **Bookman BOOKMAN** BOLD CONT. SHAD. (ITC)

58 Bookman BOOKMAN	75 Bubble BUBBLE DUBBLE	85 Caslon NEW CASLON
68 *Bookman BOOKMAN* ITAL.	75 Bubble BUBBLE OUT.	85 *Caslon NEW CASLON* ITAL.
68 Bookman BOOKMAN BOLD SWASH	76 BUFFALO BILL BUFFALO BILL	85 Caslon CASLON 471 ROMAN
69 *Bookman BOOKMAN* BOLD ITAL.	76 Bulletin Typewriter B TYPE-WRITER	86 *Caslon CASLON* 471 ITAL. SWASH
69 *Bookman BOOKMAN* BOLD ITAL. (VGC)	76 BULLION SHADOW	86 Caslon CASLON 540
69 Bookman BOOKMAN BOLD OUT.	77 BUSORAMA BUSORAMA LT. (ITC)	87 Caslon CASLON 540 ITAL.
70 Bookman BOOKMAN BLK.	77 BUSORAMA BOOK (ITC)	87 Caslon CASLON 641
70 Boulevard BOULEVe	77 BUSORAMA BUSORAMA MED. (ITC)	87 Caslon CASLON BOLD
71 Bradley BRADLEY	78 BUSORAMA BUSORAMA BOLD (ITC)	88 *Caslon CASLON* BOLD ITAL.
71 Brandywine BRANDYW	81 California CALIFORNIA GROTESK	88 Caslon CASLON OLD FACE HVY.
71 Brandywine BRANDY BOLD	81 California CALIFORNIA GROTESK MED.	88 Caslon CASLON OLD FACE ULTRA BLK.
72 Brillante BRILLANT	81 California CALIFORNIA GROTESK BOLD	89 Caslon CASLON HEADLINE (ITC)
72 Britannic BRITANNI BOLD	82 California CALIFORNIA GROTESK BLK.	89 Caslon CASLON LT. NO. 223 (ITC)
72 BROADSIDE	82 Calligraph CALLIGR	89 Caslon CASLON REG. NO. 223 (ITC)
73 Broadway BROAE	82 CALYPSO CALYPSO	90 Caslon CASLON BOLD NO. 223 (ITC)
73 Broadway BROAE BOLD	83 CAMELOT	90 Caslon CASLON X-BOLD NO. 223 (ITC)
73 BROADWAY ENGRAVED	83 CAMPAIGN	91 *Caslon CASLON* BOLD ITAL. NO. 223 (ITC)
74 Bronstein BRONS BOLD	83 Cancelleresca CANCELLE BASTARDA	91 *Caslon CASLON* X-BOLD ITAL. NO. 223 (ITC)
74 Brush American BRUSH AM	84 Carpenter Carpent	91 Caslon CASLON MODERN
74 Bubble BUBBLE LT.	84 Caslon CASLON ANTIQUE	92 Caslon CASLON SWASH (ARRIOLA)
75 Bubble BUBBLE	84 *Caslon CASLON* ANTIQUE ITAL.	92 *Caslon CASLON CASL* (AMERI-CAN) ITAL.

93 Casual Script CASUAL SCRIP	100 Cheltenham CHELTENH MED.	108 Cheltenham CHELTENHAM LIGHT COND. ITAL. (ITC)
93 Caxtonian CAXT	100 Cheltenham CHELTEN BOLD	108 Cheltenham CHELTENHAM BOOK COND. ITAL. (ITC)
93 Celtic Cursive CELTIC CU	101 Cheltenham CHELT HVY.	108 Cheltenham CHELTENH BOLD COND. ITAL. (ITC)
94 Celtic Cursive CELTIC C BOLD	101 Cheltenham CHELTENH MED. ITAL.	109 Cheltenham CHELTEN OUT. (ITC)
94 Centaur CENTAUR	101 Cheltenham CHELTEN BOLD ITAL.	109 Cheltenham CHELTEI OUT. SHAD. (ITC)
94 Centennial Script Centenn	102 Cheltenham CHELTENHAM O.S. COND.	109 Cheltenham CHELTEN CONT. (ITC)
95 Century CENTURY EXPANDED	102 Cheltenham CHELTENHAM BOLD COND.	110 Churchill CHURCHI
95 Century CENTURY O.S.	102 Cheltenham CHELTEN BOLD OUT.	110 Churchward CHURC METALLIC
95 Century CENTURY O.S. BOLD	103 Cheltenham CHELTENH LT. (ITC)	110 Churchward CHURC METALLIC ITAL.
96 Century CENTURY SCHOOL-BOOK	103 Cheltenham CHELTEN BOOK (ITC)	111 CINEMA ONE ONE
96 Century CENTURY SCHOOL-BOOK BOLD	103 Cheltenham CHELTE BOLD (ITC)	111 CINEMA TWO
96 Century CENTURY BOOK (ITC)	104 Cheltenham CHI ULTRA (ITC)	111 CINEMA THREE
97 Century CENTUR ULTRA (ITC)	104 Cheltenham CHI ULTRA ITAL. (ITC)	112 CIRCUS CAPS
97 Century CENTURY BOOK ITAL. (ITC)	105 Cheltenham CHELTENH LT. ITAL. (ITC)	112 Cirque CIRQUE
97 Century CENTU ULTRA ITAL. (ITC)	105 Cheltenham CHELTEN BOOK ITAL. (ITC)	112 City Compact CITY COMPACT LT.
98 Century CENTURY MODERN SWASH	105 Cheltenham CHELTI BOLD ITAL. (ITC)	113 City Compact CITY COMPA MED.
98 Century Litho CENTURY L SHAD	106 Cheltenham CHELTENHAM LT. COND. (ITC)	113 City Compact CITY COM BOLD
99 CERTIFIED	106 Cheltenham CHELTENHAM BOOK COND. (ITC)	113 Clarendon CLAR BOLD
99 Champion CHAMPIO	106 Cheltenham CHELTENHA BOLD COND. (ITC)	114 Clearface CLEARFACE REG. (ITC)
99 Checkmate CHECK	107 Cheltenham CHELTEN ULTRA COND. (ITC)	114 Clearface CLEARFACE BOLD (ITC)
100 Cheltenham CHELTENH O.S.	107 Cheltenham CHELTE ULTRA COND. ITAL. (ITC)	114 Clearface CLEARFACI HVY. (ITC)

115 **Clearface CLEARFAC** BLK. (ITC)	122 Columbus COLUMBUS	131 Della Robbia DELLA ROB
115 *Clearface CLEARFAC* BLK. ITAL. (ITC)	122 **Columbus COLUMBU** BOLD	132 Della Robbia DELLA ROE BOLD
115 Clearface CLEARFACE CONT. (ITC)	122 COLUMNA SOLID	132 **Della Robbia DELLA R** X-BOLD
116 **Clearface CLEARFAC** X-BOLD	123 COLUMNA OPEN	132 **Della Robbia DELLA RO** HVY.
116 **Clearface CLEARFACI** BLK.	123 Compacta COMPACTA LT.	133 DELPHIAN
116 Clearface CLEARFACE GOTHIC	123 Compacta COMPACTA	133 Delphin 2 DELPHIN NO. 2
117 **Clearface CLEARFACE** GOTHIC BOLD	124 **Compacta COMPACTA** BOLD	133 Dempsey DEMPSEY MED
117 Cloister CLOISTER O.S.	124 **Comstock COMSTO**	134 DESDEMONA
117 **Cloister CLOISTER** BOLD	124 Consort CONSORT	134 Design DESIGN FINELINE
118 **Cloister CLOISTER** X-BOLD	125 *CONSTANZE* INITIALS	134 Design DESIGN MED.
118 **Cloister CLOISTER** HVY	125 Cooper COOPER O.S.	135 Design DESIGN DEMI
118 Cloister CLOISTER BLK.	125 **Cooper COOPER** BLK. COND.	135 **Design DESIGN** X-BOLD
119 CLOISTER CLOISTER INITIALS	126 **Cooper COOPER** BLK.	135 Design DESIGN OUT.
119 Cochin COCHIN O.S.	126 *Cooper COOPER* BLK. ITAL.	136 DEUTSCH BLACK
119 Cochin COCHIN ROMAN	127 **Cooper COOPER** COMSTOCK SWASH	136 **Devinne DEVINNE** X-BOLD
120 Cochin COCHIN ROMAN BOLD	127 Cooper COOPER HILITE	136 **Devinne DEVINNE** BLK.
120 **Cochin COCHIN** ROMAN BLK.	128 Craw Clarendon CRAW CLA	137 Didi DIDI (ITC)
120 *Cochin COCHIN* ITAL.	128 **Cucumber CUCUMBER**	137 Diotima DIOTIMA
121 *Cochin COCHIN* BOLD ITAL.	128 Cushing CUSHING O.S. X-BOLD	137 *Discus DISCUS*
121 *Cochin COCHIN* BLK. ITAL.	131 DAVIDA DAVIDA BOLD	138 *Discus DISCUS* SEMI
121 Collins Collins COL BICENTENNIAL	131 Dektiv DEKTIV	138 Dragonwyck DRAGON

138 **Dynamo DYNAMO** MED.

139 **Dynamo DYNAMO**

141 **EAGLE** BOLD

141 **ECLIPSE**

141 EDDA EDDA

142 **Egizio EGIZIO** BOLD

142 *Egizio EGIZIO* BOLD ITAL.

142 Egyptian EGYPTIAN 505 LT.

143 Egyptian EGYPTIAN 505

143 Egyptian EGYPTIAN 505 MED.

143 Egyptian EGYPTIA 505 BOLD

144 Egyptian EGYPTIA 505 OUT.

144 **Egyptian EGYPTIAN** BOLD. COND.

144 **Абвгдежз АБВГДЕЁЖЗ** EGYPTIAN BOLD COND. (RUSSIAN)

145 Egyptian EGYPTIAN BOLD. COND. OUT.

145 **EGYPTIAN PATRIOT**

145 **EGYPTIAN EGYPTIAN**

146 **Ehrhardt EHRHAI** ULTRA BOLD

146 ELEKTRIK

146 ELEKTRIK MED.

147 **ELEKTRIK** BOLD

147 Elizabeth ELIZABETH ROMAN

147 *Elvira ELVIRA* BOLD ITAL.

148 *Emphasis EMPHAS*

148 Enge Etienne ENGE ETIENNE

148 **Engravers ENGRAVER** OLD ENGLISH (VGC)

149 ERAS

149 Eras ERAS LT. (ITC)

149 Eras ERAS BOOK (ITC)

150 Eras ERAS MED. (ITC)

150 **Eras ERAS** DEMI (ITC)

150 **Eras ERAS** BOLD (ITC)

151 **Eras ERAS** ULTRA (ITC)

151 Eras ERAS OUT. (ITC)

152 **Eras ERAS** CONT. (ITC)

152 Eurostile EUROS EXT.

153 **Eurostile EURO** BOLD EXT.

155 **FAT CAT**

155 **Fat Face FAT FACE** COND. (ITC)

155 *Fat Face FAT FACE* COND. ITAL. (ITC)

156 **Fat Face FAT FACE** (ITC)

156 **Firenze FIRENZE** (ITC)

156 Firmin Didot FIRMIN DI

157 Firmin Didot FIRMIN BOLD

157 **Flange FLANGE**

157 *Fleetwing '44 FLEE*

158 Flex FLEX

158 Flirt FLIRT

158 Florentine FLORENTINE

159 **Folio FOLIO** MED.

159 **Folio FOLIO** X-BOLD

159 Folio FOLIO X-BOLD OUT.

160 Folkwang FOLKWANG

160 **Fortuna FOR** X-BOLD

160 **Fraktur FRAKTUR** FRAKTUR

161 Framingham FRAMINGI

161 **Framingham FRAMIN** X-BOLD

161 **FRANKFURTER**

162 FRANKFURTER OUT. BLK.

162 **FRANKFURTER** CONT. COND.

162 **Franklin Gothic FRANI**

163 **Franklin Gothic FRAN** BLK.

163 **Franklin Gothic FRANKLIN** COND.

163 Franklin Gothic **FRANKLIN GOTHIC** X-COND	173 Galliard GALLIARD	180 *Garamond GARAMON* BOOK COND. ITAL. (ITC)
164 **Franklin Gothic FRANKLIN GOTHI** BLK X-COND	173 **Galliard GALLIARD** BOLD	180 *Garamond GARAMON* BOLD COND. ITAL. (ITC)
164 **FREDERICKSBURG**	174 **Galliard GALLIARD** BLK.	181 *Garamond GARAM* ULTRA COND. ITAL. (ITC)
164 **FRISCO**	174 **Galliard GALLIAR** ULTRA	181 Garamond GARAMON O.S.
165 FrizQuadrata FRIZQU (ITC)	174 *Galliard GALLIARD* ITAL.	181 *Garamond GARAMOND* O.S. ITAL
165 FrizQuadrata FRIZ C MED.	175 *Galliard GALLIARD* BOLD ITAL.	182 Garamond GARAMO BOLD
165 **FrizQuadrata FRIZ** DEMI	175 *Galliard GALLIARI* BLK. ITAL.	182 **Garamond GARAMC** HVY.
166 **FrizQuadrata FRIZ C** BOLD (ITC)	175 *Galliard GALLIAR* ULTRA ITAL.	182 Garamond GARAI O.S. X-BOLD
166 Futura FUTURA LT.	176 Garamond GARAMC LT. (ITC)	183 **GARDENIA**
166 Futura FUTURA BOOK	176 Garamond GARAMC BOOK (ITC)	183 **GEMINI GEMINI**
167 Futura FUTURA MED.	176 **Garamond GARA** BOLD (ITC)	183 Gesh Ortega GESHO
167 Futura FUTURA DEMI	177 **Garamond GARA** ULTRA (ITC)	184 **GETTYSBURG**
167 **Futura FUTURA** BOLD	177 *Garamond GARAM* LT. ITAL. (ITC)	184 *Gillies GILLIES* GOTHIC BOLD
168 **Futura FUTURA** X-BOLD	177 *Garamond GARAM* BOOK ITAL. (ITC)	184 Gill Sans GILL SANS LT.
168 **Futura FUTURA** BOLD COND.	178 *Garamond GARA* BOLD ITAL. (ITC)	185 Gill Sans GILL SANS MED.
168 **Futura FUTURA** X-BOLD COND.	178 *Garamond GARA* ULTRA ITAL. (ITC)	185 **Gill Sans GILL SANS** BOLD
169 **Futura FUTURA** DISPLAY	178 Garamond GARAMOND LT. COND. (ITC)	185 **Gill Sans GILL SANS** X-BOLD
169 **Futura FUTURA** BLK.	179 Garamond GARAMOND BOOK COND. (ITC)	186 **Gill Sans GILL SAN** ULTRA
169 FUTURA STENCIL LT.	179 **Garamond GARAMO** BOLD COND. (ITC)	186 *Gill Sans GILL SANS* LT. ITAL.
170 **FUTURA** STENCIL BOLD	179 **Garamond GARAMO** ULTRA COND. (ITC)	186 *Gill Sans GILL SANS* BOLD ITAL.
173 **GALLIA**	180 *Garamond GARAMOND* LT. COND. ITAL. (ITC)	187 **Gill Sans GILL SANS** BOLD COND.

187 Gill Sans GILL SANS BOLD X-COND.	194 Goudy Text GOUDY TE	204 Harry HARRY FAT
187 GIORGIO	195 Granby GRANBY LT.	205 Harry HARRY OBESE
188 Globe Gothic GLOBE GOTHIC COND.	195 Granby GRANBY	205 Harry HARRY OBESE SQUEEZED
188 Globe Gothic GLOBE GOT	195 Granby GRANBY BOLD	205 Helvetica HELVETICA X-LT.
188 Globe Gothic GLOB X-BOLD	196 Granby GRANBY X-BOLD	206 Helvetica HELVETICA LT.
189 Gorillaa GORILLA (ITC)	196 Granby GRANBY ELEPHANT	206 Helvetica HELVETICA
189 Goudy GOUDY O.S.	196 Granby GRANBY OUT. SHAD.	206 Helvetica HELVETICA MED.
189 Goudy GOUDY O.S. ITAL.	197 GRECIAN	207 Helvetica HELVETICA DEMI
190 Goudy GOUDY CATALOGUE	197 Grizzly GRIZZLY	207 Helvetica HELVETIC. BOLD
190 Goudy GOUDY BOLD	197 Grotesque No.9 GROTESQI	207 Helvetica HELVETIC. X-BOLD
190 Goudy GOUDY BOLD ITAL.	198 Grouch GRROUCH (ITC)	208 Helvetica HELVETICA LT. ITAL.
191 Goudy GOUDY X-BOLD	198 GUTZON BORGLUI GUTZON BORGLUM	208 Helvetica HELVETICA ITAL.
191 Goudy GOUDY BLK.	201 Halbstarke HALB PICA	208 Helvetica HELVETIC BOLD COMPACT ITAL.
191 Goudy GOUDY BLK. ITAL.	201 Halftone HALFTONE	209 Helvetica HELVI X-BOLD EXT.
192 Goudy GOUDY HEAVYFACE	201 Handel HANDEL GOTHIC LT.	209 Helvetica HELVETICA COMPRESSED
192 Goudy GOUDY HEAVYFACE ITAL.	202 Handel HANDEL GOTHIC	209 Helvetica HELVETICA EXTRA COMPRESSED
193 Goudy GOUDY HEAVYFACE COND.	202 Harlow HARLOW	210 Helvetica HELVETICA MED. OUT.
193 Goudy GOUDY HANDTOOLED	203 Harper's Bazaar HARPER'S L	210 Helvetica HELVETICA BOLD OUT.
193 Goudy GOUDY HANDTOOLED ITAL.	203 Harry HARRY THIN	210 Henrietta HENRIETT. MED.
194 Goudy GOUDY CURSIVE	204 Harry HARRY PLAIN	211 Henrietta HENRIET BOLD
194 GOUDY ORNATE ORNATE	204 Harry HARRY HVY.	211 Henrietta HENRIETTA BOLD COND.

211 Hensby HENSBY	221 Inserat Grotesk INSERAT GROTESK	229 Joric Joric JORIC JORIC ULTRA
212 Herkules HERKULES	221 Italia ITALIA BOOK (ITC)	231 Kabel KABEL BOOK (ITC)
212 Herold Reklame HEROLD REKLAME	222 Italia ITALIA MED. (ITC)	231 Kabel KABEL MED. (ITC)
212 Hobo HOBO	222 Italia ITALIA BOLD (ITC)	231 Kabel KABEL DEMI (ITC)
213 Hogarth HOGARTH	222 IVY LEAGUE	232 Kabel KABEL BOLD (ITC)
213 Holland HOLLAND	223 IVY LEAGUE BOLD	232 Kabel KABEL ULTRA (ITC)
213 Holland HOLLAND MED.	223 IVY LEAGUE OPEN	232 Kabel KABEL OUT. (ITC)
214 Holland HOLLAND SEMI	225 Jana JANA	233 Kabel KABEL LT.
214 Holland HOLLAND BOLD	225 Janson JANSON	233 Kabel KABEL MED.
214 Horley HORLEY O.S.	225 Janson JANSON ITAL.	233 Kabel KABEL BOLD
215 Horley HORLEY O.S. MED	226 Japanette JAPANETTE	234 Kabel KABEL HVY.
215 Horley HORLEY O.S. BOLD	226 Jay Gothic JAY GOTHIC	234 Kabel KABEL BLK. MODERN
215 Howland HOWLAND OPEN	226 Jay Gothic JAY GOTHIC BOLD	234 Kabel KABEL BOLD COND.
216 HUXLEY VERTICAL	227 Jay Gothic JAY GOTHIC OUT	235 Kabel KABEL SHAD.
219 Impact IMPACT	227 Jenson JENSON O.S.	235 KANTANAKA RED KANTANAKA RED
219 Impact IMPACT OPEN	227 Jenson JENSON	235 Kap Antiqua KAPA ANTIQUA BOLD
219 Imprint IMPRINT	228 Jenson Book JENSON BOLD	236 Karnak KARNAK BLK. COND.
220 Imprint IMPRINT BOLD	228 Jenson Book JENSON X-BOLD	236 Kaufman KAUFMAN SCRIPT
220 INDEPENDENCE	228 Jenson JENSON COND.	236 Kaufman KAUFMAN BOLD
220 INFORMAL GOTHIC INFORMAL	229 JIM CROW	237 Kismet KISMET
221 Information	229 JOCUNDA	237 Koloss KOLOSS

237 **Kompakt KOMP.**
238 Korinna KORINNA (ITC)
238 Korinna **KORINNA** BOLD (ITC)
238 **Korinna KORINNA** X-BOLD (ITC)
239 **Korinna KORINN** HVY. (ITC)
239 Korinna KORINNA OUT. (ITC)
239 Korinna KORINNA KURSIV (ITC)
240 Korinna KORINNA KURSIV BOLD (ITC)
240 **Korinna KORINNA** KURSIV X-BOLD (ITC)
240 **Korinna KORINN** KURSIV HVY. (ITC)
241 **Kubra KUBRA**
243 L & C Hairline L&C HAIRLINE
243 LED L.E.D.
243 Laertes LAERTES
244 Lafayette LAFAYETTE
244 LARGO LT.
244 Lariat LARIAT
245 Le Griffe LE GRIFFE
246 Lee LEE
246 LETTRES ORNEE ORNEES
246 Life Antiqua LIFE AN BOLD

247 Lightline LIGHTLINE GOTHIC
247 LINCOLN GOTHIC
248 Lubalin Graph LUBALIN X-LT. (ITC)
248 Lubalin Graph LUBAL BOOK (ITC)
249 Lubalin Graph LUB MED. (ITC)
249 **Lubalin Graph LUB** DEMI (ITC)
250 **Lubalin Graph LUB** BOLD (ITC)
250 Lubalin Graph LUB DEMI OUT. (ITC)
247 Lucifer LUCIFER NO. 1
251 Lys Calligraph L
253 **Macbeth MACBETH macb**
253 **MACHINE** (ITC)
253 **MACHINE** BOLD (ITC)
254 MADISON MADISON
254 Madisonian MADISO
254 **Manchester MANCHES**
255 MANDARIN
255 Mandate MANDATE
255 Manhattan MANHATT (ITC)
256 MANUSCRIPT INITIAL INITIALS
256 MARBLEHEART

256 **Marten Roman MART**
257 **Mastodon MASTOD**
257 Maxie MAXIE LINED
257 Melior MELIOR
258 Melior MELIOR SEMI
258 Melior MELIOR BOLD OUT
258 MICHELANGELO
259 **MICROGRAMMA** BOLD
259 MICROGRAMM MICRO-GRAMMA EXT.
259 **MICROGRAMM** MICRO-GRAMMA BOLD EXT.
260 Milano Roman MILAN (ITC)
260 Mistral MISTRAL
260 Modern No 20 MODE
261 **Modernique MODI**
261 Modernique MODI OUT.
261 Moonshadow MOONSHA
262 MOORE COMPUTER
262 MOORE LIBERTY
262 Musketeer MUSKETEER LT.
263 Musketeer MUSKETEER REG.
263 Musketeer MUSKETEE DEMI

263	Musketeer MUSKETI	BOLD	
264	Musketeer MUSKET	X-BOLD	
267	NATIONAL SPIRIT		
267	Neil NEIL	BOLD	
267	Neil NEIL	BOLD OPEN	
268	NEON	(ITC)	
268	Neptune NEPTUNE		
268	NEULAND		
269	NEULAND	BLK.	
269	News Gothic NEWS GOTHIC		
269	News Gothic NEWS GOT	BOLD	
270	News Gothic NEWS GOTHIC	X-COND.	
270	Newtext NEWTEX	BOOK (ITC)	
270	Newtext NEWTEX	REG. (ITC)	
271	Newtext NEWTEX	DEMI (ITC)	
271	Newtext NEWTEX	REG. ITAL. (ITC)	
271	Nova Augustea NOVA A		
272	Novel Gothic NOVEL		
275	OCTIC OCTIC	EXT.	
275	Octopuss OCTOPUSS		
276	OLD GLORY		

276	Old Gothic OLD GO	BOLD ITAL.	
276	ביטחזוהדגבא	OLD HEBREW	
277	Olden OLDEN		
277	Olive Antique OLIVE AN		
277	Olive Antique OLIVE A	MED	
278	Olive Antique OLIVE	BOLD	
278	Olive Antique OLN	BLK	
278	Olive Antique OLIVE ANTIQU	NARROW	
279	OLYMPIA OLYMPIA		
279	Onyx ONYX		
279	Optima OPTIMA		
280	Optima OPTIMA	SEMI	
280	Optima OPTIMA	BOLD	
280	Optima OPTIMA	ITAL	
281	ORLEANS OPEN		
281	ORPLID		
281	Othello OTHELLO		
282	Othello OTHELLO	OUT.	
285	P.T. Barnum P.T. BARNUM		
285	Packard PACKARD		
285	Paddington PADDING		

286	PAGEANT	INITIALS	
286	Palatino PALATINO	ROMAN	
286	Palatino PALATINO	SEMI	
287	Palatino PALATINO	BOLD (SOFT SERIF)	
287	Palatino PALATINO	BOLD (HARD SERIF)	
287	Palatino PALATINO	ITAL	
288	Palatino PALATINO	CURSIVE	
288	PALISADES GRAF	GRAPHICS	
288	Pamela PAMELA		
289	Paprika PAPRIKA		
289	Parisian PARISIAN		
289	Park Avenue PARK		
290	Parsons PARSONS		
290	Parsons PARSONS	BOLD	
291	Parsons PARSONS	HVY.	
291	Patriot PATRIOT		
291	PATTERN		
292	PEIGNOT PEIGNOT	LT.	
292	PEIGNOT PEIGNOT	DEMI	
292	PEIGNOT PEIGNOT	BOLD	
293	Pekin PEKIN		

293 PERGOLA
293 Permanent Headline PERMANENT HEAD
294 Permanent PERMANENT MASSIV
294 Permanent Headline PERMANENT HEA OPEN
294 PERPETUA TITLING LT.
295 Perpetua PERPETUA ROMAN
295 Perpetua PERPETU BOLD
295 Perpetua PERPET X-BOLD
296 Perpetua PERPEI BLK.
296 Perpetua PERPETUA ITAL.
296 Perpetua PERPETU BOLD ITAL.
297 Perpetua PERPETUA BOLD SHAD.
297 PHOTOMANIA NO. 2
297 PIONEER PIONEER (ITC)
298 Pistilli Roman PISTI
298 Pistilli Roman PISTI OPEN NO. 1
298 Pistilli PISTILLI OPEN NO. 2
299 Placard PLACARD BOLD COND.
299 Plantin PLANTIN LT.
299 Plantin PLANTIN
300 Plantin PLANTIN BOLD

300 Plantin PLANTIN BOLD COND.
300 Plantin PLANTIN BOLD COND. OUT.
301 Playbill PLAYBILL
301 Plymouth & PLY
301 PoorRichard POOR RICH
302 Post POST COND.
302 Post POST O.S. ROMAN NO. 2
302 Post POST O.S. ITAL.
303 Pretoria PRETOI
303 PRISMA
303 PRISMANIA PRISMANIA G
304 PRISMANIA PRISMAN K
304 PUBLICITY GOTH GOTHIC
307 QUENTIN
307 Quorum QUORUM LT. (ITC)
307 Quorum QUORUM BOOK (ITC)
308 Quorum QUORUM MED. (ITC)
308 Quorum QUORUM BOLD (ITC)
308 Quorum QUORUM BLK. (ITC)
311 RADIANT ANTIQI ANTIQUE
311 RAILROAD GOTHIC

311 Raleigh RALEIGH X-LT.
312 Raleigh RALEIGH LT.
312 Raleigh RALEIGH MED.
312 Raleigh RALEIGH DEMI
313 Raleigh RALEIGH BOLD
313 Raleigh RALEIGH X-BOLD
313 Raleigh RALEIGH OUT.
314 Raleigh RALEIGH CONT.
314 Raleigh RALEIGH SHAD.
314 Rebecca REBECCA
315 RELIEF
315 Reubens REUBENS WIDE
315 Revue REVUE
316 Revue REVUE X-BOLD
316 Rhythmic RHYTHMIC SHAD.
316 RIBBONETTE
317 Richmond RICHMONI O.S.
317 Richmond RICHMON O.S. BOLD
317 Richmond RICHMON O.S. HVY.
318 Richmond RICHMON O.S. ITAL.
318 Richmond RICHMOND O.S. COND.

318 Richmond RICHMOND BOLD COND	327 Sabon SABON ROMAN	334 Serpentine SERIF BOLD ITAL.
319 ROCK OPERA	327 Sabon SABON BOLD	334 SHOTGUN SHOTGUN
319 Rockwell ROCKWELL LT.	327 Sabon SABON ITAL.	334 SHOTGUN SHOTGUN BLANKS
319 Rockwell ROCKWELL MED.	328 St. Clair ST. CLAIR	335 Siegfried SIEGFRIED
320 Rockwell ROCKWEI BOLD	328 SANS SERIF CONDENSED COND. NO. 1	335 SILVER DOLLAR
320 Rockwell ROCKV X-BOLD	328 Sans Serif SANS SERIF COND. ITAL.	335 Skin & Bones SKIN & BC
320 ROCO	329 SANS SERIF ELONGATED	336 Skjald SKJALD
321 Rococo ROCOCO	329 SANS SERIF SHADED SHAD.	336 Skylark SKYLARI
321 Rodeo RODEO	329 Schadow SCHADO ANTIQUA SEMI	336 Smoke SMOKE
321 Roman ROMAN COMPRESSED NO. 3	330 Schadow SCHADO ANTIQUA BOLD	337 Smoke SMOKE SHAD.
322 Romana ROMANA NORMAL	330 SCOT GOTHIC	337 Snell Roundhand
322 Romana ROMANA BOLD	330 SCOTFORD UNCIAL	337 Solitaire SOLITAIRE
322 Romana ROMANA ULTRA	331 Serif Gothic SERIF GOTHIC LT. (ITC)	338 Souvenir, Eastern SOUVE LT.
323 Romany ROMANY RO ROUND-HAND	331 Serif Gothic SERIF GOTHI (ITC)	338 Souvenir, Eastern SOUV MED.
323 Ronda RONDA LT. (ITC)	331 Serif Gothic SERIF GOTHI BOLD (ITC)	338 Souvenir, Eastern SOUV BOLD
323 Ronda RONDA (ITC)	332 Serif Gothic SERIF GOTHI X-BOLD (ITC)	339 Souvenir, Eastern SOU X-BOLD
324 Ronda RONDA BOLD (ITC)	332 Serif Gothic SERIF GOTH HVY. (ITC)	339 Souvenir SOUVENIR LT. (ITC)
324 Roslyn Gothic ROSLYN GOTH MED.	332 Serif Gothic SERIF GO BLK. (ITC)	339 Souvenir SOUVENI MED. (ITC)
324 Roslyn Gothic ROSLYN GOT BOLD	333 Serif Gothic SERIFGOTH BOLD OUT (ITC)	340 Souvenir SOUVEN DEMI (ITC)
325 RUSTIC	333 Serif Gothic SERIF GO OPEN BOLD (ITC)	340 Souvenir SOUVEI BOLD (ITC)
325 Rustikalis RUSTIKAL MODERN-IZED GOTHIC	333 Serif Gothic SERIF GOTHIC BOLD SHAD. (ITC)	340 Souvenir SOUVENIR LT. ITAL. (ITC)

341 *Souvenir SOUVENI* MED. ITAL. (ITC)	348 STEPHEN ORNATE	357 Tavern TAVERN
341 *Souvenir SOUVEN* DEMI ITAL. (ITC)	348 STOUTHEART	358 Thalia THALIA
341 *Souvenir SOUVEI* BOLD ITAL. (ITC)	348 STREAMLINE	358 THORNE SHAD.
342 Souvenir SOUVEN OUT.	349 Stymie STYMIE HAIRLINE (ITC)	358 ThorowGOOD ROMAN
342 Souvenir SOUVEI COM. STOCK	349 Stymie STYMIE LT.	359 *ThorowGOOD* ITAL. SWASH
342 Souvenir SOUVENIR SHAD.	349 Stymie STYMIE MED.	359 Ticonderoga TICONI LT.
343 Stagecoach STAGECOACH	350 Stymie STYMIE BOLD	360 Ticonderoga TICONDI BOLD
343 STAGG SHADED	350 **Stymie STYMIE** X-BOLD	360 Tiffany TIFFANY LT. (ITC)
343 Standard STANDA X-LT. EXT.	350 SUPERSTAR	360 Tiffany TIFFANY MED. (ITC)
344 Standard STANDARD MED.	351 SUPERSTAR SHAD.	361 Tiffany TIFFANY DEMI (ITC)
344 **Standard STANDARD** BOLD	351 Syntax Antiqua SYNTAX	361 **Tiffany TIFFANY** HVY. (ITC)
344 **Standard STANDARD** X-BOLD / COND.	351 Syntax Antiqua SYNTA MED.	361 *Time Script TIME S*
345 Stark STARRK DEBONAIR	352 **Syntax Antiqua S** BOLD	362 Times Roman TIMES RO
345 Stark STARRK SEMI	355 **T.H.ALPHABET SOUP**	362 АБВГДЕЖЗ АБВГДЕЖЗ TIMES ROMAN (RUSSIAN)
345 STEAMBOAT	355 T.H.UNCLE SAM	362 *Times Roman TIMES RO* ITAL.
346 STEAMBOAT SHAD.	355 Tabasco TABASCO LT.	363 **Times Roman TIMES R** BOLD
346 Steel STEEL ELON-GATED	356 **Tabasco TABASCO** MED.	363 **Times Roman TIMES** BLK.
346 Steelplate STEELPLAT TEXT BLK.	356 **Tabasco TABASCO** BOLD	363 **Times MODIFIED NO.** BOLD NO. 1
347 Steelplate STEELPLAT TEXT OPEN	356 TABLEAU	364 **Times MODIFIED NO** BOLD NO. 2
347 Steelplate STEELPLAT TEXT SHAD.	357 Tango TANGO	364 Times New TIMES NE ROMAN SEMI
347 STENCIL	357 **Tanker TANKER**	364 *Times New TIMES NEW* ROMAN SEMI ITAL.

365	Tintopetto TINTORO	373	UMBRA	382	Visa VISA
365	Tom's Roman TOM'S RO (ITC)	373	UMBRA 57	382	Vivaldi VIVALC
365	TONIGHT	373	Unbelievable UNBEL	385	Walbaum WALBAUM
366	TOP HAT	374	UNCLE BILL	385	Washington WASHINGTON X-LT.
366	Topic Futura TOPIC FUTU	374	Univers 45 UNIVERS	385	Washington WASHINGTON LT.
366	Torino TORINO ROMAN	374	Univers 55 UNIVERS	386	Washington WASHINGTON MED.
367	TOWN HALL	375	Univers 65 UNIVERS	386	Washington WASHINGTON BOLD
367	TOWN HALL 2	375	Univers 75 UNIVERS	386	Washington WASHINGTON BLK.
367	Trafalgar TRAFALGAR	375	Univers 67 UNIVERS	387	Wedding Text WEDDING T
368	Trajanus TRAJANUS ITAL.	376	URBAN	387	Weiss Italic WEISS ITALIC
368	Trooper Roman TROOPER R LT.	379	Venture VENTURE	387	Weiss Roman WEISS RO BOLD
368	Trooper Roman TROOPER	379	Venus VENUS MED.	388	Weiss Roman WEISS RO X-BOLD
369	Trooper Roman TROO BLK.	379	Venus VENUS X-BOLD	388	WEISS INITIALS NO.2
369	Trooper Roman TROOPEI ITAL.	380	Veronese VERONESE	388	Weiss Initials WEISS INITIA LT.
369	Trump TRUMP MEDIAEVAL	380	Veronese VERONESE SEMI	389	Weiss Initials WEISS INI MED
370	Trump TRUMP MEDIAEVAL SEMI	380	Veronese VERONESI BOLD	389	Weiss Initials WEISS INI BOLD
370	Trump TRUMP MEDIAEVAL BOLD	381	VICKSBURG	389	Weiss Initials WEISS IN X-BOLD
370	Trump TRUMP MEDIAEVAL ITAL.	381	Victoria VICTORIA	390	Wexford WEXFORD MED.
371	Trump TRUMP MEDIAEVAL SEMI COND	381	VINETA OR ORNA-MENT	390	Wexford WEXFORD
371	Tulo TULO	382	Virtuoso1 VIRTUOSO	390	WINCHESTER X-BOLD
371	TypoScript			391	Windsor WINDSOR

391 **Windsor WINDSOI** BLK	403 *Zapf Book ZAPF BO* MED. ITAL. (ITC)	413-A **Benguiat BENGUIAT** GOTHIC HVY. (ITC)
391 Windsor WINDSOR LT. COND	404 **Zapf Book ZAPF B** DEMI ITAL. (ITC)	413-A Benguiat BENGUIAT GOTHIC BK. ITAL (ITC)
392 Windsor WINDSOR ELON-GATED	404 **Zapf Book ZAPF** HVY. ITAL. (ITC)	413-A Benguiat BENGUIAT GOTHIC MED ITAL (ITC)
392 **Windsor WINDSOR** HVY. COND	405 *Zapf Ch'ry ZAPF CH'R* CHAN-CERY LT. (ITC)	414-A **Benguiat BENGUIAT** GOTHIC BOLD ITAL. (ITC)
392 Windsor WINDSOR OUT	405 *Zapf Ch'ry ZAPF CH'F* CHAN-CERY MED (ITC)	414-A **Benguiat BENGUIAT** GOTHIC HVY. ITAL (ITC)
393 Windsor WINDSOI COM-STOCK	406 *Zapf Ch'ry ZAPF CH* CHAN-CERY DEMI (ITC)	414-A *Berling BERLING* ITAL.
393 Wolf Antiqua WOLF ANT	406 **Zapf Ch'ry ZAPF CI** CHAN-CERY BOLD (ITC)	415-A Berling BERLING SEMI
393 **WOODWARD**	407 *Zapf Ch'ry ZAPF CH'R* CHAN-CERY LT. ITAL. (ITC)	415-A Bodoni Campanile BODONI CAMPANI
394 Worcester WORCEST ROUND	407 *Zapf Ch'ry ZAPF CH'R* CHAN-CERY MED ITAL (ITC)	415-A **Bulletin BULLETIN 113**
394 Worcester WORCEST ROUND MED	408 Zapf Int'l ZAPF INT' LT. (ITC)	416-A *Candice CANDICE* INLINE
394 **Worcester WORCEST** ROUND BOLD	408 Zapf Int'l ZAPF IN' MED. (ITC)	416-A **CHEQUE**
395 *Worcester WORCESTEI* ROUND ITAL.	409 **Zapf Int'l ZAPF IN** DEMI (ITC)	416-A Chesterfield CHESTERFII
397 **Yagi Universal YAGI UI** NO. 2	409 **Zapf Int'l ZAPF I** HVY. (ITC)	417-A *Chopin CHOPIN* LT.
398 **YAGI LINK DOUBLE**	410 Zeppelin ZEPPELIN	417-A *Chopin CHOPIN* BOLD
398 York YORK		418-A *Cooper COOPER* BLACK ITAL. OUT.
398 **YUKON**	SUPPLEMENT 1	418-A **Egiziano EGIZIA**
401 Zapf Book ZAPF BOO LT. (ITC)	411-A **Aesthetic Aesthetic**	418-A **Egyptian Bold EGYPTI** BOLD (FRANCAIS)
401 Zapf Book ZAPF BC MED. (ITC)	411-A **Art Gothic ART GOTHIC** BOLD	419-A Fenice FENICE LT. (ITC)
402 **Zapf Book ZAPF E** DEMI (ITC)	411-A **BARNDANCE**	419-A Fenice FENICE REG (ITC)
402 **Zapf Book ZAPF** HVY. (ITC)	412-A Benguiat BENGUIAT GOTHIC BK. (ITC)	419-A **Fenice FENICE** BOLD (ITC)
403 *Zapf Book ZAPF BOO* LT. ITAL. (ITC)	412-A Benguiat BENGUIAT GOTHIC MED (ITC)	420-A **Fenice FENICE** ULTRA (ITC)
	412-A **Benguiat BENGUIAT** GOTHIC BOLD (ITC)	

420-A	*Fenice FENICE* LT ITAL (ITC)	427-A	**Glow Worm GLOW WORM**	434-A	**Omega OMEGA** X-BOLD
420-A	*Fenice FENICE* REG ITAL (ITC)	427-A	*Goudy GOUDY* HEAVYFACE OPEN	435-A	**Omega OMEGA** ULTRA
421-A	***Fenice FENICE*** BOLD ITAL (ITC)	428-A	*Goudy GOUDY* HEAVYFACE OPEN ITAL	435-A	**Plantin PLANTIN** X-BOLD
421-A	***Fenice FENICE*** ULTRA ITAL (ITC)	428-A	Harlequin HARLEQUIN	435-A	Premier Lightline PREMIER LIGHT
421-A	*Framingham FRAMING* ITAL	428-A	Hess Oldstyle HESS OL	436-A	*Razie RAZIE* SHADOW
422-A	**Frankfurter FRANKFURT** MED	429-A	Lectura LECTURA LT	436-A	Romic ROMIC LT.
422-A	Franklin Gothic FRANKL GOT/ BK (ITC)	429-A	L.E.D. ROMAN BOLD	437-A	Romic ROMIC MED.
422-A	Franklin Gothic FRANK GOTHIC MED (ITC)	429-A	Manquis MANQUIS	437-A	**Romic ROMIC** BOLD
423-A	**Franklin Gothic FRANK** GOTHIC DEMI (ITC)	430-A	**MERCHANT** BOLD	437-A	**Romic ROMIC** X-BOLD
423-A	**Franklin Gothic FRAN** GOTHIC HVY (ITC)	430-A	Novarese NOVARESE BK (ITC)	438-A	Savannah SAV
423-A	*Franklin Gothic FRANKL* GOTHIC BOOK ITAL (ITC)	430-A	Novarese NOVARESE MED (ITC)	438-A	Seagull SEAGULL LT
424-A	*Franklin Gothic FRANKL* MED ITAL (ITC)	431-A	**Novarese NOVARESE** BOLD (ITC)	438-A	Seagull SEAGULL MED
424-A	***Franklin Gothic FRANI*** DEMI ITAL (ITC)	431-A	**Novarese NOVARE** ULTRA (ITC)	439-A	**Seagull SEAGULL** BOLD
424-A	***Franklin Gothic FRAN*** HVY ITAL (ITC)	432-A	*Novarese NOVARESE* BK ITAL (ITC)	439-A	**Seagull SEAGULL** BLK
425-A	Franklin Gothic GOTHIC OUT (ITC)	432-A	*Novarese NOVARESE* MED ITAL (ITC)	439-A	**Sheraton SHERATO** BOLD
425-A	**Franklin Gothic FRANK** CONTOUR (ITC)	432-A	*Novarese NOVARESE* BOLD ITAL (ITC)	440-A	**Sheraton SHERA** BOLD EXTENDED
425-A	**Franklin Gothic FRANK** SHADOW (ITC)	433-A	**Olive Antique OLIVE ANT** BOLD COND.	440-A	Worcester WORCESTE ROUND OUT
426-A	French Elzevir No.1 FRENC	433-A	**Olive Antique OLIVE AN** BLACK COND.	440-A	**Worcester WORCESTE** ROUND CONTOUR
426-A	**Futura FUTURA** DEMI OBLIQUE	433-A	Omega OMEGA	441-A	Worcester WORCEST ROUND SHADOW
426-A	***Futura FUTURA*** BOLD OBLIQUE	434-A	Omega OMEGA DEMI	441-A	YANKEE SHADOW
427-A	**Gill Sans GILL SANS** X-BOLD COND	434-A	**Omega OMEGA** BOLD		

SUPPLEMENT 2

442-B *Alexandra ALEXANI*

442-B Arnholm ARNHOLM SANS MED.

442-B **Arnholm ARNHOLM** SANS BOLD

443-B Barcelona BARCELOI BOOK (ITC)

443-B Barcelona BARCELO MED. (ITC)

443-B **Barcelona BARCELO** BOLD (ITC)

444-B **Barcelona BARCEI** HVY (ITC)

444-B *Barcelona BARCELO* BOOK ITAL (ITC)

444-B *Barcelona BARCELO* MED. ITAL (ITC)

445-B *Barcelona BARCEL* BOLD ITAL (ITC)

445-B **Barcelona BARCE** HVY ITAL (ITC)

445-B *Baskerville BASKERVIL* ITAL. (VGC)

446-B ***Baskerville BASKERVI*** BOLD ITAL (VGC)

446-B Baskerville BASKERVI (ITC)

446-B Baskerville BASKERV SEMI (ITC)

447-B **Baskerville BASKERVI** BOLD (ITC)

447-B **Baskerville BASKER** BLK. (ITC)

447-B *Baskerville BASKERVIL* ITAL. (ITC)

448-B *Baskerville BASKERVIL* SEMI ITAL (ITC)

448-B ***Baskerville BASKERVIL*** BOLD ITAL (ITC)

448-B **Baskerville BASKER** BLK. ITAL (ITC)

449-B Berkeley BERKELEY O.S. BOOK (ITC)

449-B Berkeley BERKELEY O.S. MED. (ITC)

449-B Berkeley BERKELEY O.S. BOLD (ITC)

450-B **Berkeley BERKELEY** O.S. BLK. (ITC)

450-B *Berkeley BERKELEY* O.S. BOOK ITAL (ITC)

450-B *Berkeley BERKELEY* O.S. MED. ITAL (ITC)

451-B *Berkeley BERKELEY* O.S. BOLD ITAL (ITC)

451-B ***Berkeley BERKELEY*** O.S. BLK. ITAL (ITC)

451-B Bramley BRAMLEY LT.

452-B Bramley BRAMLEY MED.

452-B **Bramley BRAMLEY** BOLD

452-B **Bramley BRAMLEY** X-BOLD

453-B Brighton BRIGHTON LT.

453-B Brighton BRIGHTON MED.

453-B **Brighton BRIGHTON** BOLD

454-B *Brighton BRIGHTON* LT. ITAL

454-B **Broadway BROADW** ENGR.

454-B Caxton CAXTON ROMAN LT.

455-B Caxton CAXTON ROMAN BOOK

455-B **Caxton CAXTON** ROMAN BOLD

455-B *Caxton CAXTON* ROMAN LT. ITAL

456-B *Century CENTURY* EXPANDED ITAL

456-B **Chivaree CHIVAREE**

456-B **Clarendon CLAREN** SEMI

457-B **Corvinus CORVINUS** BOLD

457-B **Craw Clarendon CRA** BOLD

457-B Craw Modern CRA

458-B Else ELSE LT.

458-B Else ELSE MED.

458-B Else ELSE SEMI

459-B Else ELSE BOLD

459-B *Else ELSE* LT. ITAL

459-B *Else ELSE* MED. ITAL

460-B *Else ELSE* SEMI ITAL

460-B *Else ELSE* BOLD ITAL

460-B Fedora FEDORA

461-B **FRANKFURTER** HIGH LIGHT

461-B Futura FUTURA BOLD OUT

461-B GALADRIEL

462-B **Gill Sans GILL SANS** X-BOLD COND.

462-B HADRIANO STONEC STONECUT

462-B *Harlow HARLOW* SOLID	469-B Modern MODERN #216 MED. ITAL. (ITC)	476-B **Tiffany TIFFAN** HVY. ITAL. (ITC)
463-B Isbell ISBELL BOOK (ITC)	470-B Modern MODERN #216 BOLD ITAL. (ITC)	477-B TITLE GOTHIC X-COND. NO. 12
463-B Isbell ISBELL MED. (ITC)	470-B **Modern MODERN** #216 HVY. ITAL. (ITC)	477-B Tower TOWER
463-B **Isbell ISBELL** BOLD (ITC)	470-B *Murray Hill MURRAY* BOLD	SUPPLEMENT 3
464-B **Isbell ISBELL** HVY. (ITC)	471-B Normandia NORM OPEN	478-C *Aerolite AEROLITE* SCRIPT
464-B *Isbell ISBELL* BOOK ITAL. (ITC)	471-B **Nubian NUBIAN**	478-C **American Text AMERICAN TEXT**
464-B *Isbell ISBELL* MED. ITAL. (ITC)	471-B Palatino PALATINO SEMI OUT.	478-C BALLÉ INITIALS
465-B *Isbell ISBELL* BOLD ITAL. (ITC)	472-B **PROFILE**	479-C BALLOON LIGHT
465-B *Isbell ISBELL* HVY. ITAL. (ITC)	472-B PYGMALION PYGM	479-C *Balzac BALZAC*
465-B Kennerley KENNERLE O.S.	472-B Ringlet RINGLET	479-C **BANCO**
466-B Kennerley KENNER BOLD	473-B **Абвгд АБВГД** RODIN CYRILLIC	480-C **Berliner BERLINER** GROTESK
466-B *Lubalin Graph LUBA* X-LT. OBLIQUE (ITC)	473-B **Runaround RUNGR**	480-C **Berliner BERLINER** GROTESK BOLD
466-B Lubalin Graph LUE BOOK OBLIQUE (ITC)	473-B **Абвгдежзи АБВГД** RUSSIAN HELVETICA	480-C **Berling BERLING** BOLD
467-B Lubalin Graph LUI MED. OBLIQUE (ITC)	474-B **St. Thomas ST. THOMAS**	481-C **Berling BERLING** BOLD COND.
467-B **Lubalin Graph LU** DEMI OBLIQUE (ITC)	474-B SOUTACHE	481-C Beton BETON BOLD
467-B **Lubalin Graph LU** BOLD. OBLIQUE (ITC)	474-B *Stationers STATION* SEMISCRIPT	481-C **Block BLOCK**
468-B Modern MODERN #216 LT. (ITC)	475-B **Studio STUDIO** BOLD	482-C Bulfinch BULFINCH OLDSTYLE
468-B Modern MODERN #216 MED. (ITC)	475-B *THUNDERBOLT*	482-C Carnase Text CARNAS LT. (WTC)
468-B **Modern MODERN** #216 BOLD (ITC)	475-B *Tiffany TIFEANY* LT. ITAL. (ITC)	482-C Carnase Text CARNA REG. (WTC)
469-B **Modern MODERN** #216 HVY. (ITC)	476-B *Tiffany TIFEANY* MED. ITAL. (ITC)	483-C **Carnase Text CARNA** MED (WTC)
469-B *Modern MODERN* #216 LT. ITAL. (ITC)	476-B *Tiffany TIFEANY* DEMI ITAL. (ITC)	483-C **Carnase Text CARNA** BOLD (WTC)

483-C **Carnase Text CARNA** X-BOLD (WTC)

484-C *Carnase Text CARNAS* LT. ITAL. (WTC)

484-C *Carnase Text CARNAS* REG. ITAL. (WTC)

484-C *Carnase Text CARNAS* MED. ITAL. (WTC)

485-C *Carnase Text CARNA* BOLD ITAL. (WTC)

485-C **Carnase Text CARNA** X-BOLD ITAL. (WTC)

485-C Caslon 224 CASLON 22 BOOK (ITC)

486-C Caslon 224 CASLON 2 MED. (ITC)

486-C Caslon 224 CASLON 2 BOLD (ITC)

486-C **Caslon 224 CASLON** BLK. (ITC)

487-C *Caslon 224 CASLON 2* BOOK ITAL. (ITC)

487-C *Caslon 224 CASLON 2* MED. ITAL. (ITC)

487-C *Caslon 224 CASLON* BOLD ITAL. (ITC)

488-C *Caslon 224 CASLON* BLK. ITAL. (ITC)

488-C Абвгдеежзи АБВГД CASLON RUSSIAN

489-C Caslon CASLON SHADED

489-C Centaur CENTAUR ITALIC

489-C *Century CENTURY* BOLD ITAL

490-C Century CENTURY BOLD COND.

490-C Century CENTURY BOLD COND. ITAL

490-C Century CENTURY NOVA

491-C *Century CENTURY* O.S. ITAL

491-C *Century CENTURY* SCHOOLBOOK ITAL.

491-C Century CENTURY LT. (ITC)

492-C **Century CENTURY** BOLD (ITC)

492-C *Century CENTURY* LT. ITAL. (ITC)

492-C **Century CENTURY** BOLD ITAL. (ITC)

493-C Century CENTURY LT. COND. (ITC)

493-C Century CENTURY BOOK COND. (ITC)

493-C Century CENTURY BOLD COND. (ITC)

494-C **Century CENTURY** ULTRA COND. (ITC)

494-C *Century CENTURY* LT. COND. ITAL. (ITC)

494-C *Century CENTURY* BOOK COND. ITAL. (ITC)

495-C *Century CENTURY* BOLD COND. ITAL. (ITC)

495-C **Century CENTURY** ULTRA COND. ITAL. (ITC)

495-C *Charme CHARM* LIGHT

496-C *Charme CHARM* BOLD

496-C Chevalier CHEVALIER

496-C **Cloister CLOISTER** X-BOLD COND.

497-C **Columbia COLUMBIA** BOLD ITAL

497-C Congress CONGRESS (LYONS)

497-C Corinthian CORINTHIAN LIGHT

498-C Corinthian CORINTHIAN MEDIUM

498-C **Corinthian CORINTHIAN** BOLD

498-C **Corinthian CORINTHIA** X-BOLD

499-C *Corvinus CORVINUS* MED. ITAL.

499-C Corvinus Skyline CORVINUS SKYLINE

499-C Cushing CUSHING BOOK (ITC)

500-C Cushing CUSHING MED. (ITC)

500-C **Cushing CUSHING** BOLD (ITC)

500-C **Cushing CUSHING** HVY. (ITC)

501-C *Cushing CUSHING* BOOK ITAL. (ITC)

501-C *Cushing CUSHING* MED. ITAL. (ITC)

501-C *Cushing CUSHING* BOLD ITAL. (ITC)

502-C **Cushing CUSHING** HVY. ITAL. (ITC)

502-C DeRoos DEROOS ROMAN

502-C *Dianna DIANNA* LIGHT

503-C *Dianna DIANNA* MEDIUM

503-C *Dianna DIANNA* BOLD

503-C Dutch DUTCH O.S. COND.

504-C *Excelsior EXCELSIOR* SCRIPT

504-C *Excelsior EXCELSIOR* SEMI-BOLD SCRIPT

504-C FAMOUS MAGAZIN

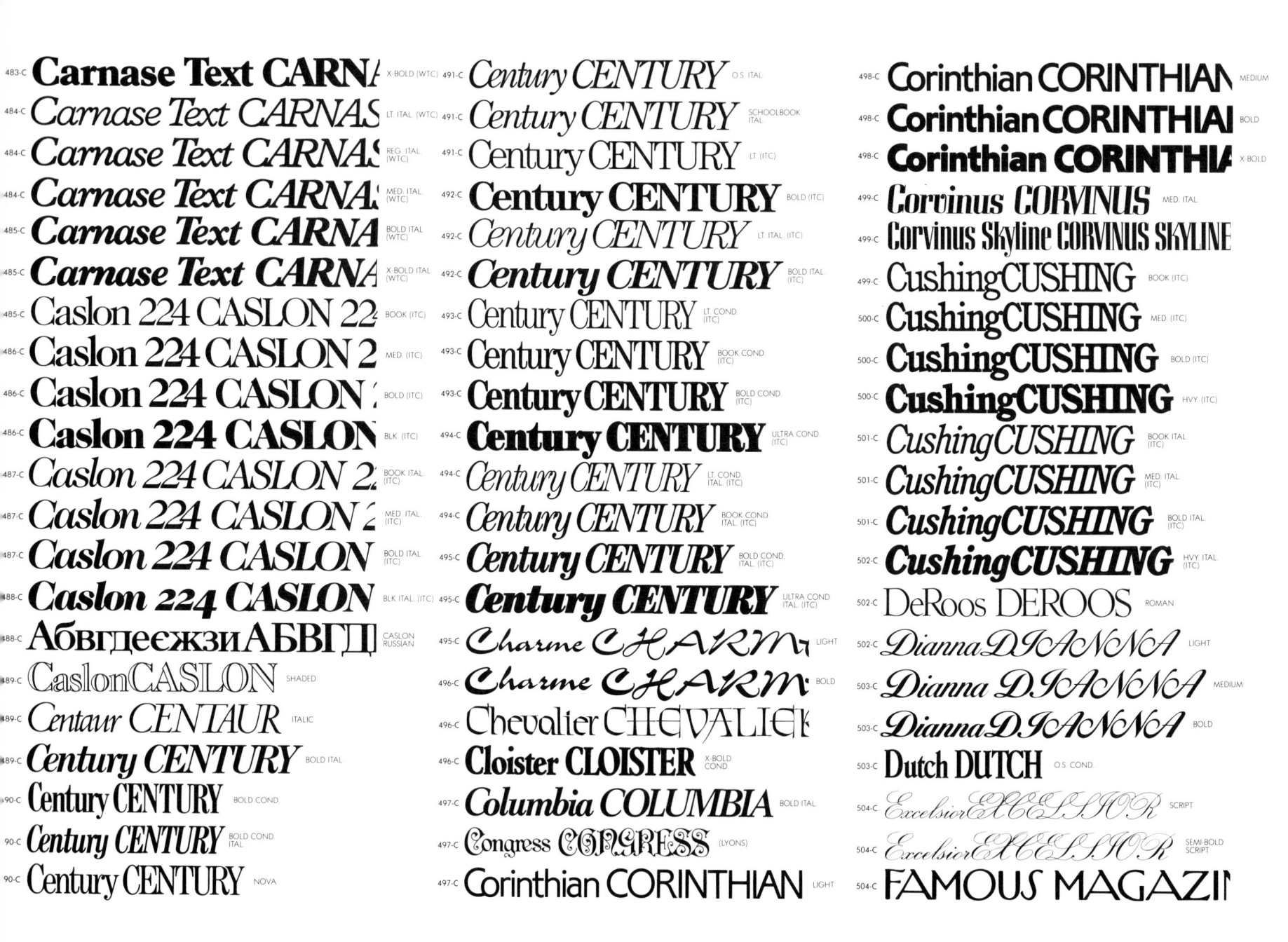

505-C Fantail FANTAIL	513-C Grotesque #9 GROTESQUE#	520-C Meridien MERIDIEN BOLD
505-C Florentine FLORENTINE CURSIVE	513-C Grouch GROUCH BLACK	520-C Meridien MERIDII X-BOLD
505-C Fox FOX	513-C Helvetica HELVETICA MED. ITAL.	520-C Meridien MERID BLACK
506-C Futura FUTURA BOLD COND. OBLIQUE	514-C Helvetica HELVETICA BOLD COND.	521-C MICROGRAMMA
506-C Futura FUTURA X-BOLD COND. OBLIQUE	514-C Helvetica HELVETICA BOLD COND. OUT.	521-C Modula MODULA
507-C Gavotte GAVOTTE	514-C Helvetica HELVETICA ROUND BOLD COND. NO. 2	521-C Modula MODULA MEDIUM
506-C Girder GIRDER HEAVY	515-C Johnston JOHNSTON RAILWAY LT.	522-C Modula MODULA BOLD
507-C GOLD RUSH	515-C Johnston JOHNSTON RAILWAY MED.	522-C Modula MODULA X-BOLD
508-C Goudy GOUDY OPEN	515-C Johnston JOHNSTON RAILWAY BOLD	522-C Normande NORMANDE COND.
508-C Goudy GOUDY OPEN ITAL.	516-C Johnston JOHNSTON RAILWAY MED. ITAL.	523-C Optima OPTIMA MEDIUM
508-C Goudy GOUDY LT. (WTC)	516-C Johnston JOHNSTON RAILWAY BOLD ITAL.	524-C Phidian PHIDIAN
509-C Goudy GOUDY REG. (WTC)	516-C Johnston JOHNSTON RAILWAY MED. COND.	523-C Primus PR
509-C Goudy GOUDY MED. (WTC)	517-C Johnston JOHNSTON RAILWAY BOLD COND.	524-C Radiant RADIANT BOLD COND.
509-C Goudy GOUDY BOLD (WTC)	517-C Karnac KARNAC	524-C Rock and Roll ROCK AN LIGHT
510-C Goudy GOUDY LT. ITAL. SWASH (WTC)	517-C Kennerley KENNERL BOLD ITAL.	525-C Rock and Roll ROCK BOLD
510-C Goudy GOUDY MED. ITAL. SWASH (WTC)	518-C Kunstler KUNSTL BOLD	525-C Rock and Roll ROCK AN LT. ITAL.
511-C Goudy GOUDY REG. ITAL. SWASH (WTC)	518-C Legend LEGEND	525-C Rock and Roll ROCK BOLD ITAL.
511-C Goudy GOUDY BOLD ITAL. SWASH (ITC)	518-C LIBRA	526-C Rondo RONDO BOLD
512-C GoudyItalian GOUDY IT	519-C Lydian LYDIAN	526-C Royal ROYAL
512-C GoudyItalian GOUD X-BOLD	519-C Meridien MERIDIEN LIGHT	526-C Sally Mae SALLY MAE LIGHT
512-C GRAPHIQUE	519-C Meridien MERIDIEN MEDIUM	527-C Sally Mae SALLY MAE MEDIUM

527-C **Sally Mae SALLY MAE** DEMI	534-C **Solon Antiqua. SOLON** BOLD	541-C *Univers 66 UNIVERS 6*
527-C **Sally Mae SALLY MA** HEAVY	534-C *Stuyvesant STUYVESANT* SCRIPT	541-C **Univers 76 UNIVERS**
528-C Sampler SAMPLER	535-C Symbol SYMBOL BOOK (ITC)	542-C Univers 59 UNIVERS 59
528-C Serifa SERIFA THIN	535-C Symbol SYMBOL MED. (ITC)	542-C **Univers 73 UNIVI**
528-C Serifa SERIFA LIGHT	535-C **Symbol SYMBOL** BOLD (ITC)	542-C *Valiant VALIANT* LIGHT
529-C Serifa SERIFA	536-C **Symbol SYMBOL** BLK. (ITC)	543-C *Valiant VALIANT* BOLD
529-C **Serifa SERIFA** BOLD	536-C *Symbol SYMBOL* BOOK ITAL. (ITC)	543-C Veljovic VELJOVIC BOOK (ITC)
529-C **Serifa SERIFA** BLACK	536-C *Symbol SYMBOL* MED. ITAL. (ITC)	543-C Veljovic VELJOVIC MED. (ITC)
530-C *Serifa SERIFA* THIN ITAL.	537-C *Symbol SYMBOL* BOLD ITAL. (ITC)	544-C **Veljovic VELJOVIC** BOLD (ITC)
530-C *Serifa SERIFA* LT. ITAL.	537-C ***Symbol SYMBOL*** BLK. ITAL. (ITC)	544-C **Veljovic VELJOVIC** BLK. (ITC)
530-C *Serifa SERIFA* ITALIC	537-C **TEA CHEST**	545-C *Veljovic VELJOVIC* BOOK ITAL. (ITC)
531-C Serpentine SERPEN LIGHT	538-C Thaddeus THADDEUS LT. (WTC)	545-C *Veljovic VELJOVIC* MED. ITAL. (ITC)
531-C **Serpentine SERPI** MEDIUM	538-C Thaddeus THADDEUS REG. (WTC)	546-C *Veljovic VELJOVIC* BOLD ITAL. (ITC)
531-C **Serpentine SER** BOLD	538-C Thaddeus THADDEUS MED. (WTC)	546-C ***Veljovic VELJOVIC*** BLK. ITAL. (ITC)
532-C *Serpentine SERPEN* LT. ITAL.	539-C **Thaddeus THADDEUS** BOLD (WTC)	547-C Weidemann WEIDEMAN BOOK (ITC)
532-C ***Serpentine SERPI*** MED. ITAL.	539-C *Thaddeus THADDEUS* LT. ITAL. (WTC)	547-C Weidemann WEIDEMAN MED. (ITC)
532-C Signum SIGNUM	539-C *Thaddeus THADDEUS* REG. ITAL. (WTC)	547-C **Weidemann WEIDEMA** BOLD (ITC)
533-C Simoncini Garamond SIMC	540-C *Thaddeus THADDEUS* MED. ITAL. (WTC)	548-C **Weidemann WEIDEI** BLK. (ITC)
533-C Solon Antiqua. SOLON AN LIGHT	540-C ***Thaddeus THADDEUS*** BOLD ITAL. (WTC)	548-C *Weidemann WEIDEMANN* BOOK ITAL. (ITC)
533-C Solon Antiqua. SOLON A NORMAL	540-C *Univers 46 UNIVERS 46*	548-C *Weidemann WEIDEMAN* MED. ITAL. (ITC)
534-C **Solon Antiqua. SOLON A** SEMI-BOLD	541-C *Univers 56 UNIVERS 56*	549-C *Weidemann WEIDEMA* BOLD ITAL. (ITC)

549-C **_Weidemann WEIDEM_** BLK. ITAL. (ITC)

549-C WTG 145 LIGHT

550-C WTG 145 REGULAR

550-C **WTG 145** MEDIUM

550-C **WTG 145** BOLD

551-C **WTG 145** X-BOLD

551-C _WTG 145_ LT. ITAL.

551-C _WTG 145_ REG. ITAL.

552-C _WTG 145_ MED. ITAL.

552-C **_WTG 145_** BOLD ITAL.

552-C **_WTG 145_** X-BOLD ITAL.

553-C _Zapf Int'l ZAPF INT'l_ LT. ITAL. (ITC)

553-C _Zapf Int'l ZAPF INT'l_ MED. ITAL. (ITC)

554-C **_Zapf Int'l ZAPF IN'_** DEMI. ITAL. (ITC)

554-C **_Zapf Int'l ZAPF I_** HVY. ITAL. (ITC)

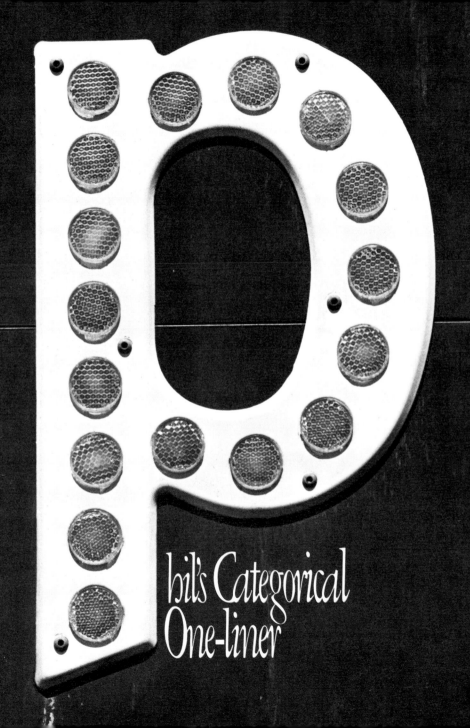

phil's Categorical
One-liner

Categories

Evenly weighted sans serifs

Thick and thin sans serifs

Bracketed serifs

Ruled serifs

Spur serifs

Soft serifs

Square serifs

Extra light

To make this categorical index easy to use for both typophiles and novices, traditional categories have been eliminated in favor of ones which better catch the "feel" of a typeface.

It was felt that borderline faces should be included in all possible categories to allow you the option of comparison. Thus Joric, which is a condensed, ultra bold, evenly weighted sans serif, stencil face is displayed in four categories.

In addition to classifying the serifs (or lack of them), workhorse categories such as "Ultra bold" allow for quick and easy comparison of the blackest of the blacks. Faces of narrow proportions have been grouped together, but it should be remembered that any face can be condensed to your specifications at an additional charge. Subheads have been inserted in some categories to help you zero in on their most telling traits.

This categorical index was completed with the first publication of this catalog, and has been revised to include the three supplements in these groups.

2321 Wisconsin Ave. NW, Washington, DC 20007
202-293-2214 / 1-800-424-2977

Evenly weighted sans serifs

2	Advertisers ADVERTISE — GOTHIC LT
3	**Advertisers ADVER** — GOTHIC
3	Advertisers Gothic ADVERTISE — GOTHIC COND.
6	**ALPHA MIDNIGI** — MIDNIGHT
7	Alternate Gothic ALTERNATE G(— NO. 3
15	**Anzeigen ANZEIGEN** — GROTESK BOLD
19	Argentica ARGENTICA — BOOK
19	Argentica ARGENTICA — MED
19	Argentica ARGENTIC — DEMI
20	**Argentica ARGENTIC** — BOLD
20	Arpad ARPAD — MED
24	Aurora AURORA AURORA — COND
25	**Aurora AURORA** — GROTESK IX
25	Avant Garde AVANT GARL — GOTHIC X-LT (ITC)
25	Avant Garde AVANT GARL — GOTHIC BOOK (ITC)
26	Avant Garde AVANT GARL — GOTHIC MED (ITC)

26	**Avant Garde AVANT GAR** — GOTHIC DEMI (ITC)
26	**Avant Garde AVANT G** — GOTHIC BOLD (ITC)
27	Avant Garde AVANT GARDE — GOTHIC BOOK COND (ITC)
27	Avant Garde AVANT GARDE — GOTHIC MED COND (ITC)
27	Avant Garde AVANT GARDE — GOTHIC DEMI COND (ITC)
28	**Avant Garde AVANT GARDE** — GOTHIC BOLD COND (ITC)
31	**BABY TEETH**
40	Bauhaus BAUHAUS — LT (ITC)
41	Bauhaus BAUHAUS — MED (ITC)
41	**Bauhaus BAUHAUS** — DEMI (ITC)
41	**Bauhaus BAUHAUS** — BOLD (ITC)
42	**Bauhaus BAUHAUS** — HVY (ITC)
51	Bernhard BERNNHAF — FASHION
51	Bernhard BERNHARD — GOTHIC LT
52	Bernhard BERNHARD — GOTHIC MED
52	**Bernhard BERNHAF** — GOTHIC X-HVY

55	Blippo BLIPPO — BOLD
55	**Blippo BLIPPO** — BLK
56	**Block Engraving BLOCK**
59	**Bolt BOLT** — BOLD (ITC)
75	Bubble BUBBLE
75	**Bubble BUBBLE** — DUBBLE
77	BUSORAMA BUSORAMA — LT (ITC)
77	BUSORAMA — BOOK (ITC)
77	BUSORAMA BUSORAMA — MED (ITC)
78	BUSORAMA BUSORAMA — BOLD (ITC)
99	**Checkmate CHECKI**
123	Compacta COMPACTA — LT.
123	**Compacta COMPACTA**
124	**Compacta COMPACTA** — BOLD
133	Dempsey DEMPSEY — MED
134	Design DESIGN — FINELINE
134	Design DESIGN — MED.
135	Design DESIGN — DEMI
135	**Design DESIGN** — X-BOLD
138	Dynamo DYNAMO — MED.
139	**Dynamo DYNAMO**

EVENLY WEIGHTED SANS SERIFS

EVENLY WEIGHTED SANS SERIFS

141 **EAGLE** BOLD

148 *Emphasis EMPHAS.*

149 ERAS

149 Eras ERAS LT. (ITC)

149 Eras ERAS BOOK (ITC)

150 Eras ERAS MED. (ITC)

150 **Eras ERAS** DEMI (ITC)

150 **Eras ERAS** BOLD (ITC)

151 **Eras ERAS** ULTRA (ITC)

152 Eurostile EUROS EXT.

153 **Eurostile EURC** BOLD EXT.

159 Folio FOLIO MED.

159 **Folio FOLIO** X-BOLD

161 **FRANKFURTER**

162 **Franklin Gothic FRANI**

163 **Franklin Gothic FRAN** BLK

163 **Franklin Gothic FRANKLIN** COND.

163 **Franklin Gothic FRANKLIN GOTHI** X-COND

164 **Franklin Gothic FRANKLIN GOTHI** BLK X-COND.

166 Futura FUTURA LT.

166 Futura FUTURA BOOK

167 Futura FUTURA MED.

167 Futura FUTURA DEMI

167 **Futura FUTURA** BOLD

168 **Futura FUTURA** X-BOLD

168 **Futura FUTURA** BOLD COND.

168 **Futura FUTURA** X-BOLD COND.

169 **Futura FUTURA** DISPLAY

184 **GETTYSBURG**

184 Gill Sans GILL SANS LT.

185 Gill Sans GILL SANS MED.

185 Gill Sans GILL SANS BOLD

185 **Gill Sans GILL SANS** X-BOLD

186 **Gill Sans GILL SAN** ULTRA

186 *Gill Sans GILL SANS* LT. ITAL.

186 *Gill Sans GILL SANS* BOLD ITAL.

187 **Gill Sans GILL SANS** BOLD COND.

187 Gill Sans GILL SANS BOLD X-COND.

195 Granby GRANBY LT.

195 Granby GRANBY

195 **Granby GRANBY** BOLD

196 **Granby GRANBY** X-BOLD

196 **Granby GRANBY** ELEPHANT

197 **Grizzly GRIZZLY**

197 **Grotesque No.9 GROTESQI**

201 **Handel HANDEL** GOTHIC LT.

202 **Handel HANDEL** GOTHIC

203 Harry HARRY THIN

204 Harry HARRY PLAIN

204 Harry HARRY HVY.

204 Harry HARRY FAT

205 **Harry HARRY** OBESE

205 **Harry HARRY** OBESE SQUEEZED

205 Helvetica HELVETICA X-LT.

206 Helvetica HELVETICA LT.

206 Helvetica HELVETICA

206 Helvetica HELVETICA MED.

207 Helvetica HELVETICA DEMI

207 **Helvetica HELVETIC** BOLD

207 **Helvetica HELVETIC** X-BOLD

208 *Helvetica HELVETICA* LT. ITAL.

208 *Helvetica HELVETICA* ITAL.

208 *Helvetica HELVETIC* BOLD COMPACT ITAL

EVENLY WEIGHTED SANS SERIFS

352 **Syntax Antiqua S** BOLD

355 **T.H.ALPHABET SOUP**

355 Tabasco TABASCO LT.

356 Tabasco TABASCO MED.

356 **Tabasco TABASCO** BOLD

366 **Topic Futura TOPIC FUTL**

374 Univers 45 UNIVERS

374 Univers 55 UNIVERS

375 Univers 65 UNIVERS

375 **Univers 75 UNIVERS**

375 Univers 67 UNIVERS

379 Venus VENUS MED.

379 **Venus VENUS** X-BOLD

385 Washington WASHINGTON X-LT.

385 Washington WASHINGTON LT.

386 Washington WASHINGTON MED.

386 **Washington WASHINGTON** BOLD

386 **Washington WASHINGTON** BLK.

390 Wexford WEXFORD MED.

390 **Wexford WEXFORD** X-BOLD

390 **WINCHESTER**

397 Yagi Universal YAGI UI NO. 2

412-A Benguiat BENGUIAT GOTHIC BK. (ITC)

412-A Benguiat BENGUIAT GOTHIC MED. (ITC)

412-A **Benguiat BENGUIAT** GOTHIC BOLD (ITC)

413-A **Benguiat BENGUIAT** GOTHIC HVY (ITC)

413-A Benguiat BENGUIAT GOTHIC BK. ITAL (ITC)

413-A Benguiat BENGUIAT GOTHIC MED ITAL (ITC)

414-A Benguiat BENGUIAT GOTHIC BOLD ITAL (ITC)

414-A **Benguiat BENGUIAT** GOTHIC HVY ITAL (ITC)

422-A **Frankfurter FRANKFURT** MED

426-A Futura FUTURA DEMI OBLIQUE

426-A **Futura FUTURA** BOLD OBLIQUE

427-A **Gill Sans GILL SANS** X-BOLD COND

433-A **Olive Antique OLIVE ANT** BOLD COND.

433-A **Olive Antique OLIVE AN** BLACK COND.

473-B **Абвгдежзи АБВГД** RUSSIAN HELVETICA

460-B Fedora FEDORA

477-B TITLE GOTHIC X-COND. NO. 12

480-C Berliner BERLINER GROTESK

480-C **Berliner BERLINER** GROTESK BOLD

481-C **Block BLOCK**

497-C Corinthian CORINTHIAN LIGHT

498-C Corinthian CORINTHIAN MEDIUM

498-C **Corinthian CORINTHIAI** BOLD

498-C **Corinthian CORINTHIA** X-BOLD

506-C *Futura FUTURA* BOLD COND. OBLIQUE

506-C *Futura FUTURA* X-BOLD COND. OBLIQUE

513-C *Helvetica HELVETICA* MED. ITAL

514-C **Helvetica HELVETICA** BOLD COND.

514-C **Helvetica HELVETICA** ROUND BOLD COND. NO. 2

515-C Johnston JOHNSTON RAILWAY LT.

515-C Johnston JOHNSTON RAILWAY MED.

515-C **Johnston JOHNSTON** RAILWAY BOLD

516-C Johnston JOHNSTON RAILWAY MED. ITAL

516-C **Johnston JOHNSTON** RAILWAY BOLD ITAL.

516-C Johnston JOHNSTON RAILWAY MED. COND.

517-C **Johnston JOHNSTON** RAILWAY BOLD COND.

526-C Sally Mae SALLY MAE LIGHT

527-C Sally Mae SALLY MAE MEDIUM

527-C **Sally Mae** **SALLY MAE** DEMI

527-C **Sally Mae** **SALLY MA** HEAVY

532-C Signum SIGNUM

540-C *Univers 46 UNIVERS 46*

541-C *Univers 56 UNIVERS 56*

541-C *Univers 66 UNIVERS 6*

541-C *Univers 76 UNIVERS*

542-C Univers 59 UNIVERS 59

542-C **Univers 73 UNIVE**

EVENLY WEIGHTED SANS SERIFS

Thick and thin sans serifs

34 Baker Signet BAKER SIGN

54 **Binner BINNER**

72 **Britannic BRITANNI** BOLD

73 **Broadway BROAD**

73 **Broadway BROAD** BOLD

81 California CALIFORNIA GROTESK

81 California CALIFORNIA GROTESK MED.

81 **California CALIFORNIA** GROTESK BOLD

82 **California CALIFORNIA** GROTESK BLK.

83 CAMELOT

116 Clearface CLEARFACE GOTHIC

117 **Clearface CLEARFACE** GOTHIC BOLD

128 Cucumber CUCUMBER

136 DEUTSCH BLACK

158 Florentine FLORENTINE

188 Globe Gothic GLOBE GOTHIC COND.

188 Globe Gothic GLOBE GO

188 **Globe Gothic GLOB**

211 Hensby HENSBY

221 **Information**

225 Jana JANA

226 Japanette JAPANETTE

237 **Koloss KOLOSS**

246 Lee LEE

247 LINCOLN GOTHIC

255 Manhattan MANHATTA (ITC)

261 **Modernique MODI**

267 **Neil NEIL** BOLD

268 **NEULAND**

269 **NEULAND** BLK.

276 *Old Gothic OLD GC* BOLD ITAL.

279 Optima OPTIMA

280 **Optima OPTIMA** SEMI

280 **Optima OPTIMA** BOLD

280 *Optima OPTIMA* ITAL.

289 Parisian PARISIAN

291 **Patriot PATRIOT**

292 Peignot PEIGNOT LT.

292 Peignot PEIGNOT DEMI

292 **Peignot PEIGNOT** BOLD

293 Pekin PEKIN

294 **Permanent PERMANENT** MASSIV

299 **Placard PLACARD** BOLD COND.

311 **RAILROAD GOTHIC**

320 ROCO

323 **Romany ROMANY ROI** ROUND HAND

325 Rustikalis RUSTIKAL MODERN-IZED GOTHIC

328 *Sans Serif SANS SERIF* COND. ITAL.

345 Stark STARRK DEBONAIR

345 Stark STARRK SEMI

SUPPLEMENT 1

422-A Franklin Gothic FRANKL GOTH BK (ITC)

422-A **Franklin Gothic FRANKI** GOTHIC MED (ITC)

Franklin Gothic FRANI GOTHIC DEMI (ITC)

Franklin Gothic FRAN GOTHIC HVY (ITC)

Franklin Gothic FRANKL GOTHIC BOOK ITAL (ITC)

Franklin Gothic FRANKL MED ITAL (ITC)

Franklin Gothic FRANI DEMI ITAL (ITC)

Franklin Gothic FRAN HVY ITAL (ITC)

423-A
423-A
423-A
424-A
424-A
424-A

SUPPLEMENT 2

442-B Arnholm ARNHOLM SANS MED.

442-B **Arnholm ARNHOLM** SANS BOLD

473-B **Абвгд АБВГД** RODIN CYRILLIC

475-B Studio STUDIO BOLD

SUPPLEMENT 3

479-C *BANCO*

504-C FAMOUS MAGAZII

513-C **Grotesque #9 GROTESQUE**

519-C Lydian LYDIAN

521-C Modula MODULA

521-C Modula MODULA MEDIUM

522-C **Modula MODULA** BOLD

522-C **Modula MODULA** X-BOLD

THICK AND THIN SANS SERIFS

523-C Optima OPTIMA MEDIUM

524-C **RadiantRADIANT** BOLD COND.

Bracketed serifs

11 Americana AMER

11 *Americana AMER* ITAL

12 Americana AMER BOLD

12 **Americana AME** X-BOLD

12 **Americana AME** BLK

13 Andrich Minerva AN

13 **Annlie ANNLIE** X-BOLD

20 Arrow ARROW

21 Art Gothic ART GOTHIC

21 Artcraft ARTCRAFT

22 Aster ASTER

22 **Aster ASTER** BOLD

22 **Aster ASTER** X-BOLD

23 **Aster ASTER** BLK

31 Baker Danmark 1 BAKE

32 Baker Danmark 2 BA

32 Baker Danmark 3 BA

32 Baker Danmark 4 BA

33 **Baker Danmark 5 B**

33 **Baker Danmark 6 I** 6

34 Baker Signet BAKER SIGN

34 **Baker Signet BAK** BLK

36 Basilea BASILEA

37 Baskerville BASKERVIL

37 **Baskerville BASKERV** BOLD

37 **Baskerville BASKE** BOLD NO. 312

39 BAUER TEXT INITIALS

43 Belwe BELWE LT.

43 **Belwe BELWE** MED

44 **Belwe BELWE** BOLD

44 Bembo BEMBO

45 *Bembo BEMBO* ITAL

45 **Bembo BEMBO** BOLD

45 **Bembo BEMBO** BLK

46 Benguiat BENGUIAT BOOK (ITC)

46 Benguiat BENGUIA MED (ITC)

46 **Benguiat BENGUI** BOLD (ITC)

47 *Benguiat BENGUIA* BOOK ITAL (ITC)

47 *Benguiat BENGUIA* MED (ITC)

47 ***Benguiat BENGU*** BOLD ITAL (ITC)

48 Benguiat BENGUIAT BOOK COND (ITC)

48 Benguiat BENGUIAT MED COND (ITC)

48 **Benguiat BENGUIAT** BOLD COND (ITC)

49 *Benguiat BENGUIAT* BOOK COND ITAL (ITC)

49 *Benguiat BENGUIAT* MED COND ITAL (ITC)

49 ***Benguiat BENGUIAT*** BOLD COND ITAL (ITC)

50 Benton BENTON

50 Berling BERLING ANTIQUA

50 **Bernase BERNASE** ROMAN (ITC)

60 Book LSC BOOK REG (ITC)

60 **Book LSC BOOK** BOLD (ITC)

60 **Book LSC BOOK** X-BOLD (ITC)

61 ***Book LSC BOOK*** X-BOLD ITAL (ITC)

62 Bookman BOOKMA LT (ITC)

62 Bookman BOOKM MED (ITC)

63 **Bookman BOOKM** DEMI (ITC)

63 **Bookman BOOK** BOLD (ITC)

64 Bookman BOOKM — LT. ITAL (ITC)	90 Caslon CASLON — BOLD NO. 223 (ITC)	100 Cheltenham CHELTENH — MED
64 Bookman BOOKM — MED. ITAL (ITC)	90 Caslon CASLON — X-BOLD NO. 223 (ITC)	100 Cheltenham CHELTEN — BOLD
65 Bookman BOOKI — DEMI ITAL (ITC)	91 Caslon CASLON — BOLD ITAL NO. 223 (ITC)	101 Cheltenham CHELT — HVY
65 Bookman BOOK — BOLD ITAL. (ITC)	91 Caslon CASLON — X-BOLD ITAL. NO 223 (ITC)	101 Cheltenham CHELTENH — MED. ITAL
68 Bookman BOOKMAN	91 Caslon CASLON — MODERN	101 Cheltenham CHELTEN — BOLD ITAL
68 Bookman BOOKMAN — ITAL.	92 Caslon CASLON — SWASH (ARRIOLA)	102 Cheltenham CHELTENHAM — O.S. COND.
69 Bookman BOOKMAN — BOLD ITAL.	92 Caslon CASLON CASL — (AMERICAN) ITAL.	102 Cheltenham CHELTENHAM — BOLD COND.
69 Bookman BOOKMAN — BOLD ITAL. (VGC)	93 Celtic Cursive CELTIC CU	103 Cheltenham CHELTENH — LT. (ITC)
85 Caslon NEW CASLON	94 Celtic Cursive CELTIC (— BOLD	103 Cheltenham CHELTEN — BOOK (ITC)
85 Caslon NEW CASLON — ITAL.	94 Centaur CENTAUR	103 Cheltenham CHELTE — BOLD (ITC)
85 Caslon CASLON — 471 ROMAN	95 Century CENTURY — EXPANDED	104 Cheltenham CHI — ULTRA (ITC)
86 Caslon CASLON — 471 ITAL SWASH	95 Century CENTURY — O.S.	104 Cheltenham CHI — ULTRA ITAL. (ITC)
86 Caslon CASLON — 540	95 Century CENTURY — O.S. BOLD	105 Cheltenham CHELTENH — LT. ITAL (ITC)
87 Caslon CASLON — 540 ITAL	96 Century CENTURY — SCHOOLBOOK	105 Cheltenham CHELTEN — BOOK ITAL. (ITC)
87 Caslon CASLON — 641	96 Century CENTURY — SCHOOLBOOK BOLD	105 Cheltenham CHELT — BOLD ITAL. (ITC)
87 Caslon CASLON — BOLD	96 Century CENTURY — BOOK (ITC)	106 Cheltenham CHELTENHAM — LT. COND. (ITC)
88 Caslon CASLON — BOLD ITAL.	97 Century CENTUR — ULTRA (ITC)	106 Cheltenham CHELTENHAM — BOOK COND. (ITC)
88 Caslon CASLON — OLD FACE HVY.	97 Century CENTURY — BOOK ITAL. (ITC)	106 Cheltenham CHELTENHA — BOLD COND. (ITC)
88 Caslon CASLON — OLD FACE ULTRA BLK.	97 Century CENTU — ULTRA ITAL. (ITC)	107 Cheltenham CHELTEN — ULTRA COND. (ITC)
89 Caslon CASLON — LT. NO. 223 (ITC)	98 Century CENTURY — MODERN SWASH	108 Cheltenham CHELTENHAM — LIGHT COND. ITAL. (ITC)
89 Caslon CASLON — REG. NO. 223 (ITC)	100 Cheltenham CHELTENH — O.S.	108 Cheltenham CHELTENHAM — BOOK COND. ITAL. (ITC)

BRACKETED SERIFS

BRACKETED SERIFS

#	Sample	Weight
108	*Cheltenham CHELTENH*	BOLD COND ITAL (ITC)
107	**Cheltenham CHELTE**	ULTRA COND ITAL (ITC)
114	Clearface CLEARFACE	REG (ITC)
114	Clearface CLEARFACE	BOLD (ITC)
114	Clearface CLEARFAC	HVY (ITC)
115	**Clearface CLEARFA**	BLK (ITC)
115	*Clearface CLEARFA*	BLK ITAL (ITC)
116	**Clearface CLEARFAC**	X-BOLD
116	**Clearface CLEARFACI**	BLK
117	Cloister CLOISTER	O.S.
117	Cloister CLOISTER	BOLD
118	**Cloister CLOISTER**	X-BOLD
118	**Cloister CLOISTER**	HVY
119	Cochin COCHIN	O.S. NO. 61
119	Cochin COCHIN	ROMAN
120	Cochin COCHIN	ROMAN BOLD
120	**Cochin COCHIN**	ROMAN BLK
120	*Cochin COCHIN*	ITAL
121	*Cochin COCHIN*	BOLD ITAL
121	*Cochin COCHIN*	BLK ITAL
122	Columbus COLUMBUS	
122	**Columbus COLUMBL**	BOLD
124	Consort CONSORT	
128	**Cushing CUSHING**	O.S. X-BOLD
131	**DAVIDA DAVIDA**	BOLD
131	Della Robbia DELLA ROI	
132	Della Robbia DELLA ROI	BOLD
132	**Della Robbia DELLA R**	X BOLD
132	**Della Robbia DELLA R**	HVY
133	*Delphin 2 DELPHIN*	NO. 2
136	**Devinne DEVINNE**	X-BOLD
136	**Devinne DEVINNE**	BLK
142	Egyptian EGYPTIAN	505 LT.
143	Egyptian EGYPTIAI	505 MED.
143	**Egyptian EGYPTIA**	505 BOLD
148	Enge Etienne ENGE ETIENNE	
157	**Flange FLANGE**	
160	Folkwang FOLKWANG	
161	Framingham FRAMING	
165	FrizQuadrata FRIZQU	(ITC)
165	FrizQuadrata FRIZ (	MED
165	**FrizQuadrata FRIZ (**	DEMI
166	**FrizQuadrata FRIZ (**	BOLD (ITC)
173	Galliard GALLIARD	
173	**Galliard GALLIARD**	BOLD
174	**Galliard GALLIARD**	BLK
174	**Galliard GALLIAR**	ULTRA
174	*Galliard GALLIARD*	ITAL
175	*Galliard GALLIARD*	BOLD ITAL
175	*Galliard GALLIARI*	BLK ITAL
175	*Galliard GALLIAR*	ULTRA ITAL
176	Garamond GARAMO	LT (ITC)
176	Garamond GARAMO	BOOK (ITC)
176	**Garamond GARA**	BOLD (ITC)
177	**Garamond GARA**	ULTRA (ITC)
177	*Garamond GARAM*	LT ITAL (ITC)
177	*Garamond GARAM*	BOOK ITAL (ITC)
178	*Garamond GARA*	BOLD ITAL (ITC)
178	*Garamond GARA*	ULTRA ITAL (ITC)
178	Garamond GARAMOND	LT COND (ITC)
179	Garamond GARAMOND	BOOK COND (ITC)
179	Garamond GARAMOI	BOLD COND (ITC)
179	**Garamond GARAMO**	ULTRA COND (ITC)

180	*Garamond GARAMOND*	LT. COND. ITAL. (ITC)
180	*Garamond GARAMON*	BOOK COND. ITAL. (ITC)
180	**Garamond GARAMON**	BOLD COND. ITAL. (ITC)
181	**Garamond GARAM**	ULTRA COND. ITAL. (ITC)
181	Garamond GARAMON	O.S.
181	*Garamond GARAMOND*	O.S. ITAL.
182	Garamond GARAMO	BOLD
182	**Garamond GARAMO**	HVY.
182	**Garamond GARAI**	O.S. X-BOLD
183	Gesh Ortega GESH OI	
189	Goudy GOUDY	O.S.
189	*Goudy GOUDY*	O.S. ITAL.
190	Goudy GOUDY	CATALOGUE
190	**Goudy GOUDY**	BOLD
190	*Goudy GOUDY*	BOLD ITAL.
191	**Goudy GOUDY**	X-BOLD
191	**Goudy GOUDY**	BLK.
191	**Goudy GOUDY**	BLK. ITAL.
194	*Goudy GOUDY*	CURSIVE
198	**Grouch GRROUCH**	(ITC)
213	Holland HOLLAND	

213	**Holland HOLLAND**	MED.
214	**Holland HOLLAND**	SEMI
214	**Holland HOLLAND**	BOLD
219	Imprint IMPRINT	
220	**Imprint IMPRINT**	BOLD
225	Janson JANSON	
225	*Janson JANSON*	ITAL.
227	Jenson JENSON	O.S.
227	**Jenson JENSON**	
228	**Jenson Book JENSC**	BOLD
228	**Jenson Book JENSON**	X-BOLD
228	Jenson JENSON	COND.
235	**Kap Antiqua KAPA**	ANTIQUA BOLD
238	Korinna KORINNA	(ITC)
238	**Korinna KORINNA**	BOLD (ITC)
238	**Korinna KORINNA**	X-BOLD (ITC)
239	**Korinna KORINN**	HVY. (ITC)
239	*Korinna KORINNA*	KURSIV (ITC)
240	*Korinna KORINNA*	KURSIV BOLD (ITC)
240	***Korinna KORINNA***	KURSIV X-BOLD (ITC)
240	***Korinna KORINN***	KURSIV HVY. (ITC)

244	Lafayette LAFAYETTE	
244	LARGO	LT.
246	**Life Antiqua LIFE ANT**	BOLD
253	**Macbeth MACBETH macB**	
256	**Marten Roman MART**	
257	Melior MELIOR	
258	**Melior MELIOR**	SEMI
258	MICHELANGELO	
260	**Milano Roman MILAN**	(ITC)
260	Modern No20 MODEI	
262	Musketeer MUSKETEER	LT.
263	Musketeer MUSKETEEI	REG.
263	Musketeer MUSKETEE	DEMI
263	**Musketeer MUSKETI**	BOLD
264	**Musketeer MUSKET**	X-BOLD
270	Newtext NEWTE>	BOOK (ITC)
270	Newtext NEWTE>	REG. (ITC)
271	**Newtext NEWTE**	DEMI (ITC)
271	*Newtext NEWTEX*	REG. ITAL. (ITC)
279	**Onyx ONYX**	
286	Palatino PALATINO	ROMAN

BRACKETED SERIFS

BRACKETED SERIFS

#		
286	**Palatino PALATINO**	SEMI
287	**Palatino PALATINO**	BOLD (SOFT SERIF)
287	**Palatino PALATINO**	BOLD (HARD SERIF)
287	*Palatino PALATINO*	ITAL.
288	*Palatino PALATINO*	CURSIVE
294	PERPETUA	TITLING LT.
295	Perpetua PERPETUA	ROMAN
295	**Perpetua PERPETU**	BOLD
295	**Perpetua PERPET**	X-BOLD
296	**Perpetua PERPE**	BLK.
296	*Perpetua PERPETUA*	ITAL.
296	***Perpetua PERPETU***	BOLD ITAL.
298	**Pistilli Roman PISTI**	
299	Plantin PLANTIN	
300	**Plantin PLANTIN**	BOLD
300	**Plantin PLANTIN**	BOLD COND.
307	Quorum QUORUM	LT. (ITC)
307	Quorum QUORUM	BOOK (ITC)
308	Quorum QUORUM	MED. (ITC)
308	Quorum QUORUM	BOLD (ITC)
308	**Quorum QUORUM**	BLK. (ITC)
311	Raleigh RALEIGH	X-LT.
312	Raleigh RALEIGH	LT.
312	Raleigh RALEIGH	MED.
312	**Raleigh RALEIGH**	DEMI
313	**Raleigh RALEIGH**	BOLD
313	**Raleigh RALEIGH**	X BOLD
315	**Reubens REUBENS**	WIDE
317	Richmond RICHMONI	O.S.
317	Richmond RICHMOI	O.S. BOLD
318	*Richmond RICHMOI*	O.S. ITAL.
318	Richmond RICHMOND	O.S. COND.
321	Rococo ROCOCO	
321	Roman ROMAN	COMPRESSED NO. 3
322	Romana ROMANA	NORMAL
322	**Romana ROMANA**	BOLD
322	**Romana ROMANA**	ULTRA
327	Sabon SABON	ROMAN
327	**Sabon SABON**	BOLD
327	*Sabon SABON*	ITAL.
358	**Thalia THALIA**	
360	Tiffany TIFFANY	LT. (ITC)
360	Tiffany TIFFANY	MED. (ITC)
361	Tiffany TIFFANY	DEMI (ITC)
361	**Tiffany TIFFANY**	HVY. (ITC)
362	Times Roman TIMES RC	
362	*Times Roman TIMES RC*	ITAL.
363	**Times Roman TIMES R**	BOLD
363	**Times Roman TIMES**	BLK.
363	**Times MODIFIED NO**	BOLD NO. 1
364	**Times MODIFIED NO**	BOLD NO. 2
364	Times New TIMES NE	ROMAN SEMI
364	*Times New TIMES NEW*	ROMAN SEMI ITAL.
365	**Tom's Roman TOM'S RC**	(ITC)
368	*Trajanus TRAJANUS*	ITAL.
368	Trooper Roman TROOPER R	LT.
368	**Trooper Roman TROOPEI**	
369	**Trooper Roman TROO**	BLK.
369	***Trooper Roman TROOPEI***	ITAL.
369	Trump TRUMP	MEDIAEVAL
370	Trump TRUMP	MEDIAEVAL SEMI
370	**Trump TRUMP**	MEDIAEVAL BOLD
370	*Trump TRUMP*	MEDIAEVAL ITAL.

371	Trump TRUMP	MEDIAEVAL SEMI COND	
385	Walbaum WALBAUM		
387	Weiss Roman WEISS RO	BOLD	
388	Weiss Roman WEISS RO	X-BOLD	
408	Zapf Int'l ZAPF INT'	LT. (ITC)	
408	Zapf Int'l ZAPF INT'	MED. (ITC)	
409	Zapf Int'l ZAPF IN	DEMI (ITC)	
409	Zapf Int'l ZAPF	HVY. (ITC)	

SUPPLEMENT 1

4-A	Berling BERLING	ITAL.
5-A	Berling BERLING	SEMI
5-A	Bodoni Campanile BODONI CAMPANI	
16-A	Chesterfield CHESTERFII	
1-A	Framingham FRAMING	ITAL.
26-A	French Elzevir No.1 FRENC	
28-A	Hess Oldstyle HESS OL	
9-A	Lectura LECTURA	LT.
9-A	Manquis MANQUIS	
0-A	Novarese NOVARESE	BK. (ITC)
0-A	Novarese NOVARESE	MED. (ITC)
1-A	Novarese NOVARESE	BOLD (ITC)

BRACKETED SERIFS

431-A	Novarese NOVARES	ULTRA (ITC)
432-A	Novarese NOVARESE	BK. ITAL. (ITC)
432-A	Novarese NOVARESE	MED. ITAL. (ITC)
432-A	Novarese NOVARESE	BOLD ITAL. (ITC)
433-A	Omega OMEGA	
434-A	Omega OMEGA	DEMI
434-A	Omega OMEGA	BOLD
434-A	Omega OMEGA	X-BOLD
435-A	Omega OMEGA	ULTRA
435-A	Plantin PLANTIN	X-BOLD
436-A	Romic ROMIC	LT.
437-A	Romic ROMIC	MED.
437-A	Romic ROMIC	BOLD
437-A	Romic ROMIC	X-BOLD
438-A	Savannah SAV	
439-A	Sheraton SHERATO	BOLD
440-A	Sheraton SHERA	BOLD EXTENDED

SUPPLEMENT 2

443-B	Barcelona BARCELO	BOOK (ITC)
443-B	Barcelona BARCELO	MED. (ITC)
443-B	Barcelona BARCELC	BOLD (ITC)

444-B	Barcelona BARCEI	HVY. (ITC)
444-B	Barcelona BARCELO	BOOK ITAL. (ITC)
444-B	Barcelona BARCELO	MED. ITAL. (ITC)
445-B	Barcelona BARCEL	BOLD ITAL. (ITC)
445-B	Barcelona BARCE	HVY. ITAL. (ITC)
445-B	Baskerville BASKERVIL	ITAL. (VGC)
446-B	Baskerville BASKERVI	BOLD ITAL. (VGC)
446-B	Baskerville BASKERVI	(ITC)
446-B	Baskerville BASKERV	SEMI (ITC)
447-B	Baskerville BASKERVI	BOLD (ITC)
447-B	Baskerville BASKER	BLK. (ITC)
447-B	Baskerville BASKERVIL	ITAL. (ITC)
448-B	Baskerville BASKERVIL	SEMI (ITC)
448-B	Baskerville BASKERVIL	BOLD ITAL. (ITC)
448-B	Baskerville BASKERV	BLK. ITAL. (ITC)
449-B	Berkeley BERKELEY	O.S. BOOK (ITC)
449-B	Berkeley BERKELEY	O.S. MED. (ITC)
449-B	Berkeley BERKELEY	O.S. BOLD (ITC)
450-B	Berkeley BERKELEY	O.S. BLK. (ITC)
450-B	Berkeley BERKELEY	O.S. BOOK ITAL. (ITC)
450-B	Berkeley BERKELEY	O.S. MED. ITAL. (ITC)

BRACKETED SERIFS

451-B *Berkeley*BERKELEY O.S. BOLD ITAL. (ITC)

451-B **Berkeley**BERKELEY O.S. BLK. ITAL. (ITC)

453-B Brighton BRIGHTON LT.

453-B Brighton BRIGHTON MED.

453-B **Brighton BRIGHTON** BOLD

454-B *Brighton*BRIGHTON LT. ITAL.

454-B Caxton CAXTON ROMAN LT.

455-B Caxton CAXTON ROMAN BOOK

455-B **Caxton CAXTON** ROMAN BOLD

455-B *Caxton CAXTON* ROMAN LT. ITAL.

456-B *Century CENTURY* EXPANDED ITAL.

457-B **Corvinus CORVINUS** BOLD

457-B Craw Modern CRA

458-B Else ELSE LT.

458-B Else ELSE MED.

458-B Else ELSE SEMI

459-B Else ELSE BOLD

459-B *Else ELSE* LT. ITAL.

459-B *Else ELSE* MED. ITAL.

460-B *Else ELSE* SEMI ITAL.

460-B *Else ELSE* BOLD ITAL.

463-B Isbell ISBELL BOOK (ITC)

463-B Isbell ISBELL MED. (ITC)

463-B **Isbell ISBELL** BOLD (ITC)

464-B **Isbell ISBELL** HVY. (ITC)

464-B *Isbell ISBELL* BOOK ITAL. (ITC)

464-B *Isbell ISBELL* MED. ITAL. (ITC)

465-B *Isbell ISBELL* BOLD ITAL. (ITC)

465-B *Isbell ISBELL* HVY. ITAL. (ITC)

465-B Kennerley KENNERLEY O.S.

466-B **Kennerley KENNERL** BOLD

468-B Modern MODERN #216 LT. (ITC)

468-B Modern MODERN #216 MED. (ITC)

468-B **Modern MODERN** #216 BOLD (ITC)

469-B **Modern MODERN** #216 HVY. (ITC)

469-B *Modern MODERN* #216 LT. ITAL. (ITC)

469-B *Modern MODERN* #216 MED. ITAL. (ITC)

470-B *Modern MODERN* #216 BOLD ITAL. (ITC)

470-B *Modern MODERN* #216 HVY. ITAL. (ITC)

475-B *Tiffany TIFFANY* LT. ITAL. (ITC)

476-B *Tiffany TIFFANY* MED. ITAL. (ITC)

476-B *Tiffany TIFFANY* DEMI ITAL. (ITC)

476-B *Tiffany TIFFAN* HVY. ITAL. (ITC)

SUPPLEMENT 3

480-C Berling BERLING BOLD

481-C **Berling BERLING** BOLD COND.

482-C Bulfinch BULFINCH OLDSTYLE

482-C Carnase Text CARN LT. (WTC)

482-C Carnase Text CARN REG. (WTC)

483-C **Carnase Text CARN** MED (WTC)

483-C **Carnase Text CARN** BOLD (WTC)

483-C **Carnase Text CARN** X-BOLD (WTC)

484-C *Carnase Text CARN* LT. ITAL. (WTC)

484-C *Carnase Text CARN* REG. ITAL. (WTC)

484-C *Carnase Text CARN* MED. ITAL. (WTC)

485-C *Carnase Text CARN* BOLD ITAL. (WTC)

485-C *Carnase Text CARN* X-BOLD ITAL. (WTC)

485-C Caslon 224 CASLON 2 BOOK (ITC)

486-C Caslon 224 CASLON MED. (ITC)

486-C Caslon 224 CASLON BOLD (ITC)

486-C **Caslon 224 CASLO** BLK. (ITC)

487-C *Caslon 224 CASLON* BOOK ITAL. (ITC)

487-C *Caslon 224 CASLON* MED. ITAL. (ITC)

487-C *Caslon 224 CASLON* BOLD ITAL. (ITC)	495-C **Century CENTURY** ULTRA COND. ITAL. (ITC)	520-C **Meridien MERIDII** X-BOLD
488-C **Caslon 224 CASLON** BLK. ITAL. (ITC)	496-C **Cloister CLOISTER** X-BOLD COND.	520-C **Meridien MERID** BLACK
488-C Абвгдеежзи АБВГДI CASLON RUSSIAN	497-C **Columbia COLUMBIA** BOLD ITAL.	522-C Normande NORMANDE COND.
489-C Centaur CENTAUR ITALIC	499-C *Corvinus CORVINUS* MED. ITAL.	523-C **Primus PR**
489-C *Century CENTURY* BOLD ITAL.	499-C **Corvinus Skyline CORVINUS SKYLINE**	524-C Rock and Roll ROCK ANI LIGHT
490-C Century CENTURY BOLD COND.	502-C DeRoos DEROOS ROMAN	525-C *Rock and Roll ROCK AN* LT. ITAL.
490-C Century CENTURY BOLD COND. ITAL.	503-C **Dutch DUTCH** O.S. COND.	533-C Simoncini Garamond SIMC
490-C Century CENTURY NOVA	508-C Goudy GOUDY LT. (WTC)	543-C Veljovic VELJOVIC BOOK (ITC)
491-C *Century CENTURY* O.S. ITAL.	509-C Goudy GOUDY REG. (WTC)	543-C Veljovic VELJOVIC MED. (ITC)
491-C *Century CENTURY* SCHOOLBOOK ITAL.	509-C **Goudy GOUDY** MED. (WTC)	544-C **Veljovic VELJOVIC** BOLD (ITC)
491-C Century CENTURY LT. (ITC)	509-C **Goudy GOUDY** BOLD (WTC)	544-C **Veljovic VELJOVI** BLK. (ITC)
492-C **Century CENTURY** BOLD (ITC)	510-C *Goudy GOUDY* LT. ITAL. SWASH (WTC)	545-C *Veljovic VELJOVIC* BOOK ITAL. (ITC)
492-C *Century CENTURY* LT. ITAL. (ITC)	510-C *Goudy GOUDY* MED. ITAL. SWASH (WTC)	545-C *Veljovic VELJOVIC* MED. ITAL. (ITC)
492-C **Century CENTURY** BOLD ITAL. (ITC)	511-C *Goudy GOUDY* REG. ITAL. SWASH (WTC)	546-C *Veljovic VELJOVIC* BOLD ITAL. (ITC)
493-C Century CENTURY LT. COND. (ITC)	511-C **Goudy GOUDY** BOLD ITAL. SWASH (ITC)	546-C **Veljovic VELJOVIC** BLK. ITAL. (ITC)
493-C Century CENTURY BOOK COND. (ITC)	512-C GoudyItalian GOUDY I1	547-C Weidemann WEIDEMAI BOOK (ITC)
493-C **Century CENTURY** BOLD COND. (ITC)	512-C **GoudyItalian GOUD** X-BOLD	547-C Weidemann WEIDEMAI MED. (ITC)
494-C **Century CENTURY** ULTRA COND. (ITC)	517-C *Kennerley KENNERLI* BOLD ITAL.	547-C **Weidemann WEIDEM** BOLD (ITC)
494-C *Century CENTURY* LT. COND. ITAL. (ITC)	519-C Meridien MERIDIEN LIGHT	548-C **Weidemann WEIDI** BLK. (ITC)
494-C *Century CENTURY* BOOK COND. ITAL. (ITC)	519-C Meridien MERIDIEN MEDIUM	548-C *Weidemann WEIDEMAN* BOOK ITAL. (ITC)
495-C *Century CENTURY* BOLD COND. ITAL. (ITC)	520-C **Meridien MERIDIEI** BOLD	548-C *Weidemann WEIDEMA* MED. ITAL. (ITC)

BRACKETED SERIFS

BRACKETED SERIFS

549-C *Weidemann WEIDEMA* BOLD ITAL. (ITC)

549-C *Weidemann WEIDEM* BLK. ITAL. (ITC)

549-C WTG 145 LIGHT

550-C WTG 145 REGULAR

550-C WTG 145 MEDIUM

550-C **WTG 145** BOLD

551-C **WTG 145** X-BOLD

551-C *WTG 145* LT. ITAL.

551-C *WTG 145* REG. ITAL.

552-C *WTG 145* MED. ITAL.

552-C *WTG 145* BOLD ITAL.

552-C *WTG 145* X-BOLD ITAL.

553-C *Zapf Int'l ZAPF INT'l* LT. ITAL. (ITC)

553-C *Zapf Int'l ZAPF INT'l* MED. ITAL. (ITC)

554-C *Zapf Int'l ZAPF IN* DEMI ITAL. (ITC)

554-C *Zapf Int'l ZAPF I* HVY. ITAL. (ITC)

Ruled serifs

RULED SERIFS

469-B *Modern MODERN* #216 MED. ITAL. (ITC)

470-B *Modern MODERN* #216 BOLD ITAL. (ITC)

470-B *Modern MODERN* #216 HVY ITAL (ITC)

| SUPPLEMENT 3 |

499-C **Corvinus CORVINUS** MED. ITAL.

499-C **Corvinus Skyline CORVINUS SKYLINE**

522-C **Normande NORMANDE** COND.

553-C *Zapf Int'l ZAPF INT'l* LT. ITAL. (ITC)

553-C *Zapf Int'l ZAPF INT'l* MED. ITAL. (ITC)

554-C *Zapf Int'l ZAPF IN'.* DEMI ITAL. (ITC)

554-C *Zapf Int'l ZAPF I* HVY. ITAL. (ITC)

Spur serifs

2 Abbott ABBOTT O.S.	131 Della Robbia DELLA ROE	331 Serif Gothic SERIF GOTHI (ITC)
4 Albertus ALBERTUS LT.	148 Enge Etienne ENGE ETIENNE	331 Serif Gothic SERIF GOTHI BOLD (ITC)
4 Albertus ALBERTUS	157 Flange FLANGE	332 Serif Gothic SERIF GOTHI X-BOLD (ITC)
5 Albertus ALBERTUS BOLD	165 FrizQuadrata FRIZQU (ITC)	332 Serif Gothic SERIF GOTH HVY. (ITC)
7 American AMERI GOTHIC LT.	165 FrizQuadrata FRIZ Q MED.	332 Serif Gothic SERIF GO BLK (ITC)
8 American AMER GOTHIC MED.	165 FrizQuadrata FRIZ DEMI	334 Serpentine SERF BOLD ITAL.
8 American AMER GOTHIC BOLD	166 FrizQuadrata FRIZ C BOLD (ITC)	379 Venture VENTURE
20 Arrow ARROW	244 Lafayette LAFAYETTE	388 WEISS INITIALS NO.2
21 Art Gothic ART GOTHIC	244 LARGO LT.	388 Weiss Initials WEISS INITIA LT.
34 Baker Signet BAKER SIGN	253 Macbeth MACBETH MACB	389 Weiss Initials WEISS INI MED
34 Baker Signet BAKI BLK	270 Newtext NEWTE BOOK (ITC)	389 Weiss Initials WEISS INI BOLD
36 Basilea BASILEA	270 Newtext NEWTE REG. (ITC)	389 Weiss Initials WEISS IN X-BOLD
39 BAUER TEXT INITIALS	271 Newtext NEWTE DEMI (ITC)	393 Wolf Antiqua WOLF ANT
50 Bernase BERNASE ROMAN (ITC)	271 Newtext NEWTEX REG. ITAL. (ITC)	
122 Columbus COLUMBUS	271 Nova Augustea NOVA A	
122 Columbus COLUMBI BOLD	315 Reubens REUBENS WIDE	
122 COLUMNA SOLID	322 Romana ROMANA ULTRA	
131 DAVIDA DAVIDA BOLD	331 Serif Gothic SERIF GOTHIC LT. (ITC)	

SUPPLEMENT 1

411-A Art Gothic ART GOTHIC BOLD
426-A French Elzevir No.1 FRENC
430-A Novarese NOVARESE BK. (ITC)
430-A Novarese NOVARESE MED (ITC)
431-A Novarese NOVARESE BOLD (ITC)
431-A Novarese NOVARE ULTRA (ITC)
432-A Novarese NOVARESE BK. ITAL. (ITC)

SPUR SERIFS

432-A Novarese NOVARESE MED. ITAL. (ITC)

432-A **Novarese NOVARESE** BOLD ITAL. (ITC)

436-A Romic ROMIC LT.

437-A Romic ROMIC MED.

437-A **Romic ROMIC** BOLD

437-A **Romic ROMIC** X-BOLD

SUPPLEMENT 3

523-C **Primus PR**

531-C Serpentine SERPEN LIGHT

531-C **Serpentine SERPI** MEDIUM

531-C **Serpentine SER** BOLD

532-C *Serpentine SERPEN* LT. ITAL.

532-C *Serpentine SERPI* MED. ITAL.

533-C Solon Antiqua. SOLON AN LIGHT

533-C Solon Antiqua. SOLON AI NORMAL

534-C Solon Antiqua. SOLON A SEMI-BOLD

534-C **Solon Antiqua. SOLON** BOLD

535-C Symbol SYMBOL BOOK (ITC)

535-C Symbol SYMBOL MED. (ITC)

535-C **Symbol SYMBOL** BOLD (ITC)

536-C **Symbol SYMBOL** BLK. (ITC)

536-C *Symbol SYMBOL* BOOK ITAL. (ITC)

536-C *Symbol SYMBOL* MED. ITAL. (ITC)

537-C **Symbol SYMBOL** BOLD ITAL. (ITC)

537-C ***Symbol SYMBOL*** BLK. ITAL. (ITC)

538-C Thaddeus THADDEUS LT. (WTC)

538-C Thaddeus THADDEUS REG. (WTC)

538-C **Thaddeus THADDEUS** MED. (WTC)

539-C **Thaddeus THADDEUS** BOLD (WTC)

539-C *Thaddeus THADDEUS* LT. ITAL. (WTC)

539-C *Thaddeus THADDEUS* REG. ITAL. (WTC)

540-C *Thaddeus THADDEUS* MED. ITAL. (WTC)

540-C ***Thaddeus THADDEUS*** BOLD ITAL. (WTC)

Soft serifs

8 American TYPEWR	TYPEWRITER LT. (ITC)	
9 American TYPEWI	TYPEWRITER MED. (ITC)	
9 **American TYPE**	TYPEWRITER BOLD (ITC)	
10 American TYPEWRITER	TYPEWRITER LT. COND. (ITC)	
10 American TYPEWRITE	TYPEWRITER MED. COND. (ITC)	
10 **American TYPEWRI**	TYPEWRITER BOLD COND. (ITC)	
14 **Antique No. 14 AN**		
15 Apollo APOLLO		
21 Artcraft ARTCRAFT	BOLD	
28 Avon AVON	REG.	
28 Avon AVON	BOLD	
29 **Avon AVON**	BLK.	
40 Bauer Text BAUER TEX		
40 Bauer Text BAUERTEX	BOLD	
51 **Bernhard BERNHA**	FAT	
56 Bocklin BOCKLIN		
72 **Brillante BRILLANT**		
76 Bulletin Typewriter B	TYPEWRITER	

89 **Caslon CASLON**	HEADLINE (ITC)	
125 Cooper COOPER	O.S.	
125 **Cooper COOPER**	BLK. COND.	
126 **Cooper COOPER**	BLK.	
126 **Cooper COOPER**	BLK. ITAL.	
147 *Elvira ELVIRA*	BOLD ITAL.	
161 **Framingham FRAMI**	X-BOLD	
176 Garamond GARAMC	LT. (ITC)	
176 Garamond GARAMC	BOOK (ITC)	
176 **Garamond GARA**	BOLD (ITC)	
177 **Garamond GARA**	ULTRA (ITC)	
177 *Garamond GARAM*	LT. ITAL. (ITC)	
177 *Garamond GARAM*	BOOK ITAL. (ITC)	
178 *Garamond GARA*	BOLD ITAL. (ITC)	
178 *Garamond GARA*	ULTRA ITAL. (ITC)	
178 Garamond GARAMOND	LT. COND. (ITC)	
179 Garamond GARAMOND	BOOK COND. (ITC)	
179 **Garamond GARAMO**	BOLD COND. (ITC)	

179 **Garamond GARAMO**	ULTRA COND. (ITC)	
180 *Garamond GARAMOND*	LT. COND. ITAL. (ITC)	
180 *Garamond GARAMON*	BOOK COND. ITAL. (ITC)	
180 *Garamond ITC GARA*	BOLD COND. ITAL. (ITC)	
181 *Garamond GARAM*	ULTRA COND. ITAL. (ITC)	
182 Garamond GARAMO	BOLD	
182 **Garamond GARA**	O.S. X-BOLD	
189 Gorillaa GORILLA	(ITC)	
190 Goudy GOUDY	CATALOGUE	
190 Goudy GOUDY	BOLD	
190 *Goudy GOUDY*	BOLD ITAL.	
191 Goudy GOUDY	X-BOLD	
191 **Goudy GOUDY**	BLK.	
191 *Goudy GOUDY*	BLK. ITAL.	
192 **Goudy GOUDY**	HEAVYFACE	
192 *Goudy GOUDY*	HEAVYFACE ITAL.	
193 **Goudy GOUDY**	HEAVYFACE COND.	
210 Henrietta HENRIETT	MED.	
211 **Henrietta HENRIET**	BOLD	
211 Henrietta HENRIETTA	BOLD COND.	
212 Herkules HERKULES		

SOFT SERIFS

SOFT SERIFS

214 Horley HORLEY O.S.	302 Post POST O.S. ITAL.	392 Windsor WINDSOR HVY. COND
215 Horley HORLEY O.S. MED.	317 Richmond RICHMOI O.S. HVY.	394 Worcester WORCEST ROUND
215 Horley HORLEY O.S. BOLD	318 Richmond RICHMOND O.S. BOLD COND	394 Worcester WORCEST ROUND MED
221 Italia ITALIA BOOK (ITC)	336 Skylark SKYLARI	394 Worcester WORCEST ROUND BOLD
222 Italia ITALIA MED. (ITC)	338 Souvenir, Eastern SOUVE LT.	395 Worcester WORCESTEI ROUND ITAL
222 Italia ITALIA BOLD (ITC)	338 Souvenir, Eastern SOUV MED.	SUPPLEMENT 1
263 Musketeer MUSKETEE DEMI	338 Souvenir, Eastern SOUV BOLD	416-A Chesterfield CHESTERFII
263 Musketeer MUSKETI BOLD	339 Souvenir, Eastern SOI X-BOLD	421-A Framingham FRAMING ITAL
264 Musketeer MUSKET X-BOLD	339 Souvenir SOUVENIR LT. (ITC)	428-A Hess Oldstyle HESS OLI
268 Neptune NEPTUNE	339 Souvenir SOUVENII MED. (ITC)	438-A Seagull SEAGULL LT
275 Octopuss OCTOPUSS	340 Souvenir SOUVEN DEMI (ITC)	438-A Seagull SEAGULL MED.
277 Olden OLDEN	340 Souvenir SOUVEI BOLD (ITC)	439-A Seagull SEAGULL BOLD
285 Packard PACKARD	340 Souvenir SOUVENIR LT. ITAL. (ITC)	439-A Seagull SEAGULL BLK.
285 Paddington PADDINC	341 Souvenir SOUVENI MED. ITAL. (ITC)	SUPPLEMENT 2
287 Palatino PALATINO BOLD (SOFT SERIF)	341 Souvenir SOUVEN DEMI ITAL. (ITC)	443-B Barcelona BARCELC BOLD (ITC)
290 Parsons PARSONS	341 Souvenir SOUVEI BOLD ITAL. (ITC)	444-B Barcelona BARCEI HVY. (ITC)
290 Parsons PARSONS BOLD	357 Tango TANGO	443-B Barcelona BARCEL BOLD ITAL (ITC)
291 Parsons PARSONS HVY.	391 Windsor WINDSOR	445-B Barcelona BARCE HVY. ITAL (ITC)
301 Poor Richard POOR RICHA	391 Windsor WINDSOI BLK.	451-B Bramley BRAMLEY LT.
302 Post POST COND.	391 Windsor WINDSOR LT. COND.	452-B Bramley BRAMLEY MED.
302 Post POST O.S. ROMAN NO. 2	392 Windsor WINDSOR ELON-GATED	452-B Bramley BRAMLEY BOLD

452-B **Bramley BRAMLEY** X-BOLD

453-B Brighton BRIGHTON LT.

453-B Brighton BRIGHTON MED.

453-B **Brighton BRIGHTON** BOLD

454-B *Brighton BRIGHTON* LT. ITAL.

465-B Kennerley KENNERLEY O.S.

466-B **Kennerley KENNERL** BOLD

SUPPLEMENT 3

508-C Goudy GOUDY REG. (WTC)

509-C Goudy GOUDY REG. (WTC)

509-C **Goudy GOUDY** MED. (WTC)

509-C **Goudy GOUDY** BOLD (WTC)

510-C *Goudy GOUDY* LT. ITAL. SWASH (WTC)

510-C *Goudy GOUDY* MED. ITAL. SWASH (WTC)

511-C *Goudy GOUDY* REG. ITAL. SWASH (WTC)

511-C ***Goudy GOUDY*** BOLD ITAL. SWASH (ITC)

512-C GoudyItalian GOUDY IT

512-C **GoudyItalian GOUD** X-BOLD

517-C *Kennerley KENNERL* BOLD ITAL.

533-C Simoncini Garamond SIM(

547-C Weidemann WEIDEMAN BOOK (ITC)

SOFT SERIFS

547-C Weidemann WEIDEMAN MED. (ITC)

547-C **Weidemann WEIDEMA** BOLD (ITC)

548-C **Weidemann WEIDE** BLK. (ITC)

548-C *Weidemann WEIDEMANN* BOOK ITAL. (ITC)

548-C *Weidemann WEIDEMAN* MED. ITAL. (ITC)

549-C ***Weidemann WEIDEM*** BOLD ITAL. (ITC)

549-C ***Weidemann WEIDEM*** BLK. ITAL. (ITC)

Square serifs

1 **Aachen AACHEN** MED.
1 **Aachen AACHEN** BOLD
15 Aquarius2 AQUARIUS
16 Aquarius4 AQUARIUS
16 Aquarius 5 AQUARIUS
16 Aquarius 6 AQUARIUS
17 **Aquarius7 AQUARIUS**
17 **Aquarius 8 AQUARIUS**
53 **Beton BETON** X-BOLD
54 Beton BETON MED. COND.
54 **Beton BETON** BOLD COND.
62 Bookman BOOKM MED. (ITC)
63 **Bookman BOOKM** DEMI (ITC)
63 **Bookman BOOKI** BOLD (ITC)
70 Bookman BOOKMAN BLK.
112 Cirque CIRQUE
112 City Compact CITY COMPACT LT.
113 City Compact CITY COMPA MED.

113 **City Compact CITY COM** BOLD
113 **Clarendon CLAR** BOLD
124 Consort CONSORT
128 **Craw Clarendon CRAW CLA**
128 Cushing CUSHING O.S. X-BOLD
142 **Egizio EGIZIO** BOLD
142 *Egizio EGIZIO* BOLD ITAL.
142 Egyptian EGYPTIAN 505 LT.
143 Egyptian EGYPTIAN 505
143 Egyptian EGYPTIAI 505 MED.
143 Egyptian EGYPTIA 505 BOLD
144 **Egyptian EGYPTIAN** BOLD COND.
145 **EGYPTIAN EGYPTIAN**
146 **Ehrhardt EHRHAI** ULTRA BOLD
160 **Fortuna FOR** X-BOLD
187 **GIORGIO**
197 **GRECIAN**
222 **IVY LEAGUE**

223 **IVY LEAGUE** BOLD
227 Jenson JENSON O.S.
227 Jenson JENSON
228 Jenson Book JENSC BOLD
228 **Jenson Book JENSON** X-BOLD
228 Jenson JENSON COND.
236 **Karnak KARNAK** BLK. COND.
239 **Korinna KORINN** HVY. (ITC)
241 **Kubra KUBRA**
248 Lubalin Graph LUBALI X-LT. (ITC)
248 Lubalin Graph LUBA BOOK (ITC)
249 **Lubalin Graph LUB** MED. (ITC)
249 **Lubalin Graph LUI** DEMI (ITC)
250 **Lubalin Graph LUI** BOLD (ITC)
257 **Mastodon MASTOD**
285 P.T. Barnum P.T. BARNUM
319 Rockwell ROCKWELL LT.
319 Rockwell ROCKWELL MED.
320 **Rockwell ROCKWEI** BOLD
320 **Rockwell ROCKW** X-BOLD
329 **Schadow SCHADO** ANTIQUA SEMI

330	**Schadow SCHADO** ANTIQUA BOLD	
345	**STEAMBOAT**	
346	**Steel STEEL** ELONGATED	
349	Stymie STYMIE HAIRLINE (ITC)	
349	Stymie STYMIE LT.	
349	Stymie STYMIE MED.	
350	Stymie **STYMIE** BOLD	
350	**Stymie STYMIE** X-BOLD	
357	**Tanker TANKER**	
371	**Tulo TULO**	
373	**UMBRA 57**	
380	Veronese VERONESE	
380	Veronese VERONESE SEMI	
380	Veronese VERONES BOLD	
381	VICKSBURG	
393	**WOODWARD**	

SUPPLEMENT 1

418-A	**Egiziano EGIZIA**
418-A	**Egyptian Bold EGYPTI** BOLD (FRANCAIS)
430-A	**MERCHANT** BOLD

SQUARE SERIFS

438-A	Seagull SEAGULL LT.
438-A	Seagull SEAGULL MED.
439-A	**Seagull SEAGULL** BOLD
439-A	**Seagull SEAGULL** BLK.

SUPPLEMENT 2

451-B	Bramley BRAMLEY LT.
452-B	Bramley BRAMLEY MED
452-B	**Bramley BRAMLEY** BOLD
452-B	**Bramley BRAMLEY** X-BOLD
456-B	**Clarendon CLAREN** SEMI
457-B	**Craw Clarendon CRA** BOLD
461-B	GALADRIEL
466-B	*Lubalin Graph LUBALI* X-LT. OBLIQUE (ITC)
466-B	*Lubalin Graph LUBA* BOOK OBLIQUE (ITC)
467-B	*Lubalin Graph LUBA* MED. OBLIQUE (ITC)
467-B	*Lubalin Graph LUBA* DEMI OBLIQUE (ITC)
467-B	*Lubalin Graph LUB* BOLD OBLIQUE (ITC)
477-B	Tower TOWER

SUPPLEMENT 3

481-C	**Beton BETON** BOLD
499-C	Cushing CUSHING BOOK (ITC)

500-C	Cushing CUSHING MED. (ITC)
500-C	**Cushing CUSHING** BOLD (ITC)
500-C	**Cushing CUSHING** HVY. (ITC)
501-C	*Cushing CUSHING* BOOK ITAL. (ITC)
501-C	*Cushing CUSHING* MED. ITAL. (ITC)
501-C	*Cushing CUSHING* BOLD ITAL. (ITC)
502-C	*Cushing CUSHING* HVY. ITAL. (ITC)
506-C	**Girder GIRDER** HEAVY
513-C	**Grouch GROUCH** BLACK
525-C	**Rock and Roll ROCK** BOLD
525-C	*Rock and Roll ROCK* BOLD ITAL
528-C	Serifa SERIFA LIGHT
529-C	Serifa SERIFA
529-C	**Serifa SERIFA** BOLD
529-C	**Serifa SERIFA** BLACK
530-C	*Serifa SERIFA* THIN ITAL.
530-C	*Serifa SERIFA* LT. ITAL.
530-C	*Serifa SERIFA* ITALIC
549-C	WTG 145 LIGHT
550-C	WTG 145 REGULAR
550-C	**WTG 145** MEDIUM

SQUARE SERIFS

550-C **WTG 145** BOLD

551-C **WTG 145** X-BOLD

551-C *WTG 145* LT. ITAL.

551-C *WTG 145* REG. ITAL.

552-C *WTG 145* MED. ITAL.

552-C *WTG 145* BOLD ITAL.

552-C *WTG 145* X-BOLD ITAL.

Extra light

8	American TYPEWR	TYPE-WRITER LT. (ITC)	
10	American TYPEWRITEF	TYPE-WRITER LT. COND. (ITC)	
15	Aquarius2 AQUARIUS		
25	Avant Garde AVANT GARD	GOTHIC X-LT. (ITC)	
40	Bauhaus BAUHAUS	LT. (ITC)	
43	Belvedere BELVEDERE	SCRIPT	
51	Bernhard BEERNNHAF	FASHION	
56	Blue Skies BLUE		
77	BUSORAMA BUSORAMA	LT. (ITC)	
77	BUSORAMA	BOOK (ITC)	
84	Carpenter Carpent		
93	Casual Script CASUAL SCRIP		
93	Celtic Cursive CELTIC CU		
134	Design DESIGN	FINELINE	
147	Elizabeth ELIZABETH	ROMAN	
149	Eras ERAS	LT. (ITC)	
160	Folkwang FOLKWANG		
166	Futura FUTURA	LT	

169	FUTURA	STENCIL LT.	
184	Gill Sans GILL SANS	LT.	
186	Gill Sans GILL SANS	LT. ITAL.	
195	Granby GRANBY	LT.	
203	Harry HARRY	THIN	
205	Helvetica HELVETICA	X-LT.	
206	Helvetica HELVETICA	LT.	
208	Helvetica HELVETICA	LT. ITAL.	
216	HUXLEY VERTICAL		
233	Kabel KABEL	LT.	
236	Kaufman KAUFMAN	SCRIPT	
243	L & C Hairline L & C HAIRLINE		
248	Lubalin Graph LUBALI		
262	Musketeer MUSKETEER	LT.	
287	Palatino PALATINO	ITAL.	
288	Palatino PALATINO	CURSIVE	
307	Quorum QUORUM	LT. (ITC)	
311	Raleigh RALEIGH	X-LT.	

314	Rebecca REBECCA		
328	Sans Serif SANS SERIF	COND. ITAL.	
331	Serif Gothic SERIF GOTHIC	LT. (ITC)	
337	Snell Roundhand		
343	Standard STANDA	X-LT. EXT.	
345	Stark STARRK	DEBONAIR	
345	Stark STARRK	SEMI	
349	Stymie STYMIE	HAIRLINE (ITC)	
349	Stymie STYMIE	LT.	
360	Tiffany TIFFANY	LT. (ITC)	
368	Trajanus TRAJANUS	ITAL.	
382	Virtuoso1 VIRTUOSO		
385	Washington WASHINGTON	X-LT.	
385	Washington WASHINGTON	LT.	
387	Weiss Italic WEISS ITALIC		
393	Wolf Antiqua WOLF ANT		
405	Zapf Ch'ry ZAPF CH'R	CHAN-CERY LT. (ITC)	
407	Zapf Ch'ry ZAPF CH'R	CHAN-CERY LT. ITAL. (ITC)	

SUPPLEMENT 1

414-A	Berling BERLING	ITAL.	
417-A	Chopin CHOPIN	LT.	

EXTRA LIGHT

EXTRA LIGHT

419-A Fenice FENICE LT (ITC)

420-A Fenice FENICE LT ITAL (ITC)

428-A Harlequin HARLEQUIN

429-A Lectura LECTURA LT

429-A Manquis MANQUIS

430-A Novarese NOVARESE BK (ITC)

432-A Novarese NOVARESE BK ITAL (ITC)

438-A Seagull SEAGULL LT

451-B Bramley BRAMLEY LT

453-B Brighton BRIGHTON LT

454-B Brighton BRIGHTON LT ITAL

454-B Caxton CAXTON ROMAN LT

455-B Caxton CAXTON ROMAN LT ITAL

458-B Else ELSE LT

459-B Else ELSE LT ITAL

460-B Fedora FEDORA

466-B Lubalin Graph LUBALIN X-LT OBLIQUE (ITC)

| SUPPLEMENT 3 |

478-C Aerolite AEROLITE SCRIPT

478-C BALLÉ INITIALS

479-C BALLOON LIGHT

489-C Centaur CENTAUR ITALIC

491-C Century CENTURY LT (ITC)

492-C Century CENTURY LT ITAL (ITC)

493-C Century CENTURY LT COND (ITC)

494-C Century CENTURY LT COND ITAL (ITC)

496-C Chevalier CHEVALIER

502-C DeRoos DEROOS ROMAN

504-C Excelsior EXCELSIOR SCRIPT

504-C Excelsior EXCELSIOR SEMI-BOLD SCRIPT

505-C Florentine FLORENTINE CURSIVE

508-C Goudy GOUDY LT (WTC)

510-C Goudy GOUDY LT ITAL SWASH (WTC)

528-C Serifa SERIFA THIN

530-C Serifa SERIFA THIN ITAL

533-C Solon Antiqua SOLON AN LIGHT

534-C Stuyvesant STUYVESANT SCRIPT

535-C Symbol SYMBOL BOOK (ITC)

536-C Symbol SYMBOL BOOK ITAL (ITC)

540-C Univers 46 UNIVERS 46

542-C Valiant VALIANT LIGHT

543-C Valiant VALIANT BOLD

Ultra bold

ULTRA BOLD

ULTRA BOLD

124 Compacta **COMPACTA** BOLD
124 Comstock **COMSTO**
125 Cooper **COOPER** BLK. COND.
126 Cooper **COOPER** BLK.
126 *Cooper* **COOPER** BLK. ITAL.
136 DEUTSCH BLACK
139 Dynamo **DYNAMO**
141 EAGLE BOLD
144 Egyptian **EGYPTIAN**
146 Ehrhardt **EHRHAF** ULTRA BOLD
150 Eras **ERAS** BOLD (ITC)
151 Eras **ERAS** ULTRA (ITC)
155 FAT CAT
157 Flange **FLANGE**
159 Folio **FOLIO** X-BOLD
160 Fortuna **FOR** X-BOLD
161 FRANKFURTER
162 Franklin Gothic **FRANI**
163 Franklin Gothic **FRAN** BLK.
164 Franklin Gothic **FRANKLIN GOTH** BLK. X-COND
166 Friz Quadrata **FRIZ Q** BOLD (ITC)

167 Futura **FUTURA** BOLD
168 Futura **FUTURA** X BOLD
168 Futura **FUTURA** BOLD COND.
168 Futura **FUTURA** X BOLD COND.
169 Futura **FUTURA** DISPLAY
169 Futura **FUTURA** BLK.
177 Garamond **GARA** ULTRA (ITC)
178 *Garamond* **GARA** ULTRA ITAL (ITC)
179 Garamond **GARAMO** ULTRA COND (ITC)
181 *Garamond* **GARAM** ULTRA COND ITAL (ITC)
184 GETTYSBURG BOLD COND.
185 Gill Sans **GILL SANS** X BOLD
186 Gill Sans **GILL SAN** ULTRA
187 GIORGIO
188 Globe Gothic **GLOB** X-BOLD
192 Goudy **GOUDY** HEAVYFACE
192 *Goudy* **GOUDY** HEAVYFACE ITAL
196 Granby **GRANBY** ELEPHANT
197 Grizzly **GRIZZLY**
197 Grotesque No.9 **GROTESQI**
205 Harry **HARRY** OBESE

205 Harry **HARRY** OBESE SQUEEZED
207 Helvetica **HELVETIC** BOLD
207 Helvetica **HELVETIC** X BOLD
208 *Helvetica* **HELVETIC** BOLD COMPACT ITAL
209 Helvetica **HELV** X BOLD EXT
209 Helvetica **HELVETICA** COMPRESSED
209 Helvetica **HELVETICA** EXTRA COMPRESSED
219 Impact **IMPACT**
221 Information
229 Joric Joric **JORIC JORIC** ULTRA
232 Kabel **KABEL** ULTRA (ITC)
234 Kabel **KABEL** HVY
234 Kabel **KABEL** BLK. MODERN
236 Karnak **KARNAK** BLK. COND.
237 Koloss **KOLOSS**
237 Kompakt **KOMP**
241 Kubra **KUBRA**
250 Lubalin Graph **LUI** BOLD (ITC)
253 Macbeth **MACBETH** macb
253 MACHINE BOLD (ITC)
256 Manchester **MANCHES**

ULTRA BOLD

418-A Egiziano EGIZIAI	457-B Corvinus CORVINUS BOLD	506-C Futura FUTURA X-BOLD COND OBLIQUE
418-A Egyptian Bold EGYPTI BOLD (FRANCAIS)	461-B FRANKFURTER HIGH LIGHT	513-C Grouch GROUCH BLACK
420-A Fenice FENICE ULTRA (ITC)	462-B Gill Sans GILL SANS X-BOLD COND	520-C Meridien MERID BLACK
421-A Fenice FENICE ULTRA ITAL. (ITC)	464-B Isbell ISBELL HVY. (ITC)	522-C Modula MODULA X-BOLD
423-A Franklin Gothic FRAN GOTHIC HVY. (ITC)	465-B Isbell ISBELL HVY. ITAL. (ITC)	523-C Primus PR
424-A Franklin Gothic FRAN HVY. ITAL. (ITC)	467-B Lubalin Graph LUB. BOLD OBLIQUE (ITC)	527-C Sally Mae SALLY MA HEAVY
427-A Gill Sans GILL SANS X-BOLD COND.	469-B Modern MODERN #216 HVY (ITC)	529-C Serifa SERIFA BLACK
430-A MERCHANT BOLD	470-B Modern MODERN #216 HVY ITAL (ITC)	531-C Serpentine SER BOLD
431-A Novarese NOVARES ULTRA (ITC)	472-B PROFILE	536-C Symbol SYMBOL BLK. (ITC)
433-A Olive Antique OLIVE AN BLACK COND.	476-B Tiffany TIFFAN HVY. ITAL. (ITC)	537-C Symbol SYMBOL BLK. ITAL. (ITC)
435-A Omega OMEGA ULTRA	SUPPLEMENT 3	541-C Univers 76 UNIVERS
435-A Plantin PLANTIN X-BOLD	479-C BANCO	544-C Veljovic VELJOVIC BLK. (ITC)
437-A Romic ROMIC X-BOLD	481-C Block BLOCK	546-C Veljovic VELJOVIC BLK. ITAL. (ITC)
439-A Seagull SEAGULL BLK.	483-C Carnase Text CARNA X-BOLD (WTC)	551-C WTG 145 X-BOLD
SUPPLEMENT 2	485-C Carnase Text CARNA X-BOLD ITAL. (WTC)	552-C WTG 145 X-BOLD ITAL.
442-B Arnholm ARNHOLM SANS BOLD	486-C Caslon 224 CASLON BLK. (ITC)	554-C Zapf Int'l ZAPF I HVY. ITAL. (ITC)
444-B Barcelona BARCEI HVY. (ITC)	488-C Caslon 224 CASLON BLK. ITAL. (ITC)	
445-B Barcelona BARCE HVY. ITAL. (ITC)	494-C Century CENTURY ULTRA COND. (ITC)	
447-B Baskerville BASKER\ BLK. (ITC)	495-C Century CENTURY ULTRA COND. ITAL. (ITC)	
448-B Baskerville BASKER\ BLK. ITAL. (ITC)	500-C Cushing CUSHING HVY. (ITC)	
452-B Bramley BRAMLEY X-BOLD	502-C Cushing CUSHING HVY. ITAL. (ITC)	

CONDENSED

299	**Placard PLACARD** BOLD COND.
300	**Plantin PLANTIN** BOLD COND.
300	Plantin PLANTIN BOLD COND. OUT.
301	**Playbill PLAYBILL**
302	**Post POST** COND.
307	**QUENTIN**
311	**RAILROAD GOTHIC**
315	**Reubens REUBENS** WIDE
318	Richmond RICHMOND O.S. COND.
318	**Richmond RICHMOND** O.S. BOLD COND.
321	Rococo ROCOCO
321	Roman ROMAN COMPRESSED NO. 3
324	Roslyn Gothic ROSLYN GOTH MED.
324	**Roslyn Gothic ROSLYN GOT** BOLD
328	**SANS SERIF CONDENSED** COND. NO. 1
328	*Sans Serif SANS SERIF* COND. ITAL.
329	SANS SERIF ELONGATED
330	SCOT GOTHIC
335	Siegfried SIEGFRIED
335	SILVER DOLLAR
336	Smoke SMOKE

CONDENSED

337	Smoke SMOKE SHAD.
343	Stagecoach STAGECOACH
344	**Standard STANDARD** X-BOLD COND.
346	**Steel STEEL** ELON-GATED
348	STOUTHEART
355	**T.H.ALPHABET SOUP**
357	Tavern TAVERN
358	Thalia THALIA
366	**Topic Futura TOPIC FUTI**
368	Trooper Roman TROOPER R LT.
368	**Trooper Roman TROOPEI**
369	*Trooper Roman TROOPEI* ITAL.
371	**Trump TRUMP** MEDIAEVAL SEMI COND
375	**Univers 67 UNIVERS**
376	**URBAN**
381	
391	Windsor WINDSOR LT. COND
392	Windsor WINDSOR ELON-GATED
392	**Windsor WINDSOR** HVY. COND.

415-A	Bodoni Campanile BODONI CAMPANI
415-A	Bulletin BULLETIN 113
418-A	**Egiziano EGIZIAI**
418-A	**Egyptian Bold EGYPTI** BOLD (FRANCAIS)
419-A	Fenice FENICE LT. (ITC)
419-A	Fenice FENICE REG. (ITC)
419-A	Fenice FENICE BOLD (ITC)
420-A	**Fenice FENICE** ULTRA (ITC)
420-A	*Fenice FENICE* LT. ITAL. (ITC)
420-A	*Fenice FENICE* REG. ITAL. (ITC)
421-A	*Fenice FENICE* BOLD ITAL (ITC)
427-A	**Gill Sans GILL SANS** X-BOLD COND
427-A	**GlowWorm GLOW WORM**
430-A	**MERCHANT** BOLD
433-A	**Olive Antique OLIVE ANT** BOLD COND.
433-A	**Olive Antique OLIVE AN** BLACK COND.

460-B	Fedora FEDORA
461-B	GALADRIEL
462-B	**Gill Sans GILL SANS** X-BOLD COND.

CONDENSED

474-B	SOUTACHE	
477-B	TITLE GOTHIC	X-COND. NO. 12
477-B	Tower TOWER	

SUPPLEMENT 3

478-C	American Text AMERICAN TEXT
479-C	BALLOON — LIGHT
479-C	BANCO
480-C	Berliner BERLINER — GROTESK
480-C	Berliner BERLINER — GROTESK BOLD
490-C	Century CENTURY — BOLD COND.
490-C	Century CENTURY — BOLD COND. ITAL.
490-C	Century CENTURY — NOVA
493-C	Century CENTURY — LT. COND. (ITC)
493-C	Century CENTURY — BOOK COND. (ITC)
493-C	Century CENTURY — BOLD COND. (ITC)
494-C	Century CENTURY — BOOK COND. ITAL. (ITC)
495-C	Century CENTURY — BOLD COND. ITAL. (ITC)
496-C	Cloister CLOISTER — X-BOLD COND.
499-C	Corvinus CORVINUS — MED. ITAL.
499-C	Corvinus Skyline CORVINUS SKYLINE
499-C	Cushing CUSHING — BOOK (ITC)

500-C	Cushing CUSHING — MED. (ITC)
500-C	Cushing CUSHING — BOLD (ITC)
500-C	Cushing CUSHING — HVY. (ITC)
501-C	Cushing CUSHING — BOOK ITAL. (ITC)
501-C	Cushing CUSHING — MED. ITAL. (ITC)
501-C	Cushing CUSHING — BOLD ITAL. (ITC)
502-C	Cushing CUSHING — HVY. ITAL. (ITC)
503-C	Dutch DUTCH — O.S. COND.
505-C	Fantail FANTAIL
506-C	Futura FUTURA — BOLD COND. OBLIQUE
506-C	Futura FUTURA — X-BOLD COND. OBLIQUE
510-C	Goudy GOUDY — LT. ITAL SWASH (WTC)
510-C	Goudy GOUDY — MED. ITAL SWASH (WTC)
512-C	GRAPHIQUE
513-C	Grotesque #9 GROTESQUE
514-C	Helvetica HELVETICA — BOLD COND.
514-C	Helvetica HELVETICA — BOLD COND. OUT.
514-C	Helvetica HELVETICA — ROUND BOLD COND. NO. 2
516-C	Johnston JOHNSTON — RAILWAY MED. COND.
517-C	Johnston JOHNSTON — RAILWAY BOLD COND.
522-C	Normande NORMANDE — COND.

524-C	Phidian PHIDIAN
524-C	Radiant RADIANT — BOLD COND.
532-C	Signum SIGNUM
537-C	TEA CHEST
542-C	Univers 59 UNIVERS 59
547-C	Weidemann WEIDEMANN — BOOK (ITC)
547-C	Weidemann WEIDEMANN — MED. (ITC)
547-C	Weidemann WEIDEMA — BOLD (ITC)
548-C	Weidemann WEIDE — BLK. (ITC)
548-C	Weidemann WEIDEMANN — BOOK ITAL. (ITC)
548-C	Weidemann WEIDEMAN — MED. ITAL. (ITC)
549-C	Weidemann WEIDEMA — BOLD ITAL. (ITC)
549-C	Weidemann WEIDEM — BLK. ITAL. (ITC)

Italics

6	**Allegro ALLEGRO**		
11	Americana AMER. *ITAL.*		
35	BALLOON		
35	**BALLOON** *BOLD*		
36	*BANK NOTE* *ITAL.*		
38	*BauerBodoni BAUER BC* *ITAL.*		
39	**Bauer Bodoni BAUI** *X-BOLD ITAL.*		
45	*Bembo BEMBO* *ITAL.*		
47	*Benguiat BENGUIA* *BOOK ITAL. (ITC)*		
47	*Benguiat BENGUIA* *MED. ITAL. (ITC)*		
47	**Benguiat BENGU** *BOLD ITAL. (ITC)*		
49	*Benguiat BENGUIAT* *BOOK COND. ITAL. (ITC)*		
49	*Benguiat BENGUIAT* *MED. COND. ITAL. (ITC)*		
49	**Benguiat BENGUIAT** *BOLD COND. ITAL. (ITC)*		
53	*Bernhard BERNHARD* *TANGO*		
58	*Bodoni BODONI* *ITAL.*		
58	*Bodoni BODONI* *BOLD ITAL.*		
61	**Book LSC BOOK** *X-BOLD ITAL. (ITC)*		

61	*Book Jacket BOOK JACKEI* *ITAL.*
64	*Bookman BOOKM* *LT. ITAL. (ITC)*
64	*Bookman BOOKM* *MED. ITAL. (ITC)*
65	**Bookman BOOKI** *DEMI ITAL. (ITC)*
65	**Bookman BOOK** *BOLD ITAL. (ITC)*
68	*Bookman BOOKMAN* *ITAL.*
69	*Bookman BOOKMAN* *BOLD ITAL.*
69	*Bookman BOOKMAN* *BOLD ITAL. (VGC)*
74	**Bronstein BRONS** *BOLD*
82	*Calligraph CALLIGR*
83	*Cancelleresca CANCELLE* *BASTARDA*
84	*Caslon CASLON* *ANTIQUE ITAL.*
85	*Caslon NEW CASLON* *ITAL.*
86	*Caslon CASLON* *471 ITAL. SWASH*
87	*Caslon CASLON* *540 ITAL.*
88	*Caslon CASLON* *BOLD ITAL.*
91	*Caslon CASLON* *BOLD ITAL. NO. 223 (ITC)*
91	*Caslon CASLON* *X-BOLD ITAL NO. 223 (ITC)*

92	*Caslon CASLON CASL* *(AMERI-CAN) ITAL.*
97	*Century CENTURY* *BOOK ITAL (ITC)*
97	**Century CENTU** *ULTRA ITAL. (ITC)*
99	*Champion CHAMPIO*
101	*Cheltenham CHELTENH* *MED. ITAL*
101	**Cheltenham CHELTEN** *BOLD ITAL.*
105	*Cheltenham CHELTENH* *LT. ITAL. (ITC)*
105	*Cheltenham CHELTEN* *BOOK ITAL. (ITC)*
105	**Cheltenham CHELTI** *BOLD ITAL. (ITC)*
104	**Cheltenham CHI** *ULTRA ITAL. (ITC)*
108	*Cheltenham CHELTENHAM* *LIGHT COND. ITAL (ITC)*
108	*Cheltenham CHELTENHAM* *BOOK COND. ITAL (ITC)*
108	*Cheltenham CHELTENH* *BOLD COND. ITAL (ITC)*
107	**Cheltenham CHELTE** *ULTRA COND. ITAL (ITC)*
110	*Churchward CHURC* *METALLIC ITAL*
115	**Clearface CLEARFA** *BLK (ITC)*
120	*Cochin COCHIN* *ITAL.*
121	*Cochin COCHIN* *BOLD ITAL.*
121	*Cochin COCHIN* *BLK. ITAL.*
126	**Cooper COOPER** *BLK ITAL.*
133	*Delphin 2 DELPHII*

ITALICS

137 Discus DISCUS
138 Discus DISCUS SEMI
142 **Egizio EGIZIO** BOLD ITAL.
147 **Elvira ELVIRA** BOLD ITAL.
148 Emphasis EMPHAS
149 ERAS
149 Eras ERAS LT. (ITC)
149 Eras ERAS BOOK (ITC)
150 Eras ERAS MED. (ITC)
150 **Eras ERAS** DEMI (ITC)
150 **Eras ERAS** BOLD (ITC)
151 **Eras ERAS** ULTRA (ITC)
155 *Fat Face FAT FACE* COND. ITAL (ITC)
157 **Fleetwing '44 FLE**
158 Flex FLEX
174 Galliard GALLIARD ITAL
175 **Galliard GALLIARD** BOLD ITAL.
175 **Galliard GALLIARI** BLK. ITAL.
175 **Galliard GALLIAR** ULTRA ITAL.
177 Garamond GARAM LT. ITAL. (ITC)
177 Garamond GARAM BOOK ITAL. (ITC)

178 **Garamond GARA** BOLD ITAL. (ITC)
178 **Garamond GARA** ULTRA ITAL. (ITC)
180 Garamond GARAMOND LT. COND. ITAL. (ITC)
180 Garamond GARAMON BOOK COND. ITAL. (ITC)
180 **Garamond GARAMON** BOLD COND. ITAL. (ITC)
181 **Garamond GARAM** ULTRA COND. ITAL. (ITC)
181 Garamond GARAMOND O.S. ITAL
184 **Gillies GILLIES** GOTHIC BOLD
186 Gill Sans GILL SANS LT. ITAL
186 **Gill Sans GILL SANS** BOLD ITAL
189 Goudy GOUDY O.S. ITAL.
190 Goudy GOUDY BOLD ITAL.
191 **Goudy GOUDY** BLK. ITAL.
192 **Goudy GOUDY** HEAVYFACE ITAL.
193 Goudy GOUDY HANDTOOLED ITAL.
194 Goudy GOUDY CURSIVE
202 Harlow HARLOW
203 Harper's Bazaar HARPER'S
208 Helvetica HELVETICA LT. ITAL.
208 Helvetica HELVETICA ITAL.
208 **Helvetica HELVETIC** BOLD COMPACT ITAL.

225 Janson JANSON ITAL
237 **Kompakt KOMF**
239 Korinna KORINNA KURSIV (ITC)
240 Korinna KORINNA KURSIV BOLD (ITC)
240 **Korinna KORINNA** KURSIV X-BOLD (ITC)
240 **Korinna KORINN** KURSIV HVY. (ITC)
243 LED L.E.D.
245 Le Griffe LE GRIFFE
251 Lys Calligraph LY
254 Madisonian MADIFO
260 Mistral MISTRAL
261 Moonshadow MOONSHA
271 Newtext NEWTEX REG. ITAL. (ITC)
276 **Old Gothic OLD GO** BOLD ITAL.
280 Optima OPTIMA ITAL
287 Palatino PALATINO ITAL.
288 Palatino PALATINO CURSIVE
289 Park Avenue PARK
296 Perpetua PERPETUA ITAL.
296 **Perpetua PERPETU** BOLD ITAL.
302 Post POST O.S. ITAL.

318	*Richmond RICHMO*ɴ	O.S. ITAL.
327	*Sabon SABON*	ITAL.
328	*Sans Serif SANS SERIF*	COND. ITAL.
334	**Serpentine SERF**	BOLD ITAL.
340	*Souvenir SOUVENIR*	LT. ITAL. (ITC)
341	*Souvenir SOUVENI*	MED. ITAL. (ITC)
341	***Souvenir SOUVEN***	DEMI ITAL. (ITC)
341	***Souvenir SOUVEı***	BOLD ITAL. (ITC)
359	***ThorbwGOOD***	ITAL. SWASH
362	*Times Roman TIMES Rᴄ*	
364	*Times New TIMES NEı*	ROMAN SEMI ITAL.
368	*Trajanus TRAJANUS*	ITAL.
369	***Trooper Roman TROOPE***	ITAL.
370	*Trump TRUMP*	MEDIAEVAL ITAL.
382	*Vivaldi VꞮⅤⱰⱢ*	
387	*Weiss Italic WEISS ITALIC*	
395	*Worcester WORCESTEı*	ROUND ITAL.
403	*Zapf Book ZAPF BOᴄ*	LT. ITAL. (ITC)
403	*Zapf Book ZAPF Bᴄ*	MED. ITAL. (ITC)
404	***Zapf Book ZAPF ʙ***	DEMI ITAL. (ITC)
404	***Zapf Book ZAPF***.	HVY. ITAL. (ITC)

ITALICS

407	*Zapf Ch'ry ZAPF CH'R*	CHANCERY LT. ITAL. (ITC)
407	*Zapf Ch'ry ZAPF CH'R*	CHANCERY MED ITAL. (ITC)

413-A	*Benguiat BENGUIAT*	GOTHIC BK. ITAL. (ITC)
413-A	*Benguiat BENGUIAT*	GOTHIC MED ITAL (ITC)
414-A	**Benguiat BENGUIAT**	GOTHIC BOLD ITAL. (ITC)
414-A	**Benguiat BENGUIAT**	GOTHIC HVY ITAL. (ITC)
414-A	*Berling BERLING*	ITAL.
420-A	*Fenice FENICE*	REG. ITAL. (ITC)
421-A	**Fenice FENICE**	BOLD ITAL. (ITC)
421-A	**Fenice FENICE**	ULTRA ITAL. (ITC)
421-A	*Framingham FRAMING*	ITAL
423-A	*Franklin Gothic FRANKL*	GOTHIC BOOK ITAL. (ITC)
424-A	*Franklin Gothic FRANKL*	MED ITAL (ITC)
424-A	**Franklin Gothic FRANı**	DEMI ITAL. (ITC)
424-A	**Franklin Gothic FRAı**	HVY ITAL (ITC)
426-A	**Futura FUTURA**	DEMI OBLIQUE
426-A	**Futura FUTURA**	BOLD OBLIQUE
432-A	*Novarese NOVARESE*	BK. ITAL. (ITC)
432-A	*Novarese NOVARESE*	MED ITAL. (ITC)
432-A	**Novarese NOVARESE**	BOLD ITAL. (ITC)

444-B	*Barcelona BARCELᴄ*	BOOK ITAL. (ITC)
444-B	*Barcelona BARCELᴄ*	MED ITAL (ITC)
445-B	**Barcelona BARCEL**	BOLD ITAL (ITC)
445-B	**Barcelona BARCE**	HVY. ITAL. (ITC)
445-B	*Baskerville BASKERVIL*	ITAL. (VGC)
446-B	**Baskerville BASKERVı**	BOLD ITAL. (VGC)
447-B	*Baskerville BASKERVILı*	ITAL. (ITC)
448-B	*Baskerville BASKERVIL*	SEMI ITAL. (ITC)
448-B	**Baskerville BASKERVIL**	BOLD ITAL. (ITC)
448-B	**Baskerville BASKERVı**	BLK. ITAL. (ITC)
450-B	*Berkeley BERKELEY*	O.S. BOOK ITAL. (ITC)
450-B	*Berkeley BERKELEY*	O.S. MED. ITAL. (ITC)
451-B	*Berkeley BERKELEY*	O.S. BOLD ITAL. (ITC)
451-B	**Berkeley BERKELEY**	O.S. BLK. ITAL. (ITC)
454-B	*Brighton BRIGHTON*	LT. ITAL.
455-B	*Caxton CAXTON*	ROMAN LT. ITAL.
456-B	*Century CENTURY*	EXPANDED ITAL.
456-B	***Chivaree CHIVAREE***	
459-B	*Else ELSE*	LT. ITAL.
459-B	*Else ELSE*	MED ITAL.

ITALICS

460-B *Else ELSE* SEMI ITAL	478-C *BALLÉ* INITIALS	494-C *Century CENTURY* LT. COND. ITAL. (ITC)
460-B **Else ELSE** BOLD ITAL	479-C *BALLOON* LIGHT	494-C *Century CENTURY* BOOK COND. ITAL. (ITC)
462-B *Harlow HARLOW* SOLID	479-C **Balzac BALZAC**	495-C **Century CENTURY** BOLD COND. ITAL. (ITC)
464-B *Isbell ISBELL* BOOK ITAL. (ITC)	479-C **BANCO**	495-C **Century CENTURY** ULTRA COND. ITAL. (ITC)
464-B *Isbell ISBELL* MED. ITAL. (ITC)	484-C *Carnase Text CARN* LT. ITAL. (WTC)	495-C *Charme CHARM* LIGHT
465-B **Isbell ISBELL** BOLD ITAL. (ITC)	484-C *Carnase Text CARN* REG. ITAL. (WTC)	496-C *Charme CHARM* BOLD
465-B **Isbell ISBELL** HVY. ITAL. (ITC)	484-C **Carnase Text CARN** MED. ITAL. (WTC)	497-C *Columbia COLUMBIA* BOLD ITAL.
466-B *Lubalin Graph LUBALII* X-LT OBLIQUE (ITC)	485-C **Carnase Text CARN** BOLD ITAL. (WTC)	499-C **Corvinus CORVINUS** MED. ITAL.
466-B *Lubalin Graph LUBA* BOOK OBLIQUE (ITC)	485-C **Carnase Text CARN** X-BOLD ITAL. (WTC)	501-C *Cushing CUSHING* BOOK ITAL. (ITC)
467-B *Lubalin Graph LUBA* MED OBLIQUE (ITC)	487-C *Caslon 224 CASLON* BOOK ITAL. (ITC)	501-C *Cushing CUSHING* MED. ITAL. (ITC)
467-B **Lubalin Graph LUBA** DEMI OBLIQUE (ITC)	487-C *Caslon 224 CASLON* MED. ITAL. (ITC)	501-C *Cushing CUSHING* BOLD ITAL. (ITC)
467-B **Lubalin Graph LUB** BOLD OBLIQUE (ITC)	487-C **Caslon 224 CASLO** BOLD ITAL. (ITC)	502-C **Cushing CUSHING** HVY. ITAL. (ITC)
469-B *Modern MODERN* #216 LT. ITAL. (ITC)	488-C **Caslon 224 CASLO** BLK ITAL. (ITC)	502-C *Dianna DIANNA* LIGHT
469-B *Modern MODERN* #216 MED. ITAL. (ITC)	489-C *Centaur CENTAUR* ITALIC	503-C *Dianna DIANNA* MEDIUM
470-B **Modern MODERN** #216 BOLD ITAL. (ITC)	489-C **Century CENTURY** BOLD ITAL.	503-C *Dianna DIANNA* BOLD
473-B **Runaround RUNCA**	490-C *Century CENTURY* BOLD COND. ITAL.	505-C *Florentine FLORENTINE* CURSIVE
474-B *Stationers STATION* SEMISCRIPT	491-C *Century CENTURY* O.S. ITAL.	506-C **Futura FUTURA** BOLD COND. OBLIQUE
475-B *THUNDERBOLT*	491-C *Century CENTURY* SCHOOLBOOK ITAL.	506-C **Futura FUTURA** X-BOLD COND OBLIQUE
475-B *Tiffany TIFFANY* LT. ITAL. (ITC)	492-C *Century CENTURY* LT. ITAL. (ITC)	507-C *Gavotte GAVOTTE*
476-B *Tiffany TIFFANY* MED. ITAL. (ITC)	492-C **Century CENTURY** BOLD ITAL. (ITC)	508-C *Goudy GOUDY* OPEN ITAL.
476-B **Tiffany TIFFANY** DEMI ITAL. (ITC)		510-C *Goudy GOUDY* LT. ITAL. SWASH (WTC)

610-C	Goudy GOUDY	MED. ITAL. SWASH (WTC)	
611-C	Goudy GOUDY	REG. ITAL. SWASH (WTC)	
611-C	**Goudy GOUDY**	BOLD ITAL. SWASH (ITC)	
613-C	**Helvetica HELVETICA**	MED. ITAL.	
516-C	Johnston JOHNSTON	RAILWAY MED. ITAL.	
516-C	**Johnston JOHNSTON**	RAILWAY BOLD ITAL.	
517-C	Kennerley KENNERLI	BOLD ITAL.	
518-C	Legend LEGEND		
525-C	Rock and Roll ROCK AN	LT. ITAL.	
525-C	**Rock and Roll ROCK**	BOLD ITAL.	
526-C	Rondo RONDO	BOLD	
526-C	Royal ROYAL		
530-C	Serifa SERIFA	THIN ITAL.	
530-C	Serifa SERIFA	LT. ITAL.	
530-C	Serifa SERIFA	ITALIC	
532-C	Serpentine SERPEN	LT. ITAL.	
532-C	**Serpentine SERPI**	MED. ITAL.	
536-C	Symbol SYMBOL	BOOK ITAL. (ITC)	
536-C	Symbol SYMBOL	MED. ITAL. (ITC)	
537-C	**Symbol SYMBOL**	BOLD ITAL. (ITC)	
537-C	**Symbol SYMBOL**	BLK. ITAL. (ITC)	

ITALICS

539-C	*Thaddeus THADDEUS*	LT. ITAL. (WTC)
539-C	*Thaddeus THADDEUS*	REG. ITAL. (WTC)
540-C	*Thaddeus THADDEUS*	MED. ITAL. (WTC)
540-C	**Thaddeus THADDEUS**	BOLD ITAL. (WTC)
540-C	Univers 46 UNIVERS 46	
541-C	Univers 56 UNIVERS 56	
541-C	**Univers 66 UNIVERS**	
541-C	**Univers 76 UNIVERS**	
543-C	Valiant VALIANT	LIGHT
542-C	Valiant VALIANT	BOLD
545-C	Veljovic VELJOVIC	BOOK ITAL. (ITC)
545-C	Veljovic VELJOVIC	MED. ITAL. (ITC)
546-C	**Veljovic VELJOVIC**	BOLD ITAL. (ITC)
546-C	**Veljovic VELJOVIC**	BLK. ITAL. (ITC)
548-C	Weidemann WEIDEMANN	BOOK ITAL. (ITC)
548-C	Weidemann WEIDEMAN	MED. ITAL. (ITC)
549-C	**Weidemann WEIDEMA**	BOLD ITAL. (ITC)
549-C	**Weidemann WEIDEM**	BLK. ITAL. (ITC)
551-C	WTG 145	LT. ITAL.
551-C	WTG 145	REG. ITAL.
552-C	WTG 145	MED. ITAL.

552-C	**WTG 145**	BOLD ITAL.
552-C	**WTG 145**	X-BOLD ITAL.
553-C	Zapf Int'l ZAPF INT	LT. ITAL. (ITC)
553-C	Zapf Int'l ZAPF IN	MED. ITAL. (ITC)
554-C	**Zapf Int'l ZAPF L**	DEMI. ITAL. (ITC)
554-C	**Zapf Int'l ZAPF**	HVY. ITAL. (ITC)

Scripts

2 Adagio ADAGIO
5 Alfereta ALFERETA
53 Bernhard BERNHARD TANGO
71 Brandywine BRANDYWINE
71 Brandywine BRANDYWINE BOLD
Centennial Script Centenn
110 Churchill CHURCHILL
184 Gillies GILLIES GOTHIC BOLD
251 Lys Calligraph LY
254 Madisonian MADISON
289 Park Avenue PARK
314 Rebecca REBECCA
371 Typo Script
382 Virtuoso 1 VIRTUOSO 1
382 Vivaldi VIVALD

CASUAL, CALLIGRAPHIC

5 Alfereta ALFERETA
42 Bazaar BAZAAR

43 Belvedere BELVEDERE SCRIPT
56 Blue Skies BLUE
61 Book Jacket BOOK JACKET ITAL.
74 Bronstein BRONST BOLD
74 Brush American BRUSH AM
82 Calligraph CALLIGR
83 Cancelleresca CANCELLE BASTARDA
84 Carpenter Carpent
93 Casual Script CASUAL SCRIPT
99 Champion CHAMPIO
137 Discus DISCUS
138 Discus DISCUS SEMI
157 Fleetwing '44 FLE
158 Flex FLEX
202 Harlow HARLOW
203 Harper's Bazaar HARPER'S B
236 Kaufman KAUFMAN SCRIPT
236 Kaufman KAUFMAN BOLD

244 Lariat LARIAT
245 Le Griffe LE GRIFFE
255 Mandate MANDATE
260 Mistral MISTRAL
261 Moonshadow MOONSHA
330 SCOTFORD UNCIAL
361 Time Script TIME S
398 York YORK
405 Zapf Ch'ry ZAPF CH'R CHANCERY LT (ITC)
405 Zapf Ch'ry ZAPF CH'R CHANCERY MED. (ITC)
406 Zapf Ch'ry ZAPF CH CHANCERY DEMI (ITC)
406 Zapf Ch'ry ZAPF CH CHANCERY BOLD (ITC)
407 Zapf Ch'ry ZAPF CH'R CHANCERY ITAL. (ITC)
407 Zapf Ch'ry ZAPF CH'R CHANCERY MED ITAL. (ITC)

SUPPLEMENT 1

417-A Chopin CHOPIN LT
417-A Chopin CHOPIN BOLD

CASUAL, CALLIGRAPHIC

416-A Candice CANDICE INLINE
436-A Razie RAZIE SHADOW

442-B *Alexandra ALEXANT*

470-B *Murray Hill MURRAY* BOLD

CASUAL, CALLIGRAPHIC

456-B **Chivaree CHIVAREE**

462-B **Harlow HARLOW** SOLID

473-B **Runaround RUNGR**

474-B **St. Thomas ST. THOMAS**

474-B *Stationers STATION* SEMISCRIPT

475-B **Studio STUDIO** BOLD

478-C *Aerolite AEROLITE* SCRIPT

478-C *BALLÉ* INITIALS

502-C *Dianna DIANNA* LIGHT

503-C *Dianna DIANNA* MEDIUM

503-C *Dianna DIANNA* BOLD

504-C *Excelsior EXCELSIOR* SCRIPT

504-C *Excelsior EXCELSIOR* SEMI-BOLD SCRIPT

505-C *Florentine FLORENTINE* CURSIVE

507-C *Gavotte GAVOTTE*

SCRIPTS

518-C *Kunstler KUNSTLR* BOLD

534-C *Stuyvesant STUYVESANT* SCRIPT

542-C *Valiant VALIANT* LIGHT

543-C *Valiant VALIANT* BOLD

CASUAL, CALLIGRAPHIC

479-C **Balzac BALZAC**

495-C *Charme CHARM* LIGHT

496-C **Charme CHARM** BOLD

505-C **Fox FOX**

518-C *Legend LEGEND*

518-C **LIBRA**

526-C *Rondo RONDO* BOLD

526-C *Royal ROYAL*

Inline/Outline/Contour/Shaded

508-C	Goudy GOUDY OPEN
508-C	Goudy GOUDY OPEN ITAL.
462-B	HADRIANO STONEC STONECUT
526-C	Royal ROYAL
534-C	Stuyvesant STUYVESANT SCRIPT

4	AKI LINES AKI LINES (ITC)	
14	Antique ANTIQUE ROMAN	
24	AUGUSTEA INLINE	
59	Bodoni BODONI OPEN	
73	BROADWAY ENGRAVED	
109	Cheltenham CHELTEI OUT. SHAD (ITC)	
110	Churchward CHURCI METALLIC	
110	Churchward CHURCI METALLIC ITAL	
127	Cooper COOPER HILITE	
131	Dektiv DEKTIV	
133	DELPHIAN	
141	ECLIPSE	
173	GALLIA	
193	Goudy GOUDY HANDTOOLED	
193	Goudy GOUDY HANDTOOLED ITAL	
194	GOUDY ORNATE ORNATE	

247	Lucifer LUCIFER NO. 1	
279	OLYMPIA OLYMPIA	
289	Paprika PAPRIKA	
303	PRISMA	
303	PRISMANIA PRISMANIA G	
304	PRISMANIA PRISMAN K	
320	ROCO	
335	Skin & Bones SKIN & BO	
366	TOP HAT	
398	YAGI LINK DOUBLE	
410	Zeppelin ZEPPELIN	

SUPPLEMENTS 2, 3

454-B	Broadway BROAD\ ENGR.	
489-C	Caslon CASLON SHADED	
461-B	FRANKFURTER HIGH LIGHT	
427-A	Glow Worm GLOW WORM	

OUTLINE

1	Aachen AACHEN BOLD OUT.	
5	Albertus ALBERTUS OUT.	
9	American TYPE TYPE- WRITER OUT. (ITC)	
13	Americana AME OUT.	
17	Aquarius AQUARIUS OUT.	
23	Aster ASTER OUT.	
33	Baker Danmark BAI OUT.	
42	Bauhaus BAUHAUS HVY. OUT. (ITC)	
55	Blippo BLIPPO BLK. OUT.	
59	BOLD EDGE	
66	Bookman BOOKM BOLD OUT. (ITC)	
69	Bookman BOOKMAN BOLD OUT.	
75	Bubble BUBBLE OUT.	
102	Cheltenham CHELTEI BOLD OUT.	
109	Cheltenham CHELTEN OUT. (ITC)	

CONTOUR (CONTINUED)

SUPPLEMENT 1

416-A	Candice CANDICE	INLINE
425-A	Franklin Gothic FRANK	CONTOUR (ITC)
440-A	Worcester WORCESTE	ROUND CONTOUR

SHADED

6	ALGERIAN ALGERI	
•11	American TYPEWRITE	TYPEWRITER SHAD. (ITC)
14	Antique ANTIQUE	ROMAN
18	Argent ARGENT	
18	Argent Open ARGENT OPEN	
31	BABY FAT BLACK	
34	Baker Danmark BAK	SHAD.
36	BANK NOTE	ITAL
36	Banque Job BANQUE JOB	BANQUE JOB
•44	Belwe BELWE	BOLD SHAD.
59	Bodoni BODONI	OPEN
•67	Bookman BOOKMAN	BOLD SHAD. (ITC)
•67	Bookman BOOKMAN	BOLD CONT. SHAD. (ITC)
72	BROADSIDE	
76	BUFFALO BILL	BUFFALO BILL
76	BULLION SHADOW	

93	Caxtonian CAXT	
98	Century Litho CENTURY L	SHAD
99	CERTIFIED	
109	Cheltenham CHELTE	OUT. SHAD. (ITC)
•111	CINEMA ONE ONE	
•111	CINEMA TWO	
•111	CINEMA THREE	
112	CIRCUS CAPS	
145	EGYPTIAN PATRIOT	
158	Flex FLEX	
164	FREDERICKSBURG	
164	FRISCO	
183	GARDENIA	
•196	Granby GRANBY	OUT. SHAD.
201	Halftone HALFTONE	
202	Harlow HARLOW	
220	INDEPENDENCE	
229	JIM CROW	
•235	Kabel KABEL	SHAD.
246	LETTRES ORNEI	ORNEES
256	MARBLEHEART	

281	ORLEANS OPEN	
281	ORPLID	
288	Pamela PAMELA	
•297	Perpetua PERPETUA	BOLD SHAD.
•297	PIONEER PIONEER	ITC
307	QUENTIN	
311	RADIANT ANTIQU	
•314	Raleigh RALEIGH	SHAD.
315	RELIEF	
•316	Rhythmic RHYTHMIC	SHAD.
325	RUSTIC	
329	SANS SERIF SHADED	
•333	Serif Gothic SERIF GOTHIC	BOLD SHAD. (ITC)
335	SILVER DOLLAR	
•337	Smoke SMOKE	SHAD.
•342	Souvenir SOUVENIR	SHAD.
343	Stagecoach STAGECOACH	
346	STEAMBOAT	SHAD.
351	SUPERSTAR	SHAD.
357	Tavern TAVERN	
358	THORNE	SHAD.

*SHADED FACES SET WITH A MASK COST MORE PER WORD. SEE PRICE LIST.

SHADED (CONTINUED)

365 Tintopetto TINTORE

365 TONIGHT

367 TOWN HALL

367 TOWN HALL 2

373 UMBRA

374 UNCLE BILL

381 VINETAOR ORNA-MENT

SUPPLEMENTS 1, 2, 3

416-A CHEQUE

425-A Franklin Gothic FRANK SHADOW (ITC)

507-C GOLD RUSH

512-C GRAPHIQUE

471-B Nubian NUBIAN

472-B PROFILE

436-A Razie RAZIE SHADOW

441-A Worcester WORCEST ROUND SHADOW

441-A YANKEE SHADOW

ORNATE

5 Alfereta ALFERETA
15 Apollo APOLLO
18 Argent ARGENT
18 Argent Open ARGENT OPEN
56 Bocklin BOCKLIN
82 Calligraph CALLIER
131 DAVIDA DAVIDA BOLD
147 Elvira ELVIRA BOLD ITAL
158 Flirt FLIRT
183 GARDENIA
194 GOUDY ORNATE ORNATE
203 Harper's Bazaar HARPER'S 1
213 Hogarth HOGARTH
237 Kismet KISMET
268 Neptune NEPTUNE
288 Pamela PAMELA
303 Pretoria PRETOI
335 Siegfried SIEGFRIED

336 Skjald SKJALD
357 Tango TANGO
358 Thalia THALIA
373 Unbelievable UNBEL.

SUPPLEMENT 1

411-A Aesthetic Aesthetic
411-A Art Gothic ART GOTHIC BOLD
411-A BARNDANCE
415-A Bulletin BULLETIN 113

SUPPLEMENT 2

461-B GALADRIEL
472-B PYGMALION PYGM
472-B Ringlet RINGLET
474-B SOUTACHE
475-B THUNDERBOLT

SUPPLEMENT 3

478-C BALLÉ INITIALS
496-C Chevalier CHEVALIEF

497-C Congress CONGRESS (LYONS)
505-C Fantail FANTAIL
517-C Karnac KARNAC
524-C Phidian PHIDIAN
526-C Royal ROYAL
528-C Sampler SAMPLER
549-C WTG 145 LIGHT
550-C WTG 145 REGULAR
550-C WTG 145 MEDIUM
550-C WTG 145 BOLD
551-C WTG 145 X-BOLD
551-C WTG 145 LT. ITAL.
551-C WTG 145 REG. ITAL.
552-C WTG 145 MED. ITAL.
552-C WTG 145 BOLD ITAL.
552-C WTG 145 X-BOLD ITAL.

STARS AND STRIPES

23 ASTRA ASTRA ASTRA
35 BANDANERO
121 Collins Collins COL BICEN-TENNIAL
198 GUTZON BORGLI GUTZON BORGLUM

STARS AND STRIPES (CONTINUED)

220 INDEPENDENCE
262 MOORE LIBERTY
267 NATIONAL SPIRIT
276 OLD GLORY
355 T.H.UNCLE SAM
367 TOWN HALL 2

HORIZON LINES

4 AKI LINES AKI LINES (ITC)
183 GARDENIA
229 JIM CROW
235 KANTANAKA EEP KANTANAKA RED
293 PERGOLA
303 PRISMANIA PRISMANIA G
304 PRISMANIA PRISMAN K
311 RADIANT ANTIQ ANTIQUE
319 ROCK OPERA
367 TOWN HALL

SHADING LINES

18 Argent ARGENT
99 CERTIFIED
201 Halftone HALFTONE

246 LETTRES ORNEE ORNEES
347 Steelplate STEELPLAT TEXT SHAD.
381 VINETA OR ORNAMENT

SUPPLEMENT 1

416-A CHEQUE

COMPUTER

7 Amelia AMELIA
128 Cucumber CUCUMBER
183 GEMINI GEMINI
243 LED L.E.D.
262 MOORE COMPUTER

SUPPLEMENT 1

429-A LED ROMAN BOLD

STENCIL

2 Advertisers ADVERTISE GOTHIC LT.
3 Advertisers ADVER GOTHIC
3 Advertisers Gothic ADVERTIS GOTHIC COND.
6 ALPHA MIDNIG MIDNIGHT
40 Bauhaus BAUHAUS LT. (ITC)
41 Bauhaus BAUHAUS MED (ITC)
41 Bauhaus BAUHAUS DEMI (ITC)

41 Bauhaus BAUHAUS BOLD (ITC)
42 Bauhaus BAUHAUS HVY. (ITC)
42 Bauhaus BAUHAUS HVY. OUT. (ITC)
55 Blippo BLIPPO BOLD
55 Blippo BLIPPO BLK
55 Blippo BLIPPO BLK. OUT.
59 BOLD EDGE
169 Futura FUTURA BLK.
169 FUTURA STENCIL LT.
170 FUTURA STENCIL BOLD
229 Joric Joric JORIC JORIC ULTRA
243 LED L.E.D.
289 Paprika PAPRIKA
315 Revue REVUE
316 Revue REVUEE X-BOLD
347 STENCIL
348 STREAMLINE
355 Tabasco TABASCO LT.
356 Tabasco TABASCO MED
356 Tabasco TABASCO BOLD
382 Visa VISA

STENCIL (CONTINUED)

SUPPLEMENT 3

537-C **TEA CHEST**

LETTERS IN LIGHTS

4 **AKI LINES AKI LINES** (ITC)

23 **ASTRA ASTRA** ASTRA

131 **Dektiv DEKTIV**

146 **ELEKTRIIK**

146 **ELEKTRIIK** MED.

147 **ELEKTRIIK** BOLD

243 *LED* L.E.D.

247 **Lucifer LUCIFER** NO.1

268 **NEON** (ITC)

365 **TONIGHT**

SUPPLEMENT 3

528-C **Sampler SAMPLER**

SQUARE INITIALS

119 **CLOISTER** CLOISTER INITIALS

286 **PAGEANT** INITIALS

LETTERS IN RIBBONS

83 **CAMPAIGN**

316 **RIBBONETTE**

348 **STEPHEN ORNATE**

356 **TABLEAU**

OLD ENGLISH, BLACK LETTER

71 **Bradley BRADLEY**

118 **Cloister CLOISTER** BLK.

148 **Engravers ENGRAVER** OLD ENGLISH (VGC)

160 **Fraktur FRAKTU** FRAKTUR

194 **Goudy Text GOUDY TE**

243 **Laertes LAERTE**

288 **Pamela PAMELA**

346 **Steelplate STEELPLAT** TEXT BLK.

347 **Steelplate STEELPLAT** TEXT OPEN

347 **Steelplate STEELPLAT** TEXT SHAD.

387 **Wedding Text WEDDING T**

SUPPLEMENT 3

478-C **American Text AMERICAN TEXT**

496-C **Chevalier CHEVALIER**

RUSTIC

14 Antique No. 14 AN
53 Bernhard BERNHARD *BOLD COND.*
56 Block Engraving BLOCK
76 Bulletin Typewriter B *TYPE-WRITER*
84 Caslon CASLON *ANTIQUE*
84 *Caslon CASLON* *ANTIQUE ITAL.*
145 EGYPTIAN EGYPTIAN
184 GETTYSBURG
189 Gorillaa GORILLA *(ITC)*
201 Halbstarke HALB *PICA*
243 Laertes LAERTES
254 MADISON MADISON
254 *Madisonian MADISO*
275 OCTIC OCTIC *EXT.*
277 Olden OLDEN
285 Packard PACKARD
290 Parsons PARSONS
290 Parsons PARSONS *BOLD*

301 Plymouth & PLY
302 Post POST *O.S. ROMAN NO. 2*
302 *Post POST* *O.S. ITAL.*
304 PUBLICITY GOTHI *GOTHIC*
311 RAILROAD GOTHIC
359 Ticonderoga TICONI *LT.*
360 Ticonderoga TICONDI *BOLD*
390 WINCHESTER *X.BOLD*
398 YUKON

SUPPLEMENTS 1, 2, 3

411-A Art Gothic ART GOTHIC *BOLD*
479-C *Balzac BALZAC*
411-A BARNDANCE
480-C Berliner BERLINER *GROTESK*
480-C Berliner BERLINER *GROTESK BOLD*
481-C Block BLOCK
418-A Egiziano EGIZIA
507-C GOLD RUSH

430-A MERCHANT *BOLD*
471-B Nubian NUBIAN
438-A Savannah SAV

THE
ALPHABETS

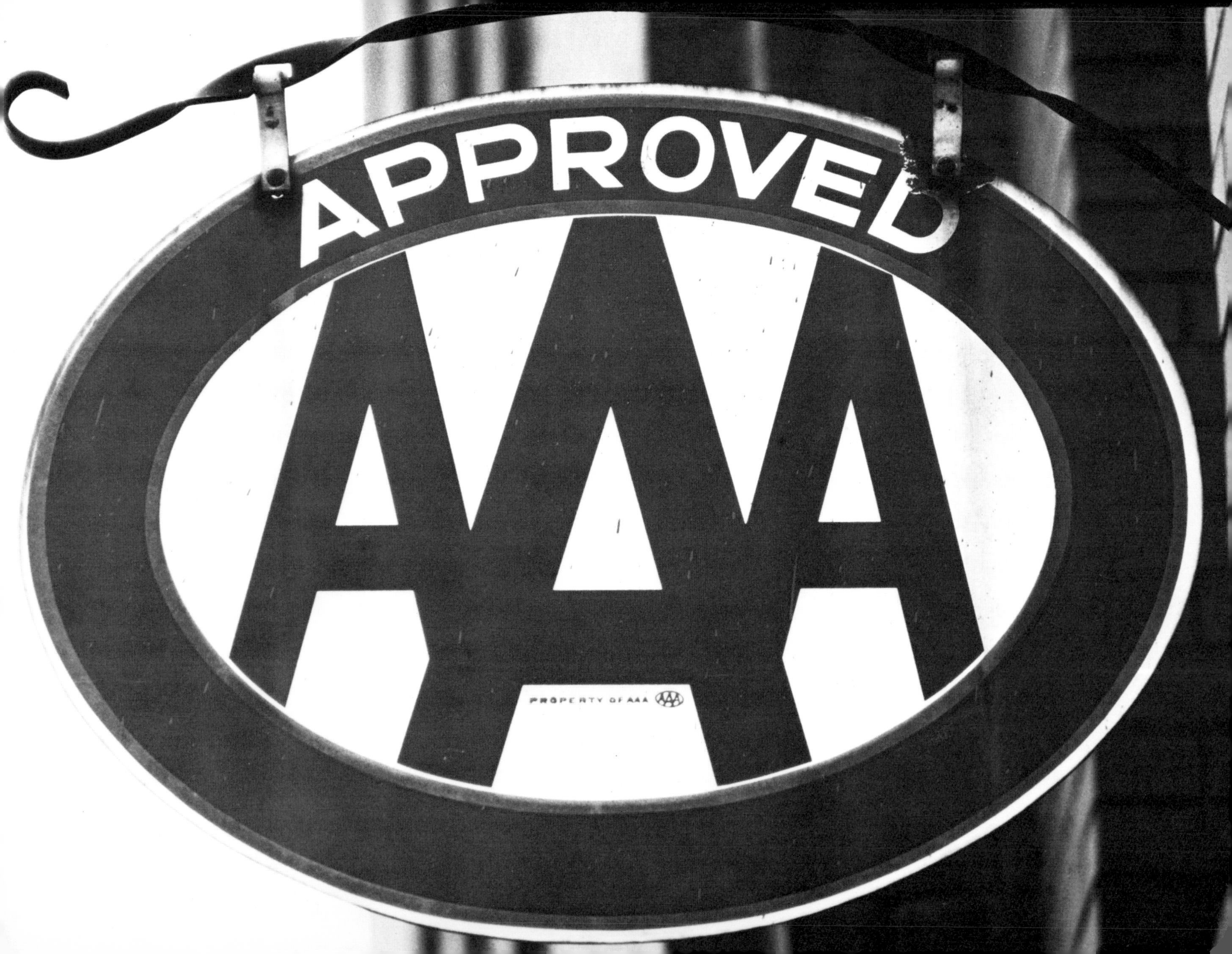
APPROVED
AAA
PROPERTY OF AAA

Aachen Medium
ABCDEFGH
IJKLMNOP
QRSTUVW
XYZ&(".::;")?!
abcdefghij
klmnopqr
stuvwxyz
$1234567
890£$/¢%
#1234567890 *

Aachen Bold
ABCDEFG
HIJKLMNOP
QRSTUVW
XYZ&(".::;")?!
=·*abcdefghi
jklmnopqrst
uvwxyz$$l
234567890
¢¢%/£#
1234567890

Aachen Bold Outline
ABCDEFGH
IJKLMNOP
QRSTUVW
XYZÇØÆŒ
&(".::;")?!
abcdefghij
klmnopqr
stuvwxyz
ßçøæœ
$1234567
890¢%£/
$1234567890¢ (wv)

Abbott Old Style

ABCCDEFG
HIJKLMNO
PQRR²STU
VWXYZ©.&
(.,=.;"*¦!?)abcd
efg_²ghijklm
nopqrr²stuv
wxyz$1234
567890£¢
%$¢1234567890

Adagio

ABCDEFG
HIJKLMN
OPQRST
UVWXYZ
&⁊₂(.,:;)?!=abbe
bercdeerfffghiijk
lllmmnnooeoerorp
qrrsssrsstuuvvve
verwwwewerwrxyyz
$12345678
90¢£%(WV)

Advertisers Gothic Light

ABCDEFG
HIJKLLM²
NOPQRS
TUVWXY
Z&("",";")?!*ab
cdefghijk
lmnopqr²
stuvwxyz
$123456
7890¢%$¢

2

Advertisers Gothic
AABCDE
FGHIJKLMN
OPQ
RSTUV
WXYZ&."::?!
ābcdefg
hijklmnop
qrstuv
wxyzß$12
34567890

Advertisers Gothic Condensed
AABCDEFGHIJ
KLMNOPQRS
TUVWXYZ
&(",:;)?!*
abcdefghi
jklmnopqrst
uvwxyz
$1234567
890¢/

Affiche Moderne
ABCDEFGHI
JKLMNO
PQRSTUV
WXYZ&.":;"?!
abcdefghij
klmnopqrstu
vwxyz$1
234567890¢

AKI LINES

ABCDEEF
GHHIIJJKLL
MNOPQRST
UVWXYY
ZƐ([≡≡])?!*≡S1
234567
890¢/sf%# (WV)

Albertus Light

AÆBCÇDEFG
HIJKLMNO
ŒØPQRSTUV
WXYZß&ᴛ(",:;")
?!*_aæbcçdefff
fiflghijklmno
œøpqrstuvwxyz
$123456789
0%$¢%₂+¿i ©® (S)

Albertus

ABCDEFG
HIJJKLMM
NOPQRS
TUVWW
XYZ&ᴛ&
ß(",:;")?!*_+
abcdefgh
ijklmnopqr
stuvwxy
zæçœø
$122344 5
678900
¢/.%■□≈¿i

4

Albertus Bold
ABCDEFG
HIJKLMN
OPQRST
UVWX
YZ&&²(',:;")
?![*=]≡©®abcde
ffffifflghijkl
mnopqrst
uvwxyz
$12345678
90¢%$%○■

Albertus Outline
ABCDEFG
HIJKLMN
OPQRST
UVWX
YZ&(',:;")
?!*≡abcde
fghijklm
nopqrst
uvwxyz
$12345678
90¢%$£% (WV)

Alfereta
ABCDE
FGHIJK
LMNOPQ
RSTUVW
XYZ&(',:;)
?!abcdefghij
klmnopq
rstuvwxyz
$123456
7890¢ (SR)

ALGERIAN

AABCDEFG
HHIJKKLM
MNNOPQRR
SSTUVWX
YZ&(;,::,-!?)
$123456789
0£/»«:..~ (WV)

Allegro

ABCDEFGHIJK
LMNOPQRSTUV
WXYZ&(.,:.;"*¡"!?)
abcdefghijklmn
opqrstuvwxyz
$£1234567890
¢%$c1234567890

ALPHA

MIDNIGHT
AABBCCDE
EFGHIJK
KLMMNN
OPQRRSS
TTUUVW
WXYYZ&
(.",:;"!?-*')$
123456
7890¢% (S)

**Alternate
Gothic No.3**
ABCDEFGH
IJKLMNO
PQRSTUVW
XYZ&('.,:;"")
?!_.abcdefgh
ijklmnopqr
stuvwxyz
$12345678
90¢/£%

Amelia
ABCDEFG
HIJKKLMN
OPQRSTUV
WXYZ&
('.,:;""!?.-—*)
abcdefgh
ijklmnopq
rstuvwxyz
£ñïï(æ)
$1234567890
¢%/ 1234567890

American
Gothic Light
ABCDEF
GHIJKLMN
OPQRSTU
VWXYZ
&('.,:;")?!*ab
cdefghijklm
nopqrst
uvwxyz
$1234567
890¢$%¢%

American
Gothic
MediumA
BCDEFG
HIJKLM
NOPQRS
TUVWXY
Z&('.;:;"")?!*
abcdefghij
klmnopqr
stuvwxyz
$1234567
890¢$¢%

American
GothicBold
ABCDEF
GHIJKLM
NOPQRS
TUVWX
YZ&('.;:;"")?!*
abcdefghij
klmnopqr
stuvwxyz
$1234567
890¢$¢%

American
Typewriter
LightABCD
EFGHIJKL
MNOPQR
RSTUVWX
YZÆÇØŒ
&&('.;:;"")?![*]
abcdefgh
ijklmnopqr
stuvwxyz
æçøoeß$
123456789
0¢$/£%#@

ITC LICENSED
American
Typewriter
Medium ABC
DEFGHIJKL
MNOPQR
RSTUVWX
YZÆÇØŒ
&&(',:,;")?!
[*]abcdeefgh
ijklmnopqr
stuvwxyz
$ßæçøœ
123456789
0¢$/£%#⌢»«@

ITC LICENSED
American
Typewriter
Bold ABCD
EFGHIJKL
MNOPQR
STUVWXY
ZÆÇØŒ
&&(',:,;")?![*]
abcdeefgh
ijklmnopqr
stuvwxyz
$ßæçøœ
123456789
0¢$/£%#⌢»«@

ITC LICENSED
American
Typewriter
Outline ABC
DEFGHIJK
LMNOPQR
STUVWX
YZÆÇØŒ
&&(',:,;")?!
[*]abcdeef
ghijklmnop
qrstuvwx
yz$ßæçøœ
123456789
0¢$/£%#⌢»«@ (WV)

ITC™ LICENSED American
Typewriter Light
Condensed ABCD
EFGHIJKLMN
OPQRRSTUV
WXYZÆÇØŒ
&&(',.;;")?![*]abcdee
fghijklmnopqrs
tuvwxyzæçøœ
ß$1234567890¢
$/£%#⁙»«@

ITC™ LICENSED American
Typewriter
Medium
Condensed ABC
DEFGHIJKL
MNOPQRRST
UVWXYZÆÇØ
Œ&&(',.;;")?![*]
abcdeefghijklm
nopqrstuvwx
yzæçøœß$12
34567890
¢$/£%#⁙»«@

ITC™ LICENSED American
Typewriter Bold
Condensed AB
CDEFGHIJK
LMNOPQRS
TUVWXYZ
ÆÇØŒ&&
(',.;;")?![*]
abcdeefghij
klmnopqrs
tuvwxyzæ
çøœß$123
4567890¢$
/£%#⁙»«@

10

ITC™ LICENSED **American Typewriter Shaded** ABCDE FGHIJKLM NOPQRSTUV WXYZÆÇ ØŒ&&(',;'""") ?![*]abcdee² fghijklm nopqrstuvw xyzæçøœß $1234567 890¢$/£%# ~´¨`˜"¸@

(WV)(CMM)

Americana ABCDEFG HIJKLM NOPQRS TUVWXY Z&(".:;"")?!?[*] abcdefg hijklmno pqrstuvw xyz$1234 567890 ¢$%¢£%

Americana ItalicABCD EFGHIJKL MNOPQ RSTUVW XYZ&(".:;"") ?![*]abcdefg hijklmnop qrstuvwx yzfffiflfffifflß $1234567 890¢¢$£%©

Americana
BoldABC
DEFGHIJ
KLMNO
PQRSTU
VWXYZ
&(";:;"")?!?[*-]a
bcdefghi
jklmnop
qrstuvw
xyz$123
456789
0¢¢/s£%

Americana
ExtraBold
ABCDEFG
HIJKLM
NOPQRS
TUVW
XYZ&(.;:;")
?!?[*-]abcd
efghijklm
nopqrstu
vwxyz$
12345678
90¢¢/s£%◗▪

Americana
BlackAÆB
CÇDEFGH
IJKLMNO
ŒØPQRST
UVWXYZ
&[";:;"")?!([*-])
aæbcçde
fghijklm
nooeøp
qrstuvw
xyzß$123
4567890
¢/%⚬❋©®▪◻⊠↯

12

Americana Outline
ABCDEFG
HIJKLMNO
PQRSTUV
WXYZ&
(✳'""·;·,""≗!??)ab
cdefghijkl
mnopqrst
uvwxyz
$12345678
90£¢%$/¢
1234567890 (WV)

Andrich Minerva
ABCDEFG
HIJKLMN
OPQRSTU
VWXYZ&
(':;,"")?!*abcd
efghijklmn
opqrstuvw
xyz$12345
67890¢/£$%‰ (WV)

**Annlie Extra Bold ABCDE
FGHIJKL
MNOPQRST
UVWXYZ&
(:;,:"!?)abcdef
ghijklmnop
qrstuvwxyz
$1234567
890¢❖«❖❖»** (WV)

ANTIETAM

ABCDEFGH
IJKLMNOP
QRSTUVW
XYZ".,:;!_ (IB)(WV)

Antique No.14A

BCDE
FGHIJK
LMNOP
QRSTUV
WXYZ
&.",:;?!*_ab
cdefghijk
lmnopqrs
tuvwxyz
$12345
67890¢/ (WV)

Antique Roman

AABCDEFFG
HIJKLLMNO
PPQRSTTUV
VwWXYYZ
&(.,:;!?)*abcd
efghijklmnop
qrstuvwxyz
$123456 7
890£¢/%$

1234567890(WV)

Anzeigen GroteskBold
ABCDEFGHIJK
LMNOPQRS
TUVWXYZ&
(‚.,:;"")?![_*_]ab
cdefghijklmn
opqrstuvwx
yz$123456
7890¢¢%£%o† (IB)

Apollo
ABCDEF
GHIJK
LMNOPQ
RSTU
VWXYZ&
(‚.,:;")?!ãbc
defghijklm
nopqrstu
vwxyz$
12345678
90¢¢/$£ᵉ

Aquarius2
ABCDEFGH
IJKLMNOPQ
RSTUVWX
YZ&(‚"'')?!*abc
defghijklmn
opqrstuv
wxyz$123
4567890
¢/£$%ᵉ (WV)

Aquarius4

ABCDEFGH
IJKLMNOPQ
RSTUVWX
YZ&(.',.:;'")?!*abc
defghijklmn
opqrstuv
wxyz$123
4567890
¢/£¢$%

Aquarius5

ABCDEFGH
IJKLMNOPQ
RSTUVWX
YZ&(.',.:;'")?!*abc
defghijklmn
opqrstuv
wxyz$123
4567890
¢/£¢$%

Aquarius6

ABCDEFGH
IJKLMNOPQ
RSTUVWX
YZ&(.',.:;'")?!*a
bcdefghijklm
nopqrstuvw
xyz$1234
567890
¢/£¢$%

Aquarius7
ABCDEFGH
IJKLMNOPQ
RSTUVWX
YZ&(',.:;")?!*ia
bcdefghijklm
nopqrstuvw
xyz$1234
567890
¢/£$%

Aquarius8
ABCDEFGH
IJKLMNOPQ
RSTUVWX
YZ&(',.:;")?!*ia
bcdefghijklm
nopqrstuvw
xyz$1234
567890
¢/£$%

Aquarius
OutlineABCD
EFGHIJKL
MNOPQRSTU
VWXYZ&
(',.:;")?!*abcd
efghijklmn
opqrstuvwxy
z$12345
67890¢$%¢£%
1234567890 (WV)

Archie

AABBCCDD
EEFFGGHH
HIIJJKKL
LMMNNO
OPPQQRR
SSTTUUVV
WWXXYYZZ
&('.,:;"")?!_ab
cdefghijklm
nopqrstuvw
xyz$12345
67890¢£% (WV)

Argent

ABCDEFG
HIJKLMNO
PQRSTUV
WXYZ&".,:;
?!abcdefgh
ijklmnopqrst
uvwxyz$12
34567890
the of and (WV)

ArgentOpen

ABCDEFG
HIJKLMNO
PQRSTUV
WXYZ&'.,:;
?!abcdefgh
ijklmnopqrst
uvwxyz$12
34567890
the of and (WV)

Argentica
BookABCDE
FGHIJKLMNO
PQRSTUVW
XYZÆÇØŒ
&(',.:;'")?!*=abc
defghijkkl
mnopqrstu
vwwxxyyz
œçœeø\$ß
1234567890
¢£%⸮¿i

Argentica
MediumAB
CDEFGHIJ
KLMNOPQ
RSTUVWXY
ZÆÇŒØ&
(',.:;'")?!*=abc
defgghijkk
lmnopqrst
uvwwxx
yyzœçœø
ß\$1234567
890¢£%⸮¿i«»

Argentica
DemiABCD
EFGHIJKLM
NOPQRST
UVWXYZÆ
ÇŒØ&(',.:;'")
?!*=abcdef
gghijkklm
nopqrstu
vwwxxy
yzœçœøß
\$12345678
90¢£%⸮¿i«»

Argentica Bold
ABCDE
FGHIJKLM
NOPQRST
UVWXYZÆ
ÇŒØ&('.,:;"")
?!*abcdef
gghijkklm
nopqrstu
vwwxxy
yzæçœøß
$12345678
90¢£%

Arpad Medium
AB
CDEFGHIJ
KLMNOP
QRSTUVW
XYZ&('.,:;"")
?!*abcdefg
hijklmnop
qrstuvwxy
z$123456
7890¢/£$%

Arrow
ABCDEFG
HIJKLMN
OPQRST
UVWXYZ
&('.,:;"")?!*abc
defghijklmn
opqrstuvw
xyz$12345
67890
¢/£%

ArtGothic

ABCCDEEFC
GHhIJKLCMN
OPQRSSTT
UVWXYZ&
(",:;)?!ābccdeef
ghijklmmnop
qrsstuvwxy
z$1234567
890¢/£

Artcraft

ABCDEFG
HIJKLMN
OOØPQRST
UVWXYZ
&(.,:;—!?)
abcdefghij
klmnoøpqr
stuvwxyz
«≈»$¢£123
4567890

Artcraft

BoldABC
DEFGHIJK
LMNOPQ
RSTUV
WXYZ&
(",:;)?!ābcd
effghijkl
mnopqr
stuvwxy
z$123456
7890¢

Aster

ABCDE
FGHIJK
LMNOP
QRSTU
VWXYZ
&(.,;:"'')?!*_a
bcdeffffi
flghijkl
mnopqr
stuvwx
yz$1234
567890
¢/£¢$%

AsterBold

ABCDE
FGHIJK
LMNOP
QRSTU
VWXYZ
&(.,;:;'')?!*_a
bcdefff
fiflffifflghij
klmnopqr
stuvwx
yz$1234
567890
¢/£¢$%

Aster Extra Bold

AB
CDEFGHIJ
KLMNO
PQRSTUV
WXYZ&
(.,;:;'')?!*_abc
deffffifl
ffifflghijkl
mnopqr
stuvwxyz
$12345
67890$/¢¢%
123456789

22

AsterBlack
ABCDEF
GHIJKLM
NOPQRS
TUVWXY
ZßÆÇŒØ
&(.,:;"")?!*+§§
abbᶜcdde
ffffffffififlflg
hhijkkll
mnopqrstu
vwxyz$12
34567890$¢
%/·○●■□

Aster
OutlineA
BCDEFG
HIJKLM
NOPQR
STUVWX
YZ&('·;:"")
?!*abcdef
ffffififlfflg
hijklmn
opqrstuv
wxyz$123
4567890
¢/£$$%(WV)

ASTER
ABCDEFGHIJK
LMNOPQRST
UVWXYZ&(.,:)?!
=*$1234567
890¢% (WV)

Athenaeum

ABCDEFGHIJ
KLMNOPQRS
TUVWXYZ
&(".;;"—!?)[†‡S*]
abcdefghijklm
nopqrstuvwx
yzffffiffiflffl
$1234567
890£¢/%
1234567890

AUGUSTEA INLINE

ABCDEFGH
IJKLMNOP
QRSTUVW
XYZ&
(".;:♡♣!9)$123
4567890£¢/%
$1234567890¢ (WV)

Aurora Condensed

AABCDEFGHIJKKLMMN
NOPQRSTUVVWWXXYY
Z&(.',::,;")?![=]abcdefgh
ijkklmnopqrstuvv
wwxxyýz$1234456
7890¢/$£%ᶜ* 12344567890 (IB)(S)

24

Aurora Grotesk IX
ABCDEFGH
IJKLMNOP
QRSTUVW
XYZÆÇŒ&
(',.;'")?!*ab
cdefghijk
lmnopqrst
uvwxyzæ
œ$123456
7890¢£

ITC™ LICENSED
Avant Garde Gothic X-Light A
AABCCAODEEA
FFAFRGGAHHTIJK
KALIALALLMMN
NTOPPRQRRAS
SSTSTTTHUUTVN
VVWWXYZ&(',.;")
?!(*)abcdefffffifl
ffifflghijklmnopq
rsttuvvvwwvxy
z$12345678
90¢/£$%#(wv)

ITC™ LICENSED
Avant Garde Gothic Book
AAABCCAODE
EAFFAFRGGAHHT
IJKKALLIALALLMM
MNNTOPPRQR
RASSSSTSTTHUUT
VNVVWWNWX
YZ&(',.;")?!(*)ab
ccdeefffffifffifl
ghijklmnop
qrsttuvvvwwvw
xyyz$1234567
890¢/£$%#

AvantGarde
GothicMedium

AAABCCACⒸDE
EAFFAFRGGAHHT
IJKKALLALALM
MNNTOPRRQR
RASSSSTSTTTHU
UTVVVWWX
YZ&(',.;"")?!(⁑)ab
ccdeefffifffiffl
ghijklmnop
qrsttuvⅤⅤⅤww
xyyz$1234567
890¢/£¢$%#

AvantGarde
GothicDemi

AAABCCACⒸDE
EAFFAFRGGAHHT
IJKKALLALALM
MNNTOPRRQR
RASSSSTSTTTHU
UTVVVWWX
YZ&(',.;"")?!(⁑)ab
ccdeefffifffiffl
ghijklmnop
qrsttuvⅤⅤⅤww
xyyz$1234567
890¢/£¢$%#

AvantGarde
GothicBoldAA

ABCCACⒸDEEAF
EAFRGGAHHTIJK
KALLALLMMⅯⅯ
NNTOPRRQRRRAS
SSSSTSTTTHUUTV
VVVⅤWWXY
Z&(','"";)?!⁑abcc
deefffifffffiflg
hijklmnopqrstt
uvⅤⅤWWWWx
yyz$11234567
890¢/£¢$%#

ITC LICENSED AvantGarde GothicBook Condensed
AABCCDEEAF
FARGGAHHTIJKKA
LLALLMMMNNTO
PRQRRASSSST
STTHUUTVVW
WWWXYZ&
(',:;")?!(*)abcdeef
ghijklmnopqrstu
vW²³³vWWW⁴WWxyy²z
$$1234567890
¢$/¢£%

ITC LICENSED AvantGarde GothicMedium CondensedAA²A³
BCCADEEAFFAR
GGAHHTIJKKAL
LALLALLMMM²M³M
NTOPRQRRAS
SSTSTTHUUTV
VV²W³VWWXYZ&
(',:;")?!(*)abcdee₂
fghijklmnopqrs
tuv²w³WWW²M³WWW⁴
xyy²z$$123456
7890¢$/¢£%#

ITC LICENSED AvantGarde GothicDemi CondensedA
AABCCADEEAF
FARGGAHHTIJK
KALLALLALLMMM
NNTOPRQRRAS
SSTSTTHUUTV
VV²W³VWWXYZ&
(',:;")?!(*)abcdee₂
fghijklmnopqr
stuv²w³WWW²M³WWW⁴
xyy²z$$123456
7890¢$/¢£%#

Avant Garde Gothic Bold Condensed

AA²A³BCDEE⁴FG
HH⁴TIJKK⁴LLL⁴L
MM²M³NNTOPR⁴
QRRASSSTSTT²
THUUTV V²V³W W²
WXYZ&(.',.:;")
?!(*)abcdeefg
hijklmnopqrs
tuv²v³ww w²ww⁴x
yyz²z$$1234567
890¢$/¢£%#

Avon Regular

ABCDEFGHIJKLMN
OPQRSTT²UVWXYZ
ÆARÇCAEAETGAE
KAIAØŒRAREST
SWThTHTETTTTWTY
&(":"..,.:;„"")?![⁰]
abcdeffghijklmnopq
rstuvwxyzßçøæœ
$1234567890¢/$%£≈⁚¿¡«»
1234567890

Avon Bold

ABCDEFGHIJKL
MNOPQRSTT²UVW
XYZÆŒRÇCAEAET
GAÆKAIAØŒRARE
STSWThTHTHETW
TITTTYTY&(",";.;;")?![≗]
abcdeffighijklmnopq
rstuvwxyzßçøæœ
$1234567890¢/
$%£⚄⚅¿¡«»1234567890

Avon Black

ABCDEFGHIJKL
MNOPQRSTT²UV
WXYZÆŒRÇCA
EAETGAÆKAIAØ
ŒRARESTSWTh
THTHETITTTWTY
&(",";.;;")?![≗]
abcdeffighijklmn
opqrstuvwxyzßçø
æœ$1234567890¢/
$%£⚄⚅¿¡«»1234567890

BABY
FAT BLACK
ABCDEFG
HIJKLMNO
PQRSTUV
WXYZ&
(()))?!
_=*$1234
567890¢
1£% (IB)

BABY
TEETH
ABCDE
FGHIJKL
MNOPQR
STUVWX
YZ&(.,:;)
??$1234
56789
O/E (WV)

Baker
Danmark1
ABCDEF
GHIJKLMN
OPQRSTUV
WXYZ
&(*,:,-"!?)abc
defghijklm
nopqrstu
vwxyz
$12345
6789
o£¢%/ (IB)

Baker
Danmark 2
ABCDEF
GHIJKLMN
OPQRSTUV
WXYZ
&(*.,;--"!?)abc
defghijklm
nopqrstu
vwxyz
$123456
7890Ł¢%/

Baker
Danmark 3
ABCDEF
GHIJKLM
NOPQRST
UVWXY
Z&(*.,;--"!?)
abcdefghij
klmnopqrs
tuvwxyz
$123456
7890Ł¢%/

Baker
Danmark 4
ABCDEF
GHIJKLMN
OPQRST
UVWXYZ
&(*.,;--"!?)ab
cdefghijk
lmnopqrs
tuvwxyz
$123456
7890Ł¢%/

**Baker
Danmark 5
ABCDEF
GHIJKLM
NOPQRST
UVWXY
Z&(‘;*:.,‘‘”!?)
abcdefghi
jklmnopq
rstuvwxyz
$1234567
890£¢%/**

**Baker
Danmark 6
ABCDEFG
HIJKLMN
OPQRSTU
VWXYZ
&(‘;*:.,‘‘”!?)
abcdefg
hijklmn
opqrstu
vwxyz
$1234567
890£¢%/**

Baker
Danmark
Outline
ABCDEFGH
IJKLMNOPQ
RSTUVW
XYZ &
(‘;*:.,‘‘”!?)ab
cdefghijkl
mnopqrstu
vwxyz$12
34567 8
90£¢%/ wv

Baker Danmark Shaded

ABCDEFGH
IJKLMNOP
QRSTUV
WX
YZ&
(°*°‚°°°°‚‚--!?) ab
cdefghijkl
mnopqrstu
vwxyz
$123456
7890£¢%/

Baker Signet

ABCDE
FGHIJKLMNO
PQRSTUVW
XYZ&(',.;:"")?!*
abcdefghijkl
mnopqrs
tuvwxyz
$1234567
890¢/£%

Baker Signet Black

ABCD
EFGHIJK
LMNOPQR
STUVWXYZ
ßÆÇŒØ&
(',.;:"")?![(*)]+ab
cdefghijk
lmnopq
qrstuvwx
yzæçœø$1
23456789
0¢¢/$%%◐■⌂

34

BALLOON
ABCDEFGHIJKL
MNOPQRSTUV
WXYZ&(',:;"'*!?)
$1234567890
£¢/%

$1234567890¢

BALLOON
BOLD
ABCDEFGHI
JKLMNOPQR
STUVWXYZ&
(',:;"")?!*=$12
3456789
0¢$%¢£%

BANDANERO
ABCDEFG
HIJKLMN
OPQRSTU
VWXYZ&
""",""123
4567890

BANK NOTE ITALIC

BANK
NOTE
ITALIC
ABBCD
DEFG
HIJKL
MNOPP
QRRSTU
VWXYZ
ÆŒ&(.,:;,)
?!$123456
7890¢/ (WV)

Banque Job

BanqueJob
ABCDEFG
HIJKLMN
OPQRST
UVWXYZ
&(.,;:;"-."!?)
abcdef flgh
ijklmnopq
rstuvwxyz
/%$¢£123
4567890 (WV)

Basilea

Basilea
ABCDEF
GHIJKLM
NOPQRST
UVWXYZ&
(".,:;)?!*_abcdefg
hijklmnopqr
stuvwxyz$1
2345678
90¢/%¢/£%

Baskerville
ABCDEF
GHIJKLM
NOPQRST
UVWXYZ
&(".,:;"?")?!*-abc
defffffffflffiffl
ghijklmno
pqrstuvwx
yz$123456
7890¢⁄¢$%

Baskerville
BoldAB
CDEFGHIJ
KLMNO
PQRSTUVW
XYZ&
(".,:;"?")?![*]abcdef
ffffffflfflg
hijklmnopq
rstuvwx
yz$1234567
890¢⁄£%

**Baskerville
BoldNo.312
ABCDEFGH
IJKLMNOP
QRSTUV
WXYZÇ
&(".,:;"?")?!*-ab
cdefghijkl
mnopqrs
tuvwxyz
$1234567890
1234567890
¢⁄£,⌢⌣** (S)

BauerBodoni
ABCDEFGHI
JKLMNOP
QRSTUVWX
YZ&(.,:;)?!ābc
deffffifflgh
ijklmnopqr
stuvwxyz
$1234567890 (WV)

*BauerBodoni
ItalicABCDE
FGHIJKL
MNOPQRST
UVWXYZ&
(.,:;?)?!*abcdef
ffffiflghijklmn
opqrstuvwx
yz$1234567
890¢/$£%* (WV)*

**BauerBodoni
Extra Bold
ABCDEFGHI
JKLMNOPQ
RSTUVWX
YZ&(.,:;!?!?)
abcdefghijk
lmnopqrstu
vwxyz$12
34567890
£¢/%$ 1234
567890¢**

**Bauer Bodoni
Extra Bold
Italic ABCDE
FGHIJKLM
NOPQRSTU
VWXYZ
&(.,":;"⸎!?)abc
defghijklmn
opqrstuvwx
yzfiflftff
$12345678
90£¢/%$123
4567890¢**

Bauer Classic
Roman A B C
DEFGHIJK
LMNOPQR
STUVWX̃
YZ&(*.,:;"!?)ab
cdeffffiflghij
klmnopqrst
uvwxyz
$123456
7890£¢/%
$1234567890¢/%

BAUER TEXT
INITIALS
ABCDEFGHI
JKLMNOP
QQRSTUV
WXYZ

BauerText
ABCDEFGH
IJKLMNO
PQRSTUVW
XYZ&(",:;)?!
ābcdefghijkl
mnopqrstuvw
xyz$1234
567890¢

**BauerText
BoldABCÇDE
FGHIJKLM
NOPQRSTU
VWXYZ&
(",:;)?!abcçdefgh
ijklmnopqr
stuvwxyz$12
34567890¢/£-**

BauhausLight
ABCDEFGHIJ
KLMMNNO
PQRSſTUVW
XXYZÆŒ
Ø&&(",:;")?![*]a
bcdeefghij
klmnopqrſsſt
uvwxxyyz
æææœœøß
$$12345678
90¢$$/£%ċ¡«#

LICENSED ITC Bauhaus
MediumAB
CDEFGHIJK
LMMNNOP
QRSSTUVW
XXYZÆŒØ
&&(".,.:;")?![*]a
bcdeefghijk
lmnopqrrsst
uvwxxyyzæ
æœœøß$
$1234567
890¢$$⊄£
%⁙¿¡«»#

LICENSED ITC Bauhaus
DemiABCD
EFGHIJKLM
MNNOPQRS
STUVWXXY
ZÆŒØ&&
(".,.:;")?![*]
abcdeefgh
ijklmnopqrr
sstuvwxxy
yzææœ
œøß$$1234
567890¢$$⊄
£%⁙¿¡«»#

LICENSED ITC Bauhaus
BoldABCD
EFGHIJKLM
MNNOPQRS
STUVWXXY
ZÆŒØ&&
(".,.:;")?![*]
abcdeefgh
ijklmnopqrr
sstuvwxxy
yzææœ
œøß$$1234
567890¢$$⊄
£%⁙¿¡«»#

Bauhaus
HeavyABC
DEFGHIJKL
MMNNOPQR
SSTUVWXXY
ZÆŒØ&&
("'•.,∷;;'"")?![*]
abcdeefgh
ijklmnopqrr
sstuvwxxy
yzæææœ
œøß$$1234
567890¢$$/¢
£%✿⁑¿¡⟫#

Bauhaus
HeavyOutline
ABCDEFGHIJ
KLMMNNOP
QRSSTUVW
XXYZÆÇŒØ
&&SS("'•.,∷;;'"")
?![*]abcdeef
ghijklmnopq
rrsstuvwxx
yyzæææçœ
œøßsß$$123
4567890¢$$//¢
£%✿⁑¿¡⟫#

Bazaar
ABCDEF
GHIJKL
MNOPQR
SSTUVWXY
Z&(∷;;)?!!.ab
cdefghijkl
mnopqrst
uvwxyz$
1234567
890¢¢/$£ (SR)

42

Belvedere Script

ABCÇDEF
GHIJKL
MNOØPQR
STUVWX
YZ&(.,:;)?!*aaal
amanarasbccçrçddeee
elemeneresffffrgghh
iïiliminirisjkkmmll
nnooolomonooorosøp
grrrssttthttuwulumun
urusvwwrxyzß$123
4567890¢%÷※i¡

Belwe Light

AAÆBCÇD
EFGHIJJKKL
MMNOŒØ
PQRSTUV
WXXYZ&
(.,:;'"*"!?)aæb
cçdefghijj
klmnoœø
pqrstuvwx
yzß$12345
67890¢/£%
$1234567890¢©℗®

Belwe Medium

AAÆ
BCÇDEFG
HIJJKLMN
OŒØPQ
RSTUVW
XYZ&(.,:;"¡"!?)
※i¿æbcc
defghijkl
mnoœøpq
rstuvwxyz
ß$11234567
890¢£%/
$1234567890¢

Belwe Bold
A A Æ B C Ç D
E F G H I J K L
M N O Œ Ø
P Q R S T U V
W X Y Z &
(',.:;"")?!_æb
cçdefghij
klmnoœø
pqrstuvwx
yzß$12345
67890¢/£%

Belwe Bold
Shaded A A Ä
Æ B C Ç D E F G
H I J K L M N
O Ö Ö Œ P Q
R S T U V W
X Y Z & (',.:;"")?
!_aäåæbcç
defghijkl
mnoøöœpq
rstuvwxyz
ß$1234567
890¢/.% (CMM) (WV)

Bembo
A B C D E
F G H I J K L
M N O P Q R
S T U V W X Y
Z Æ Œ & (',.:;"")?!
[*]abcdefffffifl
ffifflghijkl
mnopqrstuv
wxyzæœ$
123456789
0¢/ £ £ $%

44

Bembo Italic
A ÆB C D E F
G H I J K L M
N O Œ P Q R S
T U V W X Y Z
& (‚‚;‚‚)?![_]aæb*
c d e f fi fl ff ffi ffl g
h i j k l m n oœ p q
r s t u v w x y z
$1 2 3 4 5 6 7 8
9 0 ¢ ‰ £ %

Bembo Bold
A B C D E F G
H I J K L M
N O P Q R S
T U V W X Y
Z & (‚‚;‚‚ ")?!āb
c d e f ff fi fl ffi
ffl g h i j k l m
n o p q r s t u v
w x y z $1 2 3 4 5
6 7 8 9 0 / £

Bembo Black
A ÆB C Ç D
E F G H I J
K L M N O Œ
Ø P Q R S T U
V W X Y Z &
(‚;‚;)?!_aæb c ç
d e f ff fi fl g h
i j k l m n oœ
ø p q r s t u v w
x y z ß $1 2 3 4
5 6 7 8 9 0 ¢ / %

Benguiat

Book AAA 2 3

AAAÆBÆÆAH
AKÆPÆRBCD
EFGHIJKL
MMNOPQR
SSSTTUVW
XYZ&(',;;"!?)
[*]abcdefg
hijklmnopq
rstuvwxyz
fiæ$123456
7890¢£%#/@

$1234567890¢

Benguiat

Medium AAA 2 3

AAAÆBÆÆAH
AKÆPÆRBCDE
FGHIJKLMM 2
NOPQRSSST
TTUVWXYZ
&(',;;"!?)[*]ab
cdefghijklm
nopqrstuvw
xyzfiæ$1234
567890¢£%
#/@$1234567890¢

Benguiat

Bold AAA 2 3

AAAÆBÆÆAH
AKÆPÆRBCD
EFGHIJKL
MMNOPQR 2
SSSTTUV
WXYZ&[*]
(',;;"!?)abc
defghijkl
mnopqrst
uvwxyzfiæ
$12345678
90¢£%#/@$

Benguiat Book Italic

AAAÆ ÆBÆ
ÆÆHÆ ÆPÆR
BCDEFGHIJ
KLMMNOPQ
RSSSTTTUV
WXYZ&(',.;;!?)
[*]abcdefgh
ijklmnopqrs
tuvwxyzfiæ
$$12345678
90¢£%#/@
$1234567890¢

Benguiat Medium Italic

AAAÆ ÆBÆ
ÆÆHÆ ÆPÆRB
CDEFGHIJK
LMMNOPQR
SSSTTTUVW
XYZ&(',.;;!?)
[*]abcdefgh
ijklmnopqr
stuvwxyzfi
æ$123456
7890¢£%#/@
$1234567890¢

Benguiat Bold Italic

AAAÆ ÆBÆ
ÆÆHÆ ÆPÆR
BCDEFGHI
JKLMMMNO
PQRSSSST
TTUVWXYZ
&(',.;;!?)[*]a
bcdefghijkl
mnopqrstu
vwxyzfiæ
$12345678
90¢£%#@/$

Benguiat Book Condensed A A₂

A₃AAABÆÆAH
AKÆARBCDEF
GHIJKLMMNO
PQRSSSTTTUV
WXYZÐŁŒØ&
(.,:;!?)[•*]abcde
fghijklmnopqr
stuvwxyzæœ
øßfid$1234567
890¢£%#/@$
1234567890¢

Benguiat Medium Con- densed A A₂ A₃

AAABÆÆAH AK
ÆARBCDEFGH
IJKLMM₂NOPQ
RSSSTTTUVW
XYZĄÇEŒØ&
(.,:;!?)[•*]abcd
efghijklmnop
qrstuvwxyzą
eæœøßfi$123
4567890¢£%
#/@$1234567890¢

Benguiat Bold Condensed A A₂

A₃AAABÆÆAH
AKÆARBCDEF
GHIJKLMM₂N
OPQRSSSTTT
UVWXYZÐŁŒ
Ø&(.,:;!?)[•*]
abcdefghijkl
mnopqrstuv
wxyzæœøßfi
$1234567890
¢£%#/@$123456
7890¢

ITC LICENSED

Benguiat Book Condensed Italic
A A₂ A₃ AA ÆÆ
ÆFIAK Æ ÆRBC
DEFGHIJKLMM₂
NOPQRSSSTTTU
VWXYZŁŒØ&
(.,:;'!?)(≛)abcdef*
ghijklmnopqrs
tuvwxyzæœøß
fid$123456789
0¢£%#/@$
1234567890¢

ITC LICENSED

Benguiat Medium Condensed Italic A
AA₂A₃AÆÆÆFIH
AKÆRBCDEFG
HIJKLMM₂NOP
QRSSSTTTUVW
XYZŒØ&(.,:;'!?)
(≛*)abcdefghijk
lmnopqrstuv
wxyzæœøß$1
234567890¢£
%#/@$1234567890¢

ITC LICENSED

Benguiat Bold Condensed
ItalicA A A₂ AA₃
ÆÆ ÆFIAK Æ
ÆRBCDEFGHI
JKLMM₂NOPQ
RSSSTTTUVW
XYZÐŁŒØ&
(.,:;'!?)(≛*)abcd
efghijklmnop
qrstuvwxyz
ðłæœøßfi$12
34567890¢£
%#/@$1234567890¢

Benton

A Æ Å B C D E F
G H I J K L M N O
Œ Ø P Q R S T Th
U V W X Y Z &
(·:,·:·)?!*⹀aaæasb
cdefffffighijkl
mnoœøpqrst
uvwxyzß
$1234567890¢
£¢$%«⁑»+

Berling Antiqua

A Æ B C Ç D E F
G H I J K L M N
O Ø Œ P Q R S
T U V W X Y Z
&(·,·;··?!)aæbcçd
efghijklmn
oøœpqrsßtu
vwxyz$1234
567890¢£%+·/
© ® ⌣ ⌣ ∎ ∎
«» ⁑ ○ ● ∎ □

Bernase Roman

A B C C₂ D E F G G₂ H
H I J K L M M₂ N O P
Q R R₂ S T U V W X
Y Z & (·:,·:;·²)
?!*⹀aₐa₃abcdefgh
ijklmnopqrst
uvwxyy₂z
$123456789
0¢/£$%

50

Bernhard Fashion

AAABCDE
ECFGHIJKL
MNNOPQRS
STUVWWJX
YZ&.`:,;?!=abcdefghij
klmnopqrstuvwxyz$
$1234567890

Bernhard Fat

AÆBCÇDEF
GHIJKLMN
OŒØPQRST
UVWXYZ&
(.,:;')?!Ł æbc
çdefghijklm
nœøpqrstu
vwxyzß$123
4567890¢¢//$
£%»«×≈¿¡¿⌧●■

Bernhard Gothic Light

ABCDEFGH
IJKLMNOPQ
RSTUVWXY
Z&(`'""")?!*ab
cdefghijklmn
opqrstuvwx
yz$1234567
890¢/£¢$%

Bernhard
Gothic Medium
ABCDEFGH
IJKLMNOPQ
RSTUVWXY
Z&(",;:;")?!*ab
cdefghijklmn
opqrstuvwx
yz$1234567
890¢/£$%

**Bernhard
Gothic Extra
Heavy ABCDE
EFGHIJKKL
MNOPQRST
UVWXYZ&
(",;:;")?!*ab
cdefghijklm
nopqrsstuv
wxyz$1234
567890¢
/£$%**

Bernhard
Modern Roman
ABCDEFGH
IJKLMNOP
QRSTUVW
XYZ&(',;:;")?!*ab
cdefghijklmn
opqrstuvwx
yz$1234567
890¢/£%

**Bernhard
Bold Condensed**
ABCDEFGHIJKL
MNOPQRSTUV
WXYZÆŒØ&
(',';:;)?!*abcdef
ghijklmnopqr
stuvwxyzæç
œøß$12345
67890¢/£
¢$£%»®©«+≈¿¡i

Bernhard Tango
ABCDEF
GHIJKL
MNOPQ
RSTUV
WXYZ
ABCDEFGHIJ
KLMNOPQR
STUVWXY
*Z&(',';';")?!*abcdefgh*
ijklmnopqrstuvwxyz
$1234567890¢¢/$£% (wv)

**Beton Extra
Bold** ABCD
EFGHIJK
LMNOPQR
STUVWX
YZ&(',';:;)
?!*abcdefg
hijklmnop
qrstuvw
xyz$1234
567890
¢/£%

Beton Medium Condensed

ABCDEFGHIJKL
MNOPQRSTUVW
XYZ&(.,'":;'*!?)
abcdefghijklmn
opqrstuvwxyz
$£1234567890¢
/%0$1234567890¢

Beton Bold Condensed

ABCDEFGHIJK
LMNOPQRSTU
VWXYZ&(";:;/)
?!*abcdefghijkl
mnopqrstuvw
xyz$12345678
90¢%¢£%%£

Binner

ABCDEF
GHIJKL
MNOPQ
RSTUV
WXYZ&
';:;!?=ab
cdeffgbi
jklmnop
qrstuuv
wxyz$$
¢12345
67890 (s)

54

Blippo Bold

ABCDEFGHIJKL
MNOPQRSST
UVWXYZ&&&
(÷:.;·!?)aabbc
cddeeffggg
fhhiijjkklmno
ppqqrrssttu
vwxyyzß¢$/l
234567890○ (S)

Blippo Black

AABCCDDD
EEEFFGGHI
JJKKLLMN
OPPQRSSS
TUVVWX
XYZ&&(::::)?!
aabccccd
eeeffgghii
jjkklmnop
qrrssttuvvw
xxyyzøß$123
456788
90¢/%§$ (S)

Blippo Black Outline

BlippoBlack
OutlineAAÆB
CCCÇDDDEE
EFFFGGHIJJKK
LLMNOŒØPP
QRSSSTUVV
VWXXYZ&&ß
(::::)?!□ααæbcc
cccçdeeeefss
gchhiijjkklmn
oœøpqrrsstu
vvwxxyyz$12
34567890¢
¢/%□□§&i (WV)(S)

BlockEngraving

ABCDEFGHIJ
KLMNOPQRST
UVWXYZÆÅÇŒ
Ø&(".,.:;)?!*abcd
efghijklmno
pqrstuvwxyz
æçœøß$123
4567890¢/
£%‰®‱©⁂‖☐●

Blue Skies

ABCDEF
GHIJK
LMNOP2
RSTW
WXYZ
&(.,.;,?!*
aabccddeef
ffgghhliijkkk
llmmmnnoo
opqrrrrsssst
tuuvvwwxxyzz
$1234567
890¢/£% (WV)

Bocklin

ABCDEF
GHIJKL
MNOPQR
STUVWX
YZ&(".,.:;"")
?!abcdefg
hijklmno
pqrstu
vwxyz$1
234567
890¢/£ (WV)

56

Bodoni

ABCDEFGH
IJKLMNOP
QRSTUVW
XYZ&(.,:;"")
?!*_abcdefffffl
ffifflghijkl
mnopqrstu
vwxyz$12
3456789
0¢/£% (IB)

BodoniBold

ABCDEFG
HIJKLM
NOPQRS
TUVWX
YZ&(.,:;"")
?!*_abcdefg
hijklmnop
qrstuvwx
yz$12345
67890
c/£¢%$% (IB)

Ultra BodoniAB

CDEFGHIJ
KLMNOP
QRSTUVW
XYZ&(.,:;"")
?!*_abcdefg
hijklmnop
qrstuvwx
yz$123456
7890¢¢/%£
1234567890

Bodoni Italic
ABCDEFGH
IJKLMNOP
QRSTUVW
XYZ&('.,.:;"")
?!.*abcdefghi
jklmnopqrs
tuvvwwx
yz$1234567
890¢/₈£%

Bodoni
Bold Italic
ABCDEF
GHIJKLM
NOPQRST
UVWXYZ&
('.,.:; "")?!.*abc
defghijklm
nopqrstuv
wxyz$123
4567890
¢/£%

Ultra Bodoni
Extra Condensed
ABCDEFGHIJKL
MNOPQRSTUV
WXYZ&('.,:;"")?!.*
abcdefghijklmn
opqrstuvwxyz
$1234567890¢¢/₈
%£1234567890

Bodoni Open

ABCDEFGHIJ
KLMNOPQRS
TUVWXYZ
&(°,;:)?!*abcdefff
fiflffffifflghijklm
nopqrstuvwxyz
$1234567890¢
¢/$%0 1234567890

BOLD EDGE

ABCDEFGH
IiJKKLMN
NOPQRST
TUVWXYZ
&[''",□,oo:;;o]
?!/□□1234
567890¢

Bolt Bold

AABCDEF
GHIJKKLM
NOŒØPQR
STUVWXY
ZÆÇØŒ&
&(°,;:'') ?!*aa
bbcddeffffi
ffiflffiftghijk
klmnopqrrs
stuuvwxyz
æçøœß$12
34567890
¢£%⟨⟨☆⟩⟩

LSC Book
Regular A Æ
BCÇDEFGH
IJKLMNOØ
ŒPQRSTU
VWXYZ&
&(';.:,;"")?![*]aæ
bcçdeeffffifi
flfflftghijkk₂l
mnoøœpqrs
tuvwxyz
ß$12345678
90¢/£%#«»¿¡*

LSC Book
Bold A ÆBC
ÇDEFGHIJ
KLMNOŒ
ØPQRSTU
VWXYZ&
&(';.:,;"")?![*]aæ
bcçdeeffffifi
flfflftghijkk₂l
mnoøœpqrs
tuvwxyzß
$123456789
O¢/£%#$«»¿¡

LSC Book
Extra Bold A
ÆBCÇDEF
GHIJKLM
NOŒØPQ
RSTUVW
XYZ&&₂?!
(';.:,;"")[*]aæbc
çdeeffffififfl
fflftghijklm
noøœpqrstu
vwxyzß$12
34567890¢
¢/$%#«»¿¡

LSC Book Extra Bold Italic A Æ B C C C D E F G H I J K L M N O Ø Œ P Q R S S T U V W X Y Z & & (':,:;,?")?! [≛]

aæbcçdefffffffffffffffffff ghijklmnoøœpq rr stuvwxyz ß$1234567890¢ /£%#$¢

Book Jacket Italic A A B B C C D D E E F F G G H H I J J K L L M M M N N N O P P Q R R R R S S T T U V V W W X Y Z Th Th & & (.:.;) ?! (..) a a b c d e e*

f f f f f f f f f f g g h h h i j k k l l m m m n n n o p q r r s s t t u v v w w x y y y z $ 1 2 3 4 5 6 7 8 9 0 1 2 3 4 5 6 7 8 9 0 ¢ / £ %

Bookman Light

A A A B B B B C C D D
E E F F G G G H H H I I J J J
K K L L M N N O O
P P Q Q R R R S S T T U
U V V V W W W W X
X Y Y Z Z Æ Œ Th Ø
& & & (.,:;"")?!*—a b ƀ c d d
e e ff g h ħ i j k l m m n
n o o p p q g r r ſ t t u u v
v w w x y y z æ œ œ ø
ß $ 1 2 3 4 5 6 7 8 9 0 1 2 3 4 5
6 7 8 9 0 ¢ $ / ¢ £ % ※ ⁂ ¿ ¡ »« @

Bookman Medium

A A A B B B B C C
D D E E F F G G G H H I I
J J J K K L L M M N N
O O P P Q R R R S S T T
U U V V V W W W W
X X Y Y Z Z Æ Œ Ø Th
& & & (.,:;"")?!*—a b ƀ c d
d e e ff g h ħ i j k l m m
n n o o p p q g r r ſ t t u
u v v v w w x y y z æ ø
œ œ ß $ 1 2 3 4 5 6 7 8 9 0
1 2 3 4 5 6 7 8 9 0 ¢ $ / ¢ £ %
※ ⁂ »« @

Bookman Demi

A A A B B B C C D D
E E F F G G H H I I J J
J K K L L M M N N O
O P P Q R R R R S S T T
U U V V V W W W
W X X Y Y Y Z Z Æ Œ
Ø Th & & & (',.:;") ?! * a
b c d d e e f f fi g h h i j k
k l m m n n o o p p q
q r r s t t u u v v w w x y
y z æ æ œ œ ø ß $ 1 2 3 4
5 6 7 8 9 0 1 2 3 4 5 6 7 8 9
0 ¢ $ / ¢ £ % ° ⁝ ⁝ " @

Bookman Bold

A A A B B B C C D D
E E F F G G H H I I J J
J K K L L M M N N O
O P P Q R R R R S S T T
U U V V V W W W W
X X Y Y Y Z Z Æ Œ Th
Ø & & & (',.:;") ?! * a b
b c d d e e f f g h h i j k K l
m m n n o o p p q q r
r s t t u u v v w w x y y
z æ æ œ œ ø ß $ 1 2 3 4
5 6 7 8 9 0 1 2 3 4 5 6 7 8
9 0 ¢ $ / ¢ £ % ° ⁝ ⁝ " @ ¿ i

ITC™ LICENSED

Bookman Light Italic

AAABBBCC
DDEEFFGGHHI
IJJJKKLLMMN
NOOPPQQRRR
SSTTUUVVVW
WWWXXYYZZ
ÆŒØTh&&(',.:;"")?!
*abcdeeffighhhh
ijkKlmmnnoopq
qrrsttuvwxyzæœ
øß$1234567890123
4567890¢$/¢£%@¿¡
#

ITC™ LICENSED

Bookman Medium Italic

AAABB
BCCDDEEFFGG
HHIIJJJKKLLM
MNNOOPPQQRR
RSSTTUUVVV
WWWXXYYZZ
ÆŒØTh&&(',.:;"")?
!*abcdeeffighhhhi
jkKlmmnnoopq
qrrsttuvwxyzæ
œøß$1234567890
1234567890¢$/¢£%
@¿¡#

Bookman Demi Italic (ITC) A A A A B B B C C D D D E E F F G G H H I I I J J J K K K L L L M M N N O O O P P P Q R R S S T T U U V V V W W W W X X Y Y Z Z Z Æ Œ Ø Th & & & & ?!* (' , . : ; " ") a b c d e e ff i g h h h h i j k K l m m m n n o o o p p q g r r s t t u v w x y z æ œ ø ß $ 1 2 3 4 5 6 7 8 9 0 1 2 3 4 5 6 7 8 9 0 ¢ $/¢ £ % ° ‰ " " ¿ ¡ @ #

Bookman Bold Italic A A A A B B B C C D D D E E F F G G H H I I I J J J K K K L L M M N N O O O P P P Q Q Q R R R S S T T T U U V V V W W W W W X X Y Y Z Z Z Æ Œ Ø & & & (. . . , . : : ; ; " " " ")?! . . . a b c d e e ff i g h h h h h i j k K l m m m n n o o o p p q q r r s t t u v w x y z æ œ ß $ 1 2 3 4 5 6 7 8 9 0 1 2 3 4 5 6 7 8 9 0 ¢ ¢/$ £ %

BookmanOutline

A A A A B B B B C C
D D E E F F G G H H I
I J J J K K L L M M N
N O O P P P Q Q R R R S
S T T U U U V V V W
W W X X Y Y Z Z Æ
Ø Œ Ç Ş Th & & & @ ? ! *
(' , : ; °) a b c d d e e f f g h
h i j k k l m m n n o o
p p q q r r s t t u u v v
w x y y z æ æ ç œ œ ø ş ß
$ 1 2 3 4 5 6 7 8 9 0 1 2 3 4
5 6 7 8 9 0 ¢ $ / £ % ‰ ‹‹ " ' ¿ ¡

Bookman Bold
Contour A A A A B B

B C C D D E E F F G G
H H I I J J J K K L L M
M N N O O P P P Q Q R R
R S S T T U U U V V V W
W W X X Y Y Z Z Æ Ç
Th Œ Ş Ø & & @ (' , : ; " "
? !) a b c d d e e f f g h fi
i j k k l m m n n o o p
p q q r r s t t u u v v w w x
y y z fi æ æ ç œ œ ø ş ß $ $
£ 1 2 3 4 5 6 7 8 9 0 ¢ 1 2 3 4
5 6 7 8 9 0 % / # ` ; ¿ ^ ~ ` - * @

(WV)

BookmanBoldShaded

AAAABBBBCCDD
EEFFGGHHIIJJJ
KKLLMMNNOOP
PQQRRRSSTTThU
UVVVWWWXXY
YZZÆÇŒØ&Œ&?!
(.:;")[*]ab6cddeef
fighñiijkKlmmn
noopppqqrstttuuv
vwwxyyzæçœç
$$1234567890123
4567890¢/£%..""#§

ßt‡ (IB) (WV) (CMM)

BookmanBoldContour

Shaded AAAABBBBCCD
DEEFFGGHHIIJJ
JJKKLLMMNNOOO
PPQQRRRSSTT
ThUUVVVWWWX
XYYZZ&Œ&(.:;"")
[?!]ab6cddeeffigh
ñiijkKlmmnnoopp
qqrrstttuuvvwwx
yyzæçøœß
$$1234567890¢%#
1234567890/£t‡"»

(IB) (WV) (CMM)

Bookman

(ATF)A A AB
CDEFGHIJK
LM MNOPQ
RR STUVW
XYZ& &The
(.,:;"")?!abcdefff
ffififfflflghijk
lmnopqrr st
uvwxyz$123
4567890

Bookman Italic

(ATF)A ABC
DEFGHIJK
LM MNOP
QRR S T
UVWXYZ&
& (.,:;"")?!*abcd
efffffififfflflghij
klmnopqrs t
uvwxyy y z$1
234567890
¢/£$/¢%gf

Bookman Bold

Swash A A
AB BCD D
E EF FGH H
I IJ JK K KL LM
M MN NO
P PQR RR
STU UV VW
WX XY YZ
ÆŒØ& & (.,:;"")
?!*abcdefghijkl
mnopqrr stuv
wxyy zæœø$1
234567890¢$%

69

BookmanBold
ItalicAA A AB
BCCDDEEF
FGGHHIJJK
KKLLMMMM
MNNNNO
PPQRRRRR
RSSSTTUU
VVWWWXXY
YYZ&&(.':;")
?!:abcdeffffifighh
ijkklmnnopqrrr
risstuvwwxyy
z$1234567890¢¢/%(IB)

BookmanBold
Italic(VGC)AA
BBCGGDDEF
GGHIJKKLM
NNOPQRR S
STTUVVW
XYYZ&&
&(.':;")?!:abcde
fghhijkklm
mnnopqrrsst
uvwwxyy yz
g$1234567890
¢£¢/%

BookmanBold
OutlineAA AB
BCDDEEFF
GHHHIIJKK
LLMMMMN
NOPPQRR
RSTUUV
WWXXYYZ
&(.':;")?!:abcdefg
hijklmnopqrr
stuvwxyy z$12
34567890¢/%(WV)

Bookman Black

AAABBBCCDD
EEFFGGHHIIJJ
KKKKLLMMM
NNNNNNNOO
PPQQQRRRRR
SSTTUUVVV
WWWWXXYYYY
ZTh&&(',.;;;")?!*
aabbbcddeffffiflgg
hhhhhijkkkkklmmmn
noppqqrrrsstuuv
vwwxxyyz$1234
567890¢%%

Boulevard

ABCDEFGH
IJKLMNO
PQRSTUVW
XYZ&(',.;;")?![-*]abcdee
ffffifflfflghijkk lmm n
n opqrstt uvwxyzz
$1234567890¢¢/$£%IVX½¼¾

Bradley

ABCDEFGHIJ
KLMNOPQRSTU
VWXYZ&(",;;"")
?![*]abcdefghijklm
nopqrstuvwxyzß
$1234567890¢/£$%

Brandywine

ABCDEFGG
HIJKLM
NOPQRS§
TUVWXYZ
&(.:")abc
defghijklmno
pqrßsstuvw
xyzz$123456
7890¢ (SR)

Brandywine Bold

ABCDE
FGHIJKL
MNOPQRS
TUVWXY
Z&(.:;"")?!zabc
deeresex f ff fl fi
ghijklmnoooosp
pqrsttuvwxyz$12
34567890¢/£%

Brillante

Brillante
ABCDEFG
HIJKLMN
OPQRSTUV
WXYZÆCØ
Œ&('.;,)?!*a
bcdefghijk
lmnopqrst
uvwxyzæ
çœøßs12
34567890
¢/°%«°»+¿¡ (S)

Britannic

Britannic
BoldABCD
EFGHIJKL
MNOPQRS
TUVWXYZ
&(';:;)?![*]ab
cdefghijkl
mnopqrst
uvwxyz$1
23456789
0¢ᶜ/$°/o (S)

Broadside

BROADSIDE
ABCDEFGHI
JKLMNOPQ
RSTUVWX
YZ&.',.;?!-$12
34567890 (WV)

72

Broadway
ABCDEFG
HIJKLM
NOPQRS
STUVWX
YZ&(;:..ʒ̧ee)
?!abcdefg
ghijklmno
pqrstuvw
xyz$1234
567890
¢$¢%

Broadway
Bold ABCD
EFGHIJKL
MNOPQRS
STUVWX
YZ&(;:..ʒ̧ee)
?!abcdef
gghijklm
nopqrstu
vwxyz$12
34567890
¢$¢%★

BROADWAY
ENGRAVED
ABCDEFG
HIJKLMN
OPQRST
UVWXYZ
&;:..;?!-$12
34567890

Bronstein Bold
ABCDEFGHIJKLMNOPQRSTUVWXYZ&.,:;?!
abcdefghijklmnopqrstuvwxyz$1234567890¢/%

Brush American
ABCDEFGHIJKLMNOPQRSTUVWXYZ&(',.:;"')?!ābcdefghijklmnoopqrrsstuvwxyz$1234567890¢¢/%%

Bubble Light
ABCDEFGGHIJJJKLMNOPQRSTUVWXYZ&(".,";)?!*abcccdeefghhiijklmnopqqrsttuvwxyz$1234567890¢/£$/%.©

Bubble

Bubble
ABCDEFGGH
IJJKLMNOPQ
RSTUVWXYZ&
(',.:;"")?!*@abccc
deeefghhiij
klmnopqrrs
truvwxyz$12
34567890¢/
£¢%®©
$

Bubble
DubbleABCD
EFGGHIJJJK
LLMMNOPQR
STUVWWXY
Z&(',.:;"")?!ab
cccdeeefgh
hiijklmmnop
qrrsttuvwx
yz$1234567
890¢/£%¢%®©

Bubble Outline

Bubble
Outline
ABCDEFGGH
IJJJKLLMNO
PQRSTUVWX
YZ&(""'''")?!*
abccccdeeef
ghhiijklmno
pqrrsttuvw
xyz$12345
67890¢/£¢
$

®%©■ (WV)

BUFFALO

BILLABCD
EFGHIJK
LMNOPQR
STUVWX
YZÆŒ&',;;
-?!$12345
67890$ (WV)

Bulletin Typewriter

ABCDEFGHI
JKLMNOPQ
RSTUVWX
YZ&(!.,.;"")?!*
abcdefghij
klmnopqrs
tuvwxyz$
123456789
0¢$/¢£%#@

BULLION SHADOW

ABCDEF
GHIJKLM
NOPQRST
UVWXYZ
&(:;::)?!
$12345
67890£
/ (WV)

ITC LICENSED BUSORAMA LIGHT AABBC DEEFGHIJKK LMNOPQR RSSTTUUVWXY ZÅÄÆÇOEØ Ö&&("") ?!* $123456789 O¢/£$%#«»¿i (WV)

ITC LICENSED BUSORAMA BOOK AAB CDEEFGHIJ KKLMNOPQ RSTUVWXYZ &&(*.,.-!?)$12 34556 7890 O¢£%#¶/¢ 1234556 7890O2 (WV)

ITC LICENSED BUSORAMA MEDIUM AAB BCDEEFGHIJ KKLMNOoPQ QRRSSTTUVV WXYZÆOE ÇØ&&("") ?![*]$11234 567890¢/ £$%#«»¿i

BUSORAMA
BOLDAABC
DEEFGHIJ
KLMNOPQ
RSSTUVW
XYZ&(.'":;)
?!✳$12334
5567890
¢/£$%

California Grotesk
ABCDEFGHIJJKLM
NOPQRSTUVWXY
Z&(",;)?!'abcdef
fghij jklmnopq
rrsttuvwxyyz$
1234567890¢/% (IB)

California Grotesk
MediumABCDEFG
HIJJKLMNOPQRS
TUVWXYZ&(",;)
?!'abcdeffghij
jklmnopqrrst
tuvwxyyz$$12
34567890¢/% (IB)

California
Grotesk Bold
ABCDEFGHIJJK
LMNOPQRSTUV
WXYZ&(",;)?!
'abcdeffghijjk
lmnopqrrsttu
vwxyyz$1234
567890¢/% (IB)

California
Grotesk Black
ABCDEFGHIJK
LMNOPQRSTUV
WXYZ&(".,:;!")?!
abcdeffghijj
klmnopqrrs
ttuvwxyyz
$123456789
0¢/% (IB)

Calligraph
A A B C
C D E F H
I I K L M
N O O P
Q R S T U V
W X Y Z & (.,:;)
?!*−aæbccdefg
hijklmnoœøpqr
stuvwxyzß$1
234567890
¢/®%○+ ◇ ✧ » + ó í (SR)

CALYPSO
ABCDEFGHI
JKLMNOPQ
RSTUVW
YZ&(.,:;)
1&$123456
7890¢/£% (WV)

CAMELOT

CAMELOT
ABCDEFG
HIJKLMN
OPQRSTU
VWXYZ&
(".,:;)?!*$1234
567890
¢/$¢%

CAMPAIGN
ABCDEFGH
IJKLMNOP
QRSTUVW
XYZ&$.,
.'""!?=$
1234567
890 ◼

(WV)

Cancelleresca Bastarda

A A B B B C C D D D D
E E E F F F G G G H
H H I I I J J J K K K L L
L L M M M N N N O P
P P Q Q Q R R R S S S T
T T U U U U V V W W W
W X X X Y Y Y Z Z Z &
& (".,:;)?!l-Iaa bb bcc d
dd dee f f fgg hhh h
ijkkl L llmm nn o
pppqggrr stt t t t
uu v v vww wxx y
y zz ß $1234567890

Carpenter

ABCDEF
GHIJ
KLMN
OP2RST
UVWXYz
&,'"'?!⁻⁻abcd
eefgh hiij
klmnmm
oōpqrsst
mnmwwy
yzz⁻ᵗʰˢᵗᵈ$12
34567890+1$

Caslon Antique

ABCDEFGHIJ
KLMNOPQRS
TUVWXYZ&
(":.;:")?![*≡]abcdefg
hijklmnopqrstuv
wxyz$12345678
90¢/$£%

Caslon Antique
Italic

ABCDEFG
HIJKLMN
OPQRSTU
VWXYZ&
(",:.;")?!*≡abcde
fghijklmnopq
rsſtuvwxyz
$12345678
90¢/$£%

New Caslon

ABCDEF
GHIJKLM
NOPQRST
UVWXYZ
&(',:;"')?!*_abcd
effifffflffifflg
hijklmnop
qrstuvwxyz
$1234567890
¢¢/%

New Caslon Italic

ABCDEFG
HIJKLMN
OPQRST
UVWXYZ
&(',:;""-"'!?)a
bcdeffffifflffiffl
ghijklmnop
qrstuvwxyz
$1234567890¢
%$/¢£1234567890%

Caslon 471 Roman AB

CDEFGH
IJKLMNO
PQRSTUV
WXYZ&
("":;")?![*]abc
deffffifflffiffl
ghijklmnopq
rstuvwxyz
$123456789
O¢/£¢$%O%§†

Caslon 471 Italic Swash

A ABBCCCDDEEF
FFGGHH HIIJK
KLLLMMMNNOOP
PQQRRS ST TTUU
VUWWXYYZ
ÇØÆŒ&&~(:;:!?*)
abcdefffffifflffffflghijkklm
nopqrstuvwxyzzçtßçøææ&ï÷
«°»$1234567890¢%£/®™

Caslon 540

ABCDEFGHIJK
LMNOPQRSTUV
WXYZ&(.',:;"")?!*
abcdefghijklmnopqr
stuvwxyz$123456
7890¢/£$%

86

Caslon 540 Italic

ABCDEFGH
IJKLMNOPQ
RSTUVWX
YZ&(.,.:;‘’)?!_*
abcdefghijklmn
opqrstuvwxyz
$1234567890
¢//$£%

Caslon 641

ABCDEFG
HIJKLMNO
PQRSTU
VWXYZ&
(.,.:;‘’)?![*_]abcd
effffiflffifflg
hijklmnopqr
stuvwxyzct
$1234567890
¢/£$%

Caslon Bold

ABCDEFG
HIJKLM
NOPQRST
UVWXYZ
&.,.:;‘’?!ābc
ctdefghijkl
mnopqrsstt
uvwxyz
$123456789
0¢/£

Caslon Bold Italic ABCD EFGHIJK LMNOPQR STUVWX YZ&(.,:;'')?! *‡abcdefgh ijklmnopqr stuvwxyz $12345678 90¢$%£%

Caslon Old Face Heavy ABCDEFG HIJKLM NOPQRST UVWXYZ &(.,:;'')?![*] abcdefghijk lmnopqrst uvwxyz$12 34567890¢ /£%

Caslon Old Face Ultra Black ABCD EFGHIJK LMNOPQ RSTUVWX YZ&(.,::)?! [-]abcdefff fiflghijklmn opqrstuvw xyz$123456 7890¢

ITC™ LICENSED Caslon
Headline
ABCDEFG
HIJKLMNO
PQRSTUV
WXYZÆŒ
Ø&(":,;"?!*
abcdefghijkl
mnopqrstu
vwxyzæœøß
$123456789
0%£%#❖ (R) (S)

ITC™ LICENSED Caslon Light
No.223
ABCDEFG
HIJKLMNO
PQRSTUV
WXYZÆÇ
ŒØ&(":,;"?!
[*]*abcdeeff
fiffifl ffl ftghijk
lmnopqrstu
vwxyzæçoe
øß$12345678
90¢$/£%#❖◇¿¡ (WV)

ITC™ LICENSED Caslon Regular
No.223
ABCDEFG
HIJKLMNO
PQRSTUV
WXYZÆÇ
ŒØ&(":,;"?!
[*]*abcdeeff
fiffifl ffl ftghijk
lmnopqrstu
vwxyzæçoe
øß$12345678
90¢/£¢%#❖ (WV)

Caslon Bold No.223

ABCDEFGHIJ
KLMNOPQRST
UVWXYZÆÇŒØ
&(',:;")?![⁂]abcdee₂
fffffiffiflffiſtghijklmno
pqrstuvwxyzæçœøß
$1234567890¢
⅘§£%#«⁂»¿¡ (WV)

Caslon Extra Bold

No.223ABC
DEFGHIJKLMNO
PQRSTUVWXYZ
ÆÇŒØ&(',:;")?!
[⁂]abcdee₂fffffiffiflffiſtg
hijklmnopqrstuv
wxyzæçœøß$12345
67890¢/£%#«⁂»¿¡ (WV)

Caslon Bold No.223 Italic

ABCDEF
GHIJKLMN
OPQRST
UVWXYZÆ
ÇŒØ&
(';.;")?![※] abc
defffffiffffiflffl
ghijklmnopqr
stuvwxyz
æçœøß$1234
567890¢
$/₵£%#※cj

Caslon Extra Bold Italic

No.223 ABCD
EFGHIJK
LMNOPQRS
TUVWX
YZ&(';.;")?!※
abcdefffffifl
ffifflghijklmn
opqrstuv
wxyz$123456
7890¢/₵%/$%#
1234567890

Caslon Modern

ABCD
EFGHIJKL
MNOPQR
STUVWX
YZ&&(';.;.;)
?!※abcdee
fffigh
ijklmnoop
qrstuvw
xyzß$1234
5678
90¢¢$/₵£%※

Caslon Swash (Arriola)

AAAABBBCGDD
EEFFGGHHIIIJ
KKKKKKLLLM
MMMMNNNN
NOOPPQQRRRR
RRSSTTUU
VVVWWWXXXY
YYZ&(',.:;")?!āqₐb
bbcdefffghhhhhijk
kkklmmmmnnno
pqrrsstuuuuvvwwx
yyz$1234567890¢¢$% (SR) (IB)

(SR) (IB)

Caslon (American) Italic

A ABBCCD DEEF F
GGHHIIJJKLL
MMNNOPPPQu
RRSSTTUU
VWWXYYZ&(',.:;)(?!)
abcdefghijklmnopqrs
tuvvwwxyz$1234567890 (IB) (S) (R)

Casual Script

ABCDEFG
HIJKLMN
OPQRSTU
VWXYZ&(.,:;)
?!_*aaabcddeeff
ghhhiijkkklllm
mmmnnnnnnooeoe
ololpqvrrrsssttt
uuvvvevewwwewe
wlwlxxy z $12345
67890¢/£%

Caxtonian

ABCDE
FGHIJK
LMNOP
QRSTUV
WXYZ
ÆŒ&!?,;;
"="?abccdef
fffiflffifffffl
ghijklmn
opqrstuv
wxyzæœ
$£123456
7890¢%$/¢ (WV)

Celtic Cursive

AABCDEEFG
GHHIIJKKL
LMMNNOPP
QRRSTTUU
VVWWXXY
YZZ&(.,:;"")?!_
aaabcddeffg
ghhhijkkllmmnno
ppqqarrssttu
uvvWWXXXyyZZ
$1234567890¢ (SR) (WV)

Celtic Cursive

Bold AABCDE
EFGGHHIIJK
KLLMMNNO
PPQQRRSS
TTUUVVWWXX
YYZZÆÇŒØ&
(''"'"*‡!?)aaaabcd
deffgghhijkkllm
mnnoppqqrrss
ttuuvvwwxxyyzz
ææçœøß$¢12
34567890%‰

© ⸿
® ⸰ «»

Centaur

ABCDEFG
HIJKLMN
OPQRSTU
VWXYZ&
(''"'"*‡!?)abcd
efghijklmno
pqrstuvwx
yzfffififlfflffi
$123456
7890¢%/£

$1234567890¢

Centennial Script

AA BB CC DD
EE FF GG HH I
JJ KK LL MM N
NN OO PP 22
RR S SS TT U
UU VV WW X
X YY ZZ

&.,:;?!abcdefghijklm
nopqrstuvwxyz
$1234567890¢/$£%
Mr Mrs Dr VhCr

&&℃℞℟℘

(WV)

94

Century
Expanded
ABCDEFGHI
JKLMNOPQ
RSTUVWXYZ
&(',:;'''')?!*abcde
fghijklm
nopqrstuvwx
yz$1234567
890¢/£$%

Century Oldstyle
ABCDEFGH
IJKLMNOPQ
RSTUVWX
YZ&(',:;'''')?!*
abcdefffffifl
ffifflghijklm
nopqrstuvwx
yzctst$12345
67890¢/£¢$%

Century
Oldstyle Bold
ABCDEFGH
IJKLMNOP
QRSTUVW
XYZ&(.,':;'''')
?!*abcdefg
hijklmnopq
rstuvwxyz
$12345678
90¢$%¢£%

Century
Schoolbook
ABCDEFG
HIJKLMN
OPQRSTUV
WXYZ&(',:;'")
?!.*.abcdefghi
jklmnopqrstu
vwxyz$1234
567890'%$£%

Century
Schoolbook
Bold ABCDE
FGHIJKLL₂
MNOPQQR₂
STUVWX
YZ&(',:;'")?!.*.
abcdefgghi₂
jj₂klmnoppqq₂
rstuvwxy y z₂
$123456789
0¢¢/$%£

Century
Book
ABCDEFG
HIJKLMNO
PQRSTUVW
XYZÆŒÇØ
ß&(',:;'")?![*]ab
cdeffiflfffffi
fflghijklmn
opqrstuv
wxyzæçœ
ø$$123456789
0¢/£%⁒¿¡»#

Century Ultra
ABCDE
FGHIJKLM
NOPQRST
UVWXYZÆ
ÇŒØ&(;;;;"%)
?!*abcdeffifl
fffflffighij
klmnopqrs
tuvwxyz
æçœø
$$12345678
90¢/£%°≈÷¿¡»#

Century Book Italic
ABCD
EFGHIJKL
MNOPQRST
UVWXYZÆ
ÇŒØß&(.,:;")
?![*]abcdeffi
flfffffifflghij
klmnopqr
stuvwxyz
œçœø$$12345
67890¢/£%°≈
¿¡»#

Century Ultra Italic
ABCD
EFGHIJKL
MNOPQRST
UVWXYZÆ
ÇŒØ&(.,:;"%)
?!*abcdeffi
flfffflffig
hijjklmnop
qrstuvwxy
zæçœø$$
123456789
0¢/£%°≈÷¿¡»#

Century Modern Swash

AAA A AAABBCDD
E EE F FGGHH
HHI I I I LJUUJK KKL
L L L MMMMMM
MNNN NNNOOP PPP
QQRRRRRRSSSST
TTTUUUUUUVVVW
WWWWWXXXX
YYYYYZZ&-(',;:")?!*aabcc
c̃ddee ̃e ̃ff f fgghhii
jjkkllmmnnoop pqqrrsssstt
tuuyvvvww wxx
xyyyzz$1234567890¢

Century Litho Shaded

ABCDEFGH
IJKLMNOPQRS
TUVWXYZ&
(',.;:'")?!=abcd
efghijklmnop
qrstuvwxyz
$$123456789
0¢/£%

Checkmate

ABCDEFGH
IJKLMNOP
QRSTUVW
XYZ&[:;.."]
?!=abcdef
ghijklmno
pqrstuvw
xyz$1234
567890£

Champion

ABCDEF
GHIJKL
MNOPQRS
TUVWX
YZ&&
=abcdefghi
The(":;;")?!
ghijklmnopq
rstuvwxyz
$123456789
0¢%

(ww)
90

ABCDEFG
HIJKLM
NOPQRS
TUVWXY
Z&$-:;!?:
8765428

Cheltenham Old Style

ABCDEFGH
IJKLMNOP
QQRSTUV
WXYZ&(',.;'")
?!*-abcdefffffiflffi
fflghijklmnop
qrrstuvwxyzctst
$1234567890
¢/£$%¶

Cheltenham Medium

ABCDEFGH
IJKLMNOP
QRSTUVW
XYZ&(',.;'")
?!*-abcdefghijk
lmnopqrrstu
vwxyz$1234
567890¢/£¢$%

Cheltenham Bold ABCDE

FGHIJKL
MNOPQRS
TUVWXYZ
&(',.;'")?!*-ab
cdefghijklm
nopqrstuv
wxyz$1234
567890¢/$%

Cheltenham HeavyABCD EFGHIJKL MNOPQR STUVWX YZ&(':;?) ?!ābcdefg hijklmno pqrstuvw xyz$1234 567890 ¢/£%®©■□●□■○

Cheltenham Medium Italic ABCDEFGHIJ KLMNOPQRS TUVWXYZ& (':;")?!-abcdef fffiflffiffflghijkl mnopqrstuvwx yzctst$12345 67890¢/£%*

1234567890

Cheltenham Bold Italic ABC DEFGHIJKL MNOPQRST UVWXYZ &(':;-"!?)[*]ab cdefghijklm nopqrstuvw xyz$1234 567890¢/£%

$1234567890¢/%

Cheltenham Old Style Condensed

ABCDEFGHIJK
LMNOPQQR
STUVWXYZ&
(',:; ")?!*_abcde
fffiflffiffflghijklm
nopqrstuvwxyz
ctst$12345678
90¢/£¢%"

Cheltenham Bold Condensed

ABCDEFGHIJK
LMNOPQRST
UVWXYZ&
(',:; ")?!*_abcde
fghijklmnopq
rstuvwxyz$123
4567890¢/£¢%/£%

Cheltenham Bold Outline

ABCDEFG
HIJKLMN
OPQRST
UVWXYZ
&(',"·;"!?)[*·]
abcdefghij
klmnopqrst
uvwxyz$1
234567890
¢£%$/

1234567890 (WV)

ITC LICENSED Cheltenham
Light AB
CDEFGHIJ
KLMNOPQ
RSTUVWX
YZÆŒØ&
('.,:;"")?![*]abc
defflfiffiff
ghiijklmnop
qrstuvwxyz
æœøß$1234
567890¢/$£
%¢☙☸☙¿¡#12345678
90 ©™®™ ◆☙●■□

ITC LICENSED Cheltenham
Book
ABCDE
FGHIJKLM
NOPQRSTU
VWXYZÆ
ÇØŒ&('.,:;"")
?![*]abcdef
fiflfffiffflghij
klmnopqrst
uvwxyzæç
øœß$1234
567890¢/$£%
☙¿¡⟪

ITC LICENSED **Cheltenham
Bold
ABCDEFG
HIJKLMN
OPQRSTU
VWXYZÆ
ŒØ&('.,:;"")
?![*]abcdef
fffiflfffifflgh
ijklmnopqr
stuvwxyz
æœøß$123
4567890¢/$
£%¢☙☸☙¿¡⟪#**

Cheltenham Ultra

ABCDEFG
HIJKLMNOPQ
RSTUVWXYZÆ
ÇØŒ&(?;",:;""*""/?!)
abcdeffffffflffi
fflghijklmnop
qrstuvwxyzæ
çøœß£$$123456
7890¢%#

Cheltenham Ultra Italic

ABCDEFG
HIJKLMNOPQ
RSTUVWXYZÆ
ÇØŒ&(?;*:;""/?!)
abcdeffffffflffi
fflghijklmnop
qrstuvwxyzæ
æçøœß£$12345
67890¢%#

ITC LICENSED *Cheltenham Light Italic* ABCDEFGHI JKLMNOPQ RSTUVWX YZÆŒØ& (.,:;"")?![*_]abc defffffiflffifflghi jklmnopqrst uvwxyzæœø ß$123456789 0¢/$£%¢°¿!⁙⁘⁙

ITC LICENSED *Cheltenham Book Italic* ABCDEFG HIJKLMNOP QRSTUVWX YZÆØÇŒ& (.,:;"")?![*_]abcde ffiflffffifflghij klmnopqrstu vwxyzæçøœ ß$123456789 0¢/$£%#⁙«⁙»

ITC LICENSED **Cheltenham Bold Italic** **ABCD** **EFGHIJKL** **MNOPQRS** **TUVWXYZ** **ÆŒØ(.,':;"")** **?![*_]&abcd** **efffffifflffffifl** **ghijklmnop** **qrstuvwxyz** **æœøß$123** **4567890¢/$** **£%¢°¿!⁙¿¡»«#**

Cheltenham Light
Condensed
ABCDEFGHIJKL
MNOPQRSTUV
WXYZÆŒØ&
(.,:;"")?![±]abcdef
fffiflffffifflghiijklmn
opqrstuvwxyz
æœøß$1234567
890¢/$£%‰¿¡*#
1234567890©®™◆◈♦▷◁●○■◼

Cheltenham Book
Condensed
ABCDEFGHIJK
LMNOPQRST
UVWXYZÆŒ
Ø&(.,:;"")?![±]ab
cdefffffflffflgh
ijklmnopqrstuv
wxyzæœøß$1
234567890¢/$£
%‰¿¡«#1234567890
©®™◆◈♦▷◁●○■◼

Cheltenham
Bold Condensed
ABCDEF
GHIJKLMNOP
QRSTUVWXY
ZÆŒØ&(.,:;"")
?![±]abcdef
fffiflffffifflghijk
lmnopqrstuv
wxyzæœøß
$1234567890¢
/$£%‰¿¡«*#
1234567890©®™◆◈♦▷◁●○■◼

106

ITC LICENSED Cheltenham Ultra Condensed

ABCDEFGHIJKLM
NOPQRSTUVWX
YZÆŒØ&(.',:;"")?!
[±]abcdefffffflffffl
ghijklmnopqrstu
vwxyzæœøß$123
4567890¢/$£%

¿¡»#1234567890

ITC LICENSED Cheltenham Ultra Condensed Italic

ABCDEFGHI
JKLMNOPQRSTUV
WXYZÆŒØ&(.',:;"")
?![±]abcdeffffffl
ffifflghijklmnopq
rstuvwxyzæœøß
$1234567890¢/$£%

¿¡»#1234567890

ITC LICENSED

Cheltenham Light
Condensed Italic
ABCDEFG
HIJKLMNOPQR
STUVWXYZÆ
ŒØ&(.,:;'")?![*]
abcdefffffiflffiffl g
hijklmnopqrst
uvwxyzæœøß
$1234567890¢/$
£%‰¿¡×÷#1234567890

©TM ®TM ◆▶▲●■■»◀

ITC LICENSED

Cheltenham
Book Condensed
Italic ABCDEFG
HIJKLMNOP
QRSTUVWXY
ZÆŒØ&(.,:;'")
?![*]abcdeffffi
flffiffl ghijklmno
pqrstuvwxyz
æœøß$123456
7890¢/$£%‰¿
¡×÷#1234567890

©®TM ◆◆●○■ ▲▼●○■

ITC LICENSED

Cheltenham
Bold Condensed
Italic ABCDEF
GHIJKLMNOP
QRSTUVWXYZ
ÆŒØ&(.,:;'")?!
[≡]abcdefffffiflffi
ffl ghijklmnopqr
stuvwxyzæœøß
$1234567890¢/$
£%¿¡×÷¿¡»*#12345
67890

©®TM ◆◆●○■ ▼●

108

Cheltenham Outline

ITC™ LICENSED

ABCÇDEFG
HIJKLMNOP
QRSSTUVW
XYZÆŒØ&
(',.;,"")?![÷]ab
cçdefffffffffffff
ghijklmnop
qrsstuvwxy
zæœøß$123
4567890¢/$£
%¢⚊⚒☀¿¡»«"#12345
67890 ®™™ ⬛ ◯ ⬤

Cheltenham Outline Shaded

ITC™ LICENSED

ABCÇD
EFGHIJKLM
NOPQRSST
UVWXYZÆ
ŒØ&(',.;,"")?!
[÷]abcçdefff
fiflfffflffflghijkl
mnopqrsstu
vwxyzæœø
ß$12345678
90¢/$£%¢⚊⚒☀#
1234567890¿¡«»

Cheltenham Contour

ITC™ LICENSED

ABCÇDEFG
HIJKLMNOP
QRSSTUVW
XYZÆŒØ&
(',.;,"")?![÷]ab
cçdefffffffffffff
ghijklmnop
qrsstuvwxy
zæœøß$123
4567890¢/$£
%¢⚊⚒☀¿¡«»"*#123
4567890 ®™™ ⬛ ◯ ⬤

Churchward Metallic Italic

ABCDEFGHI JKLMNOP QRSTUVWXY Z&£.,-:;!?()
abcdefgh ijklmnop qrstuvwxyz 1234567890 $/£%

(W)

Churchward Metallic Italic

ABCDEFGHI JKLMNOP QRSTUVWXY Z&£.,-:;!?()
abcdefgh ijklmnop qrstuvwxyz 1234567890 $/£%

(W)

Churchill

ABCDEF GHIJKL MNOPQRST UVWXY Z&*()!;'":.,-=abc defghijklmno pqrstuvwx yz$1234567 890¢$%

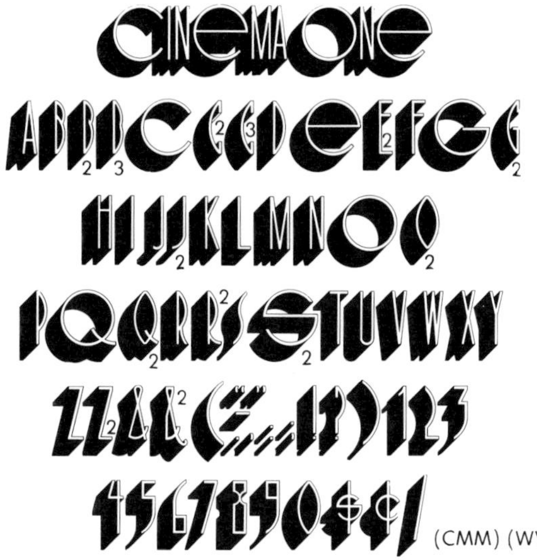

(CMM) (WV)

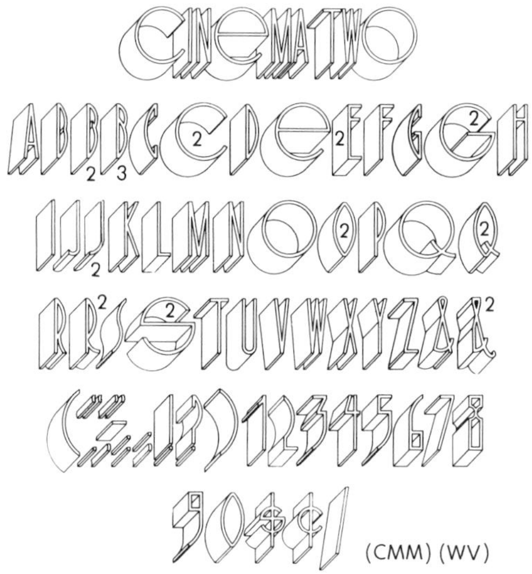

(CMM) (WV)

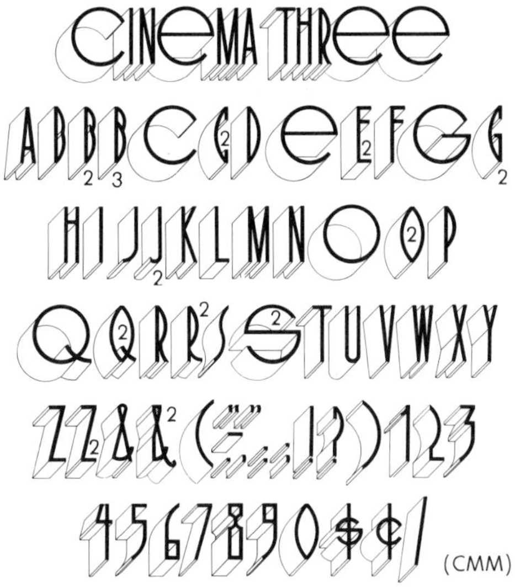

(CMM) (WV)

CIRCUS CAPS

ABCDEFG
HIJKLM
NOPQRST
UVWXYZ
&[',:.''']?!'_$1
2345678
90¢/£$% (WV)

Cirque

ABCDEFGHIJKLM
NOPQRSTUVWXYZÇ&&
(',;:i)?!'*_abcdefghijkl
mnopqrstuvwxyzç
$1234567890¢/%∴

City Compact Light

ABCDE
FGHIJKLMNO
PQRSTUVW
XYZ&('∴'"")?![*=]
abcdefghijkl
mnopqrstuv
wxyz$12345
67890¢$/£%%
†》》

CityCompact
MediumABC
DEFGHIJKL
MNOPQRST
UVWXYZ&
(\`\`\`\`\`\`\`\`\`\`)?!*_abcdef
ghijklmnopq
rstuvwxyz
$123456789
0¢%$£%

CityCompact
BoldABCDE
FGHIJKLM
NOPQRSTU
VWXYZ&[.,.;]
?!*_abcdefghi
jklmnopqrst
uvwxyz$12
34567890¢
/%o$% (IB)

Clarendon
BoldABC
DEFGHIJ
KLMNOP
QRSTUV
WXYZ&
(",.;",")?!*_ab
cdeffiflghi
jklmnop
qrstuvwx
yz$12345
67890¢$/¢£
%

ClearfaceABCD EFGHIJKLMN OPQRSTUVW XYZ&(.',:;'")?!*a bcdeffighijklm nopqrstuvwxyz $1234567890¢ ¢/$%£# 1234567890

Clearface Bold ABCDE FGHIJKLMN OPQRSTUVW XYZ&(.',:;'")?!* abcdeffighijkl mnopqrstuvwx yz$12345678 90¢¢/$%£#

1234567890

Clearface HeavyABCDE FGHIJKLMN OPQRSTUV WXYZ&(.',:;'") ?!* abcdeffig hijklmnopqrs tuvwxyz$123 4567890¢¢/$%#

1234567890

Clearface Black ABCD EFGHIJKL MNOPQRST UVWXYZ& (.',.:;%)?!* abcdeffighij klmnopqrstu vwxyz$1234 567890¢¢/$% £#1234567890

Clearface Black Italic ABCDEFGH IJKLMNOPQ RSTUVWXY Z&(.',:;%)?! *abcdeffighi jklmnopqrst uvwxyz$123 4567890¢¢/$ %£#1234567890

Clearface Contour ABC DEFGHIJKLM NOPQRSTU VWXYZ&(.',:;%)?! *abcdeffigh ijklmnopqrstuv wxyz$12345 67890¢¢/$%£ #1234567890 (WV)

Clearface Extra Bold

ABCDEFG
HIJKLMN
OPQRSTU
VWXYZ&
(‘“’‘’‘”)?![*]a
bcdefffffiflffi
fflghijklmn
opqrstuvw
xyz$12345
67890¢/£$%

Clearface Black

ABCDEFGH
IJKLMNOP
QRSTUVW
XYZÆÇŒØ
&(‘,:;”)?!*ab
cdeffifflghijk
lmnopqrst
uvwxyzæçœ
øß$123456
7890¢/%ø¿¡ (S)

Clearface Gothic

ABCDEFGHIJK
LMNOPQRSTU
VWXYZ&[.’:;”]
?!*abcdefghijkl
mnopqrstuvw
xyz$12345678
90¢$¢+/%§§■:

Clearface Gothic Bold
ABCDEFGHIJ
KLMNOPQRS
TUVWXYZ&
[.,:; "''"]?!*_abcde
fghijklmnopq
rstuvwxyz$1
234567890¢
¢®/+%‰◼◻○
$ ●

Cloister Old
Style
ABCDEFGH
IJKLMNOPQ
QuRSTUV
WXY
Z&(*.,:;-''!?)abc
&defﬁﬀﬂﬃﬄ
ghijklmnopq
rstuvwxyz$12
34567890¢%/£

Cloister Bold
ABCDEFGH
IJKLMNOPQ
QRSTUVW
XYZ&
(.,:;"''")?!*_abcdef
ﬁﬂﬀﬃﬄghijkl
mnopqrstuv
wxyz&$1234
567890¢/%

Cloister ExtraBold
ABCDEFG
HIJKLMN
OPQRSTU
VWXYZ&
(".,:;)?!ābcdefff
fiflghijklmn
opqrstuvwxy
z$123456789
0¢/%

Cloister Heavy
ABCDEFG
HIJKLMN
OPQRSTU
VWXYZ&
(".,:;)?!ābcde
ffffiflghijkl
mnopqrstuv
wxyz$12345
67890¢%

Cloister Black
ABCDEFG
HIJKLMNO
PQRSTUV
VWWXYZ&
(.',:;:"J?!*_abcdef
ghijklmnopqrst
uvwxyz$1234
567890¢/$

CLOISTER INITIALS

(WV)

Cochin Old Style No. 61

ABCDEFG
HIJKLMN
OPQRSTUV
WXYZ&
(.,-:;'!?)abcd
effiflffifflghi
jklmnopqr
stuvwxyz
$123456
7890¢£%
$/¢1234567890%/£

Cochin Roman

AÆBCDEF
GHIJKLM
NOŒPQRS
TUVWXYZ
&(',:;)?!*_ aæbc
deffiflghijklm
noœpqrstuvw
xyz1234567
890¢£$/«·»ß$12
34567890
½⅓⅔
⅛⅜⅝⅞

Cochin Roman Bold A ÆBC DEFGHIJK LMNOŒP QRSTUVW XYZ&(".,:;) ?!*.‗‗aæbcdeffi flghijklmno œpqrstuvwx yzß$1234567 890₁₂34567₈ 90¢£$/¢%«⁙» ¼½⅔⅓ ¾⅛⅜⅝⅞

Cochin Roman Black A ÆBCDE FGHIJKLM NOŒPQR STUVWXY Z&!,.:;?!*.‗‗aæb cdeffiflghij klmnoœpq rstuvwxyz ß$1234567 890 ₁₂3456 7890¢£%«⁙»

Cochin Italic A Æ BCDEFGHIJ KLMNOŒP QRSTUVWX YZ℮3(".,:;)?!‗° aæ bcdee₂ffiflghijk lmnoœpqrrₛstu vwxyzß$123456 7890₁₂34567890¢ £%«⁙»

Cochin Bold Italic A ÆBC DEFGHIJK LMNOŒPQ RSTUVWX YZ&3(.',:,;)?!* aæbcdee₂ffifl ghijklmnoœ pqrr₂sstuvwx yzß$1234567 89012345₆6 7890¢£$¢%❖

Cochin Black Italic A ÆBC DEFGHIJK LMNOŒP ORSTUVW XYZ&3('.,:,;) ?!*aæbcde ₂effiflghijkl mnoœpqrr₂ sstuvwxyzß $1234567890 1234567890¢ £$¢%❖

Collins Bicentennial ABCDEFGHIJ KLMNNOP QRSSTUVW XXYZ&& (..::..) !? abcdefghijk lmnnopqrr sstuvwxyz $1234567890 ¢/$¢%£1234567890® (WV)

Columbus

ABBCCDE
EFGHIJKK
LMNOPQQ
RRSTUVV
WXYZÆ&
(',.;"")?!abcde
fghijklmnop
qrstuvwxy
zæœ$123456
7890¢/£%

Columbus Bold

ABCDEFG
HIJKLMNO
PQRSTUV
WXYZÆÇ
ŒØ&(',.;"")?!
abcdefghij
klmnopqrs
tuvwxyzæç
œøß$1234
567890¢/%»

COLUMNA SOLID

ABCDEFGH
IJKLMNOP
QRSTUVW
XYZ&(',.;)?!
$12345678
90¢¢%%

COLUMNA OPEN

ABCDEFGH
IJKLMNOP
QRSTUVW
XYZ&(',.;'")?!
⊞⁎.$12345678
90¢¢$%

Compacta Light

ABCDEFGHIJKLMNOPQR
STUVWXYZ&(*'`"`.,:;—-'!?)
abcdefghijklmnopqr
stuvwxyz$1234567890¢
£%#$/¢1234567890 (IB)

Compacta

ABCDEFGHIJKLMNO
PQRSTUVWXYZ&
(*'`"`.,:;—-'!?)abcdefgh
ijklmnopqrstuvw
xyz$1234567890¢
£%#$/¢1234567890

Compacta Bold

ABCDEFGHIJKLM
NOPQRSTUVW
XYZ&(*'"''_-!?)ab
cdefghijklmno
pqrstuvwxyz$12
34567890¢£%
#$/¢1234567890

Comstock

ABCDEFG
HIJKLMNO
PQRSTUV
WXYZ&(',:;")
?!*abcdefg
hijklmnop
qrstuvwxyz
$1234567
890¢$/£s% (WV)

Consort

ABCDEFGHIJ
KLMNOPQR
STUVWXYZ&
(',:;"")?!*abcdef
ghijklmnopqrst
uvwxyz12345
67890¢$/%

124

CONSTANZE
INITIALS
ABCDEFG
HIJKLM
NOPQRST
UVWXYZ (WV)

Cooper Oldstyle
ABCDEFGHI
JKLMNOPQR
STUVWXYZ
&[.,:;"]?!*abcdefg
hijklmnopqrstu
vwxyz$123456
7890¢$%¢£%

**Cooper Black
Condensed A
BCDEFGHIJ
KLMNOPQR
STUVWXYZ
&[';:;"]?!*ab
cdefghijk
lmnopqrst
uvwxyz$123
4567890¢/£%c/£%**

Cooper Black

ABCDEFGHIJ
KLMNOPQRSTU
VWXYZ&[!;:;‰]?!
⸸abcdefghijklm
nopqrstuvwxyz
$1234567890
¢/% £%¢/₀$%

Cooper Black Italic

Swash A A A A
B B C C D D E E F F
G G H H I I J J K K L L
M M M M N N N N O P
P Q R R R S S T T U U
V V W W X X Y Y Z Z
&(!;:;"")?!(*)abbcdde
ffgghhijjkklmm
nnoppqdrrsttuvuw
xx yyyz$123456789
0¢/%£

Cooper Comstock Swash

A A A Æ B B
C Ç Ç D D E E F G
G H H I I I J J K K L
L L M M N N O Œ O P
P Q R R S T T U U V
V W W X X Y Y Z
&(';;;)?!*_æ æ b c ç d
d e f g h h i j k l m m n
n o œ o p q r s t u v w x
y z ß $ 1 2 3 4 5 6 7 8 9 0
¢ / £ % ©® ✕ ¿¡ ✕◻● (WV)

Cooper Hilite

A B C D E F G H I J K L
M N O P Q R S T U V W
X Y Z (',;;;)?!_abcde
f g h i j k l m n o p
q r s t u v w x y z $ 1
2 3 4 5 6 7 8 9 0 $

Craw Clarendon Condensed ABC
DEFGHIJKLMN
OPQRSTUVWX
YZ&(',.:;"")?!*abc
defghijklmnopqr
stuvwxyz$1234
567890¢%¢£%

Cucumber
ABCDEFGHIJ
KLMNOPQRS
TUVWXYZ&
(',.:; "")?!*abcdef
ghijklmnop
qrstuvwxyz
$1234567890¢€%

Cushing Old Style Extra Bold
ABCDEFGH
IJKLMNOPQ
RSTUVWXY
Z&(",.:;)?!*abcd
efghijklmno
pqrstuvwxy
z$1234567890
$¢£% (IB)

128

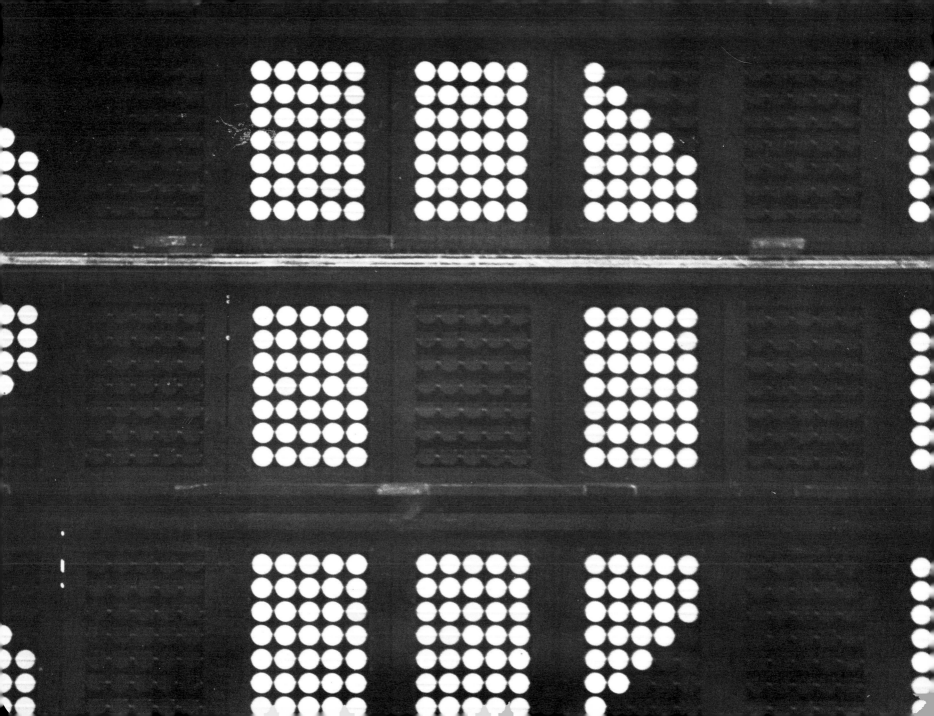

DAVIDA BOLD

AABCDEEFF
GHIJKLMNOP
QRSTUVWXY
Z&&•|'.,:;"|•?!*_$$
11223344556 67
788990¢/£%
❧

Dektiv ABC

DEFGHIJKL
MNOPQRST
UVWXYZÆ
ÇŒؕ&('.;.:,)?
!*abcdefgh
ijklmnopqr
stuvwxyz
æçœøß123
4567890/%«⁎»
©®■●§+■○

Della Robbia A

BCDEFGHIJK
LMNOPQRST
UVWXYZ&
'.,:;"abcdefghijk
lmnopqrstuvw
xyz$1234567
890¢

Della Robbia
Bold ABCDEF
GHIJKLMNO
PQRSTUVW
XYZØ&&(',:;")
?!ábcdefghijk
lmnopqrstuv
wxyzø$12345
67890$¢

Della Robbia
Extra Bold ABC
DEFGHIJKL
MNOPQRS
TUVWXY
Z&(',:;")?!ábc
defghijklmn
opqrstuvwx
yz$123
4567890¢/%

Della Robbia
Heavy ABCD
EFGHIJKL
MNOPQRST
UVWXYZ
&(',:;")?!ábcd
efghijklmnop
qrstuvwxyz$1
234567890¢/%

DELPHIANABC
DEFGHIJKLM
NOPQRSTU
VWXYZ&
(.;:)?!⁎—$12345
67890¢/£% (WV)

Delphin No.2
ABCDEFGH
IJKLMNOP
QRSTUVWXY
ZÆÇ
Œ&abcddef ff fi fl
gghijkl
mnopqrsɈtu
ʋwxyzæçœ$
¢%$£%1234567
890
(".;; "")?![★—]

Dempsey
Medium ABC
DEFGHIJKLM
NOPQRSſST
UVWXYZC
(";;;)?!lābcdef
ghijklmnopq
rɾstuvwxyzß
$1234567
890ȿ£»°«⁑

DESDEMONA
OUTLINE ABCDE
FGHIJKLMNOPQ
RSSTUVWXYZ&
(""")?!$12
34567890¢$⁄⁄£ (WV) (R)

Design Fineline A A B
C D E F G H I J K L M N
O P O R S S T
U V W X Y Z & (.,:;)?!abb
cddeefgghhijklmmnn
op pqqrrsstuvwxyyzS
12345
67890¢$⁄£ (IB) (WV)

Design Medium A A B C
D D E F G H I J K L M N
O P Q R S S T U V W X
Y Z & (.,:;)?!abbccdde
efgghhijklmmnnop
pqqrrsstuvwxyyzS12
34567890¢$⁄E (IB)

DesignDemi ÂABC
DDEÊFGHIJKLMN
OPQRSSTUVWXY
Z&(.,.::)?!*abbccdde
efgghhijklmmnnop
pqqrsstuvwxyyz$12
34567890¢$/$£ (IB)

Design ExtraBold
ÂABCDDEEFG
HIJKLMNOPQR
SSTUVWXYZ&
(.,.::)?!*abbccdde
efgghhijklmmnnop
pqqrsstuvwxyyz$1
234567890
¢$/$£ (IB)

DesignOutline
ÂABCDDEEFG
HIJKLMNOPQ
RSSTUVWXYZ
&(.,.::)?!abbccdd
eefgghhijklmm
nnoppqqrsstuvw
xyyz$1234567
890¢$/¢£ (WV) (IB)

DEUTSCH BLACK
ABCDEFGHIJKL
MNOPQRSTUV
WXYZ&(':,.)?!:
*$1234567890
¢/£% (WV)

Devinne Extra
Bold ABCDEF
GHIJKLMNO
PQRRSTUVW
XYZ&'';:;?!ab
cdefghijklm
nopqrstuvwx
yz$12345678
90¢

Devinne Black
ABCDEFGHI
JKLMNOPQ
RRSTUVWX
YZ&'';:;?!abc
defghijklm
nopqrstuvwx
yz$1234
567890¢

Didi ABCDE FGHIJKLM MNOPQRST UVWWXYZ ÆIAŒØ& (.,:;!)?!*abcd efghijklm nopqrstuvw xyzæfiœøß $$12345678 90¢/£%#✂➤◀•¡

Diotima AÅ ÆBCÇDEFG HIJKLMNO ŒØPQRST UVWXYZ &(.,:;!")?!*aåæ bcçdefghijkl mnoœøpq rsßstuvwxy z$123456789 0¢%£®/¿¡≈ã©

Discus ABC DEFGHI JKLMN OPQRSTU VWXYZ& (.,:;")?!*abcde fflghijklmnopq rsstuvwxyz$12 34567890¢$/¢£%

Discus Semi-Bold

ABCDEFG
GHIJKL
MNOPQRS
TUVWXY
Z&(.,:;")?!*abcde
ffffifflghijklmno
pqrsstuvwxyz $12
34567890¢¢/¢£%

Dragonwyck

ABCDEFGHIJ
KLMNOPQRS
TUVWXYZ&
(.,:;")?!*abcdefg
hijklmnopqrstu
vwxyz
$1234567890¢
¢/$% 1234567890

Dynamo

Medium AÄÅ
ÆBCDEFGHI
JKLMNOØÖP
QRSTUÜVWX
YZ&(.,:;)?!aäå
àæbcdeèéfg
hijklmnoöøp
qrsßtuüûvwx
yz$1234567890
£/¢

Dynamo AB
CDEFGHIJK
LMNOPQRS
STUVWXYZ
&(':;:;) ?!abc
defghijklm
nopqrstuvw
xyz$1234567
890£«⚛»

EAGLE BOLD
ABCDEFG
HIJKLMN
OPQRSTU
VWXYZ&!,
:?!$1234
567890 (IB) (SR)

ECLIPSE
ABCDEE
FGHIJKL
MNOPQRS
STUVWX
YZ&(.'..WD
?!._$12345
67890$%#☆

EDDAAABC
DEEFGHIJK
LMNOPQRS
TTUVWX
YZ&(.;.)?!S
123456789
0C¢-/£ (WV) (R)

Egizio Bold
ABCDEFG
HIJKLMN
OPQRSTU
VWXYZ&
(',.;?!abcd
efffffiflffiffl
ghijklmn
opqrstuvwx
yz$12345
67890¢/£%✿

Egizio Bold
Italic ABCD
EFGHIJKL
MNOPQRS
TUVWXY
Z&(',.;?!ab
cdefffffiflffi
fflghijklmn
opqrstuvwx
yz$1234567
890¢/$£%

Egyptian 505
Light ABCD
EFGHIJKL
MNOPQRST
UVWXYZ&
(',.;")?!*abcd
efghijklmn
opqrstuvwx
yz&$
1234567890
¢¢/$£%

Egyptian
505ABCD
EFGHIJKL
MNOPQRS
TUVWXY
ZG (.,:;«)?!*ab
cdefghijk
lmnopqrst
uvwxyzＧ$1
234567890¢
¢/s£%‥

Egyptian
505Medium
ABCDEFG
HIJKLMN
OPQRSTUV
WXYZG
(.,:;«)?!*abcd
efghijklm
nopqrstuv
wxyzＧ$123
4567890¢
¢/s£%

Egyptian
505Bold
ABCDEFG
HIJKLMN
OPQRSTU
VWXYZＧ
(.,:;«)?!*abc
defghijklm
nopqrstuv
wxyzＧ$1
234567890
¢¢/s£%

Egyptian
505 Outline
ABCDEFG
HIJKLMN
OPQRSTUV
WXYZ&
(',;:;"")?!*‡abc
defghijklm
nopqrstuv
wxyz&$
12345678
90¢%/$£%

Egyptian Bold
Condensed ABC
DEFGHIJKLM
NOPQRSTUVW
XYZ&(',;:;"")?!*
abcdefghijklmn
opqrstuvwxyz$
1234567890¢
¢/$£%

Egyptian Bold
Condensed
(Russian) АБВГ
ДЕЁЖЗИЙ
ЙКЛМНОПРС
ТУФХЦЧШ
ЩЪЫЬЭЮЯ
(:,;.:;« »!?)абвг
дежзийӣкл
мнопрстуфхц
чшщъыьэ
юя$12345678
90¢/£%

1234567890 (WV)

144

Egyptian Bold
Condensed
OutlineABCDEF
GHIJKLMNOP
QRSTUVWXY
Z&(',.,:;""")?!ābcd
efghijklmnopq
rstuvwxyz$123
4567890¢$/% (IB) (WV)

EGYPTIAN PATRIOT
ABCDEFGHIJKLM
NOPQRST
UVWXYZ (WV)

EGYPTIANAABBCC
CDDEEFFGGHIIIJKL
LLMMMNNNOOOP
PQRRRSSSTT
TUUVWWXYYZZ
&&..!$

**Ehrhardt
UltraBold AB
CDEFGHIJ
JKLMNOPQ
RSTUVWXY
ZÇ&(:;:,)?!=a
bcdefghijkl
mnopqrstuv
wxyzç$12345
67890¢/£⚥**

ELEKTRIK
ABCDEFGHI
JKLMNOPQ
RSTUVWXY
Z&(';;*""::!?)$£
1234567890
¢%$/1234567890

ELEKTRIK
MEDIUM AB
CDEFGHIJK
LMNOPQRS
TUVWXYZ&
(';;*""::!?)$£12
34567890¢%
$/1234567890

ELEKTRIK
BOLD ABCD
EFGHIJKLM
NOPQRSTU
VWXYZ&
('66*99:!?)$£12
34567890¢
%$/1234567890

Elizabeth Roman
ABCDEFGHIJK
LMNOPQRST
UVWXYZ
&(',.;:"=†*!?)abcdef
ffiflftghijklmno
pqrststuvwxyz
$1234567890£¢
/% $1234567890¢

Elvira Bold
Italic ÆŒ
BCÇDEFG
HIJKLMN
OŒ ØPQRS
TUVWXY
Z&(',:;,")?!.*
aæbcçdef
ghijklmno
œøpqrstu
vwxyzß$1
234567890
¢/£%»«®©■●▪◆≈‹i

Emphasis A
BCDEFGHIJ
KLMNOPQR
STUVWXY
Z&(.,":-")?!.ab
cdefghijklm
nopqrstuvw
xyz$12345
67890¢$/¢£
% /% (IB)

EngeEtienne ABCDEFGHIJK
LMNOPQRSTUVWXYZ&(.',::,")?!
*abcdeffffffflghijklmnopqrstuv
wxyz$1234567890¢$/¢£%

EngraversOld
EnglishABCDE
FGHIJKLMN
OPQRSTUVWX
YZ&(.",::,")?!*abcde
fghijklmnopqrst
uvwxyz$123467
890¢$/¢£% (WV)

148

ERAS ABCD
EFGHIJKLMN
OPQRSTUV
WXYZÆÇØ&
(.,;:"')?!*$123456
7890ŁĽⅩ%≈¿i

ITC™ LICENSED Eras Light AÆ
BCDEFGHIJ
KLLĿMNOŒ
ØPQRSTTTU
VWWXYZ
&&(.,;:"')?!*aaœ
æbcdeffffifflffiffl
ghijklmnooeø
pqrstttuvwxy
zß$123456789
0¢⁄$£%@#⸙⸙

ITC™ LICENSED Eras Book AÆ
BCDEFGHIJK
LLĿMNOŒ
ØPQRSTTTU
VWXYZ&&
(.,;:"')?!*⸙aaœæb
cdeffffifflffifflgh
ijklmnooeøpq
rstttuvwxyz
ß$1234567890
¢⁄$£%
@#⸙⸙¿i©®⊠▣

ErasMedium

AÆBCDEFG
HIJKLLAMNO
ŒØPQRSTTT
UVWWXYZ
&&²(.',:;"")?!*‡aa₂
œæbcdeffffiflfl
ffifflghijklmno
œøpqrstuv
wxyzttß$123
4567890¢¢/s
£%@#⚹⬡»""¿ï×⊠:©®⬛

ErasDemi

AÆBCDEFG
HIJKLLAMN
NOŒØPQR
STTTUVWX
YZ&&²(.',:;"")?!*
aa²æbcdef
ffififlffffiflffflgh
ijklmnoœøp
qrstttuvwx
yzß$1234567
890¢¢/s£%@
#⚹⬡»""¿ï×⊠:©®⬛

ErasBold

AÆBCDEF
GHIJKLLA
MNOŒØP
QRSTTTUV
WWXYZ&&²
(.',:;"")?!*‡aa²œ
æbcdeffffifl
ffifflghijklm
noœøpqrs
tttuvwxyz
ß$1234567
890¢¢/s£%@
#⚹⬡»""¿ï×⊠:©®⬛

ITC™ LICENSED Eras Ultra A Æ B
C D E F G H I J K L L A
M N O Œ Ø P Q R S
T T T U V W W W X
Y Z & & (' „ :: ;; ") ? ! * aa
æ æ b c d e f f f fi fl
ff fi ffl g h i j k l m n
o œ ø p q r s t u v w
x y z tt ß $ 1 2 3 4 5 6
7 8 9 0 ¢ ⅍ $ £ % @ #
© ®

ITC™ LICENSED Eras Outline
A B C D E F G H I J K
L L A M N O P Q R S
T T T U V W W W X
Y Z & & (' ,,::;;") ? ! * aa
b c d e f f f g h i j k l m
n o p q r s t u v
w x y z tt $ 1 2 3 4 5 6
7 8 9 0 ¢ ⅍ $ £ % @ #

ITC™ LICENSED

Eras Contour

ABCDEFGH
IJKLLAMNOP
QRSTTUVW
XYZ &&² (.',:;.°)
?!*¡=aa²bcdefffgh
ijklmnopqrsttt
uvwxyz $1234
567890¢¢/s£%@# (WV)

Eurostile Extended ABC
DEFGHIJKLM
NOPQRSTUV
WXYZ&(.',:;.'")?!
abcdefghijklmn
opqrstuvwx
yz$123456
7890¢%$£%o

152

Eurostile Bold Extended

ABCDEF
GHIJKLM
NOPQRS
TUVWX
YZ&(',:;"„)
?![*]abcd
efghijklm
nopqrstu
vwxyz$12
3456789
0¢¢/$£%

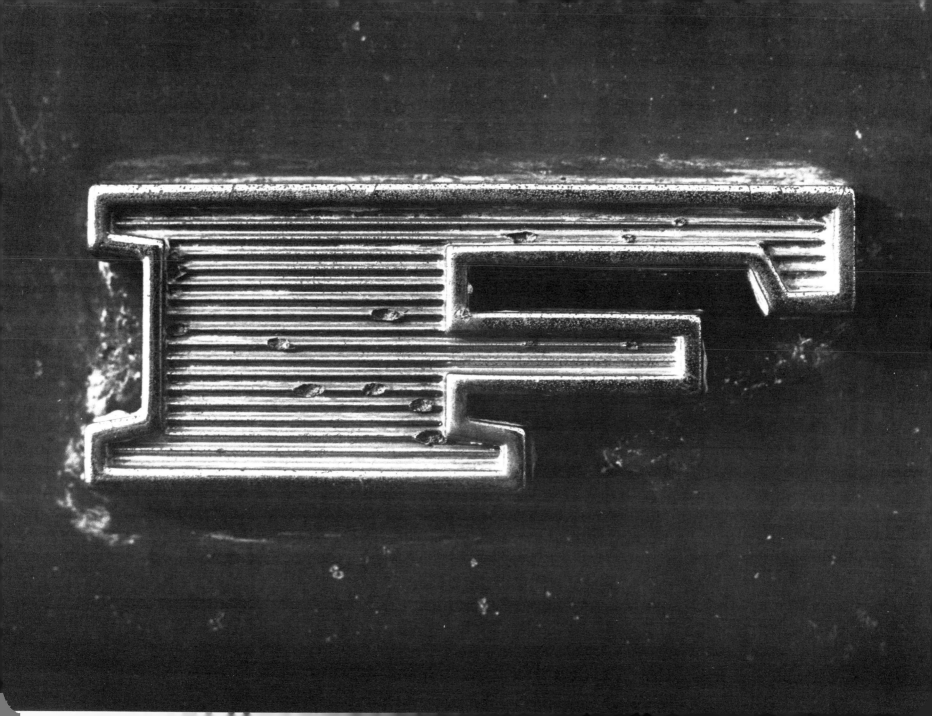

FATCAT
AÆBCCÐEF
GHIJKLM
NOÓØŒPQR
SSTUVWX
YZŁ[:::::]
?![:]¿123
4567890
¢/Σ%⟨⟩

Fat Face Condensed A ÆBC
DEFGHIJKLMNOØŒPQ
RSTUVWXYZ&(:,;.ː")?!*
aæbcctdeffffifffifflfflghij
klmnoøœpqrst
uvwxyzßß$123
4567890¢/£%#⸱⬦¶¿¡

Fat Face Condensed
Italic ABCDEFGHIJ
KLMNOPQRSTUVW
XYZ&(.;:;ː")?!*aåbc
defghijklmnopqrst
uvwxyz $123456789
0¢$/£%

FatFace

A Æ B C D E F G
H I J K L M N O Ø
Œ P Q R S T U V
W X Y Z & (' . , : ; ")
? ! ! * _ a æ b c d e f f f
fi ffi fl ffl g h i
j k l m n o o œ p q r s
t u v w x y z ß
$ 1 2 3 4 5 6 7 8
9 0 ¢ / s £ % # ‹ ❀ › ¶ ¡ ¿

Firenze

A B C D E F G
H I J K L M
N O P Q R S T
U V W X Y Z
& & (' . , : ; ")
? ! { * _ } a b c d e
f f f fi fl g h i j
k l m n o p q r s
t u v w x y z
$ 1 2 3 4 5 6 7 7
8 9 0 ¢ ¢ / s £ % # ¶

Firmin Didot

A B C D E F G H
I J K L M N O
P Q R S T U V W
X Ỳ Z & (' . , : ; ") ? ! [*]
a æ b c d e f f ff fi
fl ft g h i j k l m n o
ø p q r s t u v w
x y z ß $ 1 2 3 4 5 6
7 8 9 0 ¢ £ ¢ / $ %

Firmin Didot
Bold ABCD
EFGHIJKL
MNOPQR
STUVWXY
Z&(·;:,·?,?)?![*|]
abcdeffffi
flftffighijkl
mnopqrs
tuvwxyz$1
234567890¢
£¢/$%«†§»
1234567890

Flange
ABCDEF
GHIJKLMN
OPQRRS
TUVWXY
Z&(·;·'·;)?!·*·a
bcdeefggh
ijklmno
pqrstuvw
xyz$1234
567890¢/
£%:·

Fleetwing '44
ABCDEFG
HIJKLM
NOPQRS
TUVWXYZ
&(.;·;,")?!*_ab
bcdefghij
klmnoo
pqrstuvw
wxyzl
234567890
¢/¢£%

(IB) (SR)

Flex ABCDEF
GHIJKLMNO
PQRSTUVWX
YZ&(",:,)?!*abcde
fffffflghijklmn
opqrstuvwxyz
$1234567890/£ (WV)

Flirt ABCDEF
GHIJKLMN
OPQRSTUV
WXYZ&(",:,)?!
abcdefghijkl
mnopqrstuv
wxyz
$1234567890
¢/£

Florentine AABB
CDEEFFGHIJK
LMMNNOOPP
QRRSSTUVW
XYZ&(',:,")?!*=
aabcdeefghijk
lmnooopqrstuv
wxyyz$123456
7890¢%$£% (S)

Folio Medium Extended
AaBCDEe
FGHIJKL
MmNNOP
QRrSTUV
WXYZ&(';:;")
?!:abcdefgh
ijklmnopqr
stuvwxy
z$1234567
890¢/£%

Folio Extra Bold ABCD
EFGHIJKLM
NOPQRSTU
VWXYZ&
(';:;")?!:-ab
cdefghijkl
mnopqrstu
vwxyz$12
34567890
¢/$£%₀123456
7890

Folio Extra
Bold Outline
ABCDEFGH
IJKLMNO
PQRSTUV
WXYZ&
(';:;")?!:-a
bcdefghijk
lmnopqrst
uvwxyz$1
234567890
¢¢/$£%

Folkwang

ABCDEFGHI
JKLMNOP
QRSTUVWX
YZ&C",.,;,")?!*
abcdefffffiflghij
klmnopqrstu
vwxyz$12345
67890¢¢%$£%

Fortuna
Extra Bold

ABCDEF
GHIJKL
MNOPQ
RSTUV
WXYZ&
(",.,;,")?!*_abc
defghij
klmnop
qrstuvw
xyz$123
4567890¢
¢%$£%

Fraktur

ABCDE
FGHIJKL
MNOPQR
STUVWX
YZ&(,.,;,")?!
abcdeffifl
ghijklmnopq
rstuvwxyz
$112233445
566778
899000¢/£%

(WV)

Framingham
ABCDEFGHI
JKLMNOPQ
RSTUVWX
YZÆÇŒØ
&(':;:;")?!⁕abcdef
ghijklmnopqr
stuvwxyzæçct
œøß$12345678
90¢/%£ⁿ⊠⊡● ®©

Framingham
ExtraBold
ABCDEFGH
IJKLMNOP
QRSTUVW
XYZÆÇŒØ
&(':;:;)?!⁕abcd
efghijklmnop
qrstuvwxyz
æçœøß$1234
567890¢%£
⟨⟨⟨⟨⟩⟩⟩⟩ ◁⊠▷ ■●©
□●®

FRANKFURTER
ABCDEFGHIJ
KLMNOPQ
RSTUVWXY
Z&(':;:;)?!§12
34567890/£
⟨⟨·⟩⟩

FRANKFURTER OUTLINE

A ÆB CÇD EF
GHIJKLMNO
ŒØPQRSTU
VWXYZ&
(.'.,.:;.""')?!*¦$
1234567890
¢/£%`¨˘˜¸!
©® ⊠□◼◗»«

FRANKFURTER CONTOUR

A ÆB CÇD EFG
HIJKLMNO
ŒØPQRSTU
VWXYZ&
(.'.,.:;.""')?!¦
$123456789
0¢/£%.""»«¸□◼⊡⊠
?˜°˘˅

FranklinGothic

ABCDEFGHI
JKLMNOPQ
RSTUVWXY
Z&(.',:; "")?!*¬ab
cdefghijklmn
opqrstuv
wxyz$1234
567890¢/$£%

162

Franklin Gothic Black
AÆBCÇDE
FGHIJKLM
NOŒØPQRS
TUVWXYZ&
(",";‡!?)aæbcç
defghiıjklmn
oœøpqrstuv
wxyzß¿ïìÿ$1
234567890
£¢/%$1234567
890¢%®© (IB)

**Franklin Gothic
Condensed ABC**
DEFGHIJKLMN
OPQRSTUVW
XYZ&(',:;‰)?!*a
bcdefghijklmn
opqrstuvwxyz
$1234567890
¢%$£%

**Franklin Gothic Extra
Condensed ABCDEF**
GHIJKLMNOPQRS
TUVWXYZ&(",:;)?!*
abcdefghijklmno
pqrstuvwxyz$123
4567890¢/£%

**Franklin Gothic
Black Extra
Condensed ABCCD
EFGHIJKLMN
OPQRSTUVWXYZ
&ÆŒØ(.,:;¡"?!)
abccdefghiıjk
lmnopqrstuvwx
yzæœøß⟨❖⟩⁖¿i
$1234567890£
¢/%0$1234567890¢**®© (IB)

FREDERICKS-
BURG
ABCDEFGHIJ
KLMNOP
QRSTUVWXYZ
.,:;?!-$123457
890¢ (WV) (IB)

FRISCO
ABCDEF
GHIJKLMN
OPQRSTU
VWXYZ&
[.;:; ::]?!.*$12
34567890
¢¢/$%0«.+.»■□■● (WV)

164

ITC LICENSED Friz Quadrata AB CDEFGHIJKL MNOPQRST UVWXYZ& (.',:;"")?!⁑abc defghijklm nopqrst uvwxyz$123 4567890¢% /£12345678 90

FrizQuadrata Medium ABCDEFG HIJKLMNO PQRSTU UVWXYZ &(.',:;""")?!⁑ abcdefghij klmnopq rstuvwxyz $12345678 90¢⁹/%£123 4567890

Friz Quadrata DemiABC DEFGHIJ KLMNOP QRSTUU VWXYZ& (",:;""")?!⁑ abcdefgh ijklmno pqrstuvw xyz$123456 7890¢⁹/$%£1 234567890

FrizQuadrata BoldAÆBCÇ DEFGHIJKL MNOŒØP QRSTUVW XYZ&(":;:)?! [_*_]aæbcçdef ffffifflfiflggh ijklmnoœø pqrstuvwx yzß$$1234 567890¢/% £#123456789 o«·:·»

FuturaLight AB
ABCDEFGHI
JKLMNOPQR
STUVWXYZ&
(',:; ")?!_*_abcdefgh
ijklmnopqrstuv
wxyz$123456
7890¢¢/$£%

FuturaBook AB
CDEFGHIJKL
MNOPQRST
UVWXYZ&?!_*_
(',:;'''")abcdefff
fiftghijklmnop
qrstuvwxyz
$1234567890¢
¢/$%%/

FuturaMedium

ABCÇDEFG
HIJKLMNOP
QRSTUVWXY
Z&(',:;'')?!*abc
çdefghijklmn
opqrstuvwxy
z$123456789
0¢%$£%∴

FuturaDemi

BoldABCDEF
GHIJKLMNO
PQRSTUVW
XYZ&(',:;'')?!*
abcdefghijkl
mnopqrstuv
wxyz$1234
567890¢%$£%

FuturaBold

ABCDEFGH
IJKLMNOP
QRSTUVW
XYZ&(',:;'')
?!*abcdefg
hijklmnopq
rstuvwxyz
$12345678
90¢%$£%

Futura Extra Bold ABCD
EFGHIJKL
MNOPQR
STUVWXY
Z&(.',:;"")?!_*
abcdefghij
klmnopqrs
tuvwxyz$
123456789
0¢%/$£%

Futura Bold Condensed ABCD
EFGHIJKLMNOP
QRSTUVWXYZ
&(.',:;"")?!_*abcdef
ghijklmnopqrstu
vwxyz $12
34567890
¢$/¢£%

Futura Extra Bold Condensed
ABCDEFGHIJK
LMNOPQRSTU
VWXYZ&
(.',:;"")?!_*abcd
efghijklmnop
qrstuvwxyz$
1234567890
¢%/$£%

Futura Display
ABCDEFGHIJKL
MNOPQRSTTUV
WXYZ&[.',:;«]?!.*
abcdefghijklm
nopqrstuvwxy
z$1234567890
¢/£%

Futura Black
ABCDEFGHI
JKLMNOP
QRSTUVWX
YZ&(.',:;«»)?!.*a
bcdeffffifflfig
hijklmnopqr
stuvwxyz$
1234567890
¢c%$%%*

FUTURA
STIENCIL
LIGHT
ABCDEFGH
IJKLMNOPQ
RSTUVWX
YZ&(.,;)?!-$12
34567890O/Æ
«⚓»

FUTURA STENCIL BOLD ABCD EFGHIJKL MNOPQR STUVWXY

Z&(.,:;)?!$12 3-4567890 /&«°»

GALLIAA
BCDEFGH
IJKLMN
OPQRSST
UVWXY
ZE(.,.:;‚")?!
*$1234567
890¢/$£%‰

Galliard
ABCDEFGH
IJKLMNOP
QRSTUVW
XYZ&(.,.:;‚")?!*
aa bcctdee
ffiflghh ijkl
mnn opqrr
sstt uvwxyz
$1234567890¢£
¢/$%o# 1234567890

Galliard Bold
ABCDEFG
HIJKLMN
OPQRSTU
VWXYZ&
(.,.:;‚")?!*aa b
cctdee ffifl
ghh ijklm
nn oopqrr
sstt uvwxy
z$1234567890
¢£¢/$%o#
1234567890

Galliard Black

ABCDEFGH
IJKLMNO
PQRSTUV
WXYZ&
(;:;¿?)?!‡aa₂b
cctdee₂ffifl
ghh₂ijklm
nn₂opqrr·sst
tt₂uvwxyz
$1234567890¢
£¢/%#1234567890

Galliard

Ultra AB
CDEFGHI
JKLMNOP
QRSTUVW
XYZ&(;:;¿?)
?!‡aa₂bccd
ee₂ffiflghh₂
ijklmnn₂op
qrr₂sstt₂u
vwxyz$1234
567890¢£¢/$
%#1234567890

Galliard Italic

ABCDEFGH
IJKLMNOP
QRSTUVW
XYZ&(;:;¿?)
?!‡aa₂bcctdee₂
ffiflghijkk₂
lmnn₂opqrssʃpst
tt₂uv₂vwxyyzz₂
$1234567890¢£
¢/%#1234567890

Galliard Bold Italic ABCDE FGHIJKLM NOPQRSTU VWXYZ& (.,.;:??)?!*‿ aa‿bc ctdee‿ffifl ghi jkkl mnn‿opq rssp st tt‿ uv‿vwxyzz‿ $1234567890¢£ ¢/s%0#1234567890

Galliard Black Italic ABCDEFG HIJKLMN OPQRSTU VWXYZ& (.,.;:??)?!*‿ aa bcdee‿fghij kk‿lmnn‿opq rstt‿uv‿vwx yzz‿ctfiflspst $1234567890¢ £¢/s%0#1234567890

Galliard Ultra Italic ABCDEFG HIJKLMN OPQRSTU VWXYZ& (.,.;:??)?!*‿ aa bcctdee‿ffifl ghijkk‿lmn ‿opqrssp st tt‿uv‿vwxy zz‿$12345678 90¢£¢/s%0#

Garamond
Light ABCDE
FGHIJKLMN
OPQRSTUV
WXYZ&
(',.:;"*‥"!?) abcd
efffffiflffifflgh
ijklmnopqr
stuvwxyz$$
£12344₂5678
90¢%/#

Garamond
Book
ABCDEFGH
IJKLMNOP
QRSTUV
WXYZ&
ÆÇØŒ(',.:;"")
?![*‥]abcdeffifl
ffffffifflghijk
lmnopqrstu
vwxyzæ
çøœß$12344₂
567890¢$/£%
#☙«~»¿¡

Garamond
Bold ABC
DEFGHIJK
LMNOPQR
STUVWXY
Z& (',.:;"*‥"!?)
abcdeffffi
flffifflghi
jklmnopq
rstuvwxyz
$$£123445₂
67890¢%/# (IB)

ITC LICENSED **Garamond Ultra ABC DEFGHIJ KLMNOP QRSTUVW XYZ&(.,:;"?) abcdefghij klmnopqr stuvwxyz ?!*$12344 567890¢$%¢ £%**

ITC LICENSED Garamond Light Italic AB CDEFGHIJ KLMNOPQ RSTUVWX YZ& (.,:;""!?)abcd effff fi fl ffi ffl g hhijklmmn nopqrstuvw x yzz $$£123 4567890¢ %/#*

ITC LICENSED Garamond Book Italic A BCDEFGHIJ KLMNOPQ RSTUVWX YZÆÇØŒ& &(.,:;"?)?![*]ab cdeffffifffffffifffl ghhijklmmn nopqrstuvw xyzzæçøœß $123456789 0¢$£%#

Garamond Bold Italic

ABCDEFG
HIJKLMN
OPQRSTU
VWXYZ&&
(.,:;:*"!?)ab
cdefghhijk
lmmnnop
qrstuvwxy
zz2fffffifffffffl
$$£12345
67890¢%/#

Garamond Ultra Italic

ABCDEFG
HIJKLM
NOPQRS
TUVWXY
Z&&2(',:;")
?!*abcde
fghhijkl
mmnnopq
rstuvwxy
zz2$$12345
67890¢$$%
£%

Garamond Light Condensed ABC

DEFGHIJKLMN
OPQRSTUVWX
YZ&(',:;:*"!?)ab
cdefffifflffiffl
ghijklmnopq
rstuvwxyz$$
123456789
0¢%/#£

ITC™ LICENSED Garamond Book
Condensed ABC
DEFGHIJKLM
NOPQRSTUV
WXYZ&
(‚;:;"*̣"!?)abcde
fff fi fl ffi fflghij
klmnopqrstuv
wxyz$$£12344₂
567890¢%/#

ITC™ LICENSED Garamond
Bold Con-
densed ABCD
EFGHIJKLMN
OPQRSTUV
WXYZ&[*̣]
(‚;:;"*̣"!?)abcd
ef ff fi fl ffi ffl
ghijklmnop
qrstuvwxyz
$$£12344₂567
890¢%/#

ITC™ LICENSED Garamond
Ultra Con-
densed ABCD
EFGHIJKLM
NOPQRSTUV
WXYZ&
(‚;:;"*̣"!?) abcd
ef ff fi fl ffi ffl
ghijklmno
pqrstuvwx
yz$$£12344₂
567890¢%/#

Garamond Light Condensed Italic
ABCDEFGHIJ
KLMNOPQR
STUVWXYŽ&&
(.,:;"""!?)abcdef*
ff fi fl ffi ffl gh hh ij kl
m m n n o p q r s t
u v w x y z z $ $ £ 1
2 3 4 5 6 7 8 9
0 ¢ % / #

Garamond Book Condensed Italic ABCDEF
GHIJKLMNOP
QRSTUVWX
ŶZ&& (.,:;"""!?)*
abcdef fi fff fl ffi
ff l gh hh ij kl
m m n n o p q r s t
u v w x y z z $ $ £ 1
2 3 4 4 5 6 7 8 9 0 ¢
% / #

Garamond Bold Con-
densed Italic
ABCDEFGHI
JKLMNOPQ
RSTUVWXŶ
Z&& (.,:;"*""!?)
abcdef fff fi fl
ff i ff l gh hh ij kl
m m n n o p q r
s t u v w x y z z
$ $ £ 1 2 3 4 4 5
7 8 9 0 ¢ % / #

Garamond Ultra Con-densed Italic ABCDEFGH IJKLMNOPQ RSTUVWXY Z&&(.;:;"*.."!?) abcdefffffifl ffifflghhijkl mmnnopqr stuvwxyzz \$\$£123456 7890¢%/#

Garamond OldstyleABC DEFGHIJKL MNOPQRS TUVWXYZ &(.;:;"?!*abcctd efffffiflffifflghij klmnopqrsstt uvwxyz\$12345 67890¢/£%

Garamond Oldstyle Italic ABCDEFG HIJKLMNOP QRSTUVWX YZ&(.;:;"?!*aas bcctdefffffiflffiifflfr ghiisjkllmnopqr sspsttttuusvwxyz &\$123456 7890¢/£%

Garamond Bold
ABCDEFGH
IJKLMNOP
QRSTUVW
XYZ&(.',:;"")?!
*_abcdefghijkl
mnopqrstuv
wxyz$123456
7890¢/¢£%

Garamond
Heavy ABCD
EFGHIJKLM
NOPQRST
UVWXYZ&
(.',:;)?!*_abcdef
ghijklmnop
qrstuvwxyz$
1234567890¢

Garamond
Oldstyle Extra
Bold ABCDE
FGHIJKLM
NOPQRSTU
VWXYZ&
(.',:;)?!āābcdeffi
flffiffflghij
klmnopqrst
uvwxyz$
1234567890
¢£%

GARDENIA
ABCDEFGH
IJKLMNOPQ
RSTUVWX
YZ&$123456
7890$ (WV)

GEMINIAABCD
DEEFGHIJKLMN
OPQRSTU
VWWXYZ
[":.:]?!! * S1234
5678900¢'"
'" |:.:'

GeshOrtega
RomanAÆB
CÇDEFGHIJ
KLMNOŒØ
PQRSTUVW
XYZ&(":.:;")?!*_
aæbcçdefgh
ijklmnoøpqr
stuvwxyz
ß$12345678
90¢/£%®÷¿¡■●○

GETTYSBURG

ABCDEFGHIJKLMNO
PQRSTUVWXYZ.,:;!&$
1234567890¢ (IB) (S)

Gillies Gothic Bold

ABCDEFGH
IJKLMNOP
QRSTThUV
WXYZ&(',:;")
?!*abcdefghij
klmnopqrstuvw
xyz$1234567
890¢/$£%/%

GillSansLight

ABCDEFGHIJ
KLMNOPQRST
UVWXYZ&(':;)?!
*abcdefghijklmn
opqrstuvwxyz$1
234567890¢/% (IB)

Gill Sans Medium

AÆBCÇDEFG
HIJKLMŃNOŒ
ØPQRSTUV
WXYZ&(",;:;)?!*
aæbcçdefghijkl
mnoœøpqrstu
vwxyzß$12345
67890¢/£%⚙♟ïi®+

Gill Sans Bold

AÆBCÇDE
FGHIJKLMN
OŒØPQRST
UVWXYZ&
(",;:;")?!*‡aæbcç
defghijklmn
oœøpqrstuv
wxyzß$12345
67890¢¢/$£%

Gill Sans Extra Bold

ABCDE
FGHIJKLMN
OPQRSTUV
WXYZ&
(",;:;"")?!*‡abc
defffifflffiffl
ghijklmnop
qrstuvwxy
z$1234567
890¢⁹/$£%

GillSans UltraBold
ABCDEFG
HIJKLMNO
PQRSTUV
WXYZ&
(.,;:;"")?!*±ab
cdefffffffg
hijklmnop
qrstuvwx
yz$123456
7890¢¢/$£%

GillSansLightItalic
ABCDEFGHIJKL
MNOPQRSTUV
WXYZ&(.,;:;"")?!
±abcdefffighijk
lmnopqrstuvwx
yz$1234567890
¢¢/$£% (IB)

GillSansBold
ItalicABCDEF
GHIJKLMNO
PQRSTUVW
XYZ&(.,;:;"")?!±
abcdefffghijkl
mnopqrstuvw
xyz$1234567
890¢¢/$£%

Gill Sans Bold Condensed ABC DEFGHIJKLMNO PQRSTUVWXY Z&(":.;"")?!*ᵃᵇc deffghijklmno pqrstuvwxyz$ 1234567890 ¢%$£%

Gill Sans Bold Extra Condensed
ABCDEFGHIJKLMNOPQR STUVWXYZ&(":.;"")?!*ab cdefghijklmnopqrstuv wxyz$1234567890¢%£%

GIORGIO ABCDE FGHIJ KLMN OPQRS TUVW XYZ& (".;"")?!.$1 23456 7890¢/ £%

Globe
Gothic Condensed
ABCDEFGHIJKLM
NOPQRSTUVWXY
Z&".;:;?!ābcdefghijkl
mnopqrstuvwxy
z$1234567890¢

Globe Gothic
ABCDEFG
HIJKLMNOPQ
RSTUVWXYZ&
';:;?! ābcdefghij
klmnopqrstuv
wxyz$123456
7890¢

Globe Gothic
ExtraBold AB
CDEFGHIJK
LMNOPQRS
TUVWXYZ&
(;:;:)?!ābcdee
fghijklmnop
qrstuvwxyz
$12345678
90¢ (SR)

188

Gorilla ABCD EFGHIJKL MMNOPQRR STThe UVWX YZ@(",:;"")?! [*]aabccdefff fiflffffffghhijk lmmnnopqrst tuuvwxyz$ 1234567890 ¢¢/$£%#

Goudy Oldstyle
ABCDEFGHIJ
KLMNOPQR
STUVWXYZ
&(.',:;"")?!*abcct
defffffflffiffiflghij
klmnopqrstuv
wxyz$1234567
890¢$%%

Goudy Oldstyle
Italic ABCDEF
GHIJKLMNO
PQRSTUVW
*XYZ&(",:;"")?!*ab*
cdefghijklmnopq
rstuvwxyz$1234
567890¢$£%

GoudyCatalog

ABCDEFGH
IJKLMNOPQ
RSTUVWX
YZ&(':,:;")?!.*ab
cdefffffffflfflg
hijklmnopqrs
tuvwxyz $1234
567890 ¢/£%

GoudyBold A

BCDEFGHIJ
KLMNOPQ
RSTUVWX
YZ&(':,:;")?!.*ab
cdefffffflffifflg
hijklmnopqrs
tuvwxyz$123
4567890¢%$£%%

GoudyBold
Italic ABCDEF

GHIJKLMN
OPQRSTUV
WXYZ&
(:,"*:,"≥!?)abc
defffffflffifflgh
ijklmnopqrstu
vwxyz$12345
67890¢£%$/¢¹²
34567890

GoudyExtra
BoldABCDE
FGHIJKLM
NOPQRST
UVWXYZ&
[':;:,)?!*abcdef
fffiffiflfflghij
klmnopqrstu
vwxyz$1234
567890¢/%o

GoudyBlack
ABCDEFG
HIJKLMN
OPQRSTU
VWXYZ&
[':;:,)?!ábcdef
fffiflghijklm
nopqrstuvw
xyz$12345
67890¢% (IB) (SR)

GoudyBlack
ItalicABCDE
FGHIJKLM
NOPQRSTU
VWXYZ&':;:
;?!ábcdefghij
klmnopqrstu
vwxyz$12345
67890 (IBſ (SR)

Goudy
Heavyface A A
BCDEFGH HIJ
KLMM NNOP
QRSSTTUUVV
WW XYYYZ&
(.,:;"")?!*abcdeffg
hhijkklmmnn
opqrrsstuvwx
yyz$1234567
890¢/$%«+»■□
® ■○

Goudy
Heavyface Italic
ABCCDEFGHI
JKLMMMNOP
PQRSTUUVV
WXYZ&[.,:;"]?!
*abcdefgghijkl
mnopqrstuvw
xyz$12345678
90¢¢/$%«®●□
»+○■

**Goudy Heavyface
Condensed AB
CDEFGHIJK
LMNOPQRST
UVWXYZ&
(';:,)?![-]abcdef
ghijklmnop
qrstuvwxyz
$1234567890//**

Goudy
Handtooled
ABCDEFGH
IJKLMNOP
QRSTUVW
XYZ&(',:;"")?!*
abcdefghijk
lmnopqrstuv
wxyz$12345
67890¢/$

*Goudy
Handtooled
ItalicABCDE
FGHIJKLMN
OPQRSTUV
WXYZ&&
[.,:;""]?!*abcde
fghijklmnopqr
stuvwxyz$$12
34567890
¢¢/%*•*

Goudy Cursive
ABCDEFG
HIJKLM
NOPQRS
TUVWXY
Z&(.,:;"")?!*~a
bcdefghijklmno
pqrstuvwxyz$12
34567890¢%$£%

GOUDY
ORNATE
ABCDEFG
HIJKLMN
OPQRSTU
VWXYZ&.,

Goudy Text AB
CDEFGHIJK
LMNOPQR
STUVWXY
Z&(.,:;"")?!~abcde
ffghijklmnopqrstuv
wxyz$1234567890¢£
¶/$%1234567890

Granby Light AÆ
BCÇDEFGHIJ
KLMNOŒPQ
RSTUVWXYZ&
(';.;'')?!*═aæbcçd
efghijklmnoœø
pqrstuvwxyzß$1
234567890
¢/£«⟨⟩»

GranbyAÆBC
ÇDEFGHIJKL
MNOŒPQRS
TUVWXYZ&
(';.;'')?![*═]aæbcç
defghijklmno
œøpqrstuvw
xyz$12345678
90¢/£«⟨⟩»¿¡

GranbyBold
ABCDEFGHIJ
KLMNOPQR
STUVWXYZ&
(',:;'')?!_abcdef
ghijklmnopq
rstuvwxyz$1
234567890¢¢
/$%+®■●

Granby Extra Bold ABCDEF GHIJKLMNOP QRSTUVWX YZ&(',:;‰)?!*a bcdefghijklm nopqrstuvwx yz$123456789 0¢$/¢%‡®

Granby Elephant A BCDEFGHI JKLMNOP QRSTUVW XYZ&ÆÇ Œ(';:;"‐"/!?) abcdefghiı jklmnopqr stuvwxyz$ ¢12345678 90æçøœß £¡¿ ⟨⟩¿

Granby Outline Shaded ABC DEFGHIJK LMNOPQR STUVWXY Z&(';:;‰)?! [-]abcdefg hijklmnop qrstuvwx yz$123456 7890/£

(CMM) (IB)

GRECIAN BOLD ABCD
EFGHIJKLMNOP
QRSTUVWXYZÆŒ
&.',:;?!·$1234567890 (IB)

Grizzly ABCD
EFGGHHIJJ
KKLMNOP
QQRSTUV
WWWXYZ
&(.',:;")?!*
aabbcdeefg
hijjkklmnopq
rssttuvwxyy
z$11223456
7890o¢°/s£% (IB)

Grotesque No. 9
Heavy ABCDEFG
HIJKLMNOPQR
STUVWXYZ&
(.',:;")?!abcdefg
hijklmnopqrst
uvwxyz$1234
567890¢°/s£f (IB) (SR)

GrouchABC
DEFGHIJK
KLM NNOP
QRRSTUV
WWXYZ&
(.,:;")?!*abc
defghijkkl
mnopqrstu
vvwwxyyz
$123456789
0¢¢/s£%

GUTZON
BORGLUM
ABCDEFGH
IJKLMNOP
QRSTUVW
XYZ&""'''?!
-$1234567
890¢ (WV)

Halbstarke Pica

ABCDEFGH
IJKLMNO
PQRSTUVW
XYZ&(.,:;"")?!
ābcdefghi
jklmnopqr
stuvwxyz
$123456789
0¢

Halftone

ABCDEFGH
IJKLMNOPQR
STUVWXY
Z&(",:;,)?!āb
cdefghijklm
nopqrstuvwx
yz$123456
7890 (WV)

Handel Gothic Light

ABCD
EFGHIJKL
MNOPQRST
UVWXYZÆ
ÇŒØ&(",:;,)?!
[*]abcçdefgh
ijklmnopqr
stuvwxyzæ
œøß$1234
567890¢
%®«»☼☾☽¿¡

HandelGothic
AÆBBCÇDEFGHIJ
KLMNOŒØPP
QQRRSSSTUVWW
XYZ&ℰℓ(.,:;)?![-]
aæbcçdeefghijklm
noœøpqrrsstu
vwxyzß$123456
7890¢₵/s%‰+«»di (IB)

Harlow ABC
DEFGHIJKL
MNOPQRSTU
VWXYZ&(.,:;)?!-
aæbcdefghi jklmnoøpqr
sßtuvwxyz$1234567
890¢£ .·. (WV)

Harper's Bazaar

A A A B B T C D E F F G G H H I I R R R L L M M O P Q Q R R Y S S T T T Th U

V V V W W X X Y Y Y Z Z Z & & &

?! a b c d e f f g g h h i j k k l m m n n o o p q r r s a t T t u v w x x y y y z z

HarryThin
ABCDEFGHIJKLMNOPQR
STUVWXYZ&(.,;"")?![*]
abcdefghijklmnopqrstu
vwxyzß$1234567890
¢⅝£%§t

HarryPlain

ABCDEFGHIJK
LMNOPQRS
TUVWXYZ&(',.;")
?!(*)abcdefg
hijklmnopqr
stuvwxyz$1234
567890¢⅜£%

HarryHeavy

ABCDEFGHIJK
LMNOPQRS
TUVWXYZ&
(',.;")?![*]abcd
efghijklmno
pqrsutvwxyzß
$1234567890
¢⅜£%§†

HarryFat

ABCDEFGHIJK
LMNOPQRS
TUVWXYZ&
(',.;")?![*]abc
defghijklmnop
qrstuvwxyzß
$1234567890
¢⅜£%§†

HarryObese
ABCDEFG
HIJKLMNO
PQRSTUV
WXYZ&
(',.;:;"")?!(*)a
bcdefghijk
lmnopqr
stuvwxyz
$12345678
90¢⅝£%

HarryObese
Squeezed
ABCDEFGHIJK
LMNOPQRS
TUVWXYZ&
(',.;:;"")?!(*)ab
cdefghijklm
nopqrstuvwx
yz$1234567
890¢⅝£%

HelveticaExtra
Light ABCD
EFGHIJKLMN
OPQRSTU
VWXYZ&(',.;:;"")?!*
abcdefghijkl
mnopqrstuvw
xyz$£123
4567890/¢%
$1234567890¢ (wv)

HelveticaLight
ABCDEFG
HIJKLMNOPQ
RSTUVWXY
Z&(.,;:;"")?![*]ab
cdefghijklmno
pqrstuvwx
yz$12345678
90¢%£%

Helvetica
ABCDEFGHIJ
KLMNOPQ
RSTUVWXYZ
&(.',:;")?![*]ab
cdefghijklmn
opqrstuvw
xyz$1234567
890¢%$£%

Helvetica
MediumAÆB
CÇDEFGHIJ
KLMNOŒØ
PQRSTUV
WXYZ&(.',:;')?!
ːæbcçdef
ghijklmnoœø
pqrstuvwxyz
$12345678
90¢/£%ːːː¿¡▪◻◼◻◼

**Helvetica
DemiAÆBC
ÇDEFGHIJ
KLMNOŒØP
QRSTUV
WXYZ&(';::)?!
[*]aæbcçd
efghijklmno
œøpqrstu
vwxyzß$123
4567890¢/£
%‰#»‹‚¹²~´¿i©†®●□**

**Helvetica
BoldABCDE
FGHIJKL
MNOPQRST
UVWXYZ
&(';::)?!*abc
defghijklm
nopqrstuv
wxyz$12
34567890¢
‰$£%‱**

**Helvetica
ExtraBold
Aa²ÆBCÇD
Ee²FGHIJ
KLMm²nn²
OŒØPQR
r²STUu²VW
XYZ&(';::)
?!*aæbcçde
fghijklmn
oœøpqrstuv
wxyzß$123
4567890
¢/%®©ªº‹‚¹i¡□●◘✕** (IB)

Helvetica Light
Italic ABCDEF
GHIJKLMNOP
QRSTUVW
XYZ&(";:;-*-!?)a
bcdefghijkl
mnopqrstuv
wxyz$123456
7890¢£%/

Helvetica Italic
ABCDEFG
HIJKLMNOP
QRSTUVW
XYZ&(.,.;")?!*
abcdefghij
klmnopqrstu
vwxyz$123
4567890¢/£%

Helvetica
Bold Com-
pact Italic
ABCDEFGH
IJKLMNO
PQRSTUV
WXYZ&
(";:;'")?!*[§†]
abcdefg
hijklmnop
qrstuvw
xyz$12345
67890¢$/¢
£%/1234567890

Helvetica Extrabold Extended
ABCDEF
GHIJKLM
NOPQRS
TUVWXY
Z&(",;;)?!
⚘abcdef
ghijklmn
opqrstuv
wxyz$12
345678
90¢¢%$£%

Helvetica Compressed
ABCDEFGHIJKL
MNOPQRSTU
VWXYZ&(",;;"")
?![∗]abcdefg
hijklmnopqrstu
vwxyz$12345
67890¢¢%$£%§†

Helvetica Extra Compressed ABC
DEFGHIJKLMNOPQ
RSTUVWXYZ&
(",;,")?! ⁼ [..§†]abc
defghijklmnopqrst
uvwxyz$1234567
890¢$¢£%0123456 7890

Helvetica Medium Outline

AÆB CÇDEFGH IJKLMNOŒ ØPQRSTU VWXYZ& (.,;:;""')?!*≟aæb cçdefghijk lmnoœøpqr stuvwxyz ß$12345678 90¢/%®©⬡≋∧≪ḉi

Helvetica BoldOutline

ABCDEFG HIJKLMNOP QRSTUVW XYZ&(.,;:;"')?! *≟abcdefgh ijklmnopqr stuvwxyz$1 234567890 ¢$/¢£%

Henrietta Medium

AÆBCÇDEF GHIJKKL₂ MNOØŒPQ RSTUVW XYZ&(.;"":;"*≟!?) aæbcçdef ghijkkl₂mm₂ nn₂oøœpq rstuvwxyz ß$123456 7890/¢£%®™ ©%℠™ ⚜«»$1234567890O¢

Henrietta Bold A Æ B C Ç D E F G H I J K L M N O Ø Œ P Q R S T U V W X Y Z &(.,""'.,""*‡!?) a æ b c ç d e f g h i j k l m n o ø œ p q r s t u v w x y z ß $1 2 3 4 5 6 7 8 9 0 / ¢ £ % ® © ™ ™ $1234567890¢

Henrietta Bold Condensed A Æ B C Ç D E F G H I J K L M N O Ø Œ P Q R S T U V W X Y Z & (.,""'.,""*‡!?) a æ b c ç d e f g h i j k l m n o ø œ p q r s t u v w x y z ß $1 2 3 4 5 6 7 8 9 0 ¢ / £ % © ® ™ ™ $1234567890¢

Hensby A B C D E F G H I J K L M N O P Q R S T U V W X Y Z &(.,""'.,""*)?!. a b c d e f g h i j k l m n o p q r s t u v w x y z $1234567890¢%

Herkules
ABCDEFGHIJ
KLMNOPQ
RSTTUVWXY
ZE&(',';:,)?!/.
abcdefghijkl
mnopqrst
uvwxyz$1234
567890¢$£ℓ

Herold Reklame
ABCDEFGHIJKLMN
OPQRSTUVWXYZ
&(',';:,)?!*abcdefghij
klmnopqrstuvw
xyz$1234567890₵
/%» (R)

Hobo
ABCDEFGHIJ
KLMNOPQR
STUVWXYZ&
(',';:,'';)?!*abc
defghijklmno
pqrstuvwx
yz$12345678
90¢%$£%

Hogarth

AABCDEEFG
HHIJKKLM
NOPQRRSTU
VWXYZ&and
◆·'.,;·?!·:·abcdef
ghijklmnop
qrstuvwxyz
$1234567890¢

Holland

AÆBCÇDE
FGHIJKLM
NOŒØPQRS
TUVWXYZ
&('.,:;"")?!?*=aæb
cçdefghijk
lmnoœøpqr
stuvwxyzß
$1234567890¢
¢/$£%‰©⊠●◼

Holland Medium AÆ

BCÇDEFG
HIJKLMNO
ŒØPQRS
TUVWXYZ
&('.,:;"")?!?*
aæbcçdefgh
ijklmnoœø
pqrstuvwxy
zß$123456
7890¢¢/$£%©®
¿¡¿⊠●◼

Holland Semi-Bold

AÆBC
ÇDEFGHIJK
LMNOŒØ
PQRSTUVW
XYZ&(".,:;")
?!?.aæbccde
fghijklm
noœøpqrstuv
wxyzß$12
34567890¢¢/s
£%°«»®°¿¡©¿¡⊠●■

Holland Bold

AÆBCÇ
DEFGHIJK
LMNOŒØP
QRSTUV
WXYZ&(".,:;")
?!?*aæbcc
defghijklmn
oœøpqrst
uvwxyzß$12
34567890¢
°/s£%°«»®°©¿¡⊠●■

Horley Oldstyle

ABCDEFGHI
JKLMNOP
QRSTUVWX
YZ&(".,:;)?!ābcd
efghijklmno
pqrstuvwxyzS
1234567890¢/£%

214

Horley Oldstyle
Medium
ABCDEFGH
IJKLMNO
PQRSTUV
WXYZ&(.",:;)
?!ābcdefghij
klmnopqrstuv
wxyz$12345
67890¢/£

Horley
Oldstyle Bold
ABCDEF
GHIJKLM
NOPQRS
TUVWXY
Z&(.",:;)?!āb
cdefghijklm
nopqrstuv
wxyz$123456
7890¢/£

Howland Open
ABCDEFGHIJK
LMNOOPQRST
UVWXYZ&
[*'""..'"!?]abcdefgh
ijklmnopqrstuv
wxyz$123456789
0¢%/£$1234567890¢%/£ (WV)

HUXLEY VERTICAL

A A B C D E F G H I J K

L M M N N O P Q R S T U V W W

X Y Y Z &.,.:.?!+

$1234567890 (WV)

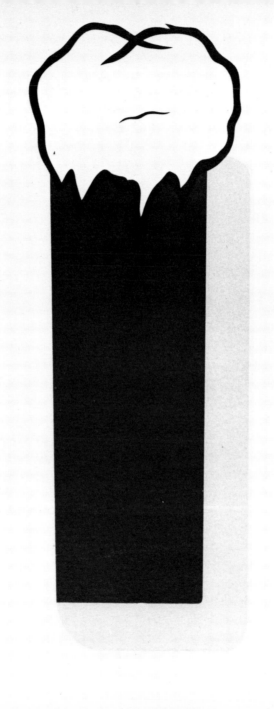

Impact
ABCDEFGHIJJK
LMNOPQRST
UVWXYZ&('.,.;")
?!*_abcdefg
hijklmnopqrr
stuvwxyz
$123456789
0¢¢/s£%

ImpactOpen
ABCDEFGHIJJK
LMNOPQRST
UVWXYZ&('.,.;")
?!*_abcdefg
hijklmnopqrr
stuvwxyz
$1234567890
¢¢/s£%

Imprint
AÆBCDEF
GHIJKLM
NOŒPQRS
TUVWX
YZ&('.,.;)?!_aæ
bcdeffifl ff
ffifflghijklmn
oœpqrstuv
wxyz$12345
67890¢/£

Imprint Bold

ABCDEF
GHIJKLMN
OPQRST
UVWXYZ
ÇØÆŒ&
(';:;"•"!?)abcde
ffffiflffiffl
ghijklmnopq
rstuvwxyz
ßçøæœ$1234
567890¢£%
¡¿≈∴/$¢ ™ ⓉⓂ ▼▲△◯□◆◀▶

INDEPENDENCE

INDEPENDENCE
ABCDEFGHIJK
LMNOPQRSTU
VWXYZ (IB) (WV)

INFORMAL GOTHIC

AaBCDEEFGHI
JKLMMNNOPQR
STUVWXYZ&
(\/\/\/)?!*_SI23456
7890c°/s%°

Informa-tionAB CDEFGHI JKLMN OPQRST UVWX YZ&("''""" .,:;""" ?![*]abc defghijk lmnopq rstuvwx yz$123 456789 0¢%$£%§†

Inserat Grotesk
ABCDEFGHIJKLMNOPQ
RSTUVWXYZ&(.',:,;''")?!
[*]abcdefghijklmnopqr
stuvwxyz$1234567890¢
£¢/$% 1234567890

(S)

Italia Book
ABCDEFGH
IJKLMNO
PQRSTUVW
XYZ&(.',:;_*_"!?)
abcdefghij
klmnopqrst
uvwxyz
$123456789
0¢£%#/
$1234567890¢

Italia Medium

ABCDEFG
HIJKLMNOP
QRSTUVW
XYZ&('.,:;"*-"!?)
abcdefghij
klmnopqrstu
vwxyz$12
34567890¢
£%#/
$1234567890¢

Italia Bold

ABCDEFGH
IJKLMNO
PQRSTUVW
XYZ&
('.,:;"*-"!?)abc
defghijkl
mnopqrstuv
wxyz$123
4567890¢£
%#/
$1234567890¢

IVY LEAGUE

ABCDEFGHIJKLM
NOPQRSTUVW
XYZ("!!)●♀&&$$1
234567890%%

IVY LEAGUE BOLD ABCDEF GHIJKLMN OPQRSTUVWX YZÇØÆŒ
[!,.:;=„!?]«*$123
4567890¢%
/£¡¿™®©®▲▼●○◆◀▶
$1234567890¢

IVY LEAGUE OPEN ABCDEF GHIJKLMN OPQRSTUVW XYZ!,?=123
4567890/

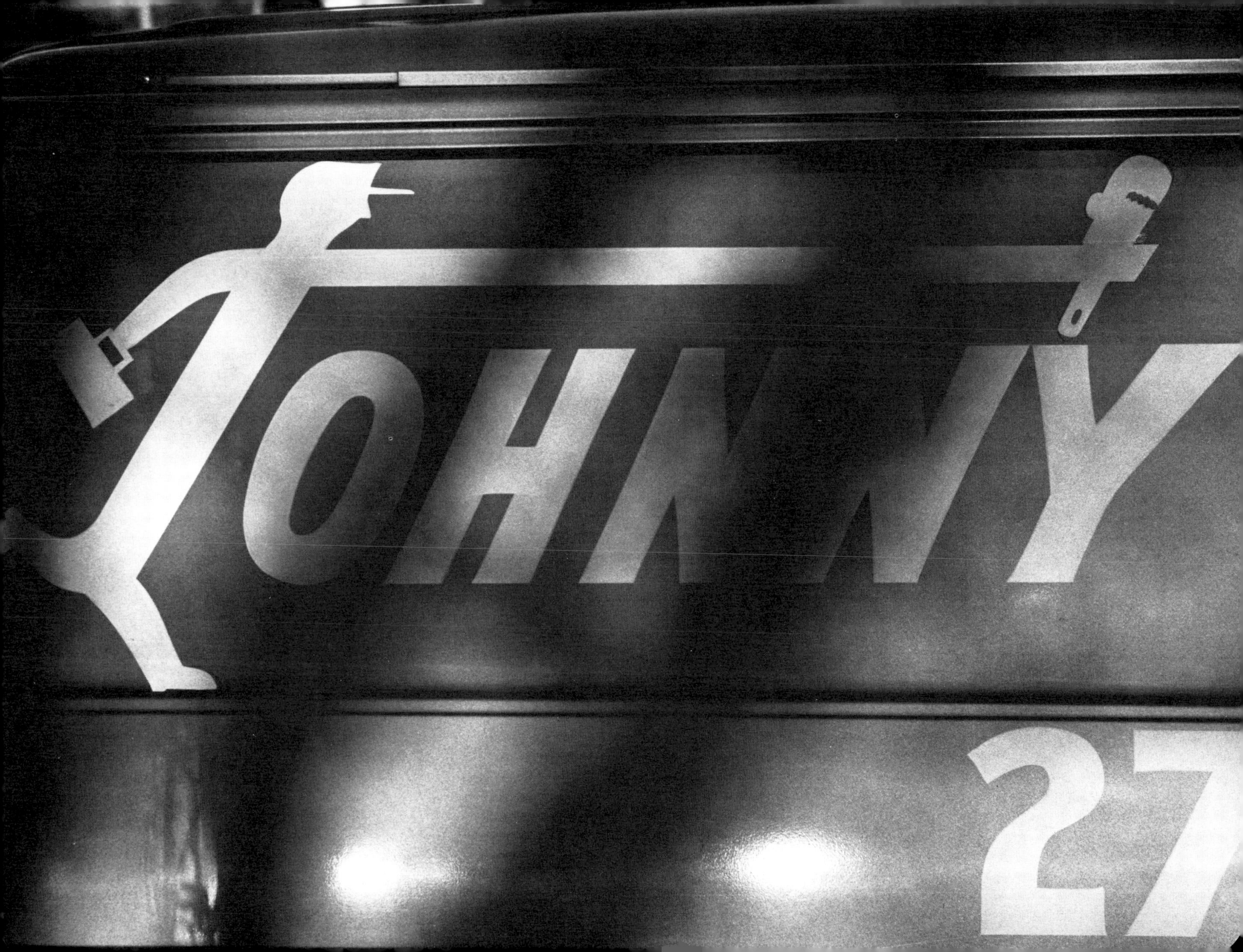
OHNNY
27

Jana ABCDEFGHIJ
KLMNOPQRSTU
VWXYZ&(.',.;;"")?!*a
bcdefghijklmnopq
rstuvwxyz$1234
567890¢⅓%‰

Janson ABCD
EFGHIJKLM
NOPQRSTU
VWXYZ&
(,".:;"-"!?)abcdeffffi
ffiflfflghijklmn
opqrstuvwxyz
$£1234567890
¢%/

Janson Italic ABC
DEFGHIJKL
MNOPQRST
UVWXYZ&
(.,".:;"-"!?)abcdeffffi
ffiflfflghijklmnop
qrstuvwxyz$£12
34567890¢%/

Japanette

JapanetteABCDE
FGHIJKLMNOP
QRSTUVWXYZ
&(',.:;«")?!*_abcdef
ghijklmnopqrstu
vwxyz$123456
7890¢/$£%%

Jay Gothic

Jay Gothic ABCDEF
GGHIJKLMNOPQRR
STUVWXYZ&(",.:;")?
!*_aáàbbcddefgggghij
jklmmnnoppqgrrst
tuuvwxyyz$12345
67890¢/£%

Jay Gothic Bold

Jay Gothic Bold AB
CDEFGGHIJKLMNO
PQRRSTUVWXYZ&
(",.:;")?!*_aaabbcdde
fgggghijjklmmnno
ppqgrrsttuuvwxy
yz$1234567890
¢$¢/s%o$/o

JayGothicOutlineA
BCDEFGGHIJKLMN
OPQRRSTUVWXYZ
&(",:;"")?![*]aaabbc
ddefgggghijjklmmn
noppqqrrsttuuvw
xyyz$1234567890
¢¢/$%

JensonOldstyle
ABCDEFGHIJ
KLMNOPQRS
TUVWXYZ&
(",:;)?!ābcdefghijkl
mnopqrstuvwx
yz$1234567890
¢/£

JensonABCD
EFGHIJKL
MNOPQRS
TUVWXYZ
&(",:;)?!*abcde
fghijklmnopq
rstuvwxyz$1
234567890¢/

Book Jenson Bold AÄÅÆB CÇDEFGHIJ KLMNOÖØ ŒPQRRST UVWXYZ&

[''!""‼°‥═˜˜~!?*]
[.,.:;;···——=·····]
[.,.;·,·;·]

aäåæbcçde
ffgghijklmn
oöøœpqrrsß
ttuvwxyyz$¢
%/1234567
890

Book Jenson ExtraBold A BCDEFGHIJ KLMNOPQ RSTUVWX YZÆÇØŒ&

(",.:;,")?!* abcde
fghijklmnop
qrstuvwxyz
æçøœß$1234
567890¢/£$
%══+®‹‹◊››❯●■□¡¿i

JensonCondensedAB CDEFGHIJKLMNOP QRSTUVWXYZ&

(.,:;)?!* abcdefghijkl
mnopqrstuvwxyz$
1234567890¢/(IB) (S)

228

JIMCROW ABCD
EFGHIJKLMNO
PQRSTUVWXY
Z&(',.:;")?!_$12
34567890¢/£
% (WV)

JOCUNDA AB
CDEFGHIJKL
MNOPQRSTU
VWXYZ ÆŒ
Ø&(':;.:;)?!*$12345
67890¢$/£%»»

Joric Ultra AAÆ
BBCCÇCDDEFGH
HIJJKLLMMNO
ŒOPPQRRSTUU
WWXYYZ&
(!.;:;")?!*:.aaaæ
bccçdeeeffghij
jklmmnoœopqr
rsttuvwwxyyz
ß$1234567890
¢//£°

ITC™ LICENSED **Kabel Book**
AÆBCÇDEFG
HIJKLMNO
ŒEØPQRSTU
VWXYZ&&
(',.;")?![*]aæb
cçdefghij
klmnoœøpqr
stuvwxyzß
$1234567890
¢$/£%˘˙´»«#

ITC™ LICENSED **Kabel Medium**
ABCDEFGHIJK
LMNOPQRS
TUVWXYZÆÇ
ŒEØ&&(',.;")?!
[*]abcdefghijk
lmnopqrstuv
wxyzæçoeøß
$1234567890
¢$/£%˘˙´»«#

ITC™ LICENSED **Kabel Demi**
ABCDEFGHIJ
KLMNOPQRS
TUVWXYZÆ
ÇŒEØ&&(',.;")
?![*]abcdefgh
ijklmnopqrst
uvwxyzæçoe
øß$12345678
90¢$/£%˘˙´»«#

KabelBoldAB CDEFGHIJKL MNOPQRST UVWXYZÆÇ ŒØ&&(',.:;"")? ![*]abcdefgh ijklmnopqrst uvwxyzæçœ øß$12345678 90¢$/£%⁙⁘#

KabelUltra ABCDEFGHIJ KLMNOPQR STUVWXYZ ÆÇŒØ&& (',.:;"")?![*]ab cdefghijkl mnopqrstuv wxyzæçœ øß$1234567 890¢$/£%⁙⁘#

Kabel OutlineABC DEFGHIJKLM NOPQRSTUV WXYZÆÇŒØ &&(',.:;"")?[*]ab cdefghijklmn opqrstuvwx yzæçœøß$1 234567890 ¢$/£%⁙⁘#

Kabel Light AÆBC
DEFGHIJKLMN
OŒPQRSTUV
WXYZ&(',;;")?![*]
aæbcdefghijklmno
œpqrstuvwxyzß$
1123456789O
¢$/£%

Kabel Medium
ABCDEFGHIJK
LMNOPQRSTU
VWXYZ&(',;:;')?!
*abcdeffffiflghijklm
nopqrstuvwxyz$
1234567890¢
¢⁄$£%

Kabel Bold ABCD
EFGHIJKLMN
OPQRSTUV
WXYZ&(',:;")?!
[*]abcchdefghijkl
mnopqrstuvw
xyz$1234567890
¢$/£%»

Kabel Heavy A
ÆBCDEFGHI
JKLMNOPQR
STUVWXYZ&
(‚'‚;:‚;"")?![‡]aæ
bcdefghijklm
noøpqrstu
vwxyzß$1234
567890¢
c/s£%°§†

Kabel Black
Modern ABC
DEFGHIJKLM
NOPQRSTU
VWXYZÆŒ
Ø&(‚'‚;:‚;"")?!
[‡]abcdefgh
ijklmnopqr
stuvwxyz
æœøß$1234
567890¢s/c£%
ü

Kabel Bold
Condensed A ÆBCD
EFGHIJKLMNOPQR
STUVWX
YZ&(‚'‚;:‚;"")?![‡]aæb
cdefghijklmnoøpqr
stuvwxyzß$1234
567890¢/s £%°§†

Kabel Shaded

A ÆB CÇD E F
G H I J K L M
N O Ø Œ P Q R
S Ş T U V W X
Y Z & & ('*;:'"")
·-?!¿¡ a æ b
c ç d e f g h i j
k l m n o ø œ p
q r s ş ß t u v w x
y z $ $ 1 2 3 4
5 6 7 8 9 0 ¢ ¢ / %
‡·¿·¿¿··‐ ¡ £

1234567890 (WV) (CMM)

KANTANAKA

RÆDABCDEF
GHIJKEELMN
OPQRRSTU
VWXYZE
(;:;#!?)?!*$¶12
3456789
&¢% (WV) (S)

Kap Antiqua

Bold ABC
DEFGHIJ
KLMNOPQ
RSTUVW
XYZ&
(.:;:;!?)[*;]ab
cdefghij
klmnopqr
stuvwxy
z$£123456
7890C%$¢
1234567890 (SR)

**KarnakBlack
Condensed ABCD
EFGHIJKLMNOP
QRSTUVWXYZ&
(",:;")?!*- abcdefg
hijklmnopqrstu
vwxyz$12345678
90¢%$%£§†**
1234567890

*KaufmanScript
ABCDEFGHIJ
KLMNOPQRST
UVWXYZ&.,:;"?!
ābcdefghijklm
nopqrstuvwxyz
$1234567890¢¢/$£*

*KaufmanBold
ABCDEFGHIJ
KLMNOP2RS
TUVWXYZ
&.,:;"?!ābcdefgh
ijklmnopqrs
tuvwxyz$1234
567890¢¢/$%£%*

Kismet ABC
DEFGHIJKL
MNOPQRS
TUVWXYZ&
·°'":;·°·?!abcdefg
hhijklmmnno
pqrstuvwxy
z$1234567890¢

Koloss
ABBCDDEF
GHIJKKKL
MNOPPQR
RRSTUVWX
YZÆÇŒOø&
(,;:;")¶!
°aabbcdde
fgghijklm
noppqqrst
uvwxyzæç
œø$123456
7890¢%«~» (R)

Kompakt A
BCDEFG
HIJKLMN
OPQRSTU
VWXYZ&
(,;:;!¡)?!*abcd
effffifl ghij
klmnopqr
stuvwxyz$
1234567
890¢/%

Korinna ABCD
EFGHIJKLM
NOPQRST
UUVWXYZ&
(',.:;"̈)?![*]abccde
efghijjklmno
pqrsstuvwxyz
$$$123456789
0¢¢'$$$/¢¢£%#@

Korinna
Bold ABCDEF
GHIJKLMNOP
QRSTUUVW
XYZ&(',.:;"̈)?!
[*]abccdeefghi
jjklmnopqr
sstuvwxyz$$
$12345678
90¢¢'$$$/¢¢%#@

Korinna Extra
Bold ABCDE
FGHIJKLM
NOPQRSTU
UVWXYZ&
(',.:;"̈)?![*]abcc
deefghijjkl
mnopqrsstu
vwxyz$$$1
234567890
¢¢'$$$/¢¢£%#@

Korinna Heavy ABC DEFGHIJ KLMNOPQ RSTUUVW XYZ&(',.:;'') ?![*]abccde effighij jklmnopqr sstuvwxyz $$$123456 7890¢¢$$$/£ %#@

Korinna Outline ABC DEFGHIJKL MNOPQRS TUUVWXYZ &ØÇÆŒ& (',.:;'')?![*]abc cdeefghij jklmnopqrs stuvwxyzæ æçøoeœß$ $$12345678 90¢¢/£%... †@

*Korinna KursivABC DEFGHIJ KLMNOPQ RSTUUVW XYZ&(',.:;"") !?*abcde fghijklmnop qrstuvw xyz$123456 7890¢/%£#@ $1234567890¢*

Korinna
Kursiv Bold
ABCDEFGH
IJKLMNOP
QRSTUUV
WXYZ&
(',.:;")!?*abcd
efghijklmno
pqrstuvwxy
z$1234567
890¢/%£@
#$1234567890¢

Korinna
Kursiv Extra
Bold ABCD
EFGHIJKL
MNOPQR
STUUVWX
YZ&(',.:;")!?*
abcdefghijk
lmnopqrstu
vwxyz
$12345678
90¢/%£@#
$1234567890¢

Korinna
Kursiv
Heavy ABC
DEFGHIJ
KLMNOPQ
RSTUUV
WXYZ&
(',.:;")?!·ab
cdefghij
klmnopqr
stuvwxyz
$123456
7890¢/%£@
#$1234567890¢

KubraABCD
EFGHIJKKL
MNOPQRR
STUVWXYZ
&abcdefghijk
klmnopqrst
uvwxyz$1234
567890

L&C Hairline A ÆBB₂
CDEFGHIJJKLMM₂
NOØPQRSTUV₂
WW₂XYZ&&₂₃-(""",;;""")
?₂?!₂!(*)a a₂b b₂c d d₂
e e₂f ff ff ff₂ ff₃ ff₄ ff₅ ff ff₂ fl fl₃ ffl ffl₄ ft t
g g₂h h₂i i j j₃k k₂k k₃k kll₂l m n o ø
p p₂q q g r r₂s s t t u u₂v w w₂
x y y₂y₃y₄z ß ß₂ $ $ 1 2 3 4
4₂ 5 6 7 8 9 0 0₁ 1 2 3 4
5 6 7 8 9 0 ¢ ¢ ¢/ ¢ $/$ £ % %
⌣⌣⌣∘ ⁵ ¶ § † ‡ # @ ⊕ ♭ ℞ ¶ # (WV)

L.E.O.
ABCDEFGHIJK
LMNOPQRS
TUVWHYZ.ŒÆ
Œ ŒC,;;;«»!?]§|
234567890¢/
£¹ ™ ⓉⓂ ●◑○ ◆◩■□
ⒸⓇ ▲◭◢ ●∙■

Laertes ÆB
CDŒFGHI
JKL MRO
PQRSTU
VWXY
ZŒC""";,,?!
abcdefghijkl
mnopqrstuv
wxyz$1234
567890¢%$£ᴱ (R)

Lafayette ABCDEFGH
IJKLMMNOPQRSTU
VWWXYZ&(",.;")
?!@abcdefghijklmn
opqrstuvwxyz$123
4567890¢%£%

LARGO
LIGHT ABC
DEFGHIJKL
MNOPQRS
TUVWXY
Z&(",.;")?!*£$1
234567890
¢%$%£1234567890

Lariat ABCDEFY
HIJKLMNOP
QRSTUVWXYZ
&(",.;")?!"abcdefgh
ijklmnopqrstu
vwxyz$12345
67890¢%£%% (WV)

244

LeGriffe AAAA

BBCDDEEFFGGHIJJ

KKLLMMNNOPPQQRRSST

TUVWXYZÆ(.,;:'*""-!?)aabbccdd

eeeffgggghhiiijjkkkllmmm

nnnoppqqqrrrsssst

tttuuuvvwwxxxyyzz

$1234567890¢£%¢/$1234567890

Lee

ABCDEFGHIJ
KLMNOPQ
RSTUVWXYZ&
(.,:;?")?!*abcde
fghijklmnop
qrstuvwxyz$
1234567890
¢ç/£%?

LETTRES
ORNEES
ABCDEFG
HIJKLMN
OPQRSTU
VWXYZ.,::
?!1234556
7890 (WV)

LifeAntiquaBold

ABCDEFGH
IJKLMNOPQ
RSTUVWXY
Z&(.,:;,")?!ābcd
efghijklmnop
qrstuvwxyz$1
234567890/

LightlineGothic
ABCDEFGHIJKL
MNOPQRSTUVW
XYZ&(',:;"')?!*abcdef
ghijklmnopqrstu
vwxyz$123456
7890¢$/£%

LINCOLN
GOTHIC
ABCDEFGH
IJKLMNOPQ
RRSTUVWX
YZ&(',:;"')?!*_$12
34567890¢¢/%®+

LuciferNo.1
ABCDEFGH
IJKLMNOP
QRSTUVW
XYZ&("':..;)?!
ābcdefghijk
lmnopqrst
uvwxyz$1
234567890
¢/£ (R)

Lubalin Graph X-Light

AAABCCⒶⒸDEEAFFA
GGⒼHHITIJKKAALAIA
MⓂMMMNNTOPRR
QRRASSSSTTHUUUVV
VWVWWXYZ&(',;;")?!
*abcdeeffffifl ffi fflghij
klmnopqrsttuvvv
wvwwxyyyz$12345
67890O¢¢/$%£# (WV)

Lubalin Graph Book

AAABCCⒶⒸDEEAFFA
GGⒼHHITIJKKAALAIA
MⓂMMMNNTOPRRQR
RASSSSTTHUUUVVW
WVWWXYZ&(',;;")?!*
abcdeeffffifl ffi fflghijk
lmnopqrsttuvvv
wvwwxyyyz$123456
7890O¢¢/$%£#

248

ITC LICENSED Lubalin Graph

Medium AAABCCACC
DEEAFFFAGGGGHHHIIJ
KKALLAMMMMNNT
OPRQRRRASSSSTUUT
VVVWWWXYZ&
(",.;")?!*abcdeefffffifl
ffifflghijklmnopqrstt
uvvVWWWwxyyz$l
234567890¢¢%£#

ITC LICENSED Lubalin Graph

Demi AAABCCACD
EEAFFFAGGGHHHTIJK
KALLAMMMMMNNT
OPQRRRASSSSTTHU
UTVVVWWWWXYZ
&(",.;")?!*abcdeeffffi
flffifflghijklmnopq
rstluvvvWWWWxyy
z$l234567890¢¢%£
#

LubalinGraph
Bold AAABCCAECDE
FFAGGHHTIJKKAL
MMMNOPQRRRASSS
STTHUVVVWW
WXYZ&(",;;")?!(*-)a
bcdeefffffifflffifflgh
ijklmnopqrstluvv
vwwwxyyz$1234
567890¢¢/₅%£#

Lubalin
Graph Demi Outline
AAABCCAECDEEAF
FAGGGAHHTIJKKAL
LAIAIMMMMMNNIOP
QRRASSSSTTHUUV
VVWWNWXYZÆÇØ
OE&(",;,;")?!(*-)abcdee
fffffiffifflfflfllghijklmnop
qrstluvVVWWWWWXYY
zæçøoe$12345
67890O¢/%£

Lys Calligraph
A ABCDE
FGHIJKL
MNOPQ
RSTTU
VWXYZ&
(""")?!ābcdeff g
hijklmnopgr
ssstuvwxyz§
1234567890¢

Macbeth AAaaÆ

BCCDEE FGHIJKL

LMMMMNNNOŒ

OPQRRRRSTUVW

XYZ&(.,;;;)?![*]a

æbccdefghfiijkk

lmnoœopqrrsttu

vwxyzß$123456

7890¢/®%°⌀≈»«+¿¡

MACHINE ABCDE

FGHIJJKLMNOPQ

RSTUVWXYZ&

(.,;;")?!*$12345

67890¢¢¢/$£%#

MACHINE BOLD AB

CDEFGHIJJKLMNO

PQRSTUVWXYZ&

(.,;;")?!*$12345

67890¢¢¢/$£%#

MADISON AABB
CCDDEEFGGHIIJ
KLMMNNOOOP
PQRRSSTTUUV
VWXYYZ&"'::.,:!!

(WV) (R)

Madisonian
ABCDEFG
HIJKLM
NOPQRS
TUVWXY
Z&(;:;)?!*abcd
efghijklmno
pqrsstuvwx
yz$12345678
90¢/£% (R)

Manchester
BoldABCDEFG
HIJKKLMNOP
QRSTUVWXY
Z&(';:;)?!*a
bcdeffgghij
jklmnopqrr
sttuvwxyz
$123456789
0¢%$% (IB)

254

MANDARIN
ABCDEFGHIJ
KLMNOPQRS
TUVWXYZ&
(.,:,;"")?!*/-

Mandate AB
CDEFGHIJK
LMNOPQR
STUVWXYZ
&(",:,;"")?![±]abc
defghijklmn
oonoforpqrst
uvwxyz$12
34567890¢$/£

ITC™ LICENSED

Manhattan
ABBCDEFG
HIJKLM
NOPQRS
SSTUVWXY
Z&(:::::"")?![❀]
aabcdeeff
fiflffffiffflghijk
lmnopqr
ssstuvwxyz
$1234567
890¢/&%#

(WV)

Manuscript Initials

A ABCDEFG
hIJKK L
MNOPQ QU
RR ST THU
VWXYZ&
(:)—.!?

Marbleheart

MARBLEHEART
ABCDEFGHIJK
LMNOPQRSTUV
WXYZ&(',.:;"")?!$
1234567890£
¢%/ 1234567890 (WV)

Marten Roman

Marten
RomanABC
CDEFGHIJK
LMNOPQRS
TUVWXYZ
&(',.:;)?!*abc
defftghiijkk
lmnopqrst
uvvwwxxy
yzzß$12345
67890
¢s$/£%

Mastodon AB CÇDEFGHIJ KLMNOŒØ PQRSTUVW XYZ&(‘.,:::)?!⁎ **aæbcçdefgg hijklmno œøpqrstuvw xyzß$12345 67890 ¢ᶜ%ₛ£** %⚇⟫⟪●■ ⚇⟫⟪●□ (S)

Maxie Lined ABCDEFGHIJ KLMNOPQ RSTUVWXYZÆ Œ&(‘.,:·) abcdefghi jklmnopqrstuvwxy zæœ$12345 67890¢% (WV)

Melior ABCD EFGHIJKLM NOPQRSTU VWXYZ& (‘.,;,'')?!⁎abcdefff fiflghijklmno pqrstuvwxyz $1234567890¢ ᶜ%£%£/%

**Melior
Semi-Bold AB
CDEFGHIJK
LMNOPQRS
TUVWXYZ&
(.,:;"")?!*_abcdef
fffiflghijklmn
opqrstuvw
xyz$123456
7890¢/$£%**

Melior Bold
Outline ABC
DEFGHIJKL
MNOPQRST
UVWXYZ&
(.,:;"")?!÷=abcd
efghijklmno
pqrstuvwxy
z$123456789
0¢/$%£*ₔ
1234567890 (wv)

MICHELANGELO
ABCDEFGHIJ
KKLMNOPQ
QRRSSTUV
WXYZ&(.,:;"")?!
*=$1234567890
¢$%£%

258

MICRO-GRAMMA BOLDABCDE FGHIJKLM NOPQRSTU VWXYZ& (.,:;"")?!*-[]$ 1234567890 ¢°/$£°lo«»§†

$1234567890¢

MICRO-GRAMMA EXTEND-ED ABCDE FGHIJKL MNOPQR STUVW XYZ&(.,:;")
?!*$12345 67890¢
¢/$£°lo
1234567890

MICRO-GRAMMA BOLD EX-TENDED ABCDE FGHIJKL MNOPQ RSTUV WXYZ& (.,:;")?!*$1 23456 7890¢¢/$ £°lo

1234567890 (IB) (S)

MilanoRoman

A ÆBCDEF
GHIJJKLM
NOŒØPQR
STUVWXYZ
&(:,;:?!)[*]aæ
bcdefffffiffiflffl
ftghijjklmn
oœøpqrrst
uvwxyzß$1
234567890¢
/£%#❄❅❆❈❉.❋ⅎ℔@

Mistral ABCDEF

GHIJKLMNOPQ
RSTUVWXYZ&
(:,;:")?!_* abcdefgh
ijkllmnoonpq
qursttuvwxyz
$1234567890¢
¢/$£%

Modern No.20

ABCDEFG
HIJKLMN
OPQRSTUV
WXYZ&(:,;:;")
?![*]abcdefffffifl
ffifflghijklmn
opqrstuvwxy
z$1234567890
¢/£%

**Modernique
ABCDEFGH
IJKLMNOP
QRSTUVW
XYZ&(.,:;'!)
?!![=]abcdef
ghijklmno
pqrstuvwx
yz$123456
7890¢$$** (IB) (R)

Modernique
Outline ABC
DEFGHIJK
LMNOØPQ
RSSTUVW
XYZ&&
(.,:;'!)?!*□abc
defghijklm
noøpqrstu
vwxyyz$ß$$
12345678
90¢/£%

*Moonshadow
ABCDEF9H
IJKLMNOP
QRSTUVWX
YZ&(.,:;'!)?!
abcdefghijk
lmnopqrstu
vwxyz$12345
67890$* (WV)

MOORE COMPUTER

MOORE
COMPUTER ABC
DEFGHIJKLMN
OPQRSTUVWXY
Z&(',:;")?![⚐]$
12345678
90¢/£%⚏

MOORE LIBERTY

MOORELIBERTY
ABCDEFGHIJKL
MNOPQRS
TUVWXYZ&[',;;"]?!
⚎$1234567890
¢¢%s% (IB) (WV)

Musketeer Light

Musketeer Light
AAAABCDE
FGHHIJKLM
MMNOPQRS
TUVVWXYZ
&ÇØÆŒ
(‘‘.;:"*!?)abcdefg
hijklmnopqrst
uvwxyzßçøæ
œi¿⚜$12345
67890¢£%©™
$1234567890¢

Musketeer
Regular A A A A A
BCDEFGHHI
JKLMMMN
OPQRSTUV
VWXYZ&ÇØ
ÆŒ(.,;:*!?)ab
cdefghijklmn
opqrstuvwxyz
ßçøæœi¿«»$1
234567890
¢£%©®™™/$12345678
90¢

Musketeer
Demi-Bold A A
A A BCDEFG
HHIJKLMM
MNOPQRST
UVVWXYZ
ÇØÆŒ&
(.,;:*!?)abcdefg
hijklmnopqr
stuvwxyzßço
æœi¿«»$123
456789
0¢£%©®™™/$12345
67890¢

Musketeer
Bold A A A A
BCDEFGH
HIJKLMM
MNOPQRS
TUVVWXY
Z&ÇØÆŒ
(.,;:*!?)abcde
fghijklmno
pqrstuvwxy
zßçøæœi¿
«»$1234567
890¢£%©®™™/$1
234567890¢

Musketeer Extra Bold

AA₂³A⁴ABCD
EFGHHₐ²HIJK
LMM₂³MNO
PQRSTUV
V²WXYZ&Ç
ØÆŒ(.,:;*!?)
abcdefghij
klmnopqrs
tuvwxyzßçø
æœ¿¡«»$123
4567890¢£
%

NATIONAL
SPIRITAABC
DEEFGHIIJ
KLLMNNOOP
QRRSSTTU
VWXYZ&'',;;
?!-123456
7890 (WV) (S)

NeilBold ABC
DEFGHIJKLM
NOPQRSTUV
WXYZ&(:::")
?!*abcdefghi
jklmnopqrst
uvwxyz
$123456789
0¢/£%

NeilBoldOpen
ABCDEFGHIJ
KLMNOPQR
STUVWXYZ&
(:::")?!*abc
defghijklmno
pqrstuvwxyz
$123456789
0¢/$£%° (WV)

NEON

NEON ABCDE
FGHIJKLMN
OPQRSTUV
WXYZ&("")
?!¦*$12345678
90¢⅝$£%# (WV)

Neptune

Neptune AÆBC
CDEFGHIJKL
MNOŒØPQR
STUVWXYZ&
(',.:;)?!—*æbcçde
fghijklmnoœøpqr
stuvwxyzß$123
4567890¢/%®
¿¡ (S)

Neuland

NEULANDA
BCDEFGHIJK
LMNOPQRS
TUVWXYZ
&(',;;'")?!([-])$1
234567890¢
⅝£%+«»†§
★ (IB)

268

NEULAND
BLACK ABC
DEFGHIJKL
MNOPQRS
TUVWXY
Z&(',.;:'"*'")
[!--◆?]$£¢
%1234567
890/$¢

News Gothic ABC
DEFGHIJKLMN
OPQRSTUVWXY
Z&(',.;:'"")?!*abcdefg
hijklmnopqrstuv
wxyz$12345678
90¢%‰£

News Gothic
Bold ABCDEFG
HIJKLMNOPQR
STUVWXYZ&
(',.;:'"")?!*abcdefg
hijklmnopqrstu
vwxyz$123456
7890¢%$‰£ (SR)

NewsGothicExtraCondensed
ABCDEFGHIJKLMNOPQRSTUV
WXYZ&(',.;:"")?!*abcdefghijklm
nopqrstuvwxyz$1234567890¢
%/£

Newtext
Book AaaB
CDEeFGHI
JKLMMN
NOPQRST
UVWWX
YZ&(',.;:;")?!
_*abcdeff
fiflftffifflg
ghijjklmno
ppqqrstuv
wxyyyyz@
$12345678
90¢$¢%£#

Newtext
Regular Aa
BCDEeFG
HIJKLMM
NNOPQRS
TUVWWX
YZ&(',.;:;")?!
*abcdefffi
flffifflftggh
ijjklmnopp
qqrstuvw
xyyyyz@
$12345678
90¢$¢%£#

270

Newtext Demi

AaBCDEeFGH
IJKLMMNNOP
QRSTUVWWX
YZ&(.":.;,")?
!=*abcdefffififlft
ffifflgghijjklmno
ppqqrstuvwx
yyyyz@$12345
67890¢$⊄%£#12
34567890

Newtext Regular Italic

AaBCDEe
FGHIJKLMM
NNOPQRSTUV
WWXYZ&(.',.;,")
?!*aabcdefffifl
ftffifflgghijjjklm
noppqqrstuvw
xyyyyz$12345
67890¢$%£#

Nova Augustea

ABCDEFGHIJ
KLMNOPQ
RSTUVWX
YZ&⁊(.,:;/X∴)9!
[⸎]abcdefffgh
ijklmnopqrst
uvwxyz$1234
567890¢%$%£

Novel Gothic

A ÆBCÇDE
FGHIJKLMN
OŒØPQRS
TUVWXYZ
&ß['.,:;'‹]?!¡a
æbcçdefghïj
klmnoœøpqr
stuvwxyz$1
23456789
0¢%$%º ¿i+«»□■

272

OCTIC EXTENDED

AABBCCD
DEEEFFGG
HIIIJKLL
MMMNN
OOOPPQR
RSSTTTTU
UVVVVWW
XXYYZ&&
(.,;:)!!_$III223
344556677
889900

Octopuss

ABCDEFGHIJKLM
NOPQQuRS
TUVWXYZ&(',.:;"?)?!
ābcdefghijklmn
opqrstuvwxyz$12
34567890£ (WV)

OLD GLORY

ABCDEFGHIJKL
MNOPQRS
TUVWXYZ&":;
.,-!?$12
34567890

OldGothic
BoldItalic

ABCDEFGHI
JKLMNOP
QRSTUVW
XYZ&(""';:;'""')
?![*]abcde
fffffflghijk
lmnopqrstu
vwxyz$12
34567890¢
¢/$£%œøßſt

Old Hebrew

1	2	2A	3	4	5
א	ב	בּ	ג	ד	ה

6	6OH	6U	7	8	9
ו	וֹ	וּ	ז	ח	ט

10	11	11A	11F	11F ALT	12
י	כ	כּ	ך	ךּ	ל

12 ALT	13	13F	14	4F	14F ALT
ל	מ	ם	נ	ן	ן

15	16	17	17A	17F	17F ALT
ס	ע	פ	פּ	ף	ף

18	18F	18F ALT	19	19 ALT	20
צ	ץ	ץ	ק	ק	ר

21	21SH	21S	22	22A	
ש	שׁ	שׂ	ת	תּ	

AW	AH	AY	EH	EE	OO	SCHWA	AW BRF	AH BRF	EH BRF

( ) ✡ Ⓤ ••• """ ✦ :-;,.!?

$1234567890

Olden

ABCDEFGH
IJKLMNO
PQRSTUVWX
YZ&(.,'::;''!)?!⚥å*
bcdefghijk
lmnopqrstu
vwxyz$12345
67890¢°/$£%

Olive Antique

ABCDEFGHIJKL
MNOPQRSTU
VWXYZ&(',:;'')?!
[±]abcdefghij
klmnopqrs
tuvwxyz$I12
34567890¢
°/$£%

Olive Antique Medium

AB
CDEFGHIJKL
MNOPQRS
TUVWXYZ&
(;:;'')?![±]ab
cdefghijklm
nopqrstu
vwxyz$I123
4567890¢
°/$£%

Olive Antique Bold
ABCDEFGHI
JKLMNOPQR
STUVWXY
Z&(",:;")?![*]a
bcdefghijkl
mnopqrst
uvwxyz$l12
34567890
¢%$£%

Olive Antique Black ABCD
EFGHIJKL
MNOPQRS
TUVWXYZ&
(,:;")?!*ab
cdefghijk
lmnopqrst
uvwxyz
$12345678
90¢%$£%

Olive Antique Narrow
ABCDEFGHIJKLM
NOPQRSTUVW
XYZ&(",:;")?![*]ab
cdefghijklmnopq
rstuvwxyz$l12
34567890¢%$£%

OLYMPIA

AABCDEEFFGH
IiJKLMMNNO
PQRSTUVUWX
YZ&(",=")?!*
$123456789
0¢%£ (S)

Onyx

ABCDEFGHIJKLMNOP
QRSTUVWXYZ&
(.,:;"")?!*abcdefghijkl
mnopqrstuvw
xyz$1234567890¢/%£

Optima

ABCDEFGHIJKL
MNOPQRST
UVWXYZ&(.,:;"")
?!*abcdefghijkl
mnopqrstuv
wxyz$1234567
890¢%$£%

Optima Semi-Bold

ABCDEFGHIJ
KLMNOPQ
RSTUVWXY
Z&(',:;«)?!*abc
defghijklm
nopqrstuvw
xyz$1234567
890¢$/%£

OptimaBold

ABCDEFGHI
JKLMNOP
QRSTUVW
XYZ&(',:;«)?!
*abcdefgh
ijklmnopqr
stuvwxyz$1
234567890
¢%$£%

Optima Italic

ABCDEFGHIJKL
MNOPQRST
UVWXYZ&(',:;«)
?!*abcdefffifl
ghijklmnopqrst
uvwxyz$123
4567890¢%/s£

Othello

ABCDEFGHIJKL
MNOPQRSTU
VWXYZÆŒÇØ
abcdefghij=Ii?[×·]*
klmnopqrstuv
wxyzæœçøß$!
1234567890¢$% (s)

ORPLID

ABCDEFGHIJ
KLMNOPQRS
TUVWWXY
123$£¡¿(.':*)!?,;:= &Z
4567890% (w)

ORLEANS OPEN

ABCDEFGH
IJKLMNOPQR
STUVWXY
12$£]:,;:[&Z
34567890¢/£ (w)

OthelloOutline

ABCDEFGHIJKL
MNOPQRSTU
VWXYZ&(";:,)?!
ābcdefghijk
lmnopqrstuvw
xyzß$12345
67890¢%./⠿ (S)

P.T. Barnum ABCD
EFGHIJKLMNOP
QRSTUVWXYZ&
(".,;;;"")?! [*]abcdeffffi
flffifflghijklmnop
qrstuvwxyz$1234
567890¢%$£%

Packard ABCÇ
DEFGHIJKLM
NOPQRST
UVWXYZÆ
ŒØ&(".,.;÷!?)abc
çdefghijklmnop
qrstuvwxyzæœø
ſ£12345678qo¢
%//®©

Paddington
AÆBCÇD
EFGHIJKLM
MNNOØ
ŒPQRSTU
VWXYZ&
(.,:;!?)aæb
cçdefghijk
lmnoœøpqr
sßtuvwx
yz$1234567
890¢£«»~

PAGEANT INITALS (WV)

PalatinoRoman
ABCDEFGHI
JKLMNOPQ
QuRSTUVW
XYZ&(.,:;")?!.*ab
cdefffffifflghij
klmnopqrstuv
wxyz$1234567
890¢%$£%

**Palatino
Semi-Bold ABC
DEFGHIJKL
MNOPQRS
TUVWXYZ
&(.,:;")?!.*abcde
fghijklmnopq
rstuvwxyz$12
34567890¢%$£
%**

Palatino Bold (Soft Serif) A BCDEFGHIJ KLMNOPQ RSTUVWX YZ&(.,:;")?!*a bcdefghijklm nopqrst uvwxyz$12 34567890¢¢/$ £%

Palatino Bold (Hard Serif) A BCDEFGHIJ KLMNOPQ RSTUVW XYZÆÇŒØ& (.,:;")?!*abcdef fffifghijklm nopqrstuvwx yzæçœøß$12 34567890¢¢/$ %

Palatino Italic ABC DEFGHIJKL MNOPQRST UVWXYZ& (.,:;")?!*abcdeefgh ijklmnopqrstuvw xyz$1234567890 ¢¢/$£%

Palatino Cursive

A A B B C D D E
E F F G G H H I J J
K K L L M M N
N O P P Q Q R R S
S T T Th U V V W
W X Y Z Z & &
(',.;;'')?!*abcdee fghij
kklmnopqrstuvwx
yzz $1234567890¢
¢/$%o£ ©®

PALISADES GRAPHIC

A B C D E F G
H I J K L M N
O P Q R S T U
V W X Y Z &
(',.;;¨)?!*‥**$12
34567890
¢/£ø (IB) (R)

Pamela

A B C D E
F G H I J K L M N
O P Q R S T U V W
X Y Z & (',.;;)?! a b
c d e f g h i j k l m n o p q
r s t u v w x y z
$1234567890¢

(WV)

288

Paprika

PaprikaAA
BCDEFGHHIJ
KKLLMMNN
OPQRRST
UUVVWWX
YYZ&(,°°°,")?!*
abcdefghhi
jkklmmnno
pqrsstuvw
wxyz$12345
67890¢%

Parisian

Parisian
ABCDEFGHI
JKLMNOPQ
RSTUVWX
YZ&(.,:;"")?!*abcd
efghijklmnopqrstuv
wxyz$123456789
0¢∫$£%

Park Avenue

Park Avenue
ABCDEFG
HIJKLMN
OPQRST
UVWXYZ&
(.,:;)?!*abcdeeres
fghijklmnopqrrsstu
vwxyz$12345678
90¢%$£/%

Parsons AAABBCC
DDEEFFJGGHH
IJ JKKLLMMM
NNOPPQQRRSS
TTUUUVVWXY
YYZ&[';:;]?!¡abbcddef
gghhijjkkllmnoppqr
sttuvwxyz
$$1234567890¢/

ParsonsBold AAAB
BCCDDEEFFJG
GHHIJ JKKLLM
MMNNOPPQQ
RRSTTUUVVWX
YYZ[';:;]?!¡abbcddef
gghhijjkkllmnoppqq
rsttuvwxyz
$$1234567890¢/

Parsons Heavy ABCD EFGHIJKLM NOPQRSTUV WXYZ&[',.:;''] ?!*÷·abcdefg hijklmnopq rstuvwxyz$ 1234567890 ¢£%/# $1234567890¢

Patriot ABCDE FGHIJKLMNO PQRSTUVW XYZ&(.,:;'')?!* abcdefghijkl mnopqrstuvw xyz$1234567 890¢£%

PATTERNAB CDEFGHIJ KLMNOPQ RSTUVWX YZ&.,:; (',.'') ?!$123456 7890¢%£ (WV) (IB)

PEIGNOT LIGHT AB
CDEFGHIJKLM
NOPQRSTUV
WXYZ&(.,:;")?!*Ab
cdefghijklmnopqr
stuvwx yz$123456
7890¢%

PEIGNOT DEMI-
BOLD ABCDEF
GHIJKLMNO
PQRSTUVWX
YZ&".,:;«?![-]Ab
cdefghijklmn
opqrstuvwxyz$
1234567890¢/£
%

PEIGNOT BOLD
ABCDEFGHI
JKLMNOPQR
STUVWXYZ&
(.,:;«)?!*abcdef
ghijklmnopqrs
tuvwxyz£1234
567890¢/%£

Pekin ABCDEFG
HIJKLMNOPQR
STUVWXYZ,.;:
;?!*_abcdefghijk
lmnopqrstuvwxy
z$1234567890

PERGOLA ABC
DEFGHIJKLM
NOPQRSTUV
WXYZ&",;:;?!- (WV)

Permanent Headline ABC
DEFGHIJKLMNOPQRST
UVWXYZ&(.,::") ?!± abcd
efgghijjklmnoppqqrstuv
wxyyz&$123456789
0c¢%/s£ %»»«§t. (IB)

Permanent Massiv ABCDEFG HIJKLMNOPQR STUVWXYZÆÇŒ Ø&(".,:;"")?![*]abc defgghijjklmnop pqqrstuvwxyyz æçœ œøßS12345 67890¢°/s£ %₀☼+»«¿¡

Permanent Headline Open A Æ B C Ç D E F G H I J K L MNOŒØPQRSTUVWXY Z&(".,:;)?!*_aɑæbcçdefgg hijjklmnoœøppqɑrstuv wxyyzß§1234567890°/ %₀‹☼›®+¿¡

PERPETUA TITLING LIGHT ABCD EFGHIJKLMN OPQRSTUV WXYZ&(".,:;"") ?!*_$123456789 0¢$%¢£%

Perpetua Roman
ABCDEFGHI
JKLMNOPQ
RSTUVWX
YZ&(.,:;‘?’)?!*_ab
cdefffffiflffiffig
hijklmnopqrst
uvwxyz$12345
67890¢$%¢£%

Perpetua Bold
ABCDEFGH
IJKLMNOP
QRSTUUV
WXYZ&(.,:;‘?’)
?!*_abcdefffffl
fiflffighijkl
mnopqrstuv
wxyz$12345
67890¢%$%

Perpetua
Extra Bold
ABCDEFG
HIJKLMN
OPQRSTU
UVWXYZ&
(.,:;‘?’)?!*_abc
defghijklm
nopqrstuv
wxyz$12345
67890¢$%¢£%

Perpetua
Black ABC
DEFGHIJK
LMNOPQR
STUUVWX
YZ&(.,;:;"")[⚹]
abcdefffifl g
hijklmnop
qrstuvwxy
z$li2345
67890o¢£
%»»«‹+●□©®

Perpetua Italic A
BCDEFGHIJK
LMNOPQRST
UVWXYZ&
(.,;:;'')?!*_abcdef
ffffiflffiffifl ghijkl
mnopqrstuv
wxyz$12345678
90¢$¢£%

Perpetua
Bold Italic AB
CDEFGHIJ
KLMNOPQ
RSTUVWX
YZ&(.,;:;'')?!*_
abcdefffffifl
ffifflghijklm
nopqrstuvw
xyz$1234567
890¢$¢£%

PerpetuaBold
Shaded ABCD
EFGHIJKL
MNOPQRS
TUUVWXY
Z&(.,;:%)?!*_
abcdefghij
klmnopqrs
tuvwxyz$
12345678
90¢/% (CMM)

PHOTOMANIA
NO.2ABCDE
FGHIJKLMN
OPQRSTUVW
XYZÆÇŒ&Ð&
[(.,;:)?!*$
1234567890¢
/£%¤®»«+&7

ITC LICENSED PIONEER
AA2B3BCDEFG
HH2IiJJKK2
LMM2M3NNÑ3OP
QQ2RR2fSTT2
UUWXYY2ZÆÇ
ŒØ&(",,")
7!2$123
4567890¢//
%#£ (WV)

Pistilli Roman

ABCDEFG
HIJKLMNO
PQRSTUV
WXYZ&&2
(.,:;'''"")?!* abcde
ff ffl ffi fi fl ft fy g h
i j j2 k l m n o p q r s
t u v w x y z @
lb $ 1 2 3 4 5 6 7 8
9 0 ¢ / $ £ % 1/2 1/3 1/4
1/5 1/8 2/3 3/4 3/8 5/8 7/8 (WV)

Pistilli Roman Open No.1

A
BCDEFGHI
JKLMNO
PQRSTUVW
XYZ&&2
(.,:;'''"")?!* abc
def ff ffl ffi fi fl ft fy
ffi g h i j j2 k
lmnopqrstuv
wxyz
$1234567890
1234567890
£ ¢ / $ % ¢ @ lb (WV)

Pistilli Roman Open No.2

A B
CDEFGHIJK
LMNOPQ
RSTUVWXY
Z&&2(.,:;'''"")
?!* abcdef ff fi fl
ft ffl ffi fy g h i j j2
klmnop
qrstuvwxyz
$1234567890
1234567890
£ $/¢ % ¢ @ lb

Placard Bold Condensed ABCDEF GHIJKLMMNOPQRS TUVWXYZ&(.,':;"")?! [⁂]aåbcdefghijkl mnopqrstuvwxyz$ 1234567890¢%$£%

(IB) (R)

Plantin Light AB CDEFGHIJK LMNOPQRS TUVWXYZ& ("",':;"")?![⁂]abcdef fffiflffffifflghijkl mnopqrstuvwx yz$1234567890¢ ¢/$£%

Plantin ABCDE FGHIJKLM NOPQRSTU VWXYZ&(',':;) ?![⁂]abcdeffffifl ffifflghijklmno pqrstuvwxyzß $1234567890¢¢/$ £%

Plantin Bold
ABCDEFGH
IJKLMNOP
QRSTUVW
XYZ&(";.;"";)?!
[⁑]abcdeffffi
flffifflghijklm
nopqrstuvwx
yz$1234567890
¢ᶜ/$$£%

Plantin Bold
Condensed ABCD
EFGHIJKLMNO
PQRSTUVWXY
ZÆŒØ&(";.:)?!⁑a
bcdefghijklmno
pqrstuvwxyzæœ
çøß$123456789
0œ/£%⁂×¿¡ (IB)

Plantin Bold
Condensed Outline
ABCDEFGHIJKL
MNOPQRSTUV
WXYZ&(';..;"/&)?!⁑a
bcdefghijklmnop
qrstuvwxyz$123
4567890¢ᶜ/$£% (WV)

300

Playbill ABCDEFGH
IJKLMNOPQRSTUVWX
YZ&(.,:;'"")?!.*abcdefg
hijklmnopqrstuvwx
yz$1234567890c%£%

Plymouth
AABBCC
DDEEFF
GGHIIJK
LLMMNN
OOPPQRR
SSTTUUV
VWWXXY
YZZ@.,;:;?!_
abcdefghij
klmnopqr
stuvwxyz$
123456789
0

PoorRichard AB
CDEFGHI JKL
MNOPQRSTU
VWXYZÆÇØ
ŒƐ(.',;:;'"")?!*ăbcd
efghijklmnopqr
stuvwxyzæçøœ
ß$1234567890
¢/$%🙂⚏⚎ (R)

Post Condensed

ABCDEFGHIJK
LMNOPQRSTU
VWXYZ&[",:;"]
?!⹀aabcdefgg₂
hijklmnopqr
stuvwxyz123
4567890

Post Old Style Roman No. 2

ABCDEFG
HIJKLMN
OPQRSTU
VWXYZ&
(",:;")?!*⹀aabc₂
defghijklm
nnopqrstu₂
uvwxyz$12₂
34567890¢$⁒
£% (R)

Post Old Style Italic

ABCDE
FGHIJKLM
NOPQRSTU
VWXYZ&
(",:;")?!⹀abcde
fffififlflflftghijkl₂
mnopqrstuvw
xyz$12345678
90¢$⁒£% (R)

**Pretoria AB
CDEFGHIJ
KLMNOPQ
RSTUVWX
YZ&!.,:;?!ābc
defghijklm
nopqrstuvw
xyz$12345
67890** (IB)

PRISMA
ABCDEFGHIJ
KLMNOPQR
STUVWXYZ&
(‚-)?!*:\$12345
67890¢¢/%% (WV)

PRISMANIA G
AABCCDEEFF
GGHIJKKLL
MMNNOPQ
QRRSTUVW
WXXYYZ&(‚:;)
?!_\$123456789
0¢%\$ (IB) (S) (R)

PRISMANIA K
AABCCDEEFF
GGHIJKKLL
MMNNOPQ
QRRSTUVW
WXXYYZ&
C::)?!-$123456
7890¢%¢ (IB) (S) (R)

PUBLICITY
GOTHIC AB
CDEFGHIJKL
MNOPQRR
SSSTTUVW
XYZC°&
(,:;()?!▾$12
34567890¢/£
%□▪▪▪◢

N.W. Q ST.

QUENTIN
ABCDEFGHIJK
LMNOPQR
STUVWXYZ&
(.,:;")?!_"$123
4567890¢/£% (WV)

ITC™ LICENSED Quorum Light
ABCDEFG
HIJKLMNOPQ
RSTUVW
XYZ&(.,:; * ”!?)
abcdefffg
hijklmnopqrs
tuvwxyztb
$123456789
0£¢%/#@

ITC™ LICENSED Quorum
Book ABCDE
FGHIJKL
MNOPQRST
UVWXYZ
&(.,:; * ”!?)ab
cdefffghij
klmnopqrst
uvwxyz
tb$1234567
890£¢%/#@

ITC LICENSED Quorum
Medium ABC
DEFGHIJ
KLMNOPQR
STUVWX
YZ&(".,:;*.*"!?)
abcdefff
ghijklmnopqr
stuvwxyz
ﬄﬅ$1234567
890£¢%
/#@

ITC LICENSED Quorum
Bold ABCDE
FGHIJKL
MNOPQRST
UVWXYZ
&(".,:;*.*"!?)ab
cdefffgh
ijklmnopqr
stuvwxyz
ﬄﬅ$1234567
890£
¢%/#@

ITC LICENSED Quorum
Black ABCD
EFGHIJ
KLMNOPQ
RSTU
VWXYZ&
(".,:;*.*"!?)
abcdefffgh
ijklmno
pqrstuvwx
yzﬄﬅ$12
34567890
£¢%/@

RADIANT
ANTIQUE AB
CDEFGHIJK
LMNOPQRS
TUVWXYZ&
:;,;-$1234567
890 (WV)

RAILROAD GOTHIC
ABCDEFGHIJKLMN
OPQRSTUVWXYZ
&(':,:;'')?!⁎$12345
67890£/% (IB)

Raleigh Extra
Light ABCDE
FGHIJKLMN
OPQRSTTU
VWXYZÇØ
ÆŒ&(':";:,⁎!?)a
bcdeffghijk
lmnopqrstuv
wxyzßçøæœ
¿»⚭$123456789
0¢£%©™®™/

Raleigh Light

ABCDEFGHI
JKLMNOPQ
RSTT²UVW̃
XYZÇØÆŒ
&(‚‘‛‚‛;!?)abcd
efſghi꜠jklm
nopqrstuvw
xyzßçøæœi꜠
»⸚⸪$1234567890
¢£%©™/$123456789
0¢

Raleigh Medium

ABC
DEFGHIJKLL²
LMNOPQRS
TT²ThT̃hŨVW
XYZÆŒÇØ
&(‚‘‛;;)?!⸚abcdeff
ghi꜠jklmnop
qrstuvwxyz
æçœøß$123456
7890¢⅜£%£©+
⊠¿¡▪□●

Raleigh Demi–Bold

ABCDE
FGHIJKLMN
OPQRSTTU
VWXYZÇØ
ÆŒ&(‚‘‛;;‛⸚!?)
abcdefſghi꜠
jklmnopqrst
uvwxyzßçø
æœi꜠»⸚⸪$12
34567890¢£%©
®
™/$1234567890¢

Raleigh Bold
ABCDEFGH
IJKLMNOP
ORSTTUVW
XYZÇØÆŒ
&(.,;"""¿!?)abc
deffghijk
lmnopqrstu
vwxyzßçøæ
œi¿«»$12
34567890¢£%
©™®™/$1234567890¢

Raleigh Extra
Bold ABCDE
FGHIJKLM
NOPQRSST
TThUVWXY
ZÆÇŒØ&
(.,;"""¿!?)abcd
effghijkl
mnopqrstu
vwxyzßçøæ
œi¿«»$12
34567890¢£
%©™®™/$1234567890¢

Raleigh
OutlineABC
DEFGHIJK
LMNOPQR
STUVWXYZ
ÇØÆŒ&
(.,;"""¿!?)abcd
efghijklmn
opqrstuvwx
yzßçøæœi¿
$1234567890
«»¢£%©™®™/
$1234567890¢ (WV)

Raleigh Contour AB CDEFGHIJ KLMNOPQ RSSTTThU VWXYZ ÇØÆOE & (‚';,;"⁙*!?)a bcdefſghi jklmnopqr stuvwxyzß çøæœi¿⁙⁙$1 234567890¢ £%©®™™/

Raleigh Shaded ABCD EFGHIJKL MNOPQRST UVWXYŽÇ ØÆOE & (‚';,;"⁙*!?)abc defghijkl mnopqrst uvwxyzßÇØ æœi¿⁙⁙$12 34567890¢/£ %©® $123456789 0¢

Rebecca ABC DEFGHIJ KLMNOP QRSTUVW XYZ&(.,.:;"?).?!_aa bbbscoddeeffgghhi ijjkkllmmmmmnnn noocosoppqrrrrss ssssttuuuuvvvvsw wwwwsxyyyz12345 67890½£% (WV)

RELIEF ABCDEF
GHIJKLMNOPQ
RSTUVWXYZ&
(.,-;:)?!£.*$123
4567890¢
¢/$£%

Reubens Wide
ABCDEFGHIJKL
MNOPQRSTUV
WXYZ&(.',:;¿?)?![*]
abcdefghijklmn
opqrstuvwxyyz
$1234567890¢/$c
%+«
®»

Revue AABC
DDEEFFGH
HIJJKLMMNN
OOPQRRSST
UVWXXYYZ
ÆŒØTH&
(.,:;«)?!=abcd
efghijklmno
pqrstuvwxyz
œœøß$12345
67890¢/$£%
»«či (IB)

Revue Extra Bold AABCÇ

DEEFFGHHIiJ
JKLMMNNO
OPQRRSSTU
VWXXYYZÆ
ÇŒØ&(".;::)?!⚹
abcdefghij
klmnopqqrst
uvwxyzœçœ
øß$12345678
90¢$%¢£⁰%⁰ᵉ⁰%·:·⟩⟩® (IB)(S)

RhythmicShaded

ABCDEFGHI
JKLMNOP
QRSTUVWX
YZ&.,!!''''
‹‹abcdefgh
ijklmnopqr
stuvwxyz¶†‡
12345678
90¢/% (CMM)

RIBONETTE

ABCDEFGHI
JKLMNOPQ
RSTUVWXY
Z&.,:;:''''!
?:—$123
4567890¢
ℋℐℋ (WV)

Richmond Old Style ABCÇD EFGHIJKLM MNOŒPQ RSTUUVW XYZÆŒØ &(.,"'";")abcçdef fiflffffiffflghijkl mnopqrstuvw xyzæœøßct $1234567890 ¢/%£/!¡?¿.:˙˙˘˚« »

$1234567890

Richmond Old Style Bold AB CÇDEFGHI JKLMNOP QRSTUVW XYZÆŒØ &(.,"'";")!?abc çdeffiflffffifflg hijklmnopqr stuvwxyzæœ øßct$123456 7890¢/%£¼½ ¾/¿¡˙.:˙˚«»ℓ

$1234567890¢©®

Richmond Old Style HeavyABCÇ DEFGHIJK LMMNOPQ RSTUUVW XYZ&ÆŒØ (.,"'";")!?abcçd efghijklmnop qrstuvwxyzß æœø$123456 7890¢/%£$1 234567890¢¡¿.:˙˚˘ »˚„«

Richmond Old Style Italic A₂A
B₂BCÇDEℰ
FGG₂HH₂HIJℱ
KLℒ₂MNOOℴ
PQRSTℒ₂UV
WXYZÆŒØ
Qu&(',;;"")!?abc
çdeffifl ff ffiffl
ghijkkℓ₂mnopq
rstuvwxyzæœ
øß$123456789
0¢/%£$1234567
890¢©®*⁎✓˘«»❀¡¿

Richmond Old Style
Condensed ABCÇ
DEFGHIJKLMM₂
NOOPQRSTUU₂
VWXYZÆŒØ&
(',;;")!?abcçdeffifl ff
ffifflghijklmnopqr
stuvwxyzæœøß
$1234567890¢
/%£$1234567890¢©®
*⁎✓˘«»¡¿

Richmond
Bold Condensed
ABCDEFGHIJ
KLMM₂NOPQR
STUUVWXYZ
&(',;;)?!ābcdefghi
jklmnopqrstuvw
xyz$1234567890
¢/£$¢

318

ROCKOPERA

ABCDEFGHI
JKLMNOP
QRSTUVWX
YZ&(".:,;)?!=$
1234567890
ŒŁ (WV)

Rockwell Light

AÆBCÇDEF
GHIJKLMNO
ŒØPQRSTU
VWXYZ&
(',:;"")?!*aæbcç
defghijklmno
œøpqrstuvw
xyzß$123456
7890¢¢/$
£%®©+«»¿¡

Rockwell Medium ABC

DEFGHIJKL
MNOPQRST
UVWXYZ&
(",:;)?!āabcdefgh
ijklmnopqrst
uvwxyz$1234
567890¢£®⊠●■□

Rockwell Bold

ABCDEFGH
IJKLMNOP
QRSTUVW
XYZÆÇŒØ
&(',:;!?)?!+*a
bcdefghijkl
mnopqrstuv
wxyzæçœø
ß$123456789
0¢⅝$%£
1234567890

Rockwell Extra Bold

ABCDEFGH
IJKLMNOP
QRSTUVW
XYZÆÇŒØ
&(',:;!?)?!+*
abcdefgh
ijklmnopq
rstuvwxyz
æçœøß$12
34567890¢
⅝$%£1234567890

ROCO

ABCDEFGH
IJKLMN
OPQRSTU
VWXYZ
(:::::) PISS123
4567
890£¥

Rococo ABCD
EFGHIJKLMN
OPQRSTUVW
XYZÆŒ&.,:;"!!*
ABCDEFGHIJKLM
NOPQRSTU
VWXYZÆŒ$1.1
2233445566778
8990o¢%$£%

Rodeo
ABCDEFG
HIJKLMN
OPQRSTU
VWXYZÆ
ÇŒŒ(".,:;)?!!*
abcdefghij
klmnopqrst
uvwxyzæç
œøß$12345
67890¢
/°/oo✿®+»«‹‹¿¡

Roman Compressed
No.3 ABCDEFGHIJ
KLMNOPQRSTUV
WXYZ&(.,:;;")?![:*]
abcdefffffifflffighij
klmnopqrstuvxw
xyz$123456789
0¢$%£1234567890

RomanaNormal

ABCÇDEFGH
IJKLMNOPQ
RSTUVWXY
Z&(';:;")?![*]aæ
bcçdefghijklmn
oœpqrstuvwxy
z$12345
67890¢$/℘%⚹†§

RomanaBold

ABCÇDEFGH
IJKLMNOP
QRSTUVWX
YZ&(';:;")?![*]
aæbcçdefghij
klmnoœpqrst
uvwxyz$1234
567890¢$/℘%⚹§

(IB)

RomanaUltra

ABCDEFGHI
JKLMNOPQ
RSTUVW
XYZÆCŒØ&
(';:;")?![*]abcd
efghijklmnop
qrstuvwxyzæç
œøß$1234567
890¢/$%⚹»«+
¿¡:■□○

Romany Roundhand

ABCDEFGHIJ
KLMNOPQRS
TUVWXYZ&
(.,:;?!*.)abcde
fghijklmnopq
rstuvwxyz
$$123456789
0¢%/$12345678
90¢

ITC LICENSED Ronda Light

AABCDEFGHIJK
KLMMNOPQQ
RSSTUVWXYZ&
&(".,:;")?![*]aabcc
deefffififtffifflgg
hijkklmnopqrrss
ttuvwxyzct$1'12
234567890o
¢/£%#@

ITC LICENSED Ronda

AABCDEFGHIJ
KKLMMNOPQ
QRSSTUVWX
YZ&&(".,:;")?![*]
aabccdeefffifl
ftffifflgghijjkklm
nopqrrssttuvw
xyyzct$1'12234
567890o¢/£%
#@

Ronda Bold

AABCDEFGHIJK
KLMMNOPQ
QRSSTUVWXY
Z&&-(',;:;'')?![*]
aabccdeefffffl
ftffifflgghijjkk
lmnopqrrsstt
uvwxyyzct$
1122334567890
o¢/£%#@

Roslyn Gothic Medium

RoslynGothic
MediumABCDEF
GHIJKLMNOPQ
RSTUVWXYZ&[',;:;'']
?!*abcdefghijklm
nopqrstuvwxyz$l
234567890¢¢/$£%

Roslyn Gothic Bold

RoslynGothic
BoldABCDEFG
HIJKLMNOPQR
STUVWXYZ&
[',;:;'']?!*abcdefgh
ijklmnopqrst
uvwxyz$1234
567890¢¢/$£%

RUSTIC
ABCDEFGHIJK
LMNOPQRST
UVWXYZ&
(';:;)!?"$123
4567890£/* (WV)

Rustikalis
Modernized
Gothic ABCDE
FGHIJKLMN
OPQRSTUVW
XYZ&(∴∗?!)
abcdefghijkl
mnopqrstu
vwxyz
$£12345678
90¢%/$12345678
90¢

Sabon Roman

ABCDEFGHI
JKLMNOPQ
RSTUVWX
YZ&(',.:;"")?!*
abcdeffifghijk
lmnopqrstuv
wxyz$1234567
890¢¢%$£•12345
67890

Sabon Bold

ABCDEFGH
IJKLMNOP
QRSTUVW
XYZ&(',.:;"")
?!*abcdeffiflg
hijklmnopqr
stuvwxyz$12
34567890¢¢%
$£#1234567890

Sabon Italic

ABCDEFGH
IJKLMNOP
QRSTUVWX
YZ&(',.:;"")?!*
abcdeffiflghijk
lmnopqrstuv
wxyz$123456
7890¢¢%$£#
1234567890

St.Clair

ABCDEFGHI
KLMNOPQRST
UVWXYZ&(";:)
?!abcdefghijk
lmnopqrstuvwxy
z$1234567890¢ (WV)

SANS SERIF CONDENSED NO.1

ABCDEFGHIJ
KLMNOPQRSTU
VWXYZ&
(";:,"-".!?)[§†*«»]
$1234567890
£¢%/
$1234567890¢

Sans Serif Condensed Italic

ABCDEFGHIJKL
MNOPQRSTUVW
XYZ&(";:,"!?)abcd
effiflff ffiffflghijkl
mnopqrstuv
wxyz$12345678
90¢%/
$1234567890¢%/

SANS SERIF ELONGATED
ABCDEFGHIJKLMN O PQRSTUVWXYZ&
(¡;,!;"""?) $1234567890¢ %/£ (IB)

SANS SERIF SHADED
AÆBCDEFG HIJKLMNOP QRSTUVWXY Z&(.',:;"")?!:$ 1234567890 ¢/£% (WV)

Schadow Antiqua Semi-Bold
ABCDE FGHIJKLM NOPQRSTU VWXYZÇŒ &(',:;"")?!.*
abcdefghijk lmnopqrstu vwxyzæçœ $1234567890 ¢$%%£«»

Schadow Antiqua Bold ABCDE FGHIJKL MNOPQR STUVWXY ZÆCŒ& (‚'‚:;'"")?!∗⁎abc defffghijkl mnopqrst uvwxyzç$ 1234567890¢ ‰$£%∴»

SCOT GOTHIC
ABCDEFGHIJKLM
NOPQRSTUVWXY
Z&ÆŒ(⋮.,.;!?)$1234
567890£¢/ (WV)

SCOTFORD
UNCIAL
ABCDEFG
HIJKLMNO
PQRSTUV
WXYZ&
(⋮⋮⋮)?!∗$
123456789
OC¢‰%£
1234567890

Serif Gothic Light

ABCDEEFGH
IJKLLMNOPQ
RSTUVWXYZ
ÆÆÇØŒŒ
ß&(',;;)?![*]aab
cdeefffffflfifl
ghijklmnopq
rrssttuvwxy
zzœœçøœœ
$12345678
8900¢/£%#

Serif Gothic

AÆÆBCÇDE
EFGHIJKLLMN
OŒŒØPQR
STUVWXYZ&
(',;;)?![*]aaœ
œbcçde effflfi
ffflghijkklmn
oœœøpqrrsst
tuvwxyzzß$
1234567890
O¢/£%#

Serif Gothic Bold

AÆÆBCÇDE
EFGHIJKLLMN
OŒŒØPQR
STUVWXYZ&
(',;;)?![*]aaœ
œbcçdeeffffl
ffiffifflghijkklm
noœœøpqrr
ssttuvwxyzz
ß$12345678
900¢/£%#

Serif Gothic
Extra Bold A A
BCDEEFGHIJKL
LMMNNOPQ
RSTUVVWW
XYZÆÆÇØ
ŒOEß&('.,:;"")
?![*]aabcdeeff
ffffififfiffiflghijkkl
mnopqrrsʃttu
vvwwxyzzœ
æœæçøœœœ$
11234456788
900¢/£%❖#»

Serif Gothic
Heavy A A B C D
EEFGHIJKLL
MMNNOPQR
STUVVWW
XYZÆÇŒOE
ØB&('.,:;"")?![*]
aabcdeeffffffi
ffflfiflghijkklm
nopqrrsʃttu
vvwwxyzzœ
æœæçøœœøø$1
1234456788
900¢/£%❖#»

Serif Gothic
Black ABCDE
EFGHIJKLLM
NOPQRSTU
VWXYZÆ
ÆÇŒOEŒøß&
('.,:;"")?![*]aa
bcdeeffffffiffl
fiflghijkklmn
opqrrsʃttuv
wxyzzœæ
æœæçøœœø$1
2345678890
0¢/£%❖#»

ITC™ LICENSED

SerifGothic
BoldOutline
ABCDEFGHI
JKLLMNOPQ
RSTUVWXYZ
&(·:'̈"')?!(*)[]a
àbcdeeffghijk
klmnopqrrsst
tuvwxyzz$1
234567889
OO0¢/$£% (WV)

ITC™ LICENSED

SerifGothic
OpenBold
AABCDEEFG
HIJKLLMMNN
OPQRSTUV
VWWXYZC
&(·:'̈"')(?!)[]
aabcdeeffffi
flffifflghijkklm
nopqrrssttu
vwxyzz$11
23445678
900¢$/¢£%

ITC™ LICENSED

SerifGothicBoldShaded
AA²ÆÆBCÇDEEF
GHIJKLLMMNNÑOE
ŒØPQRSTUV
VWWXYZ&('·:'̈")
?![(*)]aaæ æœ
æbcçdeefffmm̃
flghijkklmnoøœ
œpqrrssttuvv
wwxyzzß$1123
4456788900¢
/£%#"!'«» (IB) (CMM) (WV)

Serpentine
Bold Italic
ABCDE
FGHIJKLM
NOPQR
STUVWX
YZ&(.,:;"/)!
?!*abcd
efghijklm
nopqrs
tuvwxyz
$1234
567890¢
$/¢%£

SHOTGUN
AAABBCCD
EEFFGG
HHIiJJKELM
MMNNOP
QRRSTTUUV
VWWXXAY
YZZ&6(.,:;"%)
?!!$11238
4456778890
¢¢¢%£%/

SHOTGUN
BLANKS
AAABBCCD
EEFFGG
HHIiJJKELM
MMNNOP
QRRSTTUUV
VWWXXAYY
ZZ&6(.,:;"%)?!
!$11238 34
456778890¢
¢¢%£% (WV)

334

Siegfried ABCDEFG
HIJKLMNOPQRSTU
VWXYZÆÇŒ&(',:;)
?!*abcdcħ
defħřfghijklmnop
qrsfuvwxyzæçœøß$1
234567890¢/$%
☙☙☞®¿¡

SILVER DOLLAR
ABCDEFGHIJK
LMNOPQRST
UVWXYZ&
(',:;""!?*)12345
67890$¢%/ (WV)

Skin & Bones
AABCCDEEF
GGHIJKLLMN
OPPQRST
UVWXYZZE
(',:;":")?!‡äbced
eefgghijklmn
opqrstuvwxyz
z$123456
7890O¢%$£%

Skjald

AABCDEFG
HIFEIJKLLM
NOOOPQRRS
STUVWWX
YZ&(";:;)?!aab
cdefgghijklm
mnooopqorsst
uvwxyz$123
4567890¢£/⌀⁊⸜❧

Skylark
(LeRoburNoir)

ABCDEFG
HIJKLMNO
PQRSTUV
WXYZ&
(";:;"")?![⁅⁆]äbc
defghijklmn
opqrstuvw
xyz$12345
67890¢⅌$%

Smoke

ABCDEFGHIJK
LMNOPQRSTUV
WXYZ(";:;)?!.abcd
efghijklmnopqr
stuvwxyz$
1234567890¢

Smoke Shaded

ABCDEFGHIJ
KLMNOPQRST
UVWXYZ&('",.;'"')
fl-abcdefg
hijklmnopq
rstuvwxyz&123
4567890© (WV) (CMM)

Snell Roundhand

ABCDEFG
HIJKLMN
OPQRSTU
VWXYZ&
(.,.;'"')?!—·*abc
defghijklmn
oocpqrstu
vwxyz
$1234567890nd rdstth
£¢%$/¢ 1234567890

Solitaire

ABCDEFGHIJ
KLMNOPQR
STUVWXYZ&
('"")?!*abcdefg
hijkklmnopqr
stuvwxyz$123
4567890¢¢/%

Eastern Souvenir Light

ABCDEFGHIJ
KLMNOPQR
STUVWXYZ
&(",:;")?!*abcdef
ghijklmnopqrst
uvwxyz$$1234
567890¢⁄£%

Eastern Souvenir Medium

ABCDEFGHIJ
KLMNOPQRS
TUVWXYZ&
(",:;")?!*abcdefgh
ijklmnopqrs
tuvwxyz$123
4567890¢⁄$£%

Eastern Souvenir Bold

ABCDEFGHI
JKLMNOPQR
STUVWXYZ&
(",:;")?!*abcdefg
hijklmnopqr
stuvwxyz$$12
34567890¢
⁄£%

**Eastern
Souvenir Extra
BoldABCDEFG
HIJKLMNOPQ
RSTUVWXYZ
&(":,:;)?!*:abcdef
ghijklmnop
qrstuvwxy
z$1234567890
¢/£%:**

Souvenir
Light AAaBCD
EℯFGGHIJK
LMMNNOPQ
RSSTTUVW
XYZÆÇØŒ
&(":,:;")?![:]abcdefg
hhijklmmn
nopqrrßstuv
wxyzæçøoeß
$1234567890
¢/£%#:»«¿¡

Souvenir
Medium
AAaBCDEℯ
FGGHIJKL
MMNNOPQ
RSSTTUV
WXYZÆÇØ
Œ&(":,:;")?![:]a
bcdefghhijkl
mmnnopqrrß
tuvwxyzæçø
œß$1234567
890¢/$£#:»«¿¡

Souvenir Demi

AAaB CDEeFGGH IJKLMMNN OPQRSSTT UVWXYZÆ ÇØŒ&(",.:;") ?![*]abcdefgh hijklmmnno pqrſsstuvwx yzæçøœß$ 1234567890¢ /$£%#⚬»«¿¡

Souvenir Bold

AAaB CDEeFGGH IJKLM MNNOPQ RSSTTUV WXYZÆÇ ØŒ&(",.:;")?! [*]abcdefgh hijklmmnn opqrſsstuv wxyzæçøœ ß$123456789 0¢/$£%#⚬»«¿¡

SouvenirLight Italic

AAaœÆB CÇDEeFGG HIJKLMm NnOŒøPQR SSTTUVWX YZ&(",.:;")?![*]a æbcçdefghhij klmmnnœøpq rrſsstuvwxyz ß$$12345678 90¢/£%#⚬»«¿¡

ITC LICENSED *Souvenir*
Medium Italic
AAⓐBCDEℯ
FGGHIJKLM
MNNOPQR
SSTTUVWX
YZÆÇØŒ&
(".,:;")?![⁂]abcde
fghhijklmmn
nopqrrßstuvw
xyzæçøœß$1
234567890¢
/$£%#⸮»«¿¡

ITC LICENSED *Souvenir*
Demi Italic
AAⓐBCDEℯ
FGGHIJKLM
MNNOPQRS
STUVWX
YZÆÇØŒ
&(".,:;")?![⁂]abc
defghhijklm
mnnopqrißßt
uvwxyzæçøœ
ß$123456789
0¢/$£%#⸮»«¿¡

ITC LICENSED **Souvenir**
Bold Italic
AAⓐBCDE
ℯFGGHIJK
LMMNNOP
QRSSTTUV
WXYZÆÇØ
Œ&(".,:;")?![⁂]
*abcdefghhij
klmmnnopq
rrßstuvwxy
zæçøœß$1
234567890
¢/$£%#⸮»«¿¡

Souvenir
Outline AAAa
BCDEeFGGG
HIJKLM
MNNOPQ
RSSTTUV
WXYZÆÇØ
Œ&(',.;;")?![⁕]
abcdefghh
ijklmmnnop
qrrsstuvw
xyzæçøœßß$
123456789
0¢$/£%#⁕:⁖⟩⟨ (WV)

Souvenir
Comstock
AAaBCDE
eFGGHIJK
LMMNNOP
QRSSTTU
VWXYZÆÇ
ØŒ&(',.;;")?!
[⁕]abcdefg
hhijklmmn
nopqrrsstu
vwxyzæçøœ
ß$12345678
90¢$/£%#⁕:⁖⟩⟨ (WV)

SouvenirShaded
A AaBCDEeF
GgHIJKLMM
NNOPQRSSTT
UVWXYZÆ
ÇŒØ&(',.;;")?!
[⁕]abcdefghhi
jklmmnnopqrr
sstuvwxyzæç
œøß$1234567
890¢/$%£#⟩⟨⟩⟨
Y (CMM) (WV)

STAGECOACH
ABCDEFGHIJ
KLMNOPQRST
UVWXYZ&
(.',:;"")?!*_abcdefg
hijklmnopqr
stuvwxyz
$1234567890¢$%

(WV)

STAGG
SHADED
ABCDEFGH
IJKLMNOP
QRSTUVW
XYZ&(.,;:"")?!.*
$12345678
90C¢/s%®±:■○●

Standard
Extra Light
Extended AB
CDEFGHIJK
LMNOPQR
STUVWXY
Z&(.,:;")?!*_abc
defghijklmno
pqrstuvwxy
z$12345678
90¢¢/$%£

Standard
Medium ABC
DEFGHIJKLMN
OPQRSTUVW
XYZ&(.,':;"")?!_*
abcdefghijklm
nopqrstuvwxy
z$12345678
90¢/%

Standard
Bold ABCDE
FGHIJKLM
NOPQRSTU
VWXYZ&
(.,'""*/;:)!?abc
defghijklmn
opqrstuvwx
yz12345678
90$¢£%

Standard
Extra Bold
Condensed ABC
DEFGHIJKLMNO
PQRSTUVWXYZ
&(.,'"–"::;)?!abcde
fghijklmnopq
rstuvwxyz$£
1234567890
¢/%*«<>»

(IB) (R)

344

Stark Debonair

ABCDEFGHIJKL
MNOPQRRST
UVWWXYZ&(""")
?!abcdefgghijkl
mnopqrstuvww
xyz$12345678
90¢/£%$

Stark Semi-Bold

ABCDEFGHIJKL
MNOPQRRSTU
VWWXYZ&(""")?!*
abcdefgghijklm
nopqrstuvwwx
yyz$12345678
90¢/£%$

STEAMBOAT

ABCDEFG
HIJKLM
NOPQRS
TUVWXY
Z&(";:;")?!$
1234567
890¢/£%

STEAM·BOAT SHADED

ABCDEFG
HIJKLMN
OPQRSTU
VWXYZ&
(.,:;""")?!$123
4567890¢
/£%

Steel Elongated

ABCDEFGHIJKLMM
NOPQRSTUUVWWXY
YZ£(.,:;!)?!_abcdefg
hijklmnopqrstuvwxy
z$1234567890¢/£

Steelplate Text

BlackABCD
EFGHIJKLM
NOPQRSTU
VWXYZ&(.,:;)?!
abcdefghijkl
mnopqrstuvw
xyz$123456
7890 (WV)

Steelplate Text Open ABCD EFGHIJKLM NOPQRST UVWXYZ&.,:;'
?!abcdefghijk lmnopqrstu wxyz$12345 67890 (WV)

Steelplate Text Shaded ABC DEFGHIJK LMNOPQRS TUVWXYZ& .,:;'?!abcdefghij klmnopqrstuv wxyz$123456 7890 (WV)

STENCIL ABCDEFGHIJ KLMNOPQ RSTUVWXYZ &(.,:;:?)?!*$1234 567890¢/s% (WV)

STEPHEN ORNATE

ABCDEFGHIJKL
MNOPQRSTUVWX
YZ&!,;:?'?!-$123
4567890

(WV)

STOUTHEART

ABCDEFGHIJK
LMNOPQRSTU
VWXYZ&!-:,'?
Sc1234567890 (R)

STREAMLINE

ABCDEFG
HIJKLMNOP
QRSTUVW
XYZ&(',:;'%)?!*• (WV)

Stymie Hairline

AAABCDEFG
HIJKLMN
OPQRRSTU
VWXYZ&("")?!*
aabcdeff
fflftffifflghijklm
nopqrstuvw
xyz$12345678
900¢/£%#

Stymie Light AA

BCDEFGHIJK
LMNOPQRST
UVWXYZ&(".")
?!*abcdefghijk
lmnopqrstuvw
xyz$12345678
90¢/£%

Stymie Medium

ABCDEFG
HIJKLMNOP
QRSTUV
WXYZ&(".")
?!*abcdefghijk
lmnopqrstu
vwxyz
$1234567890
¢/£%/

Stymie Bold
ABCDEFGH
IJKLMNO
PQRSTUVW
XYZ&[",:;"]?!*a
bcdefghijkl
mnopqrstuvw
xyz$123456
7890¢¢%$%

Stymie Extra
Bold ABCDEF
GHIJKLMN
OPQRSTUVW
XYZ&(.,/:;«)?!*
abcdefghij
klmnopqrst
uvwxyz$123
4567890
¢/£% (IB)

SUPERSTAR
AÆBCÇDEFGHI
JKLMŃNOŒO
PQRSTUVWX
YZ&(";:;)?!=
$12345678
90C°%$£%¿¡i⊠●■ (WV)

SUPERSTAR
SHADOW ABCD
EFGHIJKLMN
OPQRSTUVW
XYZ&
[{:;,"'*!?)
$1234567B
90£¢%#°/c
1234567890

Syntax Antiqua
ABCDEFGHIJ
KLMNOPQRS
TUVWXYZ
&(.,:;"'')?!*abcde
fghijklmnopqrs
tuvwxyz$123
4567890¢¢/$%
»©«+●◐■□

Syntax Antiqua
Medium
ABCDEFGH
IJKLMNOPQ
RSTUVWXYZ
&(.,:;"'')?!*abcd
efghijklmno
pqrstuvwxy
z$123456789
0¢¢/$%»✳«©○■
®●□

Syntax Antiqua Bold

ABCDEFGH
IJKLMNO
PQRSTU
VWXYZ&
(.,;:"")?!-_ab
cdefghijk
lmnopqrst
uvwxyz$
123456789
0¢¢/$%+©®◯■●□

T.H.ALPHABET SOUP
ABCDEFGHIJK
LMNOPQR
STUVWXYZ&
(.,.;,")?!*_$12
34567890¢$/
£%

T.H.UNCLE SAM
ABC
DEFGHIJKL
MNOPQ
RSTUVWX
YZ&
(.,.;,")!?.*
$£1234
567890¢%
$/¢1234567890

Tabasco Light
AABCDEFG
HHIJKKLLMM
NNOPQRR
STUUVVWW
XYYZÆÇ
ØŒ&(.,.;,")?!*
abcdefghh
ijkklmmnnop
qrsstuvv
wxyzæçøœ
ß$12345678
90¢£%

(IB)

Tabasco Medium

Tabasco
MediumAAB
CDEFGHH
IJKKLLMMN
NOPQRRS
TUUVVWW
XYYZ&(.',:;'')
?!*_abcdefg
hhïijkklmm
nnopqrsstuv
vwwxyz$1
234567S90¢%

(IB)

TabascoBold

TabascoBold
AABCDEFG
HIJKKLLMMN
NOPQRRS
TUUVVWWX
YYZÆÇØŒ
&(.',:;'')?!*_abc
defghhij
kklmmnnop
qrsstuvv
WwxyzæÇØ
œß$12345
67S90¢£%⚓

《》 (IB)

TABLEAU

TABLEAU
ABCDEFGHIJ
KLMNOPQR
STUVWXYZ&
01183171 -
$1234567890
¢/£%1§1
11311119

(WV)

Tango

AÆBÇCDE
FGHIJK
LMNOOØŒ
PQRST
UVWXYZ&
(',.:;"="")?!aæb
cçdefghijklmnoø
œpqrsßtuvw
xyz$12345678
90£¢%//«»˘˜˙˙ɩ¡
$1234567890¢

Tanker

ABCDEFG
HIJKLM
NOPQRST
UVWXY
Z&(".,.;:;",")
!?!*¡¡abcc
defghijkl
mnopqr
stuvwxyz
$£1234
567890¢
%/
$1234567890¢

Tavern

ABCDEFGHIJKLMN
OPQRSTUVWXYZ
&(".¨)?!:abcdefghijklm
nopqrstuvwxyz$1
234567890¢/$£%

Thalia

ABCDEFGHIJKL
MNOPQRSTU
VWXYZ&&&&(.,.:;'")
?!*abcdefghijk
lmnopqrstuvwxyz
æœøß$123456
7890¢/%ⁿ¿¡

THORNE SHADED

ABCD
EFGHIJ
KLMN
OPQRST
UVWX
YZ&[',.:;']
?!_$1234
567890¢/

Thorowgood Roman

ABCDEF
GHIJKLM
NOPQRS
TUVWXYZ
&(;:;'"?)
?!|*±|abcde
ffffifflffg
hijklmno
pqrstuv
wxyz$123
45678
90¢/£°%»«§†

Thorowgood Italic

A A A B B C
D D E E F F G G H
H H I I J J K K
K L L M M M M N N
N O P P P Q K R R
R S S S S T T T U U
U V V V V W W
W X X X X Y Y Y Z &
(. , . : . ; . " ") ? ! a a a b c c d
e e f f f g h h h i j k k l l m m n
n o p p q q r r r s s
s t t u u v v w x y z $ 1 2 3
4 5 6 7 8 9 0 ¢

Ticonderoga

Light ABCDEFGH
IJKLMNOP
QRSTUVWXY
Z&(";.:;)?!–abc
defſſſghijklmnopqr
stuvwxyz
$1234567890¢/$

Ticonderoga
BoldABCDE
FGHIJKL
MNOPQRST
UVWXYZ
&(:;,::)?!=abcde
fffghijklm
nopqrstuvwx
yz$123456
7890¢$/

TiffanyLight
ABCDEF
GHIJJKKL
MNOPQR
RSTUVWX
YZ&(&(':;;")
?![*]abcdeeffl
ghijkklm
nopqrstuvw
xyz$1234
567890¢$/¢£
%#

Tiffany
MediumAB
CDEFGH
IJJKKLMN
OPQRRS
TUVWXY
Z&(&(':;;")
?![*]abcdeef
flghijkkl
mnopqrstu
vwxyz
$123456789
O¢$/¢£%#

Tiffany Demi

ABCDEF
GHIJJKK
LMNOPQ
RRSTUV
WXYZ&&
(",;;,"")?![*]
abcdeeffl g
hijkklm
nopqrstuv
wxyz$12
34567890¢
/¢£%#

Tiffany Heavy

ABC
DEFGHI
JKLMNO
PQRST
UVWXYZ
&&(:,;;:)
?![*]ab
cdeeffgh
ijklmno
pqrstuvw
xyz$12
34567890
¢$/£%#

Time Script

ABCDEFG
HIJKLM
NOPQRST
UVWXY
Z&(',;;")*!2
abcddef
fffiflgghijklm
nopqrss
tuvwxyz$1
23456789
0£¢%/
$1234567890¢

Times Roman

ABCDEFGHI
JKLMNOPQ
RSTUVWXY
Z&(',.:;"")?!*abcd
effffiflffiffflghijk
lmnopqrstuvw
xyz$123456789
0¢/%£ $1234567¢

Times Roman Russian

АБВГДЕЁЖЗ
ИЙКЛМНО
ПРСТУФХЦ
ЧШЩЪЫЬЭ
ЮЯ(',.:;"")?!*абв
гдежзийклм
нопрстуфхцч
шщъыьэюя$1
234567890¢/£
1234567890

Times Roman Italic

ABCDEFGH
IJKLMNO
PQRSTUVW
XYZ&
(',"":;"")*!?abcd
efghijklmn
opqrstuvwxyz
$123456789
0£¢/%
$1234567890¢

362

Times Roman Bold ABC
DEFGHIJKL
MNOPQR
STUVWXYZ
&(.,.:,;??)?!_*_
abcdefffffiffffi
ffghijklm
nopqrstuvwxyz
$12345
67890¢£$¢%

Times Roman Black ABCD
EFGHIJKL
MNOPQRS
TUVWXYZ
&(.,.:,;??)?!_*_abc
defghijklmn
opqrstuvwxy
z$123456789
0¢¢%$%£

Times Bold Modified No.1
ABCDEF
GHIJKLMN
OPQRST
UVWXYZ&
(.,:,;??)?!_*_ab
cdeffffflghijkl
mnopqrst
uvwxyz
$1234567890¢
¢$£%

Times Bold Modified No.2

A.ABCD
EFFGHIJKL
MNOPQR
STUVWXYZ
&(.,':;?")?!*_ab
cdeefflftgghij
klmnopq
rrssttuvwxyz
$12345
67890¢¢%£%

Times New Roman Semi-Bold AB
CDEFG
HIJKLMN
OPQRST
UVWXYZ&
(':,.;")?!
[*]abcdef
fffiflffifflghij
klmnopq
rstuvwxyz
$12345678
90¢¢%$%£«§†»

Times New Roman Semi-Bold Italic

A ÆBCÇDEF
GHIJKL
MNOŒPQR
STUVW
XYZ&(":,.;)?![-]
aæbcçde
ffffifflghijklm
noœpqrst
uvwxyz
ß$1234567890
¢/£%‹¿☺›»

Tintopetto

ABCDEFG
HIJKLM
NOPQRST
UVWXYZ
&.,'?!àbcde
fghijklmnop
qrstuv
wxyz$12345
67890¢ (WV)

ITC LICENSED Tom's Roman

ABCDEF
GHIJKKLMN
OPQQRR
STUVWXYZ
ÆØŒ&(".,;")
?!*·*abcdeffffi
ffiflfflſtgg
hijklmnopqrs
tuvwxyzæ
øœß$1234567
890¢/£%#

TONIGHT

AÆBCÇDE
FGHIJK
LMNOŒØ
PQRST
UVWXYZ&
([".,;"]?!*
$¢1234567
890¢/%
®⁑©+$1

TOP HAT
ABCDE
FGHIJKLM
NOPQRR₂
STUVWXY
Z123456
7890

Topic Futura
ABCDEFGHIJK
LMNOPQ
RSTUVWXYZ&
(.,'.:;«»)?!*a
bcdefghijklm
nopqrstu
vwxyz$12345
67890¢/$£%

Torino Roman
ABCDEFGHIJ
KLMNOPQRST
UVWXYZ&(.,:;")
?!_* abcdeffffifl
ffifflghijklmno
pqrstuvwxyz$1
234567890¢%£
¢/$1234567890

TOWN HALL

ABCDEFGHIJK
LMNOPQRS
TUVWXYZ&
(".:;")?!≡±*$12
34567890
¢/&%&1 (WV)

TOWN HALL NO.2

ABCDEFGH
IJKLMNOPQRS
TUVWXYZ&
(".:;")?!≡±*$1
234567
890¢/&%&1 (WV)

Trafalgar

ABCDEEFGH
HIJKLL
MMNOPQRS
TCUVWX
YZ&(".:;)?!ābcd
efghijklmn
opqrstuvwxy
z$12345
67890¢/€$¢ (IB) (R)

Trajanus Italic

ABCDEFGHIJ
KLMNOPQRS
TUVWXYZ&
(.',.:;"")?!⁑abcdefffffifl
ghijklmnopqrstuv
wxyz$1234567890¢
¢/$%£1234567890

Trooper Roman
Light ABCD

EFGHIJKLMN
OPQRSTTh
UVWXYZ&
(.',.:;"")?!⁑abcdeffi
flfyghijklm
nopqrstuvwx
yz$1234
567890¢$%c£%

Trooper Roman

ABCDEFG
HIJKLMNOP
QRSTThUV
WXYZ&(.',.:;"")?!
⁑abcdeffifl
fygghijklmnoo
pqrstuvw
xyyz$1234567
890¢%$%£

Trooper Roman Black
ABCDEF
GHIJKLMN
OPQRST
ThUVWXYZ
&(.',:;?)?¿
[¡¿]abcdeffiffl
gghijkl
mnooopqrs
tuvwx
yẏz$123456
7890¢$¢£%

TrooperRoman
ItalicABC
DEFGHIJKLM
NOPQRS
TUVWXYZ&
(.',:;"")?![¡¿]
abcdeffiflghij
klmnopq
rstuvwxyz
$1234567890
¢%£%

Trump
Mediæval
ABCDEFGH
IJKLM
NOPQQRST
UVWXYZ
ÆÇŒ&(.',:;'')?!*
abcdefff
fiflghijklmno
pqrstuvw
xyzæçœ$123
4567890
¢$£%/%

Trump
Mediæval
Semi-Bold ABC
DEFGHIJ
KLMNOPQ
QRSTU
VWXYZÆÇ
Œ&(.,:;'')?!*
abcdefffffiflgh
ijklmno
pqrstuvwxyz
æçœ$123
4567890¢$£
%'%»

Trump
Mediæval
Bold ABCD
EFGHI
JKLMNOP
QRSTU
VWXYZÆ
ÇŒ&(.,:;'')
?!*abcdeffffi
flghijkl
mnopqrstu
vwxyzæç
œ$123456789
0¢$£%'%«

Trump
Mediæval Italic
ABCDEF
GHIJKLMNO
PQRSTU
VWXYZÆÇ
Œ&(.,:;'')?!*
abcdefflfiffgh
ijklmno
pqrstuvwxyz
æçœ$1234
567890¢$£%»

Trump Mediæval Semi-Bold Condensed

ABCDEFGH
IJKLMNOPQRS
TUVWXY
ZÆÇŒ&(.',:;'')?!*
abcdeffflfi
ghijklmnopq
rstuvwxyz
æçœ$123456789
0¢$%c£0%/£§§

Tulo

ABCDEFGHIJK
LMNOPQRSTUVWX
YZÆÇŒ&('')?
!*abcdefghijklmn
opqrstuvwxyzæç
œ$1234567890¢
/&◯■§®©⊠◇♦

TypoScript

ABCDEFGH
IJKLMN
OPQRSTUV
WXYZ&
(,'')?!*-abcdefgh
ijklmnopqr
stuvwxyz$123456
7890¢/8c%

UMBRA

UMBRA
ABCDEFGHIJ
KLMNOPQRST
UVWXYZ&
[(:;!)?!£=+$1234
567890¢*% (WV)

UMBRA NO. 57

UMBRA NO. 57
ABCDEFG
HIJKLMNOP
QRSTUVW
XYZ&(",;,,)?!*
$1234567
890¢/£%⊠©®⊠
◻●⅃⅃

Unbelievable

Unbelievable
ABCDEF
GHIJKLMN
OPQRS
STUVWXY
Z&(',;.;§§)?!
[*]abcdefghijk
lmnopqrs
stuvwxyz$12
34567890¢
$/¢%»«+®©◻●
◼●○

UNCLE BILL

ABCDEFGHI
JKLMNOP
QRSTUVWX
YZ&(.',:;%)?!$I
234567890 (wv)

Univers45

ABCDEFGHIJK
LMNOPQRS
TUVWXYZ&
(".:;")?![*]abcde
fghijklmnopqrst
uvwxyz$123
4567890¢$¢£%

Univers55

ABCDEFGHIJ
KLMNOPQ
RSTUVWXY
Z&(".:;)?!*ab
cdefghijklmno
pqrstuvwx
yz$12345678
90¢%

Univers65
ABCDEFGHI
JKLMNOP
QRSTUVWX
YZ&[.'.:;/]?!
[*]abcdefghijk
lmnopqrs
tuvwxyz$12
34567890
¢$/¢£%/«»§†

Univers75
ABCDEFGHI
JKLMNO
PQRSTUVW
XYZ&
(.'.:;'"")?!*-abc
defghijkl
mnopqrstu
vwxyz$1
234567890
¢$/¢£%/

Univers67
ABCDEFGGHIJ
KLMNOPQRSTU
VWXYZ&
(.'.:;'"")?![*-]abcde
fghijklmnopq
rstuvwxyzßS11
234567890¢
$/¢£%§†

URBAN

ABCDEFGHIJK
LMNOPQRSTUVW
XYZ&.'.,:;""?!
$1234567890¢

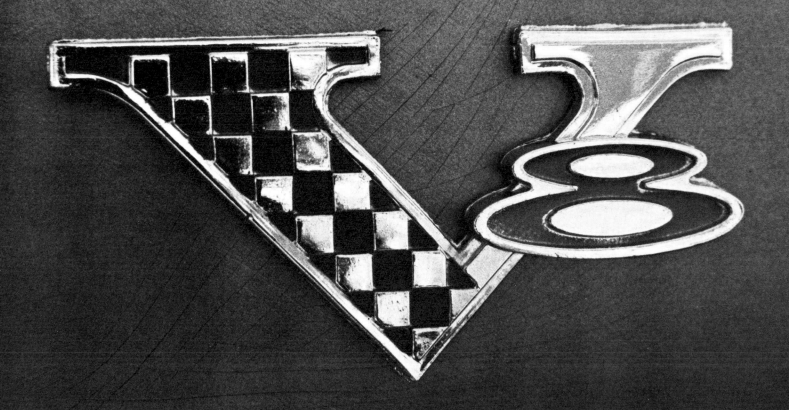

Venture

ABABCDEFG
HIJKLMN
OPQRSTUV
WXYZ&&
[',.;"]?!*abcd
efghijklm
nopqrstuvw
xyz$123
4567890¢%$
£%

Venus Medium

ABCDEFG
HIJKLMNOPQ
RSTUVW
XYZ&(',:;")?!*ab
cdefghijklmn
opqrstuvwxyz
$123456
7890¢/£%$/¢%

Venus Extra Bold AB

CDEFGHIJK
LMNOP
QRSTUVW
XYZ&(',:;")
?!*abcdefgh
ijklmnopq
rstuvwxyz
$123456
7890¢/£%$

Veronese
ABCDEFGH
IJKLMNO
PQRSTUV
WXYZ&
(':;:,)?![-]abcdef
ghijklmnop
qrstuvwxyz$1
$123456789
0¢£

Veronese
Semi-Bold ABC
DEFGHIJ
KLMNOPQ
RSTUVW
XYZ&(':;:,)?![-]
abcdefghijk
lmnopqrstuv
wxyz$123
4567890¢£

Veronese Bold
ABCDEF
GHIJKLMN
OPQRST
UVWXYZ&
(':;:,)?![':;:,]?!āb
cdefghijklmn
opqrstuv
wxyz$123456
7890¢£

VICKSBURG

ABCDEFGHIJKLMNOPQR

STUVWXYZ&¡¿ ''! (R) (IB) (WV)

Victoria
ABCDEFGH
IJKLMNO
PQRSTUVW
XYZ&(.,:;")
?![*]abcdeffgh
hijklmmnn
opqrsstuvwxyz
$12345
67890¢¢$/¢%■● (S)

VINETA
ORNA-
MENT
ABCDEF
GHIJ
KLMNO
PQRS
TUVW
XYZ
&(",;'")?!:$
1234
567890
¢$/¢£% (WV)

Virtuoso 1

A A B B C C
C D D E E F
F G G H H I I
J J K K L
L M M M N N O
O P P Q Q Q R
R S S T T T U U
V V W W X
X Y Y Z Z &
(.,.;"!?)abcdefgghij
klmnopqrstuvwxyyz
$1234567890¢
£%/$1234567890¢

Visa

ABCDEFGH
IJKLMNOP
QRSTUVWXY
Z&(.,.;"')?!*
abcdefghijkl
mnopqrstu
vwxyz
$1234567890
¢/£%‰

Vivaldi

A B C D E
F G H
H I J K L
M M N
O P Q R S T
U V W
W X Y Z &
(.,;"")?!*-abcdde
fgghhijklmnopqrs
tuvwxyzz$12
34567890¢/£% (WV)

Walbaum

ABCDEFGHI
JKLMNOPQ
RSTUVWXY
Z&('.,:.;")?![*]ab
cdeffffiflghijk
lmnopqrstuv
wxyz
$1234567890
¢/£%»†§

Washington Extra Light

AÆBÇDEFGHIJKLM
NOŒØPQRST
UVWXYZ&(',;,")?![*]a
æbbcçddefghhijkкllmn
ooeøpqrssstuvwxyz
BS1234567890
¢/£%ö (wv)

Washington Light

ABCDEFGHIJKLMN
OPQRSTUVWX
YZ&('.,;")?![*]abbcdde
fghhijkкllmnopqrssss
tuvwxyzBS12345678
90¢/£%

Washington Medium

ABCDEFGHIJKLM
NOPQRSTUVWXY
Z&(',;;"")?![*]abb
cddefghhijkkllmnop
qrssstuvwxyz
ß$1234567890
¢/£%

Washington Bold

ABCDEFGHIJKLMN
OPQRSTUVWXY
Z&(',;;"")?![*]abbc
ddefghhijkkllmnop
qrssstuvwxyz
ß$1234567890
¢/£%

Washington Black

ABCDEFGHIJKLM
NOPQRSTUVW
XYZ&(',;;"")?![*]
abcddefghhijkkllm
nopqrssstuvwxyz
ß$1234567890
¢£%

Wedding Text

ABCDEFGH
IJKLMNOP
QRSTUVWX
YZ&(',.:;")?!*
abcdefghijklmn
opqrstuvwxyz
$1234567890¢%$
%£ 1234567890 (WV)

Weiss Italic

AABBCCDDEEF
FGGHHIIIJKK
LLMMNNO
PPQQRRS
TTThUUVW
WWXXYYZZ
&(',.:;"")?!(*)+abcEdeet
ffffiflftghijklmnopqr
sstt uvwxyz
$1234567890¢$/¢£%

Weiss Roman Bold

ABCDEF
GHIJKLMNO
PQQRSTUV
WXYZ&(';:;)?![*]
abcdeEtffffiflSt
ghijklmnopqrst
uvwxyz$1234
567890¢/$£%ot

**Weiss Roman
Extra Bold ABC
DEFGHIJKL
MNOPQQR
STUVWXYZ
&(',:;#)?![*]
abcctdeetffffi
flftghijklmno
pqrstuvwxy
z$1234567890
¢$%£³%%o†**

WEISS INITIALS
NO.2 AABCDE
EFGGHIJKLM
NOPQRSTUV
WXYZ&
(',:;. ÷ .!?)$123
4567890¢/£%

Weiss Initials Light
ABCDEFGHIJKL
MNOPQRSTU
VWXYZ&(',:;)?!
ābcdefghijklm
nopqrstuvwxyz
$123456789
O¢$

Weiss Initials
Medium ABCD
EFGHIJKLMN
OPQRSTUV
WXYZ&(",:;)?!āa
bcdefghijkl
mnopqrstuv
wxyz
$12345
67890¢$⁑

Weiss Initials
Bold ABCDEF
GHIJKLMNO
PQRSTUVW
XYZ&",:;?!āb
cdefghijklmn
opqrstuvwxyz
$1234567890

Weiss Initials
Extra Bold AB
CDEFGHIJKL
MNOPQRST
UVWXYZ
&",:;?!āabcdefg
hijklmnopqr
stuvwxyz
$12345
67890

Wexford Medium
ABCDEFGHIJK
LMⁿANOPQRS
TUVWWXYZ&
(.,;!?*:)abcdefg
hijklmnopqrstu
vwxyz
$£12345
67890¢%$/¢
1234567890

Wexford Extra
Bold ABCDE
FGHIJKLMⁿAN
OPQRSTUVW
VWXYZ&(.',:;*")?!
*_abcdefghijk
lmnopqrstuvw
xyz $12345
67890¢/£%$¢

WIN-
CHESTER
ABCDEFG
HIJKLMN
OPQRSTU
VWXYZ
(.;:;)?!!;;?!-12
34567890 _{(SR) (IB)}

Windsor AB CDEFGHIJ KLMNOPQ RSTUVWX YZ&(.,:;"")?![*_] abcdefghijk lmnopqrstu vwxyz$123 4567890¢/%

$/
¢%

Windsor Black ABCD EFGHIJKL MNOPQRS TUVWXYZ &ÆÇŒO (.,:;)?!.abcdef ghijklmno pqrstuvwx yzæçœo ß$123456789 0¢/%+ॐ◼●

Windsor Light Condensed ABCD EFGHIJKLMN OPQRSTUVWX YZ&(.,:;"")?![*_] abcdefghijklm nopqrstuvwxyz$ 1234567890 ¢/£%$§†

WindsorElongated
ABCDEFGHIJKLM
NOPQRSTUVWXYZ&
(,'.:;"")?![*]abcdefghijkl
mnopqrstuvwx
yz$1234567890¢/£%

(IB)

WindsorHeavy
CondensedABCDE
FGHIJKLMNOPQ
RSTUVWXYZ&
(,'.:;"")?![*]abcdefg
hijklmnopqrstuvw
xyz$123456789
0¢/% (SR)

Windsor
OutlineABC
DEFGHIJK
LMNOPQR
STUVWX
YZ&(,'.:;"")?![*]
abcdefghijkl
mnopqrstuv
wxyz$1234
567890¢/£
%$¢

Windsor Comstock

ABCDEFG
HIJKLMN
OPQRSTU
VWXYZ&
(",:,)?![*-]abcd
efghijklmno
pqrstuvwx
yz$12345
67890¢/$%®©

(WV)

Wolf Antiqua

ABCDEFGHI
JKLMNOPQ
RSTUVWXY
Z&(",:,")?![*]abcde
fghijklmnopqrs
tuvwxyzß$123
4567890¢¢/$£
%»«§†

WOODWARD

ABCDEFGH
IJKLMNOP
QRSTUVWX
YZ6[",:,]?!-$12
34567890¢

(IB)

WorcesterRound
ABCDEFGHI
JKLLMNOP
QRSTUVWX
YZÆŒ&(':;:;)?!ā
bcdefghijklmn
opqrstuvwxyz
$1234567890
¢/£

Worcester
RoundMedium
ABCDEFGH
IJKLLMNOP
QRSTUVWX
YZÆŒ&(':;:;)?!
=abcdefghijkl
mnopqrstuvw
xyz$12345678
90¢/£

Worcester
RoundBold
ABCDEFGH
IJKLLMNOP
QRSTUVWX
YZÆŒ&(':;:;)?!
=abcdefghijk
lmnopqrstuv
wxyz
$123456789
0¢/£

WorcesterRound
Italic ABCDEF
GHIJKLMN
OPQRSTUV
WXYZÆŒ&
.,":;?!abcdefghijkl
mnopqrstuvwxy
zæœ$12345678
90¢/£

YagiUniversalNo.2

AAAAAAAAABBB
BCCCCDDDDDEEEFFFF
GGGGHHIIIIIJJJJKKK
KLLMMMMMMNNNOP
PPPPQQQRRRRRS
SSSTUUUUUUVVV
VVVWWWWXXXYY
YYYYZ&C'.,;"?!?*=aab
bccddeeeffffggggghhh
hiijkklmmmmmnnnnopp
qqrsssssttuuuuuvv
vvvwwwwxxyyyyyz
$1234567890¢/$¢0%®+■○□●

YAGI LINK DOUBLE
AAAABBBCCDDD
EFFGHHHIIIJJKLL
MMMNNOOPPPQQRR
RRRSSSSSTTT
UUVVVWWXXY
YYYZ&&('.,;'')?!?*=$1
234567890¢$/¢0%
»®©□●
«+■□○

York

ABCDEFGHIJ
KLMNOPQR
STUVWXYZ
&(`,:;”)?!|*|Ṣab
cdefghijklmn
opqrstuvwxy
zß$123456789
0¢%₵£%ö

YUKON

ABCDEFG
HIJKLMN
OPQRSTU
VWXYZ&
.,:;:1234567
890/ (WV)

398

Zapf Book Light

ABCDEFGHIJJKL
MNOPQRST
UVWXYZÆŒØ&
(".",,"::,;;)?!*abcdeff
fffififlffiafflghijklm
nopqrstuv
wxyyzæœøß$12
34567890¢¢/$
%£#1234567890«»

Zapf Book Medium

ABCDEFGH
IJKLMNOPQRST
UVWXYZ&
ÆŒØ(".",,"::,;;)?!*abcd
effffififlffiafflgh
ijklmnopqrstuvw
xyzßæœø$1
234567890¢¢/$%£
1234567890«»

Zapf Book Demi # Zapf Book Heavy

ABCDEFG
HIJKLMNOPQR
STUVWXY
ZÆŒØ&("'"".,;.::;;)?!*
abcdefg
hijklmnopqr
stuvwxyz
ßæœø$1234567
890¢¢/$%£
1234567890

ABCDEF
GHIJKLMNO
PQRSTUV
WXYZÆŒØ&
("'"".,;.::;;)?!*
abcdeffffffiflffi
fflghijklm
nopqrstuvw
xyzæœøß
$1234567890¢
¢/$%£12
34567890

Zapf Book Light Italic
ABCDEFGHIJ
KLMNOPQRSTU
VWXYZÆ
ŒØ&(".,",.:;;)?!*abc
defffffifffiffflg
hijjklmnopqrstuvwx
yyzæœøß$1
234567890¢¢/$%£#
1234567890«☺»

Zapf Book
Medium Italic AB
CDEFGHIJK
LMNOPQRST
UVWXYZ
ÆŒØ&(".,",.:;;)?!*ab
cdefffffifffi
fflghijklmnopqr
stuvwxyzæ
œøß$12345678
90¢¢/$%£#
1234567890«☺»

Zapf Book Demi Italic ABCD EFGHIJKLMN OPQRSTUV WXYZÆŒØ&

(.'"",;,::;,)?!*ab cdeffffififfifflgh ijklmnopqr stuvwxyzæœøß $123456789 0¢¢/$%£# 1234567890

«☺»

Zapf Book Heavy Italic AB CDEFGHI JKLMNOPQRST TUVWXYZ ÆŒØ&(.'"",;,::;,) ?!*abcde ffififfffffiifflgghijk klmnopqrst uvvwwxxyyzz æœøß$12 34567890¢¢/$%# 1234567890

«☺»

ITC LICENSED ZapfChanceryLight ITC LICENSED ZapfChanceryMedium

AAABBCCDDEEE

FFGGHHIIJJ

KKLLLMMNNOPP

QRRSSTTUUV

VWWXYYZZ&&

(',:;")??!*abcddd

ee²e³ffgghijkklmnop

qrrsttuvv²v³w²wₓ

xxyyyyy³yzzₓ

$1234567890¢¢/%£#

1234567890

AAABBCCDD

EEEFFGGHHIIJJJK

KLLLMMMNN

OPPQRRSSTTUUV

VWWXYYZZ

&&(',:;")??!*abcddd

ee²e³ffgghijkklmn

opqrrsttuvv²v³wₓw

xxyyyy⁴y⁵zzₓ

$1234567890¢¢/%£#

1234567890

Zapf Chancery Demi

AAABBBCCCDD
EEEFFGGGHHHIIJJ
KKLLLMM
NNOPPQRRSSTT
UUVVW
WXXYyZZ&(,:;/)
??!*abcddDLee'e
ffgghijkklmnopqrr
sttuvvvw
wwxxyyyyyzz$1
234567890¢
¢/$%£#1234567890

Zapf Chancery Bold

AAABBBCCCDDDEE
EFFGGGHHHIIJJ
KKLLLMM MNNOP
PQRRSSTT
UUVVVWWXYY
ZZ&(,:;/)??!*abc
ddDLee'e ffgg
hijkklmnopqrrstt
uv vvvwwww
xxyyyyyz
$1234567890
1234567890
¢¢/$%£#

Zapf Chancery Light Italic

AAAABBCCDDEEEFFGGHHIJIJKKLLLMMNNOPPQRRSSTTTUUVVWWXYYZZZ&(.,:;"")??![*]abcdddeeeffgghijkklmnopqrrsttuvvvwwwxxxyyyyyyzz

$1234567890¢¢⁄$%

£1234567890

《◆》

Zapf Chancery Medium Italic

AAAABBCCDDEEEFFGGHHIJIJKKLLLMMNNOPPQRRSSTTTUUVVWWXYYZZZ&(.,:;"")??!*abcdddeeeffgghijkklmnopqorrsttuvvvwwwxxxyyyyyyzz

$1234567890¢¢⁄$%£#

1234567890

Zapf International Light ABCDE FGHIJKLMNOPQR STUVWXYZ& (,.:;??)?!*abcdeffighij klmnopqr stuvwxyz $1234567890 ¢¢/$%£# 1234567890

Zapf International Medium ABC DEFGHIJKLM NOPQRST UVWXYZ&(,.:;??)?! *abcdeffighij klmnopqrstuv wxyz $1234567890 ¢¢/$%£# 1234567890

Zapf International Demi ABCDE FGHIJKLMNOP QRSTUV WXYZ&(',.:;'')?!* abcdeffighij klmnopqrstuv wxyz$1 234567890¢¢/$%£# 1234567890

Zapf International Heavy ABC DEFGHIJKLM NOPQRST UVWXYZ&(',.:;'') ?!*abcde ffighijklmnop qrstuvwx yz$1234567890 ¢¢/$%£#123 4567890

Zeppelin

ABCDEFGHIJ
KLMNOPQ
RSTUVWXY
ZÆCŒØ
&ß(",;:;-+*"?!)ab
cdefghiijklm
nopqrstuvwxy
zæçœø
$1234567890
¢%/£

(WV) (R) (IB)

PHIL'S *Supplement* # **1**

Aesthetic

ABCDEFG
HIJKKLMM
NNOPQRSTUUV
WUXYZ& (:,;!?)
AABCDEFGHIJK
LMMNOPQRSTU
VWXYZÆŒ
$1234567890¢

Art Gothic Bold

ABCDEEFGH
HIJKLMNOPQR
SSTUVWXY
Z&(.,:;")?!-abc
deefghijkmm
nopqrsstuvwx
yz$12345678
90¢£

BARN-DANCE

ABCDEF
GHIJK
LMNOPQ
RSTUV
WXYZ&
(';,;) ?!$$12
34567890

Benguiat
Gothic Book
ABCDEEFFGHI
JKLMNOPQ
RSTUVWXYZ&
(':,";/="*)!?abcde
ffighijklmnopq
rstuvwxyz
$$£1234567
890¢¢%/.;
1234567890

Benguiat
Gothic Medium
ABCDEEFF
GHIJKLMNOP
QRSTUVW
XYZ&(':,";/="*)!?
abcdeffighijkl
mnopqrstuvw
xyz$$£123
4567890¢¢%/.;
1234567890

Benguiat
Gothic Bold
ABCDEEFFGH
IJKLMNOPQ
RSTUVWXYZ
&(':,";/="*)!?abc
deffighijklmno
pqrstuvwxyz
$$£123456
7890¢¢%/.;
1234567890

ITC LICENSED **Benguiat Gothic Heavy**
ABCDEEFF[2]
GHIJKLMNOP
QRSTUVW
XYZ& (·,;:¤;'⌣')
!?abcdeffi
ghijklmnopq
rstuvwxyz
$$£123456
7890¢¢%/.;

1234567890

ITC LICENSED Benguiat Gothic Book Italic ABCDEE[2]
FF[2]GHIJKLM
NOPQRSTUVW
XYZ& (",";:".)!?*
abcdeffighijkl
mnopqrstuvw
xyz$$$123456
7890¢¢£%/#

1234567890

ITC LICENSED Benguiat Gothic Medium Italic ABCDEE[2]
FF[2]GHIJKLMNO
PQRSTUVW
XYZ& (",";:".)!?*
abcdeffighijkl
mnopqrstuvw
xyz$$$£1234
567890¢¢%/#

1234567890

Benguiat Gothic Bold Italic ABCDEE₂ FF₂GHIJKLM NOPQRSTUV WXYZ&(·.;;"*)!?
abcdeffighijkl mnopqrstuvw xyz$$$£123 4567890¢¢ %/# 1234567890

Benguiat Gothic Heavy Italic ABCDE E₂FF₂GHIJKLM NOPQRSTU VWXYZ& (·.;;")!?abc deffighijklmn opqrstuvwxy z$$$£12345 67890¢¢%/#

1234567890

Berling Italic ABCDEFGHI JKLMNO PQRSTUV WXYZÆŒ& (":.;)?!abcdefghi jklmnopqrs tuvwxyzæœ $1234567890£¢ ¢/$1234567890

Berling SemiBold

ABCDEFGH
IJKLMNOP
QQQQQQ 2 3 4 5 6
RSTUVWX
YZ&(',:;")?!*
abcdefghijk
lmnopqrstuv
wxyz$12345
67890¢£%$¢
1234567890

Bodoni Campanile

ABCDEFGHIJ
KLMNOPQRST
UVWXYZ&
(':.:/‑)[!?]
abcdefghijkl
mnopqrst
uvwxyz$
1234567890 (IB)

Bulletin 113

ABCDEFG
HIJKLM
NOPQRST
UVWXYZ
&(':;«)?!*
abcdefg
hijklmn
opqrstuv
wxyzß$
1234567
890¢%Ł/

Candice Inline

A Å Ä Ắ B C
D E F G H I
J K L M N O
Ö P Q R S T
Th U Ü V W X
Y Z & (';:;) !?=
a å ä à æ b c d e
è é f f g h i j k l m n
o ö ø p q r s ß
t u ü û v w x y z
$1234567890
¢ £ « ° ̈ ̈ » (WV)

CHEQUE

A B C D E F
G H I J K L
M N O P Q R
S T U V W
X Y Z Æ Œ
& (,,:; ''') ! ? -
$ £ 1 2 3 4 5 6
7 8 9 0 ¢ / (WV)

Chesterfield

A B C D E F G H I J
K L M N O P Q
R S T U V W X Y Z
Æ Ç Œ Ø & (':;:")
? ! * = a b c d e f g
h h i j k l m m n n
o p q r s ş t u v w
x y z æ ç œ ø ß
$1234567890¢
¢ / % £ ❉ ⊠ ◨ ●
○
1234567890

Chopin Light

A A B C C D
D E E F F G H I
I J K L L M M
N O P P 2 R R S S
T U V W X Y
Z Æ C O Œ E(.,:.;'')!?[*]

a b b c d e f f f f f f f f g h h i j k l l
m n o p q r r s s t t t u v w x y z z
æ ç œ œ ß $1234567890¢$/%£

1234567890

Chopin Bold

A A B C C D
D E E F F G H I
I J K L L M M
N O P P 2 R R S S
T U V W X Y
Z Æ C O Œ E(.,:.;'')!?

a b b c d d e f f f f f f f f f g h h i j k l l
m n o p q r r s s t t l t u v w x y z
æ ç œ œ ß $1234567890¢$/%£

1234567890

Cooper
Black Italic
Outline

AₐABB₂BCD D₂DE
E F₂FGG₂GHIJ
KLMₘMNₙN₂N
OPₚPQRR₂RS
TₜTUVW
XYZ& (.,;;'')
?![∗]abcde
fghijklmnop
qrstuvwxyz
$1234
567890¢%£ (WV)

EGIZIANO
ABCDE
FGHIJK
LMNO
PQRSTU
VWXYZ
& (.,;;'' ⨪∶)!?
abcdefffffifl
ghijklmn
opqrstuvw
xyz$$£
123456
7890¢ᶜ%/
1234567890 (S)

Egyptian Bold
(Français)
ABCDEFGHIJ
KLMNOPQR
STUVWXYZ
ÆÇØŒ&(∵;∴)?!
⁑abcdefg
hijklmnopqrs
tuvwxyzæ
çøœß$
1234567890¢
%$1234567890/£

»×⋮«

418-A

ITC™ LICENSED **Fenice Light**
ABCDEFG
HIJKLMNOPQ
RSTUVWXYZ
ĄÆÇĐĘŁØŒ&
('.,:;"")?![*]abcd
effighijklmnopq
rstuvwxyząæ
çđęłøœß $123456
7890¢/$%£
#1234567890
1234567890

ITC™ LICENSED **Fenice Regular**
ABCDEFGH
IJKLMNOPQ
RSTUVWXYZĄ
ÆÇĐĘŁØŒ&
('.,:;"")?![*]abcdef
fighijklmnopq
rstuvwxyząæç
đęłøœß$12345
67890¢/$%£#
1234567890
1234567890

ITC™ LICENSED **Fenice Bold**
ABCDEFG
HIJKLMNOP
QRSTUVWXY
ZĄÆÇĐĘŁØŒ
&('.,:;"")?![*]ab
cdeffighijklm
nopqrstuvwx
yząæçđęłøœß
$1234567890
¢/$%£#
1234567890
1234567890

Fenice Ultra
ABCDEFG
HIJKLMNOP
QRSTUVWX
YZĄÆÇĐEŁ
ØŒ&(.,:;""）?!
|⊡|abcdeffi
ghijklmnop
qrstuvwxyz
ąæçđełøœß
$123456789
0¢/$%£#
1234567890
1234567890

Fenice Light
Italic ABCDEF
GHIJKLMNOPQ
RSTUVWXYZ
ĄÆÇĐĘŁØŒ&
(.,:;"")?!|⊡|abcd
effighijklmnopq
rstuvwxyząæ
çđełøœß$12345
67890¢/$%£#
1234567890

Fenice Regular
Italic ABCD
EFGHIJKLMN
OPQRSTUVWX
YZĄÆÇĐĘŁØ
Œ&(.,:;"")?!|⊡|ab
cdeffighijklmn
opqrstuvwxyz
ąæçđełøœß$12
34567890¢/$%£
#1234567890
1234567890

Fenice Bold ItalicABCDEF GHIJKLMNO PQRSTUVWX YZĄÆÇĐĘŁØ Œ&(.,:;")?! [‡*]abcdeffig hijklmnopqr stuvwxyząæ çđęłøœß $123456789 0¢/$%£# 1234567890 1234567890

Fenice Ultra Italic ABCD EFGHIJKL MNOPQRST UVWXYZĄÆ ÇĐĘŁØŒ& (.,:;")?![‡*]ab cdeffighijk lmnopqrstu vwxyząæçđ ęłøßœ$1234 567890¢/$%£ 1234567890 1234567890

*Framingham Italic ABCDEFGHI JKLMNNOP QRSTUVWX YZÆÇŒØ& (.,:;)?!*abcdefff fifififflghijklmno pqrstuvwxyz æçœøß$123 4567890¢/$%£*

FRANKFURTER MEDIUM

ABCDEFGHIJ
KLMNOPQRS
TUVWXYZÆ
ÇŒØ&(":,:;"''')
⚇?!aabcde
fghijklmnop
qrstuvwxyz
æçœøß$123
4567890¢
/%£⁙⁘⁖.©®◆▲◼◆
□●○◯™
$1234567890¢

Franklin Gothic Book

ABCDEF
GHIJKLMNOP
QRSTUVWX
YZĄÆÇÐĘØ
Œ&(.',:;"")?![⚇]*
abcdefghijklm
nopqrstuvwx
yząæçdęøœ
ß$12345678
90¢/$£ŁĮ§%⁙«
††#1234567890

Franklin Gothic Medium

ABCDEFGHIJK
LMNOPQRSTU
VWXYZĄÆÇÐ
ĘØŒ&(.',:;"")?![⚇]
abcdefghijklm
nopqrstuvwxy
ząæçdęøœß
$1234567890
¢$/£%#«⁙»ŁĮ§††
1234567890

Franklin Gothic Demi ABC DEFGHIJ KLMNOPQR STUVWXYZĄ ÆÇĐĘØŒ& (.',:;"")?![*] abc defghijklm nopqrstuvw xyząæçdę øœß$1234 567890¢$/£ %#«*»ŁŁ§†† 1234567890

Franklin Gothic Heavy ABCDEFG HIJKLMNO PQRSTUVW XYZĄÆÇĐ ĘŁØŒ&(.',:;"") ?![*]*abcde fghijklmnop qrstuvwxy ząæçdęłø œß§$12345 67890¢$/% £#1234567890

Franklin Gothic Book Italic ABCDEFGHIJ KLMNOPQRS TUVWXYZĄÆ ÇĐĘØŒ&(.',:;"") ?![*]abcdefghi jklmnopqrstu vwxyząæçdę øœß$12345 67890¢$/£%# «»ŁŁ§†† 1234567890*

Franklin Gothic Medium Italic ABCDE FGHIJKLMN OPQRSTUVW XYZĄÆÇĐĘØ Œ&(.',:;"")?![⊛] abcdefghijk lmnopqrstuvw xyząæçđęøœ ß$12345678 90¢$/£%#☙«‹›»ŁĮŞ ††1234567890

Franklin Gothic Demi Italic ABCDEFG HIJKLMNOP QRSTUVWXYZ AÆÇĐĘØŒ& (.',:;"")?![⊛]abc defghijklm nopqrstuvwx yząæçđęø œß$123456 7890¢$/£% #☙«‹›»ŁĮŞ†† 1234567890

Franklin Gothic Heavy Italic ABC DEFGHIJKL MNOPQRS TUVWXYZĄ ÆÇĐĘŁØŒ& (.',:;"")?![⊥]*ab cdefghijklm nopqrstuvwx yząæçđełø œß§$123456 7890¢$/%£# 1234567890

JTC™ LICENSED Franklin
Gothic Outline
ABCDEFG
HIJKLMNOPQ
RSTUVWXYZ
ĄÆÇĐĘØŒ&
(.,:;"")?![☐]*abc
defghijklmno
pqrstuvwxyz
ąæçđęøœß
Łł§$12345
67890
¢$/%£#

JTC™ LICENSED Franklin Gothic
Contour
ABCDEFGHI
JKLMNOPQR
STUVWXYZ
ĄÆÇĐĘØŒ
&(.,:;"")?![☐]*
abcdefghijk
lmnopqrstuv
wxyząæçdę
øœß$123
4567890
¢/$£%#

JTC™ LICENSED Franklin
Gothic Shaded
ABCDEF
GHIJKLMN
PQRSTUVW
XYZĄÆÇĐĘ
ØŒ&(.,:;"")?!
[☐]*abcdefg
hijklmnopqr
stuvwxyzą
æçđęøœß$
1234567890
¢/$£%#«⛯»††

French Elzevir No. 1

ABCDEFGH
IJKLMNO
PQRSTUVW
XYZ&(",.:;)?!
abcdefghijklm
nopqrstuvw
xyz$12345
67890¢/

Futura Demi Oblique

ABCDEFGH
IJKLMNOP
QRSTUVW
XYZ&(',.:;;)?!
*-abcdefgh
ijklmnopqrst
uvwxyz$
1234567890
¢/%1234567890

Futura Bold Oblique

ABCDEFGHI
JKLMNOPQR
STUVWXYZ
&(".":;)?!-*
abcdefghij
klmnopqrstu
vwxyz$12
34567890¢/$
£%1234567890

Gill Sans Extra Bold Condensed ABCDEFGHIJ KLMNOPQRS TUVWXYZÆ ÇŒØ&(".,'':;") ?!≗*abcdefgh ijklmnopqrstu vwxyzæçœøß $1234567890¢ $/%1234567890

Glow Worm ABCDEFGHIJK LMNOPQRSTU VWXYZÆŒÇØ& (".,:;%)?!≗abcd efghijklmnopq rstuvwxyzæ œçøß$123456 7890¢/‰%£$ 1234567890¢

Goudy Heavyface Open ABCDEFG HIJKLM NOPQRSTU VWXYZ & &((",;:;)? !!-abcdefg hijklmnop qrstuvw xyz$1234 567890 (WV)

Goudy Heavyface Open Italic

ABCCDE
FGHIJKL
MMNOPPP
QRSTUV
UWXYZ&
(''""")?!![—]}ab
cdeffiggghij
klmnopqrs
tuvwxyz$
1234567890
$/# 1234567890¢ (WV)

Harlequin

AABCDEFG
HIJKLMNO
PQRRS
TUVWXYZ
&',:,;?!-
abcdefg
hijklmnopq
rstuvwxyz
$123456
7890¢£X (IB)

Hess Oldstyle

ABCDEF
GHIJKLM
NOPQRS
TUVWXY
Z&('':;)?!abc
deffffiflghijk
lmnopqrst
uvwxyz$12
34567890¢$

Lectura Light

ABCDEFGHI
JKLMNOP
QRSTUVWX
YZÆÇŒØ
&(";.:;")?!⁼*abcd
efghijklmn
opqrstuvwx
yzæçœøß$
1234567890¢
¢/$%£1234567890

L.E.D. Roman Bold

ABC
DEFGH
IJKL
MNOP
QRSTU
VWX
YZÆ
ÇØŒE
C,,71⁼
$1234
56789
0Ç/E

Manquis

ABCDEFGHIJ
KLMNOPQ
RSTUVWXY
ZÆÇØŒ&
(";.:;")?!⁼*abcd
efghijklmn
opqrstuvwxy
zßçøæoe$
1234567890
¢/%£¡¿ ™©®™

$1234567890¢

MERCHANT
BOLD
ABCDEFGH
IJKLMNOP
QRRSTUVW
XYZ&(.',:;")?!
=$123456
7890¢%

ITC™ LICENSED Novarese
Book
ABCDEFGH
IJKLMNOP
QRSTUVWX
YZ&ĄÆÇĐ
EŁØŒ(.',:;")[?!≜]
abcdeffighijk
lmnopqrst
uvwxyząæçd
ełøœ§ß£†+$
¢%%1234567890
#1234567890
1234567890

ITC™ LICENSED Novarese
Medium
ABCDEFG
HIJKLMNOP
QRSTUVW
XYZĄÆÇĐĘ
ŁØŒ&(.',:;")
[?!≜]abcdeffig
hijklmnopqrst
uvwxyząæçd
ełøœ§ß£†+$123
4567890¢%%#
1234567890
1234567890

ITC LICENSED Novarese Bold
ABCDEFGHI
JKLMNOPQRS
TUVWXYZĄÆÇ
ĐĘŁØŒ&(.',:;")[?!≟]
abcdefghijklmn
opqrstuvwxyz
ąæçdęłøœ§ß£†‡
$1234567890¢%%
#1234567890

1234567890

ITC LICENSED Novarese Ultra
ABCDEF
GHIJKLMNOP
QRSTUVWX
YZ ĄÆÇĐĘŁØ
Œ&(.',:;")[?!≟]
abcdefghijkl
mnopqrstuvw
xyząæçdęłøœ§
ß£†‡$1234
567890¢%%#
1234567890

1234567890

Novarese Book
Italic ABC
DEFGHIJKLM
NOPQRSTU
VWXYZĄÆÇ
ĐĘŁØŒ&(.'.:;")
[?!≛]abcdefff
ghijklmnopqrstu
vwxyząæçđ
ęłøœ§ßɛ†+$12
34567890¢%%#
1234567890

Novarese Medium
Italic ABC
DEFGHIJKL
MNOPQRSTU
VWXYZĄÆÇ
ĐĘŁØŒ&(.'.:;")
[?!≛]abcdefffg
hijklmnopqrst
uvwxyząæç
đęłøœ§ßɛ†+$12
34567890¢%%
#1234567890

Novarese Bold
Italic AB
CDEFGHIJKL
MNOPQRS
TUVWXYZĄ
ÆÇĐĘŁØŒ
&(.'.:;")[?!≛]abc
defffghijklm
nopqrstuvwx
yząæçđęłøœ
§ßɛ†+$123
4567890¢%%
#1234567890
1234567890

Olive Antique Bold Condensed
ABCDEFG
HIJKLMNOPQ
RSTUVW
XYZ&(".;:,)?!
abcdefghi
jklmnopqrstu
vwxyz $123
4567890 (S)

Olive Antique Black Condensed
ABCDEFGHIJKL
MNOPQRST
UVWXYZ
&(".;:,)?!-abc
defghijklmno
pqrstuvw
xyz$123456
7890¢£ (S)

Omega
ABCDEFG
HIJKLM
NOPQRRS
TUVWX
YZÇ& (".;:;")
?!*aabcd
effffiflghij
klmnopq
rstuvwxyz
çß$12345
67890¢£%

Omega
Demi-Bold
ABCDEFG
HIJKLMNO
PQRRSTU
VWXYZÇ&
(‚;:;‚')?!*=aaa
bcdeffffiflgh
ijklmnopq
rstuvwxyzç
ß$1234567
890¢£%

Omega Bold
ABCDEFG
HIJKLMNO
PQRRSTU
VWXYZ&
(‚;:;)?!*=aab
cdeffffiflgh
ijklmnop
qrstuvwxy
zß$12345
67890¢
£/%

Omega
Extra Bold
ABCDEFGH
IJKLMNO
PQRRSTUV
WXYZÇ&
(‚;:;‚')?!*=aabc
defghijklm
nopqrstuvw
xyzß$1234
567890¢£
%/

Omega Ultra Bold

ABCDEFG
HIJKLMNO
PQRRSTU
VWXYZÇ&
(';:;")?!*⁻aa
bcdefghijkl
mnopqrstu
vwxyzçß$
1234567890
¢£%⚬∴⚬⚬⚬

Plantin Extra Bold

ABCDEFGH
IJKLMNOP
QRSTUVWX
YZÆÇŒØ&
(';:;")?!*⁻abc
defghijklmn
opqrstuvwx
yzæçœøß$123
4567890¢⚬$%
£⚬∴⚬⚬◯●◻TM
⚬◊◁◇◻■TM®©

Premier Lightline

AABCDEFGHIJKKL
MNOPQRRSsT
UVWWXYZÆŒ
Ø&(':;"*⁻)?!abc
defghijklmnopqrsst
uvwwxyzæœøß
$1234567890¢
/$%€#
1234567890 ⚬⚬⚬ (WV)

Razie Shadow

A A Æ B C Ç D E F
G H I J K L M N O O
P Q R S T U V
W X Y Z & (. , : ; ")
? ! _ a a a a æ b b b
c c c ç d d d e e e f f f g
g g h h h i i i j j j k k k
l l l m m m n n n o o o
œ p p p q q r r r s s s
ß t t t u u u u u u u u
x x x y y y z z z $ 1 2 3
4 5 6 7 8 9 0 ¢ £ % /   (WV)

Romic Light

ABCDEFGH
IJKLMNOP
QRSTUVW
XYZÄÅÖ&
(`´,;:)?!_*_abcd
efghijklmn
opqrstuvwx
yzäèéöøü
ûæß$12345
67890%£

Romic Medium

ABCDEFGHIJK
LMNOPQRST
UVWXYZÅÄÖ
ØÆ&(`´,;:)‗*?!
abcdefghijklm
nopqrstuvwx
yzäèéöøüûæß$
1234567890
%£

Romic Bold

ABCDEFGH
IJKLMNOPQ
RSTUVWX
YZÅÄÖØÆ&
(`´,;:)?!‗*abcd
efghijklmno
pqrstuvwx
yzäèéöøüûæ
ß$1234567
890%£

Romic
Extra Bold

ABCDEFGH
IJKLMNOPQ
RSTUVWX
YZÅÄÖØÆ&
(`´,;:)*‗?!abcd
efghijklmn
opqrstuvwx
yzäèéöøüûæ
ß$1234567
890%£

Savannah

ABCDE
FGHIJK
LMNOP
QRSTU
VWXYZ
&(."''.'?)?!ab
cdefghijkl
mnopqrs
tuvwxyz
$123456
7890¢/$%

1234567890 (IB) (S)

Seagull Light

ABCDEFGHI
JKLMNOPQR
STUVWXYZ
ÆÇŒØ&(.",:;)?!
=abcdefghij
klmnopqrstu
vwxyzæçœ
øß$1234567
890¢%/£

Seagull Medium

ABCDEFGHI
JKLMNOPQR
STUVWXYZ
ÆÇŒØ&(.",:;)?!
=abcdefghi
jklmnopqrst
uvwxyzæç
œøß$123456
7890¢%/£

Seagull Bold
ABCDEFGHIJK
LMNOPQRST
UVWXYZÆÇŒ
Ø&(.,;:;)?!=abc
defghijklmnop
qrstuvwxyz
æçœøß$12345
67890¢%/£

Seagull Black
ABCDEFGHI
JKLMNOPQR
STUVWXYZ
ÆÇŒØ&(.,;:;)?!
=abcdefghi
jklmnopqrst
uvwxyzæç
œøß$123456
7890¢%/£

Sheraton Bold
ABCDEFG
HIJKLMNO
PQRSTUV
WXYZ&(.,:;;")
?!=abcdefg
hijklmnopq
rstuvwxyz
$$123456
7890¢¢
%/

Sheraton Bold Extended

ABCDEF
GHIJKLM
NOPQRS
TUVWXY
Z&(.',.:;"")?!_*
abcdefghi
jklmnop
qrstuvwx
yz$$1234
567890
¢¢°%/

Worcester Round Outline

ABCDEFG
HIJKLMNO
PQRSTUV
WXYZÆŒÇ
&(.',.:;)?!*_abcd
efghijklmnop
qrstuvwxyz
æœçß$12345
67890%¢£
«˘˘»ˆ (WV)

Worcester Round Contour

ABCDEFGHIJ
KLMNOPQR
STUVWXYZ
ÆŒÇ&('.:;)
?!_abcdefghij
klmnopqrst
uvwxyzæœçß
$123456789
0%¢£«˘˘»ˆ (WV)

Worcester
Round Shaded
ABCDEFG
HIJKLMNO
PQRSTUV
WXYZÆŒÇ
&(":;)?!.abcd
efghijklmnop
qrstuvwxyz
æœçß$12345
67890%¢£
(WV)

YANKEE
SHADOW
ABCDEFGH
IJKLMNO
PQRSTUVW
XYZÆŒÇ0
E([:::#])?!.$
12345678
90¢/%£
$1234567890¢ (WV)

Two is company. The Commodore is alone with Mitzy at last.

Alexandra

ABCDE
FGHIJK
LMNOP
QRSTU
VWXY
Z&₊₂/(.,.;'") ⁼.?!

abbcdefghi
ijklmmnnooeorpqr
rsssrsstuuvve
wwwewrxyyz

$1234567890
¢%/$1234567890

Arnholm Sans
Medium
ABCDEFGH
IJKLMNO
PQRSTUV
WXYZ&
(.,:;'")?!*÷abc
defghijkl
mnopqrstu
vwxyz
$1234567890
¢/$£% (S)

Arnholm
Sans Bold
ABCDEFG
HIJKLM
NOPQRST
UVWX
YZ&(;:'")?!
*÷abcdef
ghijklmno
pqrstuv
wxyz$123
4567890
%¢£%•

Barcelona Book

AABCDEFG
HIJKLMM
NNOPQRST
UVWXYZ
ÆÇØŒ&&
(',.:;")?!(*)abcd
effighijklm
nopqrstuvwx
yz æçøœ$
1234567890¢
/%#@ 12345
67890

Barcelona Medium

AABCDEF
GHIJKLMM
NNOPQRS
TUVWXYZ
ÆÇØŒ&&
(',.:;")?!(*)abc
defffighijklm
nopqrstuvwx
yzæçøœ$12
34567890¢/
%#@1234
567890

Barcelona Bold

AABCDEFG
HIJKLMM
NNOPQRST
UVWXYZÆ
ÇØŒ&&
(',.:;")?!(*)abcd
efghijklmn
opqrstuvwx
yzæçøœ$12
34567890¢/
%#@
1234567890

Barcelona Heavy

AABCDEFG
HIJKLM
MNNOPQR
STUVWX
YZÆÇØŒ&
&®([',.;"]?!(±)*
abcdeffighij
klmnopqr
stuvwxyzæ
çøœ$1234
567890¢/%#
@1234567890

Barcelona Book Italic

*AABCDEFG
HIJKLMN
NOPQRSTU
VWXYZÆÇ
ØŒ&&®(",.;")
?!(±)*abcdef
fighijklmnop
qrstuvwxy
zæçøœ$123
4567890¢
/$%#@123456
7890*

Barcelona Medium Italic

*AABCDEF
GHIJKLMN
NOPQRST
UVWXYZÆ
ÇØŒ&&®(",.;")
?!(±)*ab
cdeffighijkl
mnopqrstu
vwxyzæçøœ
$12345678
90¢/$%#@1234
567890*

Barcelona Bold Italic
AABCDEFG
HIJKLMN
NOPQRSTU
VWXYZÆÇ
ØŒ&&⊗ ("‚''";)
?!(≟)*abcdef
fighijklmnop
qrstuvwxy
zæçøœ$123
4567890¢
/$%#@

Barcelona Heavy Italic
AABCDEFG
HIJKLMN
NOPQRSTU
VWXYZÆÇ
ØŒ&&⊗ ("‚''";)
?!(≟)*abcde
ffighijklmn
opqrstuvw
xyzæçøœ$1
23456789
0¢/$%#@

Baskerville Italic
ABCDEFG
HIJKLMNOP
QRSTUVW
XYZÆØŒ&
('‚''";)?!*abcde
ffffflflffiffflg
hijklmnopqrstuv
wxyzæøœ
$1234567890¢$/
%#1234567890

445-B

Baskerville Bold Italic

ABCDEFGHIJ
KLMNOPQ
RSTUVWXYZ
ÆØŒ&
(.,:;")?!*abcde
ffffifflfffifflgh
ijklmnopqrstuv
wxyzæøœ
$1234567890¢$
/%#1234567890

New Baskerville

ABCDEFGH
IJKLMNO
PQRSTUV
WXYZÆÇØ
Œ&(.,:;")?!
[*]·abcdeffigh
ijklmnopqrs
tuvwxyzæçøœ
$123456789
0123456789o¢$
/%#@
1234567890

New Baskerville Semi-Bold

ABCDEFGHI
JKLMNOP
QRSTUV
WXYZÆÇØ
Œ&(.,:;")?!
[*]·abcdeffigh
ijklmnopqrs
tuvwxyzæçøœ
$1234567890
1234567890¢$/
%#@1234567890

New Baskerville Bold

ABCDEFGHI
JKLMNOP
QRSTUVWX
ŶZÆÇØŒ&
(.,;:?'')?![_*_]•abc
deffighijkl
mnopqrstuvw
xyzæçøœ
$1234567890₁₂
34567890¢$
%#@₁₂₃₄₅₆₇₈₉₀ ❈

New Baskerville Black

ABCDEFGHI
JKLMNOP
QRSTUVWX
ŶZÆÇØŒ&
(.,;:?'')?![_*_]•abc
deffighijkl
mnopqrstuv
wxyzæçøœ$1
234567890₁₂
34567890¢$/%
#@₁₂₃₄₅₆₇₈₉₀ ❈

New Baskerville Italic

ABCDEFGHIJ
KLMNOPQ
RSTUVWXY
ZÆÇØŒ&
(.,;:?'')?![_*_]•abcde
ffighijklmno
pqrstuvwxyzæç
øœ$1234567
890₁₂₃₄₅₆₇₈₉₀
¢$/%#@
₁₂₃₄₅₆₇₈₉₀ ❈

ITC LICENSED *New Baskerville*
Semi-Bold Italic
ABCDEFG
HIJKLMNO
PQRSTUV
WXYZÆÇØŒ
&(',.:;")?![⁎]·
abcdeffighijkl
mnopqrstuvwx
yzæçøœ$123
4567890123456
7890¢$/%#@
1234567890

ITC LICENSED *New*
Baskerville Bold
Italic ABCD
EFGHIJKLM
NOPQRSTU
VWXYZÆÇØ
Œ&(',;:'")?!
[⁎]·abcdeffigh
ijklmnopqr
stuvwxyzæçøœ
$1234567890
1234567890¢$%
#@1234567890

ITC LICENSED *New*
Baskerville
Black Italic
ABCDEFG
HIJKLMNOP
QRSTUVW
XYZÆÇØŒ&
(',;:'")?![⁎]·ab
cdeffighijklm
nopqrstu
vwxyzæçøœ
$1234567890
1234567890¢$/
%#@1234567890

Berkeley
Old Style Book
ABCDEFG
HIJKLMNOPQ
RSTUVWX
YZÆÇØŒ&
(.,"";,")?![*]•
abcdeffighijk
lmnopqrst
uvwxyzæçøœ
$1234567890
1234567890
¢$/%#@
1234567890

Berkeley
Old Style
MediumABC
DEFGHIJKL
MNOPQRSTU
VWXYZÆÇ
ØŒ&(.,"";,")?![*]•
abcdeffighi
jklmnopqrstuv
wxyzæçøœ
$1234567890
1234567890
¢$/%#@
1234567890

Berkeley
Old Style Bold
ABCDEFGH
IJKLMNOPQR
STUVWX
YZÆÇØŒ&
(.,"";,")?![*]•
abcdeffighijkl
mnopqrstu
vwxyzæçøœ
$1234567890
1234567890
¢$/%#@
1234567890

ITC LICENSED

Berkeley Old Style Black
ABCDEFGHIJ
KLMNOPQ
RSTUVWXY
ZÆÇØŒ&
(.,;:")?![*].•
abcdeffighijkl
mnopqrstu
vwxyzæçøœ
$1234567890
1234567890
¢$/%#@
1234567890

ITC LICENSED

Berkeley
Old Style Book
Italic
ABCDEFGHI
JKLMNOP
QRSTUVWXY
ZÆÇØŒ&&
(.,;:")?![*].•
abcdeffighijklm
nopqrstuvwx
yzæçøœ$123
4567890123456
7890¢$/%#@
1234567890

ITC LICENSED

Berkeley
Old Style
Medium Italic
ABCDEFG
HIJKLMNOPQ
RSTUVWX
YZÆÇØŒ&&
(.,;:")?![*].•abc
deffighijklmno
pqrstuvwxy
zæçøœ$123456
789012345
67890¢$/%#@
1234567890

Berkeley Old Style Bold Italic
ABCDEFGH
IJKLMNOPQR
STUVWXYZ
ÆÇØŒ&℘₂
(',":;'")?![⚹]•abcde
ffighijklmno
pqrstuvwxyzæ
çøœ$123456
7890123456789
o¢$/%#@
1234567890⚹℘

Berkeley Old Style Black Italic ABCDEF
GHIJKLMN
OPQRSTUV
WXYZÆ
ÇØŒ&℘₂(',":;'")
?![⚹]•abcde
ffighijklmnop
qrstuvwxyz
æçøœ$12345
67890l2345
67890¢$/%#@
1234567890⚹℘

Bramley
Light
ABCDEF
GHIJKLM
NOPQR
STUVWX
YZÆØ&
(',:;'")?!* abcd
efghijklm
nopqrstuv
wxyzæø
$12345678
90£ß¿¡
⚹℘

Bramley
Medium
ABCDEFGH
IJKLMNO
PQRSTUVW
XYZÆØ&
(',.:;"")?!abcdef
ghijklmn
opqrstuvwx
yzæø$123
4567890%£ß
¿¡⁓⁏«·»

Bramley Bold
ABCDEFGH
IJKLMNO
PQRSTUV
WXYZÆ
Ø&(',.:;"")?!abc
defghijkl
mnopqrstuv
wxyzæø$12
34567890
£ß¿¡⁓⁏«»

Bramley
Extra Bold
ABCDEFGH
IJKLMNO
PQRSTUV
WXYZÆØ&
(:⁞)?!⁓abcde
fghijklmn
opqrstuvwx
yz$12345
67890
£ß«⁞»⁏

Brighton Light

ABCDEFG
HIJKKLLM
NOPQR
RSTUVW
XYZÆØ&
(".:;)?!⁑abcd
efghijkkl
mnopqrsttu
vwxyzæø
$1234567
890%£ß
«»⸿⁂

Brighton Medium

ABCDEFGH
IJKKLLM
NOPQRRST
UVWXYZ
ÆØ&(".:;)?!⁑ab
cdefghijkk
lmnopqrsttuv
wxyzæø$
1234567890
%£ß«»⸿⁂

Brighton Bold

ABCDEFG
HIJKKLLMNO
PQRRSTU
VWXYZÆØ&
(".:;")?!⁑abc
defghijkklmn
opqrsttuvw
xyzæø$123456
7890%£ß
«»⸿⁂

Brighton Light Italic

ABCDEFGHI
JKKLLMN
OPQRRSTU
VWXYZÆØ
&(".;:,)?!*ab
cdefghijkklm
nopqrsttu
vwxyzæø$
1234567890
%£ß«»÷

Broadway Engraved

ABCDEFG
HIJKLMNO
PQRSTUV
WXYZ&
(.,:;'')?!*
abcdefghi
jklmnopqrss
tuvwxyz
¢℮%/#$$12
34567890
1234567890

Caxton Roman Light

ABCDEFGHIJK
LMNOPQRS
TUVWXYZÆ
Ø&(".;:,")?!*
abcdefghijklmn
opqrstuvwx
yzæø$123456
7890¢$/%£
1234567890 ÷⚬¡¿«»

Caxton Roman Book

ABCDEFGHIJ
KLMNOPQ
RSTUVWXYZ
ÆØ&(".,:;")?!*
abcdefghijklm
nopqrstuvw
xyzæø$12345
67890¢$/%£
1234567890⚹º¡¿«»

Caxton Roman Bold

ABCDEFG
HIJKLMNOP
QRSTUVWX
YZÆØ&(".,:;")
?!*abcdefg
hijklmnopqr
stuvwxyz
æø$12345678
90¢$/%£
1234567890⚹º¡¿«»

Caxton Roman Light Italic

ABCDEFGHIJK
LMNOPQR
STThUVWXYZ
ÆØ&&(".,:;")
?!*abcdefffffifl
ffifflghijkl
mnopqrstuvwx
yzæø$123
4567890¢$/%£
1234567890⚹º¡¿«»

Century Expanded
Italic ABCDEF
GHIJKLMNOP
QRSTUVWX
YZ&(.,:;'')?!*-abc
defghijklmnopqrs
tuvwxyz$1234
567890¢%/
$1234567890

Chivaree
ABCDEFGHIJ
KLMNOPQRST
UVWXYZ&
[.,:;"]*?!abcdeee
fffghijklmnooo
pqrsttuvwxyz
1234567890
¢%/£
$1234567890

Clarendon
Semi-Bold
ABCDEF
GHIJKLM
NOPQRST
UVWXYZ&
(.,:;;'')?!*abc
defghijklm
nopqrstuvw
xyz$12345
67890
¢¢$%£

Corvinus Bold
ABCDEFG
HIJKLMNOPQ
RSTUVW
XYZ&(.,:;//)?!-*
abcdefffffi
fflghijklmnop
qrstuvwxyz
$123456
7890¢
/£%

Craw Clarendon Bold
ABCDEFG
HIJKLM
NOPQRST
UVWXYZ&
(.,:;";)?!*
abcdefghijk
lmnopqrs
tuvwxyz$12
34567890
¢$/%1234567890 (IB)

Craw Modern
ABCDEF
GHIJKL
MNOPQ
RSTUVW
XYZ&(.,:;";)
?!*abcdefg
hijklmn
opqrstuv
wxyz$12
34567890
¢%/£$123
4567890 (IB)

Else Light

ABCDEFGHIJ
KLMNOPQ
RSTUVWXY
ZÆÇØŒ&
(':.;"")?![*]abcde
ffffifflffiffl
ghijklmnopqrs
tuvwxyzæçœ
$1234567890
1234567890¢$⁄
%#@1234567890

Else Medium

ABCDEFG
HIJKLMNOP
QRSTUVW
XYZÆÇØŒ&
(':.;"")?![*]
abcdeffffifflffiffl
ghijklmnopq
rstuvwxyzæçø
œ$123456
7890123456789
0¢$⁄%#@
1234567890

Else Semi-Bold

ABCDEFG
HIJKLMN
PQRSTUV
WXYZÆÇØŒ
&(':.;"")?![*]
abcdeffffifflffi
fflghijklmnop
qrstuvwxyz
æçøœ$123456
789012345
67890¢$⁄%#@
1234567890

Else Bold

ABCDEFGHIJ
KLMNOPQ
RSTUVWXY
ZÆÇØŒ&
(.,.;‘’„")?![*]abc
defffffifffffiffl
ghijklmnopqr
stuvwxyzæç
øœ$123456789
01234567
890¢$/%#@
1234567890⁂

Else Light Italic

ABCDEFG
HIJKLMNOP
QRSTUVW
XYZÆÇØŒ&
(.,.;‘’„")?![*]
abcdeffffifffffiffl
ghijklmnopq
rstuvwxyzæçøœ
$123456
7890¢$/%#@
1234567890⁂

Else

Medium Italic

ABCDEFG
HIJKLMNOP
QRSTUVW
XYZÆÇØŒ&
(.,.;‘’„")?![*]
abcdeffffifffffiffl
ghijklmnopq
rstuvwxyzæçøœ
$1234567890
¢$/%#@
1234567890⁂

Else Semi-Bold Italic

ABCDEFGHI
JKLMNOP
QRSTUVWX
YZÆÇØŒ&
(.",:;"„,")?![*]
abcdefffffiflffiffl
ghijklmnopqrs
tuvwxyz
æçøœ$1234567
890¢$/%#@
1234567890 ✲ ⚬

Else Bold Italic

ABCDEFG
HIJKLMNO
PQRSTUV
WXYZÆÇØ
Œ&(.",:;"„,")?!
[*]abcdefffffifl
ffifflghijklmn
opqrstuvwxyz
æçøœ$12
34567890¢$/%#
@1234567890 ✲ ⚬

Fedora

ABCDEFGHIJKLMM N
2
NOPQRRSSTUVWXYZ&("::,)
2 2 2
?![*]·aabcdefgghij
2   2
klmnopqrssttuvwxyz
2   2
$1234567890¢/% 1234567890

(WV)(IB)

FRANKFURTER

HIGH LIGHT

ABCD
EFGHIJK
LMNO
PQRSTU
VWX
YZÆÇ
ØŒƐ
(''...)?!$
12345
67890$
1234567890
¢/§§£∷∻~

Futura Bold
Outline
ABCDEFG
HIJKL
MNOPQR
STUVW
XYZ&('',°∴'"")
?!.∴* abcde
fghijklmno
pqrstuv
wxyz $1234
567890£
¢%/ 1234567890

GALADRIEL
ABCD
EFGHI
JKLM
NOPQRS
TUVW
XYZ&(''.:;)
!?«★»$
12345
67890
£⧖™™◄©

**Gill Sans
Extra Bold
Condensed
ABCDEFGHIJ
KLMNOP
QRSTUVW
XYZ&
(':;:;")?!≛abc
defghijk
lmnopqrstu
vwxyz$
1234567890
¢¢/$£%**

HADRIANO
STONECUT
ABCDE
FGHIJK
LMNO
PQRSTU
VWX
YZ&
(',;:;")?!$
12345
67890
¢/£% (WV)

*Harlow Solid
A B C D E F
G H I J K
L M N O P Q
R S T U V
W X Y Z &
(':;:;")?!abcdefgh
ijklmnopq
rstuvwxyzæœ
$1234567
890$1234567
890¢/%ß£
¡¿«»::~*

Isbell Book Isbell Medium Isbell Bold

Isbell Book

ABCDEFGH
IJKLMNOPQR
STUVWXYZ
ÆÇØŒ&
(',:;‹›)?![≈≠*]abc
defghijklmn
opqrstuvwx
yzæçøœ$12
34567890$
1234567890¢
/#%

Isbell Medium

ABCDEFGH
IJKLMNOPQ
RSTUVWX
YZÆÇØŒ&
(',:;‹›)?![≈≠*]
abcdefghi
jklmnopqrst
uvwxyzæç
øœ$12345
67890$
1234567890
¢/#%

Isbell Bold

ABCDEFG
HIJKLLMN
OPQRSTU
VWXYZÆÇ
ØŒ&(',:;‹›)
?![≈≠*]abcdef
ghijklm
nopqrstuv
wxyzæçø
œ$1234567
890$12345
67890¢/#
%

Isbell Heavy

ABCDEFG HIJKLLMN OPQRSTU VWXYZÆÇ ØŒ&(':,:;¤) ?![≃*]abcde fghijkl mnopqrstu vwxyzæç øœ$12345 67890$123 4567890¢/# %ᵛₒ꜀ ꜀ₓᵥ꜀

Isbell Book Italic

ABCDEFGH IJKLMNOPQ RSTUVWX YZÆÇØŒ& (':,:;¤)?![≃]abcd efghijklmn opqrstuvwxy zæçøœ$12 34567890$ 1234567890 ¢/#%¡¿ᵛₒ꜀ᵥ꜀*

Isbell Medium Italic

ABCDEFGHI JKLMNOPQ RSTUVWXY ZÆÇØŒ& (':,:;¤)?![≃]abc defghijkl mnopqrstu vwxyzæç øœ$123456 7890$12345 67890¢/#% ¡¿ᵛₒ꜀ᵥ꜀*

Isbell
Bold Italic

ABCDEFG
HIJKLLMN
OPQRSTU
VWXYZÆÇ
ØŒ&('.,:;!)
?![≚*]abcdef
ghijklmn
opqrstuvwx
yzæçœ $1
234567890
$1234567
890¢/#%¿¡ˇˆˇˇ

Isbell
Heavy Italic

ABCDEFG
HIJKLMN
OPQRSTUV
WXYZÆÇ
ØŒ&('.,:;!)?!
[≚*]abcdef
ghijklmno
pqrstuvw
xyzæçøœ$1
23456789
0$1234567
890¢/#%

Kennerley
Oldstyle

ABCDEFGHI
JKLMNOP
QRSTUVW
XYZØ&
(',:;)?!-abcdefgh
ijklmnopqr
stuvwxyzø
$1234567890*-

465-B

Kennerley Bold
ABCDEFG
HIJKLM
NOPQRST
UVWXY
ZØ&[';:;]?!-
abcdefg
hijklmnopq
rstuvw
xyzø$12345
67890✳·°
(R)

ITC LICENSED Lubalin Graph X-Light Oblique
ABCDEFGH
IJKLMNOPQ
RSTUVWX
YZÆÇØŒ&
(';:;")?!(*)abc
deffighijklmn
opqrstuvw
xyzæçøœ
$1234567890
¢$%/£ß#
(WV)

ITC LICENSED Lubalin Graph Book Oblique
ABCDEFGHI
JKLMNOP
QRSTUVWX
YZÆÇØŒ&
(';:;")?!(*)abcd
efghijklm
nopqrstuvw
xyzæçøœ
$1234567890
¢$%/£ß#
(S)

Lubalin Graph Medium Oblique

ABCDEFGHI
JKLMNOPQ
RSTUVWXY
ZÆÇØŒ&
(.,:;"")?!(*)abcd
efghijklmn
opqrstuvwx
yzæçøœ$12
34567890
¢$%/£ß# (S)

Lubalin Graph Demi Oblique

ABCDEFGH
IJKLMNOP
QRSTUVWX
YZÆÇØŒ&
(.,:;"")?!(*)abc
defffffiflffiffig
hijklmnop
qrstuvwxyz
œçøœ$1234
567890¢
$%/#

Lubalin Graph Bold Oblique

ABCDEFGHI
JKLMNOPQ
RSTUVWXY
ZÆÇØŒ&
(.,:;"")?!(*)ab
cdefffffiflffiffi
ghijklmnop
qrstuvwxyz
œçøœ$1234
567890¢$
%/£ß#

Modern #216 Light

ABCDEFGH
IJKLMNO
PQRSTUVW
XYZÆÇØŒ
&(.,:;")?![*]ab
cdeffighi
jklmnopqrs
tuvwxyzæç
øœ$12345
67890¢/$%
#@

Modern #216 Medium

ABCDEFGH
IJKLMNOPQ
RSTUVWX
YZÆÇØŒ&
(.,:;")?![*]abc
deffighijkl
mnopqrstu
vwxyzæçø
œ$1234567
890¢/$
%#@

Modern #216 Bold

ABCDEFG
HIJKLMN
OPQRSTU
VWXYZÆÇ
ØŒ&(.,:;")?!
[*]abcdeffi
ghijklmnop
qrstuvwxy
zæçøœ$123
4567890¢ $
%#@

Modern #216 Heavy

ABCDEFG
HIJKLMN
OPQRSTU
VWXYZÆ
ÇØŒ&(.,'"::;?")
?![≡*]abcdef
ffighijkl
mnopqrst
uvwxyzæç
øœ$12345
67890¢$/
%#ₐ⚘⚔

Modern #216
Light Italic

ABCDEFGH
IJKLMNOPQ
RSTUVWX
YZÆÇØŒ&
(.,"";:;)?![≡]abcd*
effighijklmn
opqrstuvwx
yzæçøœ$12
34567890¢
$/%#@⚘⚔

Modern
#216 Medium
Italic

ABCDEFG
HIJKLMNO
PQRSTUV
WXYZÆÇØ
Œ&(.,"";:;)?![≡]*
abcdeffigh
ijklmnopqr
stuvwxyzæ
çøœ$123
4567890¢$/%
#@⚘⚔

469-B

Modern #216 Bold Italic
ABCDEFG
HIJKLMN
OPQRSTU
VWXYZÆÇ
ØŒ&(.,:;'")
?![⚏*]abcde
ffighijklm
nopqrstuv
wxyzæçøœ
$123456789
0¢$ %#@⚘⚜

Modern #216 Heavy Italic ABC
DEFGHIJK
LMNOPQR
STUVWXY
ZÆÇØŒ&
(.,:;'")?![⚏*]abc
deffighijkl
mnopqrs
tuvwxyzæç
øœ$123
4567890¢
$/%#@⚘⚜

Murray Hill Bold
ABCDEFG
HIJKLMN
OPQRSTU
VWXYZ&(.,:;)
?!*-abcdefghij
klmnopqrstuvwxyz
$1234567890¢%/£

Normandia Open

ABCDEFG
HIJKLM
NOPQRST
UVWXY
Z&(.,;:'''")-a
bcdefffffi
flffifffffighijk
lmmopq
rstuvwxyz
$123456
7890¢%/£

Nubian

ABCDEFG
HIJKLM
NOPQRST
UVWXY
Z&(.,;:;)?!-
abcdefflghij
klmnopqr
stuvwxyz
æœ$1234
567890¢/

Palatino Semibold Outline

ABCDEFGHI
JKLMNOP
QRSTUVWX
YZ&('.,;:#")÷
?!abcdefffffifl
ghijklmnopq
rstuvwxyz
$$1234567890
¢¢%/£1234567890

PROFILE
ABCDE
FGHIJK
LMNO
PQRSTU
VWXYZ
&(.,:;!)?
!=*$123
4567890
¢ᶜ/$
%£ (WV)

PYGMALION
AAABB
BCCDDEE
EEFFGG
HHIIJJKK
KLLMM
NNNOPP
QQ RR
R SSITUU
VVVWW
W XXYYZ
Z&(.°°°°°°)?!*$
1234567
890¢£%/

Ringlet
AABCDEF
GHIJKL
MMNOPQR
STUVW
XYZÆŒ&
(.,:;")abcde
fghhijklmm
nnopqrs
tuvwxyzæ
œ$£1234
567890¢/

Rodin Cyrillic

АБВГГЃДЂЕ
ЁЄЖЗЅИЙ
ЍІЇЈКЌЛЉМ
НЊОПРСТ
ЋУЎФХЦЧЏ
ШЩЪЬЫЭЮ
Яᴅ(„„)?!⸺абв
ггѓдђеёєжз
ѕийѝіїјкќллљ
мнњопрсћ
уфхцчџшщъ
ыьэюя$$1234
567890£ᶜᶜ%
/«»

Runaround

ABCDEF
GHJJKL
MNOPQ
RSTUVWX
YZ&(„„)?!
⸗abcdefg
hijklmno
pqrstuvw
xyz$1223
4567890
£/⸚""»»

Russian Helvetica

АБВГДЕЁЖЗ
ИЙКЛМН
ОПРСТУФХЦ
ЧШЩЪЬЫ
ЭЮЯ&(„„)?!
абвгдежзи
йклмнопрсту
фхцчшщъ
ыьэюя$12345
67890
¢/£%

St.Thomas

AAABCCDDE
FGGHIJJK
LMMNNOPQ
RSTTUVW
XYZ&(.'.:.;"")?!
*-aabcdefg
hijklmnopqr
sttuvwxyyz
$12345
67890¢
/% (IB)

SOUTACHE

ABCDEFGHI
JKLMNOP
QRSTUVWX
YZ&(",;;)?!-
$1234567890¢ (WV)

Stationers Semiscript

AABCD
EFGHIJ
KLMN
OPQRST
UVWX
YZZ &(.,.:;"")?!*=
abcdeef fffifl
ghijklmno
pqrrsqtt uvwxyz
$1234567890
$/¢£%

Studio Bold

ABCDEFGHIJ
KLMNOPQ
RSTUVWXYZ
&(":,:;"")?!!*
abcdefffffffffff
 fflghijklmn
opqrstuvwxyz
$123456789
0¢/$%£
1234567890 (IB)

THUNDERBOLT

ABCDE
FGHIJKL
MNOP
QRSTUV
WXYZ
&.,,;"?!=
123456
7890
$¢

Tiffany Light Italic

ABCDEFGH
IJJKKLM
NOPQRRST
UVWXYZ
&&(.,:;")?![*]
abcdeffighij
klmnopqrstuv
vwwxyyz$
1234567890¢
$/£%#

Tiffany
Medium Italic

A B C D E
F G H I J J K K
L M N O P Q R R
S T U V W X
Y Z & & (',.:;")?!
[*] a b c d e f f i
g h i j k l m n o p q r
s t u v v w w x y y z
$ 1 2 3 4 5 6
7 8 9 0 ¢ $ / £ % #

Tiffany
Demi Italic

A B C D E F G
H I J J K K L M
N O P Q R R
S T U V W X Y
Z & & (',.:;")?!
[*] a b c d e f f i g
h i j k l m n o p
q r s t u v v w w x
y y z $ 1 2 3 4 5
6 7 8 9 0 ¢ $ / £ % #

Tiffany
Heavy Italic

A B C D E F G
H I J K L M
N O P Q R S T
U V W X Y Z
& & (',.:;")
?! [*] a b c
d e f f i g h i j k
l m n o p q r s t
u v v w w x y y
z $ 1 2 3 4 5 6
7 8 9 0 ¢ $ / £ % #

TITLE GOTHIC
EXTRA CONDENSED NO.12
ABCDEFGHIJK
LMNOPQRSTUVWXYZ&
(;,:;)?!*-$1234567890¢/%

1234567890 (IB)

Tower
ABCDEFGHIJKLM
NOPQRSTUVW
XYZ&[',:;']?!*-abcdef
ghijklmnopqrs
tuvwxyz$1234567890
¢$/% 1234567890

PHIL'S Supplement #3

End of the line for the Commodore. McClusky makes it a crowd.

Aerolite Script

A A A B C D
E F S G H I J
K K L M N O P
Q R S T U U
U V W X Y Z Y
(.,:;"")?!_*aaabb
cccdddeeefffggg
hhhiiijkkklll
mmmmmmmmnnnn
nnnooopqrrrrrr
sssssstttuuuvvv
vwwwwxxyyyz
$1234567890¢¢/%

American Text

ABCDEFGHIJ
KLMNOPQRSTUV
WXYZ&[.,:;!?''":-]
abcdefghijk
lmnopqrstuvwxyz
$1234567890¢¢%/£

BALLÉ INITIALS

ABCDEFGH
IJKLMNOPQR
STUVWXYZ

BALLOON LIGHT

ABCDEFGHIJ
KLMNOPQRSTUVW
XYZ&(."'")?!-
$1234567890¢%£I

$£1234567890¢%I

Balzac

ABCDEFGH
IJKLMNO
PQRSTUVW
XYZ&(",:;"")?!-*
abcdefg
hijklmnopqrst
uvwxyz
$1234567890¢
%//.,1234567890

BANCO

ABCDEFGHIJ
KLMNOPQ
RSTUVWXYZ&
(;,:;:")?! ±$⁵1
234567890¢¢
%£/
1234567890

Berliner Grotesk

ABCDEFG
HIJJKLMNOPQ
RSTUVWX
YZÆØŒ&(.,:;"";)
?![⸸]⌗abc
defghijklmno
pqrstu
vwxyzæøœß
$£1123456
7890%

Berliner Grotesk Bold

ABCDEFGHIJ
KLMNOP
QRSTUVWXYZ
ÆØŒ&
(.,:;"«»)abcd
efghijklm
nopqrstuvwx
yzæøœß
$£123456789
0%

Berling Bold

ABCDEF
GHIJKLMN
OPQRST
UVWXYZ&
(.,:;¿)?!»ab
cdefghijklm
nopqrstu
vwxyzäèß
$£1234567890

Berling Bold Condensed

ABCDEFGHIJ
KLMNOP
QRSTUVWX
YZ&(";:;")?!
abbcddeffgg
hhijkkll
mnopqrstuvwx
yz$1234
567890¢$£%

Beton Bold

ABCDEFGH
IJKLMN
OPQRSTUV
WXYZ&
(".;.:;;") ⁎⁄ ?!
abcdefg
hijklmnopqr
stuvwxyz
$1234567890¢
£$¢/% 1234567890
(S)

Block

ABCDEFGHI
JKLMNO
PQRSTUVW
XYZÆŒ
ÇØ&(.,.;;""'';;)
?! abc
defghijkl
mnopqr
stuvwxyz
æœçøß
$123456789
0¢$/%%#
1234567890≋!

Bulfinch Oldstyle

ABCDEFGH
IJKLMN
OPQRSTUVW
XYZ&
(.,:;'‸)?!-abcdef
ghijklmn
opqrstuvwxyz
$1234567890 (s)

Carnase Text Light

ABCDEFGHI
JKLMN
OPQRSTU
VWXYZÆÐ
ŁØŒ&(‷;:;§)
?![⁎]abcd
effffifflffifflghi
jklmnopqr
stuvwxyzæø
œ$12345
67890¢$/%#@
1234567890 ⁂

Carnase Text Regular

ABCDEF
GHIJKLMN
OPQRS
TUVWXYZ
ÆØŒ&
(‷;:;§)?![⁎]
abcde
fffffifflffiffflghi
jklmnopq
rstuvwxyzæø
œ$1234567
890¢$/%#@⁂

Carnase Text Medium

ABCDEFGH
IJKLMNO
PQRSTUVW
XYZÆØŒ
&(';:;'')?![⚊*⚊]
abcdefffi
flffifflghijklm
nopqrstuv
wxyzæøœ
$1234567890
¢$/%#@
1234567890❧⚬

Carnase Text Bold ABCDE

FGHIJKL
MNOPQRST
UVWXYZ
ÆØŒ&(';:;'')
?![⚊*⚊]abc
defffififlffiffl
ghijklmn
opqrstuvwx
yzæøœ $12
34567890¢$/
%#@
1234567890❧⚬

Carnase Text Extra Bold

ABCDEFGH
IJKLMNO
PQRSTUVW
XYZÆØŒ
&(';:;'')?![⚊*⚊]
abcdefffi
flffifflghijkl
mnopqrstuv
wxyzæøœ
$1234567890
¢$/%#@
1234567890❧⚬

Carnase Text
Light Italic
ABCDEFGH
IJKLMNO
PQRSTUVW
XYZÆØŒ
&(.,':.;,'';")?![ ]a*
bcdefffffi
flffiffflghijklm
nopqrst
uvwxyzæøœ
$12345
67890¢$/%#@
1234567890

Carnase Text
Regular Italic
ABCDEF
GHIJKLMN
OPQRST
UVWXYZÆ
ØŒ&(.,':.;,'';")
?![ ]abcdefff*
fiflffiffflg
hijklmnopq
rstuvw
xyzæøœ$1234
567890¢$/%
#@1234567890

Carnase Text
Medium Italic
ABCDEFGH
IJKLMNO
PQRSTUV
WXYZÆØŒ
&(.,':.;,'';")?![ ]*
abcdefffffi
flffiffflghijkl
mnopqrst
uvwxyzæøœ
$1234567
890¢$/%#@
1234567890

Carnase Text
Bold Italic
ABCDEFGH
IJKLMNO
PQRSTUVW
XYZÆØ
Œ&(.,:;‚‟)?!
[≛]abcdefffffi
flffifflghijkl
mnopqrstuv
wxyzæøœ
$1234567890
¢$/%#@
1234567890 ⚜⚜

Carnase Text
Extra Bold Italic
ABCDEF
GHIJKLMN
OPQRSTU
VWXYZÆØ
Œ&(.,:;‚‟)?!
[≛]abcdefff
fiflffifflghi
jklmnopqrst
uvwxyzæøœ
$1234567
890¢$/%#@
1234567890 ⚜⚜

Caslon 224
Book
ABCDEFGHIJ
KLMNOPQR
STUVWX
YZÆÇŁØŒ&
(.,:;‚‟)?![≛]ab
cdefghijklmn
opqrstuvw
xyz$123456
78901234567
890$¢/%
#@1234567890 ⚜⚜

ITC LICENSED **Caslon 224**
Medium
ABCDEFGHI
JKLMNOP
QRSTUVWX
YZÆÇŁØŒ
&(.,;;"")?![≛]abc
deefghijklm
nopqrstuvwx
yzææçflø
œœ$1234567
890123456
7890¢$/%#@
1234567890⁖°

ITC LICENSED **Caslon 224**
Bold ABCDE
FGHIJKL
MNOPQRST
UVWXYZ
ÆŁØŒ&
(.,;;"")?![≛]abcd
eefghijklm
nopqrstuvw
xyz$12345
67890123456
7890¢$/%#
@1234567890⁖°

ITC LICENSED **Caslon 224**
Black
ABCDEFGH
IJKLMNO
PQRSTUV
WXYZÆŁØ
Œ&(.,;;"")?!
[≛]abcdeefgh
ijklmnopq
rstuvwxyz
$123456789
0123456
7890¢$/%#@
1234567890⁖°

Caslon 224
Book Italic

ABCDEFGHI
JKLMNOP
QRSTUVWX
YZÆÇŁØŒ
&(.,:;""")?!abcdef
ghijklmno
pqrstuvwxyz
æçfłøœß$
1234567890
1234567890¢$/
£%#@
1234567890 «⁚⁞⁝
»◊○≈

Caslon 224
Medium Italic

ABCDEF
GHIJKLMNO
PQRSTUV
WXYZÆŒ
&(.,:;""")?![*]
abcdefghijkl
mnopqrst
uvwxyz$123
4567890
1234567890¢$
%#@
1234567890◊○

Caslon 224
Bold Italic

ABCDEFGH
IJKLMNO
PQRSTUVW
XYZÆŁØ
Œ&(.,:;""")?![*]
abcdefgh
ijklmnopqrs
tuvwxyz
$1234567890
1234567890
¢$/%#@
1234567890◊○

ITC LICENSED

Caslon 224
Black Italic
ABCDEFGH
IJKLMNO
PQRSTUVW
XYZ&(.,:;!?")
?!/[*‡]abcdefg
hijklmno
pqrstuvwxyz
$1234567
89012345678
90¢$/%#@
1234567890

Caslon Russian
АБВГЃҒДДЋЂЕЁЄЖЗЅИ
ЙЍЊІЇЈКЌҚЛЛ
ЉЉЬМНҢЊҢОПРСТ
ЋУЎЎҮҰФѲХ
ҲЦЧҶЧҨШЩЪЫЬЭЮ
ЯӘ&(.,:;")?!/[*‡]
абвгѓғддђеёєжзѕ
ийѝһіїјкќқллљљьмнњ
ҥопрстћуўўүұфѳ
ххҳцчҷчҩшщъыьэюяә
$12345677890¢¢//%LV№
1234567890

Caslon Shaded

ABCDEFG
HIJKLMNOP
QRSTUV
WXYZ&(⁹₀⁹₉⁸₉⁶⁶₉₉)
?!*≡abcdefghi
jklmnopqrstu
vwxyz
$1234567890¢
¢/%1234567890

Centaur Italic

ABCDEFGHIJ
KLMNOPQ
RSTUV
WXYZ&(';,;:';)
?!abcdefffffifffiffl
ggggy
hijklmnopqrstuv
wxyzzy$123
4567890
¢¢/%1234567890

Century Bold Italic

ABCDEFGHI
JKLMNO
PQRSTUVWX
YZ&(.;.;.')?!-*
abcdefghijklm
nopqrstuvw
xyz$123456789
0¢$ᶜ%/1234567890

Century Bold Condensed

ABCDEFGHIJKL
MNOPQRSTU
VWXYZ&(.,:;"")?!
abcdefffffiflffiffl
ghijklmnopqrstuv
wxyz$1
234567890¢ (IB)

Century Bold Condensed Italic

ABCDEFGHI
JKLMNOPQRST
UVWXYZ&
(.,:;"",)?![*]abcdef
fffiflffiffl ghi
jklmnopqrstuvw
xyz$1234567
890£¢$/%1234567890 (IB)

Century Nova

ABCDEFGHIJK
LMNOPQRS
TUVWXYZ&(.,:;"")
*abcdefghijk
lmnopqrstuvwx
yz$1234567
890¢/$¢%£1234567890 (IB)

Century Oldstyle Italic
ABCDEF
GHIJKLMNO
PQRSTU
VWXYZ&
(.,:;"")*abcc̄tdef
fffifĺfffifflgh
ijklmnopqrsŝt
tuvwxyz
$1234567890
¢$¢/%£
1234567890

Century Schoolbook Italic
ABCDEFG
HIJKLMNOP
QRSTUV
WXYZ&(.,:;")?!*-
abcdeffffifl
ffifflghijklmnopq
rstuvwxyz
$1234567890¢£
%/1234567890$¢%/

Century Light
ABCDEFG
HIJKLMNOPQ
RSTUVWX
YZĄÆÇĐEŁ
ØŒ&("")
?![*]abcdeffffifl
ffifflghijkl
mnopqrstuvw
xyząæçđę
łøoeß$1234567
890¢$£%/#@
1234567890†‡§f«»°

Century Bold ABCDE FGHIJKL MNOPQRST UVWXYZ ĄÆÇĐĘŁØŒ &(',;:;'')?! [*]abcdefff fiflffifflghijk lmnopqrst uvwxyz ąæçđęłøœß$1 234567890¢ $£%/#@1234567890

Century Light Italic ABCDEFGHI JKLMNOP QRSTUVWX YZĄÆÇĐ ĘŁØŒ&(',;:;'')?! [*]abcdefff fiflffifflghijklm nopqrstuv wxyząæçđęłø œß$12345 67890¢$£%/#@ 1234567890†‡§ƒ«»o

Century Bold Italic AB CDEFGHIJK LMNOPQR STUVWXYZ ĄÆÇĐĘŁ ØŒ&(',;:;'')?![*] abcdefffffi fiflffifflghijkl mnopqrst uvwxyząæçđ ęłøœß$123 4567890¢$£%/ #@1234567890

Century Light Condensed

ABCDEFGH
IJKLMNOPQRST
UVWXYZ
ĄÆÇĐEŁØŒ&
(‚""')?![*]abcde
 fffiflffifflghijklm
nopqrstuvw
xyząæçđełøœß$1
234567890¢$
£%/#@1234567890†‡
§ƒ«»o

Century Book Condensed

ABCDEFGHIJK
LMNOPQRS
TUVWXYZĄÆ
ÇĐEŁØŒ&
(‚""')?![*]abcdeffffi
flffifflghijkl
mnopqrstuvw
xyząæçđełøœß$
1234567890¢$
£%/#@1234567890
†‡§ƒ«»o

Century Bold Condensed

ABCDEFG
HIJKLMNOPQ
RSTUVW
XYZĄÆÇĐEŁ
ØŒ&(‚""')
?![*]abcdef
fffiflffifflghijkl
mnopqrstuv
wxyząæçđełø
œß$123456
7890¢$£%/#@
1234567890†‡§ƒ«»o

ITC™ LICENSED

Century Ultra Condensed
ABCDEFGHI
JKLMNOP
QRSTUVWXY
ZAÆÇÐEŁØ
Œ&(.,,;;'')?!
[*]abcdefffi
flffifflgh
ijklmnopqr
stuvwxyz
aæçðełøœß$1
234567890¢$
£%/#@1234567890

ITC™ LICENSED

Century Light
Condensed Italic
ABCDEFGHI
JKLMNOPQRST
UVWXYZA
ÆÇÐEŁØŒ&(.,,;;'')
?![*]abcdef
ffiflffifflghijklm
nopqrstuvw
xyzaæçðełøœß
$1234567890
¢$£%/#@1234567890
†‡§ƒ«»o

ITC™ LICENSED

Century Book
Condensed Italic
ABCDEFGHIJK
LMNOPQRS
TUVWXYZAÆ
CÐEŁØŒ&
(.,,;;'')?![*]abcdefff
fiflffifflghij
klmnopqrstuvw
xyzaæçðeł
øœß$1234567890
¢$£%/#@
1234567890†‡§ƒ«»o

ITC™ LICENSED **Century Bold Condensed Italic**

ABCDEFGHIJ
KLMNOPQ
RSTUVWXYZ
ĄÆÇĐĘ
ŁØŒ&(.,:;'"")?!
[≗]*abcdefffffffi
flffifflgh
ijklmnopqrstu
vwxyząæçđę
łøœß$12345678
90¢$£%/#@

ITC™ LICENSED **Century Ultra Condensed Italic ABCD**

EFGHIJK
LMNOPQRS
TUVWXYZ
ĄÆÇĐĘŁØŒ
&(.,:;'"")?![≗]*
abcdeffffi
flffifflghijjk
lmnopqrst
uvwxyząæçđ
ęłøœß$123
4567890¢$%/#

Charme Light

ABCDE
FGHIJKL
MNOP
QRSTUV
WXYZ&
(.,:;'"")=?!abcdefghi
jklmnopqr
stuvwxyz$$1234
567890¢¢%£/
1234567890

Charme Bold

ABCDE
FGHIJKL
MNOPQ
RSTUVW
XYZ&(,;:'"")*?!
abcdefghi
jklmnopqrstu
vwxyz$$
1234567890¢¢%
£/1234567890

Chevalier

ABCDEFGH
IJKLMNO
PQRSTUV
WXYZZ&
(.,:;"")*abcdefghij
klmnopqrst
uvwxyz$1234
567890$¢
%£1234567890

Cloister Extra Bold Condensed

ABCDEFGHIJ
KLMNOP
QQRSTUVWXY
Z&(:,;:,)
?!-abcdeffffi
ffifflghijklmnop
qrstuvwxyz
$1234567890¢$¢/
1234567890

Columbia Bold Italic

ABCDEFGHIJ
KLMNOP
QRSTUVWXY
Z&(.,:;"")?![*]
abcdefffffiflffiffl
ghijklmnop
qrstuvwxyz$123
4567890¢
$¢£%/1234567890

Congress/Lyons

ABCDEFGHIJK
LMMNOP
QRSTUVWXY
Z.,:;?! abcdeffiff
ghijklmnopqrstuvwx
yz$1234567890
¢$£%/1234567890

Corinthian Light

ABCDEF
GHIJKLMNOP
QRSTUV
WXYZ&(.,:;"")*
?!abcdefghij
klmnopq
rstuvwxyz
$1234567890¢
$1234567890¢%/£

Corinthian Medium
ABCDEFGHIJ
KLMNOPQ
RSTUV
WXYZÆØ&
(',;:;'')±?!
abcdefghijkl
mnopqrs
tuvwxyzæøß
$123456
7890¢ $123456789
0¢/£%

Corinthian Bold
ABCDEF
GHIJKLMNO
PQRST
UVWXYZÆØ
&(',;:;'')?!±
abcdefghijklm
nopqrstuv
wxyzæøß$12
34567890
¢$1234567890¢/
£%«»

Corinthian Extra Bold
ABCDE
FGHIJKLMN
OPQRST
UVWXYZÆØ
&(',;:;'')±?!
abcdefghijkl
mnopqrst
uvwxyzæøß
$123456
7890¢ $1234567
890¢/£%«»

Corvinus
Medium Italic
AABCDEFGGHIJ
KKLMMNN
OPQRSTUVW
XYZ&(.;;;)?!†*
abcdefghi
jklmnopqrstuv
wtwxyz$1234
567890¢$¢%£/
1234567890

Corvinus Skyline
ABCDEFGHIJKLMNOPQ
RSTUVWXY
ZÆŒ&(.;;;)?![*]
abcdefghijkl
mnopqrstuvwxyzæ
çœß$1234567
890¢$¢%£1234567890

Cushing Book
ABCDEF
GHIJJKLM
NOPQRSTUV
WXYZÆ
ÇØŒ&(.;;;)?![*]
abcdeffigh
ijklmnopqrstu
vwxyz
æçøœ$12345
67890123
4567890¢$/%#@
1234567890

ITC LICENSED Cushing Medium
ABCDEFGHI
JJKLMNO
PQRSTUVWX
YZÆØŒ
&(.,'::;"")?![*]ab
cdeffighijk
lmnopqrstuvw
xyzæøœ
$1234567890
1234567890¢$/
%#@
1234567890 ⚒ ⚘

ITC LICENSED Cushing Bold
ABCDEF
GHIJJKLMNO
PQRSTUV
WXYZ
ÆØŒ&(.,'::;"")
?![*]abcde
ffighijklmnop
qrstuvwxyz
$123456
7890123456
7890¢$/%#
@1234567890 ⚒ ⚘

ITC LICENSED Cushing Heavy ABCDE
FGHIJJK
LMNOPQRS
TUVWXYZ
ÆØŒ&(.,'::;"")
?![*]abcdef
fighijklm
nopqrstuvwx
yzæøœ
$1234567890
1234567
890¢$/%#@1234
567890 ⚒ ⚘

Cushing
Book Italic

ABCDEFGH
IJJKLM
NOPQRSTU
VWXYZÆØŒ
&(.,':;"")?![*]
abcdeffighijklm
nopqrstuv
wxyzæøœ$1234
567890
1234567890¢$/%
#@1234567890

Cushing Medium
Italic

ABCDEFGH
IJJKLMN
OPQRSTUVW
XYZÆØ
Œ&(.,':;"")?![*]
abcdeffighij
klmnopqrstuvwx
yzæøœ$123
45678901234 5
67890¢$/
%#@1234567890 ⚹ ⚲

Cushing
Bold Italic

ABCDE
FGHIJJKLM
NOPQRS
TUVWXYZÆ
ŁØŒ&
(.,':;"")?![*]ab
cdeffighij
klmnopqrstuvw
xyz$1234
56789012345
67890¢$/%
#@1234567890 ⚹ ⚲

Cushing Heavy Italic

ITC LICENSED

ABCDEFGH
IJJKLMN
OPQRSTUV
WXYZÆ
ØŒ&(.',:,;")?!
[*]abcdeffi
ghijklmnopqrs
tuvwxyzæ
øœ$12345678
90123456
7890¢$/%#@
1234567890

DeRoos Roman

ABCDEFG
HIJKLMNOPQ
RSTUV
WXYZÆŒØ&
(".":;")?![*]«»
abcdefghijklmn
opqrstuvwx
yzæœø$12345
67890¢$¢%£/
1234567890

Dianna Light

ABCDEF
GHIJK
LLMNOPQ
RSTU
VWXYZ&&(,,:;")
?!=abcdeeer
esexf ff fiflghijkl
mnooeros
ppqrstthuvwxyz
$1234567890¢£%/

Dianna Medium

ABCDE
FGHIJKL
LMNOP
QRSTUVW
XYZ&&
(",:")!=.?!abcdeee
eresexfffffifl
ghijklmnoooros
ppqrstthuv
wxyz$1234567
890¢£%

Dianna Bold

ABCDEFG
HIJKL
LMNOPQR
STUVW
XYZ&&(",:")?!=
abcdeee eres
exfff fifl ghijklmno
oorosppqr
stthuvwxyz$1234
567890¢£%/

Dutch Oldstyle Condensed

ABCDEFGHIJKLM
NOPQRST
UVWXYZ&(',,:)?!*
abcdefghijk
lmnopqrstuvwxyz
$1234567890
¢£/%+¨~

Excelsior Script

A B C D E F
G H I J K
L M N O P Q R
S T U V
W X Y Z & (.,:;"!*)?!
abcdefghijk
lmnopqrstuvwxyz
$1234567890¢/$¢%

1234567890 (WV)

Excelsior Semi-Bold
Script

A B C D E
F G H
I J K L M N
O P Q R S
T U V W X
Y Z & (.,:;")(*)?!
abcdefghijklmnop
qrstuvwxyz
$1234567890¢/$%

1234567890 (WV)

FAMOUS
MAGAZINE
ABCDEE
FGHIJKLMN
OPQR
STUVWXY
Z.,:;!?"""~
11223345 67
7888900 (IB)(R)

Fantail

ABCDEFGHIJ
KLMNOPQ
RSTUVWXYZ
ÆŒ&(',:,)?!
abcdefghijklmno
pqrstuvwxy
zæœ$1234567890¢

Florentine Cursive

ABCDEFGHI
JKLMNO
PQRSTUVW
XYZ&(.,:;)?![·]
abcdefghijklmnopqrstuvwxyz
$1234567890¢%£

Fox

ABCDEF
GHIJKLMNO
PQRS
TUVWXYZ
ÆŒ&
(:;.:;::)?![±]abcdefgh
ijklmnopqrst
uvwxyzæ$1234
567890¢$/% 1234567890

Futura Bold Condensed Oblique
ABCDEFGHI
JKLMNOPQRST
UVWXYZ
ÆŒØ&(.',:;'')?!—*
abcdefghijk
lmnopqrstuvwx
yzæœøß$1
234567890¢$¢/
£%#12345
67890

Futura Extra Bold Condensed Oblique
ABCDEFGHIJ
KLMNOP
QRSTUVWXYZ
&(.',:;'')?!—*
abcdefgh
ijklmnopqrst
uvwxyz
$1234567890¢
$/%1234567890

Girder Heavy
ABCDE
FGHIJKLM
NOPQ
RSTUVWXY
Z&(.',:;'')?!-*
abcdefghijk
lmnopq
rstuvwxyz
$1234
567890¢$/%
1234567890 (IB)

Gavotte

A A B B C C C D D D E E E F F J J

G G G H H H I I J J K

K L L M M N N N O O P P

Q Q Q R R S S S T T Th

U u u U U W W X X X Y Y Y Z Z

Ø & (,,:;') «‡» ¿?¿!¡

a b c d ð ð ð e e e f f f f f f i f l g g g h i j k k l m

n n n o p q r r r s t t t u v v v v w x y z z

œ œ ø ß $ 1 2 3 4 5 6 7 8 9 0 ¢

£ $ ¢ / % 1 2 3 4 5 6 7 8 9 0

GOLD RUSH

GOLD
RUSH
ABCDEF
GHIJ
KLMNOP
QRST
UVWXYZ
&(.,;:;;'')?!
*-$123456
7890¢
$/% 1234567890

Goudy Open

A
BCDEFGHIJ
KLMNOP
QRSTUVW
XYZ&
(‚'.;„"")?!-/ab
cdefghijklm
nopqrs
tuvwxyz$1
234567
890¢ 1234567890$¢.(R)

Goudy Open Italic

ABCDEF
GHIJKLMN
OP
QRSTUVW
XYZ&
(‚'.;„"")?!-abc
defghijk
lmnopqrstu
vwxyz
$12345678
90¢
$¢1234567890 (R)

WTC Goudy Light

ABCDEF
GHIJKLMNOP
QRSTUV
WXYZÆØŒ
&(‚'.;„")?!
[⁎]abcdefff
fiflffifflghi
jklmnopqrst
uvwxy
zæøœ$12345
67890¢$/%
#@1234567890¥¢

Goudy Regular
ABCDE
FGHIJKLMN
OPQRSTU
VWXYZ
ÆØŒ&(',;:;"")
?![⊥]*
abcdeffffifl
ffifflghij
klmnopqrstu
vwxyzæøœ
$123456
7890¢/¢$££%
1234567890⁓

Goudy Medium
ABCDEFGH
IJKLMN
OPQRSTUV
WXYZ
ÆØŒ&(.,;:;"")
?![⊥]•*
abcdeffffiflffi
fflghijklm
nopqrstuvw
xyzæøœ
$1234567890
¢/¢$%⁓

Goudy Bold
ABCDE
FGHIJKLM
NOPQRS
TUVWXYZ
ÆØŒ&
(',;:;"")?![⊥]*•
abcdefgh
ijklmnopqr
stuvwx
yzæøœ$123
4567890
¢/¢$£%1234567
890⁓

Goudy Light Italic Swash

AABBCCD DEE
FFGGHHIJJKKLL
MMNNOOPP
QQRRSSTTTTThUU
VVWWXYYZZÆØŒ
&&('.,:;'')?![‗]*abcde
fffffiflffifflghijklmnopqrs
tuvwxyzœøœ
$1234567890¢$/%#@
1234567890

Goudy Regular Italic Swash

AABBCCD DEE
FFGGHHIJJKKLL
MMNNOOPPQQRR
SSTTTTThUUVV
WWXXYYZZÆĐŁØ
Œ&&('.,:;'')?![‗]
abcdeffffffiflffiftghijk
lmnopqrstuvwxyzœđłøœ
$1234567890¢$/%#@
1234567890

Goudy Medium
Italic Swash
A A B B C C D D E E
F F G G H H I J J J K K L
L M M N N O O P P
Q R R S S T T T T Th U V
V V W W X X Y Y Z Z
Æ Ð Ł Ø Œ & T (;:;'")
?![*]abcdefffffifl
ffifflghijklmnopqr
stuvwxyzæðłøœ
$1234567890¢$/%
#@1234567890

Goudy Bold
Italic Swash
A A B B C C D D E E
F F G G H H I J J J
K K L L M M N N O O
P P Q R R S S T T T
Th U V V V W W
X X Y Y Z Z Æ Ð Ł Ø Œ
& T (;:;'")?![*]abc
deffffiflffifflghijklm
nopqrstuvwxyz
œðłøœ$12345678
90¢$/%#@1234567890

Goudy Italian
ABCDEFGHIJ
KLMNOP
QRSTUVWX
YZÆØŒ
&(",:,)?!*⁻̣abcd
effffiflghijkl
mnopqrstuvwx
yzæøœß$12
34567890₁₂₃₄
567890¢£%/†«»

**Goudy Italian
Extra Bold
ABCDEFGH
IJKLMNO
PQRSTUVW
XYZÆ
ØŒ&(",:,)?![*⁻̣]
abcdeffffifl
ghijklmnopq
rstuvwxy
zæøœß$1234
567890₁₂
345⁶7890¢
%/£†«»**

GRAPHIQUE
ABCDEFGHIJKLMNOPQRST
UVWXYZ&(",:,)?!§12
34567890¢%/₁₂₃₄₅₆₇₈₉₀%£
(WV)

Grotesque #9

ABCDEFGHIJKL
MNOPQRST
UVWXYZ&(',:;"")
?!_*_abcdefg
hijklmnopqrs
tuvwxyz$1
234567890£¢$¢
/%#1234567890

Grouch Black

ABCDEF
GHIJK
KLMNNO
PQRRST
UVWXYZ&
(:;.:;"")?!_*_
abcdeefgh
ijkklmnop
qrstuvvw
wxyyzß
$12345678
90¢/£%®

Helvetica Medium Italic

ABCDEFG
HIJKLMNOP
QRSTUV
WXYZÆŒØ
&(',:;"")?!_*_a
bcdefghijkl
mnopqrst
uvwxyzæœ
øß$12345
67890¢¢%/
1234567890

513-C

Helvetica Bold
Condensed
ABCDEFGHIJKLMN
OPQRSTUVW
XYZ&(",;;")?! *abcdefgh
ijklmnopqrstuv
wxyz$1234567890
¢$¢£%/1234567890

Helvetica Bold
Condensed Outline
ABCDEFGHIJK
LMNOPQRSTUVWXY
Z&(",;;")?!
abcdefghijklm
nopqrstuvw
xyz$1234567890
¢/%£$1234567890¢

(WV)

Helvetica Round
Bold Condensed #2
ABCDEFGHIJ
KLMNOPQRSTU
VWXYZÆ
ŒØ&(",;;")?¿!¡«–»
abcdefghijkl
mnopqrstuvwx
yzæœøß$1
234567890¢
$¢/£%#1234567890

Johnston
Railway Light
ABCDEF
GHIJKLMNO
PQRSTUV
WXYZ&(':,:!?)
-*-abcdef
ghijklmnop
qrstuvw
xyz£123456
7890 (IB)

Johnston
Railway
Medium
ABCDEF
GHIJKLMNO
PQRSTU
VWXYZ&(':,:)
?!*abcdef
ghijklmnopq
rstuvwxyz
£1234567890/ (IB)

Johnston
Railway Bold
ABCDEF
GHIJKLMNO
PQRSTUV
WXYZ&(':,:)?!
*abcdefg
hijklmnopq
rstuvwx
yz£123456
7890 (IB)

515-C

Johnston
Railway
Medium Italic
ABCDEF
GHIJKLMNO
PQRSTUV
WXYZ&(':,:,!?)
-*-abcdefg
hijklmnopqrs
tuvwxyz£
1234567890/

Johnston
Railway Bold
Italic
ABCDEFG
HIJKLM
NOPQRST
UVWXY
Z&(':,:,!?)*abc
defghijkl
mnopqrstu
vwxyz£
1234567890

Johnston
Railway Medium
Condensed
ABCDEF
GHIJKLMNOP
QRSTUV
WXYZ&(':,:,!?)-*-
abcdefghij
klmnopqrstu
vwxyz£
1234567890

Johnston Railway Bold Condensed

ABCDEFGHIJK
LMNOPQ
RSTUVWXYZ
&(',;:,!?)-*-ab
cdefghij
klmnopqrst
uvwxyz
£1234567890

KARNAC

ABCDEFGHI
JKLMNOPQ
RRSTUVWXY
Z&(',:,)?!abcd
efghijklmnopqr
stuvwxyz$123
4567890¢/£ (WV)

Kennerley Bold Italic

ABCCDEE
FGGHIJ
KLMNOPQ
RSTTU
VUWXYZ
&.,-:;"!?abc
cdefghijk
lmnopqrss
tuvwxyz
$1234567890 (R)

517-C

Kunstler Bold

A B C D
E F G H I J
K L M N
O P Q R S T
U V W X
Y Z Æ Œ Œ &
(.,"::;).?&!!'-abc
defghijklmno
pqrstuv
wxyzæœoß
$1234567890¢
£/% "‹›"

Legend

A B C D D E
E F G H H
I J K L L M N
O P Q R R
S S T T Th U V W X
Y Z & (.,;"")?!
*≐abcdefghij
klmnopqrstthuv
wxyz$1234
567890¢¢%/ 1234567890

LIBRA

ABCDDEFF
GhIjKLMNOP
QRSTUV
WXYZ&[.,":;]?!*
$123456789
0¢%/£ 1234567890

Lydian

ABCDEFGHIJK
LMNOPQR
STUVWXYZ&
(.,:;'""")?!-*-ab
cdefghijklmno
pqrstuvwxy
z$1234567890¢
£%/1234567890

Meridien Light

ABCDE
FGHIJKLM
NOPQRST
UVWXYZÆ
ŒØ&(.,:;'")
?!-«*»abcdef
fffiflfffiffl
ghijklmnopq
rstuvwxyz
æœøß$12345
67890¢¢$£
%/1234567890

Meridien Medium

ABCDEFG
HIJKL
MNOPQR
STUVWXY
Z&(.,:;'")?!-*
abcdefff
fiflfffifflgh
ijklmn
opqrstuvw
xyz$1234
567890¢¢$£%/
1234567890

519-C

Meridien Bold

ABCDEFG
HIJKLM
NOPQRSTU
VWXYZ
&(.,:;'')?!–·*
abcdef
ff fi fl ffi ffl g
hijklmn
opqrstuvw
xyz$1234
567890¢¢$£
%/1234567890

Meridien Extra Bold

ABCDE
FGHIJKL
MNOPQ
RSTUVW
XYZ&(.,:;'')
·abcdef
ff fi fl ffi ffl g
hijklmn
opqrstuv
wxyz$1234
567890¢¢
$£%/1234567890

Meridien Black

ABCDEFG
HIJKLM
NOPQRST
UVWXY
Z&(.,:;'')?!–·
*abcdefff
fi fl ffi ffl gh
ijklmno
pqrstuvw
xyz$1234
567890¢¢$£
%/1234567890

MICROGRAMMA
ABCDEFGH
IJKLMNOPQR
STUVWX
YZ&(',:;'')?!☀☀*
$1123456
7890¢£°lo/
1234567890

Modula
ABCDEFGH
IJKLMNOP
QRSTUVWX
YZÆŒØ
&(.,:;)?![*]abc
defghijkl
mnopqrstuv
wxyzæœ
ø$12345678
90¢¢/%#
1234567890

Modula
Medium
ABCDEFG
HIJKLMN
OPQRSTUV
WXYZÆ
ŒØ&(.,:;'')?![*]
abcdefgh
ijklmnopqrs
tuvwxyz
æœø$1234
567890¢
¢/%#1234567890

Modula Bold
ABCDEF
GHIJKLMN
OPQRST
UVWXYZ
ÆŒØ&(''.;;")?!
[*]abcde
fghijklmnop
qrstuvwx
yzæœø
$12345678
90¢/%
#1234567890

Modula Extra Bold
ABCDEF
GHIJKLMN
OPQRSTU
VWXYZ
ÆŒØ&(',.;;")
?![*]abcd
efghijklmn
opqrstuvwx
yzæœø$1
234567890¢
/%#1234567890

Normande Condensed
ABCDEFGHIJKL
MNOPQRSTU
VWXYZ&(',.;;'.')
?!*abcdefghijklmn
opqrstuvwxy
z$1234567890¢/%
1234567890

Optima Medium
ABCDEFGHIJKLMN
OPQRSTUV
WXYZÆŒØ&(.,'::;")
?!⸪«*»abcdeffffifl
ghijklmnopqrstuvwx
yzæœøß$$£123
4567890¢¢%/#1234567890

Primus
ABCD
EFGHIJK
LMNOP
QRSTUVW
XYZ&(.,:;"")
?!*⸪abc
defghijkl
mnopqr
stuvwxyz
$1234567
890¢$¢£%/
1234567890

Phidian

ABCDEFGHIJKL
MNOPQRSTUVWXYZ&
(.;:;)?!abcdefghijklm
nopqrstuvwxyz (S)

Radiant Bold Condensed

ABCDEFGHIJKLMN
OPQRSTUVWXY
Z&(",.:;",")?!*abcdefgh
ijklmnopqrst
uvwxyz$1234567890
¢%/£$1234567890¢%/

Rock and Roll Light

ABCDEFG
HIJKLM
NOPQQRST
UVWXYZ
&(",.:;)?!abcdefgh
ijklmnop
qrstuvwxyz
$1234567
890¢/★®©™▶◀•●○■

Rock and Roll
Bold
ABCDEFG
HIJKLM
NOPQRSTU
VWXYZ&
(.',:;)?!abcdefg
hijklmno
pqrstuvwxyz
$123456
7890¢/

Rock and Roll
Light Italic
ABCDEFG
HIJKLMNOP
QRSTUV
WXYZÆÇØ
Œ&(.',:;)?!ab
cdefffffiflffifflgh
ijklmnopq
rrstuvwxyzæ
çøœß$123
4567890¢/£

Rock and Roll
Bold Italic
ABCDEFG
HIJKLM
NOPQQRSTU
VWXYZ&
(.',:;)?! =abcdef
fffiflffifflgh
ijklmnopqrr
stuvwxyz
$1234567890¢

Rondo Bold
ABCD
EFGHIJK
LMNOP
QQRSTIU
VWX
YZ&(.,:;")?!.* ab
cdee fghij
klmnn oo pqrr
stt uvwxyz
$1234567890¢$¢£
%/1234567890

Royal
ABCDEF
GHIJK
LMNOPQR
STUVW
XYZ(.,:;")(.,:;)?!
abcdefffffi
flghijklmnop
qrstuvwxyz
$12345
67890¢$¢/%
1234567890

Sally Mae Light
ABCDEFG
HIJKLMNOPQ
RSTUVW
XYZØ&(.,:;)?!
abcdefg
hijklmnopqrst
uvwxyzø
$1234567890¢

Sally Mae Medium

ABCDEFGH
IJKLMNO
PQRSTUVWX
YZØ&(".;:;")
?![-]abcdefgh
ijklmnop
qrstuvwxyz
ø$123456
7890¢

Sally Mae Demi

ABCDEFGH
IJKLMN
OPQRSTUV
WXYZØ
&(".;:;")?!*-ab
cdefghijk
lmnopqrstuv
wxyzø$12
34567890¢/

Sally Mae Heavy

ABCDEFGH
IJKLMN
OPQRSTUV
WXYZ&
(".;:;)?!abc
defghijk
lmnopqrst
uvwxyz
$12345678
90%

Sampler
ABCDEFGHIJ
KLMNOPQ
RSTUVWXYZ&
[`,;:]abcdefg
hijklmnopqrs
tuvwxyz$
1234567890¢% (IB)

Serifa 35 Thin
ABCDEF
GHIJKLMNO
PQRSTUV
WXYZÆŒØ
&(„"")?!«—*—»
abcdefghijkl
mnopqrst
uvwxyzæœø
$12345678
90¢$¢%£/#123
4567890

Serifa 45 Light
ABCDEFG
HIJKL
MNOPQRS
TUVWX
YZÆŒØ&(„"")
?!«—*—»abcde
fghijklmnop
qrstuvwx
yzæœø$1234
567890¢
¢$%£/#1234567890

Serifa 55

ABCDEFGH
IJKLM
NOPQRST
UVWXY
ZÆŒØ&(',:;'')
?!«⁎»abc
defghijklm
nopqrs
tuvwxyzæ
œø$1234
567890¢$¢%£
/#1234567890

Serifa 65
Bold

ABCDEFGH
IJKLM
NOPQRST
UVWX
YZÆŒØ&
(',:;'')?!«⁎»
abcdefgh
ijklmn
opqrstuvw
xyzæœø$
1234567890
¢$¢%£/#

Serifa 75
Black

ABCDE
FGHIJKLM
NOPQRS
TUVWXYZ
ÆŒØ&
(',:;'')?!«⁎»a
bcdefgh
ijklmnopq
rstuvw
xyzæœø$1
2345678
90¢$¢%£/#

Serifa 36
Thin Italic
ABCDEFGHI
JKLMNO
PQRSTUVW
XYZÆŒØ
&(„"")?!«——»abc*
defghijkl
mnopqrstuvw
xyzæœø
$1234567890
¢$¢%£/#

Serifa 46
Light Italic
ABCD
EFGHIJKL
MNOPQ
RSTUVWXY
ZÆŒØ&
(„.;")?!«——»abcd*
efghijklmn
opqrstuvwx
yzæœø$1
234567890
¢$¢%£/#

Serifa 56
Italic
ABCDEFGH
IJKLM
NOPQRST
UVWX
YZÆŒØ&
(„.;")?!«——»*
abcdefghijk
lmnopq
rstuvwxyz
æœø$1
234567890
¢$¢%£/#

Serpentine
Light
ABCDEFG
HIJKLM
NOPQRSTU
VWXYZ
&(.,:;")*-?!ab
cdefghijkl
mnopqrst
uvwxyz
$12345678
90¢$¢%₤
1234567890

Serpentine
Medium
ABCDEFGH
IJKLMN
OPQRSTU
VWXYZ
&(.,:;")*-?!ab
cdefghijk
lmnopqrst
uvwxyz
$1234567
890¢$¢%
#₤1234567890

Serpen-
tine Bold
ABCDEF
GHIJKLMN
OPQRST
UVWXYZ
&(.,:;")*-?!
abcdefgh
ijklmnop
qrstuvwx
yz$123
4567890¢
$¢%₤#
1234567890

Serpentine
Light Italic
ABCDEFGHI
JKLMNOP
QRSTUVWX
YZ&(.,:;"")_*?!
abcdefghijk
lmnopq
rstuvwxyz
$123456
7890¢$‰%£
1234567890

Serpentine
Medium
Italic
ABCDEFG
HIJKLM
NOPQRSTU
VWXYZ&
(.,:;"")_*?!ab
cdefgh
ijklmnopqr
stuvwxy
z$123456
7890¢$‰%
£1234567890#

Signum
ABCDEFGHIJKLMNOPQRSTUV
WXYZÆŒ&(.,:;"")?!*-«
abcdefffgghijklmnopqrstuv
wxyzæœ$12345
67890¢%/£$1234567890¢%/£

Simoncini Garamond

ABC
DEFGHIJK
LMNOP
QRSTUVWX
YZÆŒØ
&&(„;;"")?![_*_]ab
cdefghijklm
nopqrstuvwx
yz$1234
567890%¢

Solon Antiqua Light

ABCDEFG
HIJKLMN
OPQRSTUVW
XYZ&[„;;"]?!*=
abcdefghijklmn
opqrstuv
wxyz$123
456
7890¢$¢£%/

Solon Antiqua Normal

ABCDEFGHI
JKLMNO
PQRSTUVW
XYZÆ
ŒØ&[„;;"]?!*=
abcde
fghijklmno
pqrstuvwxyzæ
œøß$1
234567890¢¢
%/1234567890

Solon Antiqua
Semi Bold
ABCDEFGHI
JKLMNO
PQRSTUVWX
YZÆŒØ
&[',.:;"]?!*≛abcd
efghijklm
nopqrstuvw
xyzæœøß
$1234567890¢
¢%/1234567890

Solon Antiqua
Bold
ABCDEFGHI
JKLMNOP
QRSTU
VWXYZÆŒ
Ø&[',.:;"]?!*≛
abcdefghijkl
mnopqr
stuvwxyz
æœøß$
1234567890$
¢¢%/1234567890

Stuyvesant Script
ABCDEFGH
IJKLMN
OPQRSTUVW
XYZÆŒØ&
¿¡~«»/!i?¿‾
abcdefghijklmnopqrs
tuvwxyzæœøß
1234567890£/ (WV)

Symbol Book
ABCDEFG
HIJKLMNOPQ
RSTUVWX
YZÆÇŒØŞ&
(".;:,;"")?![⁎]{}
abcdefffffiflffiffl
ghijklmnopqr
stuvwxyzæçœø
ß$1234567
89012345678 9
0¢¢£%/#
1234567890§†‡«»

Symbol Medium
ABCDE
FGHIJKLMNO
PQRSTUV
WXYZÆÇŒØ
Ş&(".;:,;"")?![⁎]{}
abcdefffffiflffi
fflghijklm
nopqrstuvw
xyzæçœøß
$123456789012
34567890
¢¢£%/#1234567890

Symbol Bold
ABCDEFG
HIJKLMNOP
QRSTUVW
XYZÆÇŒØŞ
&(".;:,;"")?![⁎]{}
abcdefffffifl
ffifflghijk
lmnopqrstuvw
xyzæçœøß
$1234567890
12345678
90¢¢£%/#1234
567890§†‡«»

Symbol Black
ABCDEFGH
IJKLMN
OPQRSTUV
WXYZÆÇ
ŒØŞ&(':,;:,")?!
[≡]*{}abcd
efffffifIffifflg
hijklmnop
qrstuvwxyz
æçœøß$12
34567890 12
34567890¢
£%/#1234567890

Symbol Book
Italic
ABCDEFGHIJK
LMNOPQ
RSTUVWXYZ
ÆÇŒØŞ&
(',;:"")?![≡]{}abcdef
ffffifIffiff lghij
klmnopqrstuv
wxyzæçœøß
$1234567890 12
34567890¢
¢£%/#1234567890
§†‡«»

Symbol
Medium Italic
ABCDEFG
HIJKLMNOPQ
RSTUVWX
YZÆÇŒØŞ&
(',;:"")?![≡]{}
abcdeffffifIffiffl
ghijklmnop
qrstuvwxyzœ
çœøß$12345
67890 1234567
890¢¢£/#
1234567890§†‡«»

ITC LICENSED Symbol Bold Italic

ABCDEFGHI
JKLMNOP
QRSTUVWX
YZÆÇŒØ
Ş&(.,:;"")?![±]{}
abcdeffffi
flffifflghijklmn
opqrstuvwx
yzæçœøß$123
4567890
1234567890¢
¢£%/#§†‡«»

ITC LICENSED Symbol Black Italic

ABCDEFG
HIJKLMNOP
QRSTUV
WXYZÆÇŒ
ØŞ&(.,:;"")?!
[±]{}abcdef
fffiflffifflgh
ijklmnopqrs
tuvwxyzæç
œøß$123456
789012345
67890¢£%/#

TEA CHEST

ABCDEFGHIJKLM
NOPQRSTU
VWXYZ&(.,:;")?!
*$$£1234567
890¢°%/1234567890

537-C

Thaddeus Light
ABCDEFGH
IJKLMNOPQRS
TUVWXYZ
ÆÐŁØŒ&(".,.;")
?![*☐]abcdef
fffififlfffiffflghijklmn
opqrstuvw
xyzæðłøoeß
$1234567
890¢$¢££%/#@
1234567890††§¶

Thaddeus
Regular
ABCDEFG
HIJKLMNOPQ
RSTUVWX
YZÆÐŁØŒ&
(".,.;")?![*☐]a
bcdefffffifloffffflg
hijklmnopq
rstuvwxyzæð
fłøoeß
$1234567890¢
$¢££%/#@
1234567890††§¶

Thaddeus
Medium
ABCDEFGHIJK
LMNOPQ
RSTUVWXY
ZÆÐŁØŒ
&(".,.;")?![*☐]ab
cdefffffifffi
fflghijklmnopqr
stuvwxyz
æðfłøoeß$123
4567890¢$
¢££%/#@12345
67890††§¶

Thaddeus Bold

ABCDEFG
HIJKLMNOPQ
RSTUVW
XYZÆÐŁØŒ
&(".,.;"')?![※ ⊿]
abcdefffffifflffiffl
ghijklmno
pqrstuvwxyz
ædfłøœß
$1234567890¢$
¢£€%/#@
1234567890†‡§¶

Thaddeus Light Italic

ABCDEFGHIJ
KLMNOP
QRSTUVWX
YZÆÐŁØŒ
&(".,.;"')?![※ ⊿]
abcdefffffifflffiffl
ghijklmno
pqrstuvwxyzæ
ðfłøœß$1234
567890¢$¢£€%/
#@1234567890
†‡§¶

Thaddeus Regular Italic

ABCDEFG
HIJKLMNOPQ
RSTUVW
XYZÆÐŁØ
Œ&(".,.;"')?![※ ⊿]ab
cdefffffifl
ffifflghijklmno
pqrstuvw
xyzædfłøœß
$1234567890
¢$¢£€%/#@12345
67890†‡§¶

539-C

**Thaddeus
Medium Italic**
ABCDEF
GHIJKLMNOP
QRSTUV
WXYZÆÐŁØ
Œ&(.,:;"")?!
[*]abcdefffi
flffifflghijk
lmnopqrstuvw
xyzæðfłø
œß$12345678
90¢$¢£%/#
@1234567890††§¶

**Thaddeus Bold
Italic**
ABCDEFGH
IJKLMN
OPQRSTUVW
XYZÆÐŁ
ØŒ&(.,:;")?![*]
abcdefffifl
ffifflghijklmno
pqrstuv
wxyzæðfłøœß
$1234567890
¢$¢£%/#@12345
67890††§¶

Univers 46
ABCDEFGHIJK
LMNOPQR
STUVWXYZÆ
ŒØ&(.,:;"")?!
[*]abcdefghij
klmnopq
rstuvwxyzæœ
øß$123456
7890¢$¢£%/#
1234567890

Univers 56

ABCDEFGHIJK
LMNOPQ
RSTUVWXYZ
ÆŒØ&(.,:;")
?!*̣abcdefghijk
lmnopqrstuv
wxyzæœøß$123
4567890¢$¢
£%/#1234567890

Univers 66

ABCDEF
GHIJKLMNOP
QRSTUV
WXYZ&(.,:;")?!
*̣abcdefgh
ijklmnopqrst
uvwxyz
$12345678
90¢$¢£%
/#1234567890

Univers 76

ABCDEFGHI
JKLMNO
PQRSTUV
WXYZ
ÆŒØ&(.,:;")
?![*̣]abcd
efghijklmnop
qrstuvw
xyzæœøß$
1234567
890¢$¢£%/#
1234567890 (S)(IB)

Univers 59
ABCDEFGGHIJKLM
NOPQRSTUV
WXYZ&(.,:;")?!*
abcdefghijkl
mnopqrstuvwxyz$12
34567890¢£$¢/%
1234567890

Univers 73
ABCDEF
GHIJKLM
NOPQR
STUVWXY
Z&&(.,:;")
?!*abcde
fghijkl
mnopqrstu
vwxyz$
123456789
0¢$¢/%£
1234567890

Valiant Light
ABCDEFG
HIJKL
MNOPQRS
TUVWX
YZÆÇØŒ
&(.,:;")[.?¿!¡]*
abcdefghijklmnopqrst
uvwxyzæçøœß
$1234567890¢
£$¢/%1234567890

Valiant Bold

ABCDEFG
HIJKL
MNOPQRS
TUVWX
YZÆÇØOE
&(,;:)[?!*]
abcdefghijklmnopq
rstuvwxyzæçø
œß$1234567890
¢£$¢/%1234567890

Veljovic Book

ABCDEFG
HIJKLMNO
PQRSTU
VWXYZÆ
ŒØ&(,;:)
?![*]abcdefgh
ijklmnop
qrstuvwxy
zæœø$12
34567890 1234
567890¢%/
#@1234567890

Veljovic Medium

ABCDEF
GHIJKLMN
OPQRST
UVWXYZ
ÆŒØ&(,;:)
?![*]abcdefg
hijklm
nopqrstuvw
xyzæœø$
1234567890 1
234567890¢%
/#@1234567890

543-C

ITC LICENSED Veljovic Bold
ABCDEFGHIJK
LMNOPQRST
UVWXYZÆŒØ&
(.,;:'"')?![*]abcde
ffffifflffifflghijklm
nopqrstuvwxyz
æœøß$123456
7890123456789o¢$£
%/#@1234567890

ITC LICENSED Veljovic Black
ABCDEFG
HIJKLMNOPQ
RSTUVWXY
ZÆŒØ&(.,;:'"')?![*]
abcdeffffifl
ffifflghijklmno
pqrstuvwxy
zæœøß$12345
67890012345
67890¢$£%/#@
1234567890

Veljovic Book Italic *Veljovic Medium Italic*

ABCDEFGHIJKLM
NOPQRSTUV
WXYZÆŒØ&(.,:;"'")
?![*]abcdefffffifl
ffifflghijklmnopqrstuv
wxyzæœøß$12345
67890123456789¢$£
%/#@1234567890

ABCDEFGHIJ
KLMNOPQRSTU
VWXYZÆŒØ&
(.,:;"'")?![*]abcdefghijk
lmnopqrstuvwx
yzæœø$123456789
01234567890¢%
/#@1234567890

545-C

ITC LICENSED **Veljovic Bold Italic**
ABCDEFGHIJK
LMNOPQRSTUVW
XYZÆŒØ&
(.,;:"")?![*]abcdeffffi
flffifflghijklm
nopqrstuvwxyzæ
œøß$12345678
901234567890¢$£
%/#@1234567890

ITC LICENSED **Veljovic Black
Italic**
ABCDEFG
HIJKLMNOPQR
STUVWXYZÆ
ŒØ&(.,;:")?![*]abc
deffffiflffifflgh
ijklmnopqrstuvw
xyzæœøß$123
45678901234567
890¢$£%/#@
1234567890

Weidemann
Book
ABCDEFGHIJK
LMNOPQ
RSTUVWXYZ
ÆØŒ&(.',:;"")
?![±]abcdeffighij
klmnopqrs
tuvwxyzæøœß
$1234567890
¢$$/¢¢%£#@†‡§
1234567890 «» ´`ˆ˜¯˘
‘‘’’

Weidemann
Medium
ABCDEFG
HIJKLMNOPQ
RSTUVW
XYZÆØŒ&
(.',:;"")?![±]
abcdeffighijklm
nopqrstuvw
xyzæøœß$123
4567890123
4567890¢$$/¢¢%
£#@†‡§12
34567890 «» ´`ˆ˜¯˘°
‘‘’’

Weidemann
Bold
ABCDEFGHIJ
KLMNOP
QRSTUVWX
YZÆØŒ&
(.',:;"")?![±]abcde
ffighijklm
nopqrstuvw
xyzæøœß
$1234567890
1234567890
¢$$/¢¢%£#@†
‡§«» ´`ˆ˜¯˘°
‘‘’’

ITC LICENSED **Weidemann Black**
ABCDEFGH
IJKLMN
OPQRSTU
VWXYZ
ÆØŒ&(.',:;"")
?![⬚]abcde
ffighijklmn
opqrstuvw
xyzæøœßЅ1
234567890
1234567890¢
ЅЅ/¢¢%£†‡§

ITC LICENSED *Weidemann Book Italic*
ABCDEFG
HIJKLMNOPQ
RSTUVWX
YZÆØŒ&(.',:;"")?!
[⬚]abcdeffi
ghijklmnopqrstu
vwxyzæøœß
Ѕ1234567890¢ЅЅ
/¢¢%£#@
†‡Ѕ 1234567890 «»
ˆˇˉ˘˙˜˚˛
ˌˌ

ITC LICENSED *Weidemann Medium Italic*
ABCDEF
GHIJKLMN
OPQRSTUVW
XYZÆØŒ&
(.',:;"")?![⬚]abcdef
fighijklmno
pqrstuvwxyz
æøœßЅ123
4567890 123456
7890¢ЅЅ/¢¢%
£#@†‡Ѕ«»
ˆˇˉ˘˙˜˚˛
"ˌˌ

Weidemann
Bold Italic
ABCDEFGHIJ
KLMNOP
QRSTUVWX
YZÆØŒ&
(.,:;"')?![‡]abcde
ffighijklm
nopqrstuvw
xyzæøœß
$1234567890
1234567890
¢$$/¢¢%£#@†
‡§‹‹›› ^˘¯˜°°
" "

Weidemann
Black Italic
ABCDE
FGHIJKLMN
OPQRST
UVWXYZÆØ
Œ&(.,:;"')?!
[‡]abcdeffig
hijklmno
pqrstuvwxyz
æøœß$12
34567890¢$$/
¢¢%£#@
†‡§1234567890

WTG 145
Light
ABCDEFGHI
JKLMNO
PQRSTUVW
XYZÆŒ
Ø&(.,:;"')?![*]ab
cdefffffffffffl
ghijklmnopqrs
tuvwxyz
æœøß$12345
67890¢¢%/
1234567890

WTG 145
Regular
ABCDEFGH
IJKLMNO
PQRSTUVW
XYZÆŒ
Ø&(';:;'.')?![*]a
bcdefffffifl
ffifflghijklmno
pqrstuvw
xyzæœøß$12
3456789
0¢¢%/#@
1234567890

WTG 145
Medium
ABCDEF
GHIJKLMNO
PQRSTU
VWXYZÆŒ
Ø&(';:;'.')
?![*]abcdefg
hijklmno
pqrstuvwxyz
æœø$1234
567890¢$/%#
@1234567890

WTG 145
Bold
ABCDEFGH
IJKLMNO
PQRSTUVW
XYZÆŒ
Ø&(';:;'.')?![*]
abcdefgh
ijklmnopqrst
uvwxyz
æœø$123456
7890¢$/
%#@1234567890

WTG 145
Extra Bold
ABCDE
FGHIJKLM
NOPQRS
TUVWXYZÆ
ŒØ&(',;,;'')
?![*]abcdefff
fiflffffifflghi
jklmnopqrstu
vwxyzæ
œøß$123456
7890¢$¢£
%/#1234567890@

WTG 145
Light Italic
ABCDEFGH
IJKLMNO
PQRSTUVW
XYZÆŒ
Ø&(",;,"")?![*]a
bcdefff fifl
ffifflghijklmno
pqrstuvw
xyzæœøß$123
4567890¢
¢%/#@1234567890

WTG 145
Regular Italic
ABCDE
FGHIJKLM
NOPQRS
TUVWXYZÆ
ŒØ&(',;,;'')
?![*]abcdefff fi
flffifflghijkl
mnopqrstuvw
xyzæœøß$1
234567890¢¢/
%/#@1234567890

WTG 145 Medium Italic

ABCDE
FGHIJKLM
NOPQRS
TUVWXYZÆ
ŒØ&(.,:;"')
?![*]abcdefff
fiflffifflghij
klmnopqrstuv
wxyzæœø
$1234567890
¢$/%#@
1234567890

WTG 145 Bold Italic

ABCDEFG
HIJKLM
NOPQRSTU
VWXYZ
ÆŒØ&(.,:;"')
?![*]abc
defff fiflffifflgh
ijklmnop
qrstuvwxyzæ
œø$1234567
890¢$/%
#@1234567890

WTG 145 Extra Bold Italic

ABCDEFGH
IJKLMN
OPQRSTUV
WXYZÆŒ
Ø&(.,:;"')?![*]
abcdefff fi
flffifflghijklmn
opqrstuv
wxyzæœø$123
4567890¢
$/%#@1234567890

Zapf International Light Italic

AABCDDÆEFGGH
IJKKLMM
NNOPQRRSSTTU
VVWWXYYZ
ÆÇØŒ&(;;;;"")?![[*]]
abcdeeffigghij
kklmnnopqrrsstt
uvwxyyzzæ
çøœß
$1234567890 1
234567890¢$¢$$£%/#
1234567890§†‡‹›«»

Zapf International Medium Italic

AABCDDÆEFGG
HIJKKLMM
NNOPQRRSSTTU
VVWWX
YYZÆÇØŒ&(;;;;"")
?![[*]]abcd
eeffigghijkklmnn
opqrrsstt uv
wxyyzzæçøœß$1234
56789012
34567890¢$¢$$£%/#
1234567890§†‡‹›«»

ITC LICENSED **Zapf Interna-**
tional Demi Italic
AABCDDEE
FGGHIJKKLMM
NNOPQRRSS
TTUVVWWXYY
ZÆÇØŒ&
(",;;;")?![[*]]abc
deeffigghijkklm
nnopqrrrsstt
uvwxyyzzæçøœß
$1234567890
1234567890¢$£%
#§†‡‹›«»*

ITC LICENSED **Zapf Internation-**
al Heavy Italic
AABCDDEEFGG
HIJKKLMM
NNOPQRRSS
TTUVVW
WXYYZÆÇØŒ&
(",;;;")?![[*]]*
abcdeefgghij
kklmmnnopqrr
sstt'uvwxyyz
zæçøœß$123456
7890123456 78
90¢$¢$$£%/#§†‡‹›«»*

INDEX

ITC Zapf Chancery Light, 405
ITC Zapf Chancery Medium, 405
ITC Zapf Chancery Demi, 406
ITC Zapf Chancery Bold, 406

ITC Zapf Chancery Light Italic, 407
ITC Zapf Chancery Medium Italic, 407
ITC Zapf International Light, 408
ITC Zapf International Medium, 408

ITC Zapf International Demi, 409
ITC Zapf International Heavy, 409
ITC Zapf International Light Italic, 553
ITC Zapf International Medium Italic, 553

ITC Zapf International Demi Italic, 554
ITC Zapf International Heavy Italic, 554
Zeppelin, 410